Praise for *Black Ball*

"Long before the NBA became an international brand, and before Larry Bird, Magic Johnson, and Michael Jordan made it a national obsession, a generation of Black ball players helped transition the sport from a cultural wasteland to must-see spectacle. In *Black Ball*, Theresa Runstedtler brilliantly tells the story of men famous and not-so-famous, who through sheer innovation and an articulation of self-worth, transformed how the game would be played, how it would be watched, and ultimately how it would be valued."

—Mark Anthony Neal, author of *Black Ephemera: The Crisis and Challenge of the Musical Archive*

"Theresa Runstedtler's *Black Ball* is great: deeply researched and foundational, a necessary reminder that the dunks and three-pointers, behind-the-back passes, and mid-air poetry everybody loves are the byproduct of an often-unwelcome player movement. The NBA is cool. The story of the Black players who transformed the game into what it is today is even cooler."

—Howard Bryant, author of *The Heritage: Black Athletes, a Divided America, and the Politics of Patriotism*

"In the 1970s Black basketball players quite literally changed the game. But as Runstedtler shows in this superb book, not in the way we think. Black players had to fight on the court and in court—before judges and in the court of public opinion—to secure rights, dignity, fair treatment, and equitable pay. In the face of racist backlash, economic crisis, and corporate owners who treated players as chattel, these men brought energy, style, a new consciousness, and an imperative for justice. Compelling and beautifully written, *Black Ball* is further proof why Runstedtler is one of sport's most perceptive and incisive historians."

—Robin D. G. Kelley, author of *Thelonious Monk: The Life and Times of an American Original*

"In her brilliant book *Black Ball*, Runstedtler reminds us there was nothing inevitable about the NBA's rise as 'a global profit machine' built around Black stars. She uncovers an overlooked but important history of how the league's Black players challenged a white monopoly that controlled the sport. In a fascinating and sobering read, Runstedtler reconstructs a pivotal decade—the 1970s—a time when Black players, full of frustration and determination, redefined the NBA's place in American culture. A must-read for anyone interested in basketball."

—Johnny Smith, author of *The Sons of Westwood: John Wooden, UCLA, and the Dynasty That Changed College Basketball*

"It was almost a Dickensian world. For many white traditionalists, professional basketball in the 1970s was the worst of times. Instead of earthbound, paint-by-number offensives, the game became a free-form, be-bop ballet played above the rim. Connie Hawkins, Spencer Haywood, Kareem Abdul-Jabbar, and other Black players took over the game and made it their own, thrilling a new generation of spectators. And following the lead of Oscar Robinson, they demanded more rights, greater diversity in coaching, and increased pay. Runstedtler brilliantly chronicles the decade that forever changed the game."

—Randy Roberts, coauthor of *Blood Brothers: The Fatal Friendship Between Muhammad Ali and Malcolm X*

"With *Black Ball*, Runstedtler isn't so much rewriting history as reclaiming it. The 1970s were an utterly transformative incubation period for the development of the game we see today. It also was the first time the players had a taste of actual labor power. While the NBA portrays this period as a time that almost wrecked the league, Runstedtler gives us a far more nuanced and honest reading. This is a necessary—and antiracist—correction and should inspire more of us to re-examine the 1970s—a period of pain, but also progress."

—Dave Zirin, sports editor, *The Nation*

"A half century before African American athletes became the vanguard of sport's century awakening, a generation of players in the NBA picked up the torch lit by their predecessors during the 1960s. Runstedtler adeptly captures the complex sporting landscape of those times and the backlash these players endured. With panache and perspective, she explores a profoundly compelling story of unfairly reviled players who changed how the game was played and the power relations shaping it. Though often overlooked, this generation laid the foundation for basketball's increasing cultural cachet, its rise as a global game, and its renewed commitment to social justice."

—Rob Ruck, professor of sport history, University of Pittsburgh, and author of *Tropic of Football: The Long and Perilous Journey of Samoans to the NFL*

Black Ball

Black Ball

Kareem Abdul-Jabbar,
Spencer Haywood,
and the Generation
that Saved
the Soul of the NBA

Theresa
Runstedtler

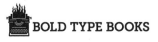

BOLD TYPE BOOKS

New York

Bold Type Books
30 Irving Place, 10th Floor New York, NY 10003
www.boldtypebooks.org
@BoldTypeBooks

Printed in the United States of America

First Edition: March 2023

Published by Bold Type Books, an imprint of Perseus Books, LLC, a subsidiary of Hachette Book Group, Inc. Bold Type Books is a co-publishing venture of the Type Media Center and Perseus Books.

The Hachette Speakers Bureau provides a wide range of authors for speaking events. To find out more, go to www.hachettespeakersbureau.com or email HachetteSpeakers@hbgusa.com.

Bold Type books may be purchased in bulk for business, educational, or promotional use. For information, please contact your local bookseller or Hachette Book Group Special Markets Department at special.markets@hbgusa.com.

The publisher is not responsible for websites (or their content) that are not owned by the publisher.

Print book interior design by Amy Quinn.

Library of Congress Cataloging-in-Publication Data

Names: Runstedtler, Theresa, author.
Title: Black ball : Kareem Abdul-Jabbar, Spencer Haywood, and the generation that saved the soul of the NBA / Theresa Runstedtler.
Description: First edition. | New York, N.Y. : Bold Type Books, 2023 | Includes bibliographical references and index.
Identifiers: LCCN 2022029151 | ISBN 9781645036951 (hardcover) | ISBN 9781645036968 (ebook)
Subjects: LCSH: National Basketball Association—History—20th century. | African American basketball players—History—20th century. | Basketball—Social aspects—United States—History—20th century. | Discrimination in sports—United States—History—20th century. | Race relations—United States—History—20th century.
Classification: LCC GV885.515.N37 R86 2023 | DDC 796.323/640973—dc23/eng/20220722
LC record available at https://lccn.loc.gov/2022029151

ISBNs: 9781645036951 (hardcover), 9781645036968 (ebook)

LSC-C

Printing 1, 2022

For John Runstedtler. Dad, you were my first teacher in critical thinking. I hope you're relaxing in heaven.

For Gus, my miracle child. You've already taught me so much about life and love.

Contents

Introduction

"NBA and Cocaine: Nothing to Snort At," declared the *Los Angeles Times* headline wryly. "There are no reliable figures on the use of cocaine by players," *Times* staff writer Chris Cobbs admitted, "but estimates by people in the game range from 40 to 75%, with perhaps as many as 10% getting high with freebase."[1]

When that story ran in August 1980, the National Basketball Association (NBA) appeared to be a league in crisis. And given that around 75 percent of the league's players were African American, it appeared to be a *Black* crisis. Cobbs's exposé came in the wake of the well-publicized drug arrests of several Black players for possession of minor quantities of cocaine. Not only had game attendance and television ratings dipped in recent years, but now professional basketball seemed to be on the verge of a cocaine epidemic. This was a public relations nightmare for a majority-Black league that white sports fans already perceived as being violent, criminal, and out of control.

Black ballplayers' use of cocaine—an expensive drug typically associated with white celebrities, jet-setters, and professionals—was yet another reminder of their undeserved fortune. At a time when the rest of the United States was still reeling from a decade of stagflation and economic recession, NBA players had become some of the highest paid professional athletes in the world. Many of them, Cobbs noted, came from "unstable families in inner-city ghettoes" and could not

1

seem to handle their sudden wealth. Also, as one anonymous source told Cobbs, "The players are so street-smart, their sophistication is just below that of a hardened convict. They know every angle on how to get women and drugs. They are so far ahead of the security men it's unbelievable. They know every hustle." The chaos in the NBA seemed to mirror the chaos, crime, and violence in the streets of American cities. In both cases, young Black men were to blame. For his reporting, Cobbs won the Investigative Series award from the Basketball Writers' Association of America.[2]

Although rife with rumor and speculation, Cobbs's exposé has, for the most part, been accepted uncritically as emblematic of the supposed decline of professional basketball throughout the 1970s. As the oft-repeated narrative goes, Black players had brought their immaturity, selfishness, drug abuse, violence, and criminality—a very microcosm of America's "urban crisis"—to the NBA. They lacked character and morality, and it showed not only in how they conducted themselves off the court but also in how they played basketball. They had imported their aggressive, flashy, individualistic, and above-the-rim style from the playgrounds of Black neighborhoods to the pro game. A once honorable and disciplined white game of teamwork and set plays had devolved into anarchy. As African American players came to dominate professional basketball over the course of the seventies, their bad behavior had tarnished its reputation, and their exorbitant salary demands had pushed it to the brink of financial ruin.[3]

Yet rather than revealing the truth of the NBA's so-called Dark Ages, Cobbs's sensationalistic story throws into relief the fault lines of a decade-long struggle over the future of the sport—one that intersected with broader racial politics. This dynamic tended to pit the white basketball establishment (team owners, front-office executives, coaches, sportswriters) and the pro game's still majority-white fan base against its increasingly Black labor force—a labor force that came of age amid urban rebellions from Watts to Baltimore, the rise of the Black Power movement, and the numerous protests and boycotts that made up the "revolt of the Black athlete" in the late 1960s. With their racial consciousness forged in the heat of these battles, Black players found ways to extend the athletic revolt into the professional ranks, albeit with different goals and different strategies. In the years leading up to Cobbs's account, they led the fight for free agency and a greater share of the profits. They introduced the moves and attitude of Black street basketball to the league. Above all, they demanded respect as professionals and as men—on their own terms. And they did this against the backdrop of continuing white resistance to racial integration. Alongside Black workers accused of unfairly capitalizing on affirmative action's "racial quotas" and rising protests against the busing of Black children to white school districts, Black ballplayers also faced opposition to their own fight for racial justice.

As Black ball became a referendum on Black freedom, the pro game emerged as a kind of morality play about the shifting place of African Americans in US society—a site where the contours of Black citizenship and belonging in the post–civil rights era were rehashed and reshaped. The white-controlled business of professional basketball, much like the nation at large, had to reckon with rising Black demands for not just equality of opportunity but also equality of results. The supposed decline of pro basketball became a metaphor for the first decades of racial integration in America: the rules of the game had changed, allowing more Black people onto a formerly white playing field, and now they were ruining everything.

DESPITE SUCH NOSTALGIA ABOUT THE GAME'S HALLOWED TRADItions and all of the hand-wringing over the seeming loss of fans, the NBA was the youngest and still the least popular of the US major professional sports leagues even into the early 1980s. Basketball had neither the cultural cachet of baseball, with its long history as America's pastime, nor the near-religious fervor of football, with its embodiment of US manhood and militarism. The Canadian-born physical educator James Naismith first developed the game of basketball in the 1890s at the International Young Men's Christian Association Training School in Springfield, Massachusetts. A middle-class, Progressive Era reformer, he designed the amateur sport to help manage the baser instincts of young immigrant/migrant working-class men in America's growing cities and to socialize them in the discipline and mores of industrial capitalism. Regardless of Naismith's intentions, working people on both sides of the color line made basketball their own, and rough play, brawls, and professional games became part of the ever-evolving sport. Up until the late 1940s, professional basketball remained a largely regional and small-town sport, composed of competing circuits and numerous independent barnstorming teams. With no central institution or league running pro ball in the first half of the twentieth century, no formal color line existed. Instead, the game followed the local rules of race in different parts of the country.[4]

This all began to change in 1949, after the formation of the National Basketball Association as the result of a merger of the Basketball Association of America and the National Basketball League. Contrary to popular NBA lore, this was by no means a peaceful merger. Ownership groups in the two rival leagues had battled it out in the late 1940s, but they eventually came together to avoid mutual destruction and collectively assert control over the game. They hoped to take advantage of the post–World War II economic boom and the expansion of consumer culture. Over the next few decades, advances in technology, from television to commercial air travel, helped the league begin its pursuit of a national footprint. The NBA desired to cement its control and construct a monopoly over the pro game. It also wanted to enter the big time. It pushed its franchises to relocate from small towns to major metropolitan areas. It favored the use of white players and enacted strict measures of control over how they entered the league and whom they could play for, which kept them underpaid and disempowered.[5]

Despite the NBA's current-day reputation as a politically progressive league dominated by Black athletes and defined by urban Black culture, its embrace of African Americans, whether as players, coaches, executives, or fans, was slow and hesitant, if not downright reluctant. The first Black ballplayers entered the league in 1950, when the Boston Celtics drafted Charles "Chuck" Cooper and the Washington Capitols selected Earl Lloyd and Harold Hunter. Although Hunter was cut before he ever played a game, he was the first African American to sign an NBA contract. A few months later, the New York Knicks purchased the contract of Nat "Sweetwater" Clifton from the Harlem Globetrotters.[6] The league's approach to Black players was one of "controlled integration," complete with an informal racial quota that restricted the number of African American players on any one team.[7]

NBA club owners chose men like Chuck Cooper as much for their unblemished reputations and diplomatic character as for their talent. Like other Black pioneers in the United States' major professional sports leagues, Cooper and his generation faced blatant racism on and off the court, whether it was the anti-Black slurs of opposing players and fans or the refusal of service at southern establishments while on the road.[8] Looking back on his career, Cooper recalled, "No black superstars were permitted in basketball then. White management couldn't afford it because they knew white spectators wouldn't put up with it. You had to sort of fit in, if you were going to get in, make your contributions in a subordinate role."[9] Cooper, Lloyd, and Clifton all played supporting roles on their respective teams, primarily as rebounders and defenders. The 1950s was also a time when all players, but especially Black players, were poorly compensated and were subject to the whims of white coaches, management, and team owners about everything from trades to exhibition schedules. In light of their precarious situation, Cooper's generation endured the abuse in stoic defiance rather than challenging it publicly.[10]

The early fifties also marked the first stirrings of unionization in the league. Led by Boston Celtics point guard Bob Cousy, the National

Basketball Players Association (NBPA) was, in its early days, largely the province of white stars, and its stance with the owners was conciliatory rather than antagonistic. The fledgling association drew up and delivered its first set of formal demands to the NBA in 1955; however, league president Maurice Podoloff blew them off for as long as he could. The NBPA forced his hand in 1957 by meeting with the American Guild of Variety Artists. Fearing that the players might affiliate with a larger, more established union, Podoloff organized a meeting between the NBPA and the team owners. In addition to granting a few minor concessions, the league's board of governors recognized the NBPA as the formal body representing the players' interests and agreed to meet with it once a year. Yet Podoloff's evasion of more substantive issues, including a pension plan, continued.[11]

By the late 1950s, the NBA was a league on the verge of racial and labor transformation. Elgin Baylor and the next generation of African American pros arrived just as the civil rights movement was picking up steam, and they were no longer willing to suffer in silence while playing subordinate roles. As a rookie for the Minnesota Lakers in 1958, Baylor became an instant star. The six-foot-five forward showed the league that Black players could be high scorers. He also showed that Black players were willing to flex their newfound star power against racial discrimination. In January 1959, when the Lakers arrived in Charleston, West Virginia, to play an exhibition game, Baylor and his African American teammates were denied accommodation at a local hotel. In a notable show of solidarity, Lakers coach John Kundla chose to move the entire squad to a Black hotel. Baylor was incensed but still on track to play the next day. But when a restaurant denied him service before the game, he could no longer stomach the indignity and refused to take the court. Although Baylor was not the first to take such a stand, his one-man strike in West Virginia pushed NBA owners to declare that they would no longer schedule games where Black players would be forced to experience the "embarrassment" of segregation. Franchises did not always follow through on that promise, but it was no longer acceptable to simply assume that African Americans would stay at separate hotels on the road.[12]

And Black players remained vulnerable in other ways. During the 1955–1956 season, the Cincinnati Royals' six-foot-seven forward Maurice Stokes became, in some respects, the NBA's first major Black star. Stokes won Rookie of the Year and made the All-NBA Second Team three years in a row. Despite the promising start to his career, by March 1958 it was over. In an exhibition game against the Minnesota Lakers, Stokes went up for a shot, got bumped in the air, and landed heavily on the floor. Game-day medical care for players was rudimentary in those days. Unconscious for three minutes, Stokes finally came to with the help of smelling salts. Less than fifteen minutes later, he was back in the game. Over the next few days, Stokes felt weak, lethargic, and nauseated—all now recognized as hallmarks of a possible head injury. However, he continued to travel and play through the discomfort, with no medical intervention on the part of the team. His decision to get on a plane from Detroit to Cincinnati almost killed him. Partway through the flight, he began bleeding out of his mouth and ears, vomiting, and convulsing. Incoherent and unable to speak, Stokes was rushed to St. Elizabeth's Hospital upon arrival in Cincinnati, where doctors managed to stabilize him. However, his brain was severely damaged. Although he endured vigorous rehabilitation, he never fully recovered, and he died just twelve years later in 1970 at the age of thirty-six.[13]

NBA president Podoloff had been on that fateful flight and had witnessed Stokes's near-death experience. But the league essentially washed its hands of the injured athlete and his mounting medical bills. The players stepped into the breach, raising more than $10,000 for Stokes from two exhibition games played in 1958. Over the next decade they continued to hold annual charity games, collecting around $750,000 for Stokes's medical care. The NBA's callous refusal to help their fallen brother had stoked the ire of the players. Black players, in particular, realized just how vulnerable and disposable they remained.[14] Coupled with their experiences of being Jim Crowed, the league's abandonment of Stokes in his time of need prompted African American players to become even more militant in their demands.

As more African Americans entered the league in the sixties, they joined the NBPA and began to reshape the goals and ethos of the organization. They brought the tenor and tactics of civil rights into the union with them, refusing to accept the status quo. "Playing conditions at that time just weren't appropriate for a professional league," Cincinnati Royals star guard Oscar Robertson recalled of the early 1960s. "Players didn't have health insurance. We always stayed in second-class hotels. Teams refused to send their trainers on the road trips. Players didn't get paid for preseason."[15] Meanwhile, Podoloff continued to brush off the NBPA's calls for a pension. When a new NBA commissioner, J. Walter Kennedy, replaced Podoloff in 1963, the issue remained unresolved.[16] When NBPA president Tommy Heinsohn requested a meeting with the team owners at the 1964 All-Star Game to discuss a pension plan, they predictably refused.

The players realized that they had to raise the stakes, so they chose the biggest stage to play on. Scheduled for prime time on ABC on January 14, the 1964 All-Star Game in Boston was critical to the team owners' plans to catapult the NBA into the big time. On the line was a national television contract. If the game brought in good ratings, ABC would consider adding the NBA to its regular sports programming. Fed up with the years of stonewalling, the players were prepared to mount a boycott in order to get a signed deal for a pension.[17]

With the game scheduled to start at 9:00 p.m., all the players had gathered in one locker room, awaiting an update from Kennedy. At 8:25 the commissioner entered the room and sheepishly explained that there would be no signed agreement that night. However, he insisted that the owners had agreed to work out a pension plan with the players. They would just have to trust Kennedy at his word. With league executives and team owners banging on the door with threats and warnings about their future careers, the players discussed their next move. They continued to hold out until 8:50 p.m.—just ten minutes before the scheduled tip-off.[18] At the very last minute, Kennedy returned and told them to have NBPA lawyer Larry Fleisher draw up a pension-plan proposal and send it to his office the next day. The players then voted to proceed with the game. A few months later the league got its television contract with ABC, and the players got their first pension plan. It was not the best deal, but it was a small victory. Retired players would receive a total of $20,000 over ten years, with the NBA and the union to share the cost of the plan.[19]

At the same time that the NBPA began to flex its muscles, the style of professional ball began to shift. The game had already become quicker and more spectator friendly because of the widening of the lane from six to twelve feet in 1951 and the introduction of the twenty-four-second shot clock in the 1954–1955 season. These strategic rule changes coincided with the advent of players steeped in a Black hoops tradition that came of age under Jim Crow—from the establishment of the Black Fives to the rise of the Harlem Rens to the expansion of Black college ball to the exploding popularity of playground ball. With moves that made the game more aerial, aggressive, and improvisational, they introduced the NBA's still largely white fan base to the exhilaration of slam dunks and the weightless artistry of hang time.[20] For a league still struggling to find its footing next to the more established Major League Baseball (MLB) and National Football League (NFL), a league with relatively small television revenues whose popularity lagged behind that of National Collegiate Athletic Association (NCAA) ball and the Harlem Globetrotters, this seemed like a potential recipe for profit. Yet Black players were both cheered *and* chastised for their innovation. White basketball purists decried their exuberant play as a contamination of Naismith's hallowed vision, a corrupting influence, even though the game had always been a "dynamic, social, and embodied process of continual invention."[21] The inspired play of Elgin Baylor, Bill Russell, Wilt Chamberlain, and other African American stars may have offered a glimpse of pro basketball's future, but the NBA of the 1960s remained a white-controlled league marketed to white spectators.

By the latter part of the decade, however, the league was reaching a racial tipping point. The emergence of the baby boomers and their countercultural rebellion, alongside the successes of the civil rights–Black Power era, helped usher in the increasing acceptance of Black entertainers and athletes on the national stage. Pro basketball, with its growing firmament of freewheeling African American stars, seemed poised to become the "sport of the seventies," and optimistic sportswriters forecast its rapid expansion and increasing profitability. But there was nothing inevitable or easy about Black players' rise to dominance in the NBA—nor was the league a breakout success. Pro basketball became emblematic of the seventies but not for the reasons that journalists had predicted. Instead, Black players' various fights to reshape the professional game during this decade came to embody ongoing battles over race and labor beyond the sport. As the NBA worked to maintain its fraying monopoly and mechanisms of labor control, a new generation of African American players became a force to be reckoned with.

I CAME TO THIS PROJECT AS SOMEONE WITH A LONG-STANDING TIE to the NBA. Back in the late 1990s I was a member of the Toronto Raptors Dance Pak (now known as the North Side Crew). I remain part of the Raptors' extended family. We still keep in touch and have reunions on significant team anniversaries. They will forever be a part of my life. But as much as I love the league, my time with the Raptors also gave me a glimpse of the game's enduring racial and labor struggles on the court, in the media, and behind the scenes.

Even from the vantage point of a dancer, it was hard to miss the league's unspoken racial politics. In the early years, with Isiah Thomas as general manager and a shifting slate of owners, the Dance Pak had a surprising amount of freedom. We didn't look like the typical NBA dance team. We were more urban athletic than sexy glamour. There was no fixation on weight. Paying homage to African American hip-hop culture, we wore coveralls, bandannas, and sequined jerseys, and we danced to the latest rap and R & B hits. Our team was made up of women and men of all different races and ethnicities.

After Thomas left and the team was later sold to Maple Leaf Sports & Entertainment (then owners of the Toronto Maple Leafs of the National Hockey League), things changed. As a group, the Dance Pak became skinnier, whiter, and blonder. Our outfits became tighter, smaller, shinier, and lower cut. Will Smith and Motown replaced Busta Rhymes and Biggie Smalls on the sound system. And when we moved to the newly built Air Canada Centre (now Scotiabank Arena) in 1999, it became even more apparent that we were performing for wealthy white season-ticket holders on the floor rather than the regular (often nonwhite) fans in the nosebleeds. In some respects this book has been more than two decades in the making—a way for me to make sense of what I became a part of in the late 1990s.

Now, as a scholar of African American history, I have turned my critical eye to our received wisdom about the supposedly apolitical nature of Black professional basketball players in the seventies. After writing *Jack Johnson, Rebel Sojourner,* a book about the first-ever Black world heavyweight champion—a man who challenged global white supremacy and Western imperialism in the early 1900s—I could not help but see these players as part of what sportswriter Howard Bryant calls "the Heritage," the time-honored tradition of African American athletes amplifying the hopes and concerns of their people.[22] Like Jack Johnson, they have also been misunderstood, overlooked for their political importance in the context of their time and for how their stories can inform our present struggles.

Although the men in this book won numerous battles, many of the issues they faced, both on and off the court, remain unresolved. I began this research just as star quarterback Colin Kaepernick was being blacklisted by the NFL for daring to take a knee during the national anthem, a peaceful gesture devised to protest police brutality and systemic anti-Blackness in the United States. Kaepernick's demonstration came on the heels of an uptick in Black sporting activism that coalesced with the broader #BlackLivesMatter movement. In 2012 LeBron James and the Miami Heat took a pregame photo wearing hoodies in support of Trayvon Martin, the Black teenager gunned down by vigilante George Zimmerman in Florida. In 2014, after a New York City police officer choked African American Eric Garner to death, Black NBA and NFL players wore "I Can't Breathe" on their warm-ups, demanding justice for Garner. In many respects, Black players' hard-won battles for higher compensation and labor protections in the seventies opened up the space for this vibrant critique decades later. Although most of them were not out in their communities organizing protests against hyper-policing, endemic poverty, and other forms of structural racism, their battles against the white basketball establishment's monopolistic control of the sport deserve recognition as a significant part of the enduring Black freedom struggle.

Contrary to how the NBA now markets itself and its history, the league was by no means an uncomplicated champion of African American advancement in this earlier moment. In an effort to discipline its majority-Black players, it frequently sought the support of white fans and the white-dominated sports media. It also worked in tandem with NCAA officials to control the flow of labor into the professional ranks. As in other aspects of US society, African American ballplayers had to fight for recognition and rights in the face of strong resistance. At the same time, they held an ambivalent position in Black America. They had both proximity and distance from their communities; they were role models yet not representative. They had a degree of power, but especially for those who were not stars, their grasp on economic and social mobility remained tenuous. They embodied the "double consciousness" of the Black male professional athlete in post–civil rights America.[23]

Even though all of the major US professional leagues had desegregated by the 1970s, race still mattered. Black players' growing dominance in professional basketball was hardly a racial panacea; it was a double-edged sword. As some of the most visible Black male professionals who had "made it" in white American society, they became icons of Black success for some and symbols of inherent Black inferiority for others. Although they challenged white authority and many became financially prosperous beyond their dreams, public debates about their "pathologies" often reinforced negative ideas about Black men and about Black culture and politics more broadly. With their relative fame, wealth, and clout, they became easy targets amid the economic hardships caused by seventies stagflation and deindustrialization, the violence of the "urban crisis," the white backlash against the Black Power movement, the emergence of the "silent majority," and the anti-Black politics of "law and order." How team owners and league executives dealt with them, how the white media reported on them, and how white fans reacted to them sometimes reflected and often foreshadowed racialized policy debates outside of sport. Because they dared to push for the right to sell their talents on the free market and challenge the overwhelming whiteness of the basketball establishment, they were labeled as ungrateful, undisciplined, and even immoral. The idea of the "troublesome" Black basketball player came to define the decade.

That trouble, however, was ultimately "good trouble." The 1970s were pivotal to the rise of the dazzling, star-laden NBA we know today, largely because of the efforts of African American players who challenged the status quo. They rejected the rigidity of the professional game, bringing with them masculine bravado, broken backboards, and Black joy personified. Black players also leveraged the existence of the NBA's competing league, the American Basketball Association (ABA, 1967–1976), and turned to legal strategies and union organizing in order to push for better salaries and benefits as well as more control over whom they played for and under what conditions. For African Americans in professional basketball, this was hardly a bleak decade: their growing prominence helped to usher in some of the first

Black coaches, general managers, and even league executives. They took advantage of their increasing visibility in the media to express new forms of Black masculine identity and to weigh in on current affairs. In so doing, they demonstrated Black economic and cultural possibilities in the post–civil rights era.

Black Ball traces how these players, some household names, others more obscure, ultimately transformed professional basketball in this neglected yet crucial period. It moves from the antitrust lawsuits involving Connie Hawkins, Spencer Haywood, and Oscar Robertson and the NBPA, to the innovative playing style of Earl "the Pearl" Monroe and Julius "Dr. J" Erving, to the challenges facing outspoken and unapologetically Black players such as Kareem Abdul-Jabbar and Wali Jones, and finally to the emergence of African American front-office pioneers such as Wayne Embry and Simon Gourdine, who sought to change the NBA from within. These rapid developments bred racial resentments: white fans, league officials, and sportswriters blamed Black players' supposed pathologies for the NBA's declining fortunes, whether embodied by Kermit Washington's infamous punch of Rudy Tomjanovich and the uptick in on-court violence or the overlapping "cocaine crisis" of the late 1970s involving the likes of Bernard King, Terry Furlow, and Eddie Johnson. Though sometimes disparaged and often disregarded, this earlier generation helped pave the way for the growth of the NBA as a global profit machine and cultural force. Without their skills, style, and savvy, there would be no Michael Jordan, Allen Iverson, LeBron James, or James Harden today.

Part 1

Battling Monopoly

Chapter 1

Exile

Connie Hawkins's Long Journey to the NBA

There is a lot of disappointment . . . a lot of years wasted. Now I just want to prove what kind of player I am in the NBA and clear my name.

—Connie Hawkins, *Life*, 1969

IN SPRING 1968, AT THE RIPE AGE OF TWENTY-SIX, THE SIX-FOOT-eight African American power forward Cornelius "Connie" Hawkins took to the court for his first playoffs as a professional in the American Basketball Association (ABA). He had waited years to showcase his skills as a pro, but now he was the Pittsburgh Pipers' breakout star and the fledgling league's Most Valuable Player. After leading his team in a three-game rout of the Indiana Pacers, Hawkins, also known as "the Hawk," prepared to play the Minnesota Muskies in the Eastern Division Finals. Although Pipers owner Gabe Rubin was counting on big playoff gates at the Civic Arena, located in the city's Hill District, racial politics off the court intervened.

At 6:00 on the evening of April 4, civil rights leader Martin Luther King Jr. was shot on the balcony of the Lorraine Motel in Memphis, Tennessee. King was rushed to a nearby hospital but was pronounced dead about an hour later. That same night, as King's life hung in the balance, the Pipers faced the Muskies at home, beating them 125–117. It was a come-from-behind win, thanks in part to the Hawk's 26 points.[1]

As news of King's murder began to circulate, it sparked uprisings in more than a hundred cities across the United States, including Pittsburgh, where persistent racial inequality had created a tinderbox of Black grievances. Civil unrest—violence, vandalism, arson, and looting—erupted in the city's impoverished African American neighborhoods, including the Hill District, Homewood, and the North Side (where Hawkins and his family lived). Over the next few days, around 3,650 National Guardsmen and 300 state troopers were deployed to restore order.

In the midst of this chaos, on April 6 the Pipers lost at home to the Muskies in front of a smattering of only the most intrepid spectators. By the time the unrest died down on April 11, one Pittsburgher was dead, 36 were injured, and around 1,000 were arrested. After winning the next two games in Minnesota, the Pipers returned home on April 14 for game 4, and Rubin hoped that ticket sales would rebound. Playing to the crowd, Hawkins "toyed around with some behind-the-back dribbles and one-handed pass-catching," leading his team to a 114–105 victory over the Muskies.[2] The Pipers had clinched the Eastern Division title four games to one, but Rubin's anticipated profits failed to materialize. In the aftermath of the uprising, white fans had stayed away from the Civic Arena, fearful for their safety.[3] Although King's tragic death had cast a pall over the series, it was not the first time that Hawkins found himself at the intersection of basketball and the Black freedom struggle.

TWO YEARS EARLIER, ON NOVEMBER 3, 1966, HAWKINS HAD LITTLE idea that his lawsuit against the NBA marked the beginning of a new chapter in professional basketball, one that would radically change the balance of power between team owners and players over the course of the next decade. His attorneys, David and Roslyn (Roz) Litman of Pittsburgh, had filed the $6 million treble-damage antitrust suit in the US District Court of Western Pennsylvania as a last resort. They had first met the quiet, lanky nineteen-year-old when he played for David's brother's team, the Pittsburgh Rens, in the short-lived American Basketball League (ABL). Since fall 1963, the Litmans' successive letters to NBA commissioner Walter Kennedy and the individual NBA teams about their client's eligibility to play starting in 1964 (the year his college class graduated) had fallen on deaf ears.[4] First unjustly blacklisted by the NCAA and then by the NBA for his alleged ties to the 1961 college game-fixing scandal, Hawkins had bounced around professional basketball's bush leagues in the 1960s. Despite his professed innocence, even the Eastern League, a haven for Black players overlooked by the NBA, wanted nothing to do with him, so he ended up playing a season in the ABL and then toured for four years with the Harlem Globetrotters.[5]

In May 1966, while Hawkins was in Europe with the Globetrotters, David Litman had stepped up the pressure with a face-to-face meeting with Commissioner Kennedy. It had gone badly. Kennedy made it clear that the league had no interest in investigating the veracity of the allegations against Hawkins. The next week, the Litmans received a letter from Kennedy. In it, the commissioner claimed that his hands were tied. Franchises made their own draft choices, and he had nothing to do with their lack of interest in the Hawk.[6] Without any due process for Hawkins, the league had effectively shut out one of professional basketball's top prospects of the decade. Known from his masterful summer-league play in New York City, Hawkins was touted as "a mixture of Bill Russell, Oscar Robertson and Elgin Baylor."[7]

The Litmans decided that the time had come for their law firm to formally take on Hawkins as a client. The couple had long been involved in local civil rights and civil liberties cases as active members of the Pittsburgh branch of the American Civil Liberties Union (ACLU). Their partner Howard Specter joined Roz and David in building the case. Although the Litmans believed that Hawkins's antitrust suit stood on solid legal ground, at the time there was little precedent to suggest that their strategy would succeed.[8] The suit alleged that the NBA had conspired "to bar him from player membership" in the league.[9] They hoped that suing the league and its teams for engaging in a group boycott of Hawkins as a restraint of trade and violation of the Sherman Antitrust Act would compensate him for his years of lost earnings and also open the door to a career in the NBA.

Hawkins did too. He was unemployed and out of money. Just a few months earlier, he had left the Globetrotters after impresario Abe Saperstein refused to put an escape clause in his contract that would allow him to leave on his own terms. Despite his years of playing, Hawkins and his extended family still lived in "a small, run-down three-story frame house" in the middle of the Black North Side neighborhood. With no income and emptied of savings, Hawkins had to borrow money to feed his family. What else could he do? He had no college degree. He had no training in anything other than basketball. Yet the NBA, the only real game in town, refused to give him a chance to play. "Connie has been hurt irreparably by the NBA's blindness," David Litman complained. "He's never had an endorsement, he's earning a fraction of what he's worth and, with no widespread reputation, what kind of job opportunities do you think a person like him will have when he can't play anymore?"[10] Operating as a monopoly, the NBA was depriving Hawkins of his right to earn a living commensurate with his talent in his chosen profession. With the help of the Litmans, Hawkins readied himself for the fight of his life.

As the details of Hawkins's case came to light, in large part thanks to the dogged reporting of journalist and biographer David Wolf, they exposed the myriad forms of manipulation and exploitation faced by young African American ballplayers, both on and off the court. His treatment by the white basketball establishment—the powers that be who controlled the NCAA and NBA—mirrored his treatment in the criminal-justice system. In the summer of 1960 the eighteen-year-old Hawkins had been playing on the courts in Manhattan Beach, Brooklyn, "when a tall man with dark, receding hair walked over and extended a hand that was almost as large as Connie's." Little did Hawkins realize that it was Jack Molinas, a former NBA player whom the league had effectively banned for life in 1954 for betting on games. Now a lawyer in New York City, the gregarious six-foot-six man "was the mastermind of a nationwide gambling ring that was in the process of paying 36 college players $70,000 to fix 43 games." Molinas used the city's playgrounds to meet vulnerable young players, particularly poor Black youths, for his game-fixing operation. But Hawkins knew nothing of Molinas's shady dealings, past or present. To Hawkins, he was an older white fan who loved basketball and happened to pick up the tab at restaurants after tournament games. "I just thought Jack was a nice guy," Hawkins later told Wolf. "He'd buy us food, drive us home from the beach or lend us his car. One time he told me he knew how hard it was for poor kids their first year at school and if I needed help or money, just let him know. He said he liked me."[11]

Later that summer, Molinas had invited Hawkins and friend Roger Brown (another top African American college prospect from Brooklyn) to his law office. He gave them $10 each for transportation and dinner and introduced them to his client "Joey." It all seemed harmless. Molinas and Brown left the room while Hawkins chatted with "Joey" about hoops. Hawkins thought nothing of the conversation. "Joe started talking about basketball: who was better Wilt or Russell? Then he asked did I know any good college players," Hawkins recalled. No stranger to playground ball in New York City, Hawkins knew many college athletes. At the time, it was not uncommon for pros, collegians, and high schoolers to play each other in three-on-three games in the off-season. "I told him Wilky Gilmore of Colorado,

Vinnie Brewer of Iowa State and some others." Then "Joey" asked if Hawkins could introduce him to them, and Hawkins said, "Sure." Hawkins thought "Joey" was just another rabid New York basketball fan—another white guy attempting to live vicariously through the athletic prowess of young Black ballplayers. However, "Joey" was Joe Hacken, "a Molinas lieutenant with nine bookmaking convictions."[12]

Given the aggressive and corrupt college recruitment tactics that Hawkins experienced, his interactions with Molinas and Hacken would have seemed innocent, if not benign. By the time he met them, he was primed to expect that receiving cash and favors from white men was a normal part of being a talented Black basketball prospect. Hawkins had played for the Bedford-Stuyvesant powerhouse Boys High School with the goal of getting a scholarship to play NCAA ball. Even as a teenager, his talent was undeniable. "I can recall seeing Connie while still in high school play against a team of pros that included Wilt Chamberlain, and Connie held his own," Harlem native and former Indiana Pacers point guard Jerry Harkness noted. "He was already as good as the pros when he was 16."[13] Heavily recruited by hundreds of colleges, Hawkins had scouts regularly slipping him cash and coaches promising him free clothes, plane tickets, and even a salary. Local promoters also slid him cash when he played in amateur tournaments. Hawkins had no qualms about taking the money. Everybody else was doing it, and he needed it. His father had left the family when he was just ten years old, leaving his mother to raise six children on her own. By his senior year at Boys High in 1960, Hawkins was six-foot-seven and recognized as one of the finest ballplayers to ever come out of the Big Apple.[14]

Even though he was weak academically, Hawkins went on to play college ball for the University of Iowa Hawkeyes. His time at Iowa involved more of the same white paternalism. Because of his poor scholastic record, he was not eligible for an athletic scholarship. Instead, Iowa admitted him on probation and arranged for him to pay his own way. An Iowa alumnus got him a job at a local filling station. Whether or not Hawkins actually had to show up to be paid is unclear, but this "job" provided for his tuition, books, room and board, and spending money. For its part, Iowa's Athletic Department set him up with tutors and hoped for the best.[15] Because freshmen were ineligible to play NCAA ball (the rule remained in place for basketball and football until 1972), the Hawk had a year to get his academics in order.

Hawkins returned to New York City for Christmas vacation in 1960. Excited to be back home and eager to show his old friends how well he was doing as an NCAA player, he blew through $200. Now he had no money to cover his dormitory fees for the upcoming semester. Desperate for cash, he remembered what Molinas had said to him back in the summer. He called Molinas and asked for a $200 loan. Molinas brought the money to Hawkins's home the day before he went back to school. Shortly thereafter, Fred Hawkins, Connie's older brother, repaid the loan on his behalf.[16]

Meanwhile, the New York County District Attorney's office was closing in on Molinas's gambling operation. In spring 1961, former collegiate player and schoolteacher David Budin admitted to arranging several fixed games as part of Molinas's nationwide network. During his interrogation, perhaps hoping to take some of the heat off of himself, Budin implicated several NCAA players, including Hawkins and Brown. Although he gave no specifics about their alleged involvement, Budin reputedly said that Molinas had them "in the bag."[17]

Hawkins became the DA's next target. On April 27, 1961, Coach Sharm Scheuerman summoned the Hawk to Iowa's fieldhouse. Detective Anthony Bernhard was there to question him about Molinas and the man he knew only as "Joey." Hawkins seemed confused. He didn't even appear to know what a "point spread" was. Still, Bernhard ordered the young player to come to New York to help with the investigation of Molinas's gambling network. Bernhard promised Scheuerman that Hawkins would be back at school in three days. Three days turned into two weeks, throwing Hawkins's life into chaos. Back in New York City, Hawkins was put under protective custody and forced to stay at the Prince George Hotel on East 28th Street with other NCAA players who were also part of the investigation. He was not allowed to call his mother, nor was he informed of his rights or offered legal counsel. Because he thought he would be in New York only for the weekend, he didn't even have a change of clothes. Detectives questioned the teenager extensively. Despite being interrogated at least twenty times over a six-day period, Hawkins told a consistent story—one that did not implicate him in the scandal.[18]

Hawkins's harrowing experience was not unlike those of other young Black men caught up in New York's criminal-justice system in the early 1960s. Although President Richard Nixon's federal War on Crime was still a few years away, by 1964 New York state anti-crime laws, including the "stop-and-frisk" and "no-knock" bills, had codified the already disproportionate policing of African American neighborhoods. Hawkins's ability to play ball offered no protection from harsh treatment. He and other Black youths bore the brunt of a system that increasingly "denied their innocence and presumed their criminality."[19]

Finding himself increasingly isolated, exhausted, confused, and afraid, he decided to change his story. "They kept saying I'd go to jail if I lied," Hawkins recounted. "Then they'd say they thought I was lying. So I thought I'd go to jail if I didn't tell a different story. And I knew what they wanted me to say. They were always saying 'Didn't you get offered $500 for introducing players?' I just decided I'd never get out if I kept telling the truth."[20] In subsequent interrogations over the next eight days and in front of a New York County grand jury on May 10, Hawkins falsely confessed to connecting gamblers with college players. Thanks to Hawkins's testimony, Hacken was indicted. The DA's office had hoped Hacken would then flip on Molinas, but Hacken pled guilty and kept his lips sealed.

New York district attorney Frank Hogan told the press that Hawkins was an "intermediary" in Molinas's gambling ring, having "introduced Hacken to a number of college players." Although Hawkins was never charged with anything, the Black freshman's face was splashed all over the newspapers.[21] The African American *Philadelphia Tribune* was saddened to hear that Hawkins and Brown "were involved on the fringes of this dirty, rotten, stinking business." The *Tribune* lamented, "Gamblers have a way of getting to young, unsuspecting and susceptible athletes."[22] Crooks like Molinas trolled the playground courts looking for talented but naive Black teens with uncertain economic futures.

The white basketball establishment was much less sympathetic to their situation. After the grand jury, an assistant DA gave Hawkins a plane ticket back to Iowa City. Coach Scheuerman was waiting for him at the airport and told him that he had to leave college because of his alleged involvement in the scandal. Publicly, though, Scheuerman claimed that Hawkins had quit "because of scholastic and financial difficulties."[23] DA Hogan's statement, along with Hawkins's coerced confession, effectively derailed the budding basketball star's career for the next eight years.

WHEN THE LITMANS FILED THE HAWK'S LAWSUIT IN NOVEMBER 1966, there had been only two other unsuccessful antitrust suits lodged against the NBA—one of which involved none other than Jack Molinas. Even though Molinas was still a compulsive gambler (he and Hacken were involved in a game-fixing scheme by 1957, just three years after the NBA had barred him for life), he had sought reinstatement to the league in 1958. When the league rebuffed him, he filed a $3 million antitrust suit that took aim at the reserve clause—a clause in professional contracts that effectively bound a player to one team until that team decided to trade or release him—as "an unreasonable restraint of trade." Molinas's suit also argued that his suspension by the league and its subsequent refusal to reinstate him were "the result of a conspiracy" and therefore violations of the Sherman Act.[24] Concerned about the case's potential repercussions for the league's reserve system, and ultimately its monopoly power, the NBA had offered Molinas a small settlement. Molinas turned it down, hoping for a bigger windfall. However, in 1961 a New York district court dismissed Molinas's case for lack of proof.

Nor was Hawkins the first African American player to find himself blacklisted from the NBA. Cleo Hill offered another cautionary tale. In the early 1960s, the talented six-foot-one guard from Newark, New Jersey, was pushed out of the league for refusing to abide by the NBA's still rigid racial etiquette. Hill became the first player from a historically Black school (Winston-Salem Teachers College) to be picked up in the first round of the 1961 NBA draft. The St. Louis Hawks, enticed by Hill's electrifying play, had signed him to a one-year, no-cut contract for $7,500. However, the high-flying and high-scoring rookie ruffled the feathers of the Hawks' white veterans.[25] In those days, Black players were supposed to be the supporting cast, not the stars, and after only one season St. Louis cut him. No other NBA team picked him up, and no attorneys came to his aid. In 1963 Hill began a five-year career in the Eastern League, which, at the time, was filled with many talented African American players who had been passed over or blacklisted by the NBA for equally dubious reasons.

The odds did not look good for Hawkins, but unlike Hill he had sympathetic white lawyers to strategize on his behalf. On November 3, 1966, a US marshal served Kennedy with the $6 million suit while the commissioner was in Pittsburgh to gauge the city's suitability for a future NBA franchise. When journalists asked for his reaction, Kennedy refused to comment.[26] Although Kennedy likely viewed it as little more than an annoyance, the lawsuit signaled something much bigger. It heralded the rise of a new generation of Black ballplayers whose legal and labor challenges would shake the racial and economic structure of pro sports.

As the out-of-work Hawkins awaited his day in court, the establishment of the ABA in 1967 opened up another opportunity for him to play professionally. The existence of this rival league changed the game not only for Hawkins but also for every other player, especially Black players who had been left out in the cold by the NBA. Even though the NBA had technically desegregated in the early 1950s, an informal racial quota system had continued to limit the number of African Americans in the league up until the late 1960s. Ray Scott, a six-foot-nine forward/center who played in the league from 1961 to 1970, recalled that on any given team "there was a quota—sometimes two or three, and the highest was four." According to Scott, "You had hard-core owners who were trying to market to the public. It was where they saw their public, and they didn't look at the black community."[27] Making matters worse, NBA scouts tended to overlook talented athletes from Black colleges and universities at a time when relatively few attended predominantly white institutions. The NBA brass also routinely rejected Black ballplayers, like Hawkins, who had less than spotless reputations. Now the ABA wanted them.

Hawkins initially greeted news of the ABA with cautious optimism. "I was happy when I first read articles about the league," he told David Wolf, "but I thought they was bullshittin'."[28] He had already seen Abe Saperstein's ABL collapse after one season. Even the NBA was still trying to cement its position as a viable sports property alongside the more popular MLB and NFL. "The [NBA's] television contract was still weak," recalled Mike Storen, the first vice president and general manager of the ABA's Indiana Pacers. "The NBA was a very distant third in the eyes of the sports fan."[29] In this weakness, the ABA's collection of opportunistic entrepreneurs saw an opening.

The origins of the ABA are a bit hazy. Some credit the "lean, smooth Yaleman" Constantine Seredin, then head of a New York City public relations firm that connected athletes with advertisers, for coming up with the idea for a rival league.[30] Others point to Dennis Murphy, a one-term mayor of Buena Park, California, turned marketing executive, as the one who led the charge to establish the ABA. Murphy's original idea had been to launch an American Football League (AFL) franchise in Anaheim, believing that a merger between the AFL and

NFL was imminent. But the two leagues consolidated in 1966, before Murphy and his investors could get their plan off the ground. They shifted their sights to founding a new professional basketball league to rival the NBA. They hoped to replicate what the AFL team owners had achieved: to create just enough competition to force a merger with the NBA.[31]

ABA team owners were banking on the fact that their franchises would grow in value once they became part of the NBA. "We heard that there would be an ABA investors meeting in New York," Dick Tinkham, former legal counsel for the Pacers, recounted. "You brought a check for $5,000 and you were in—not just in the meeting, but in the league! So we got the five grand and we were in."[32] Although the performance bond was eventually set at $50,000, the barrier to entry remained relatively low, and many ABA investors were willing to take the risk in joining this new enterprise, hoping that it would pay off sooner rather than later.[33]

This speculative gamble by a set of scrappy and irreverent white entrepreneurs proved to have unintended consequences. It not only opened up new opportunities for Hawkins and other African Americans to enter the professional ranks, but it also undermined the NBA team owners' autocratic control over their players. Although initially dubbed the "lively league," the ABA soon gained a reputation as an "outlaw league" because of how it flouted the traditions of pro basketball both on and off the court, paving the way for the racial transformation of the game.

To help create an aura of legitimacy and pull in more investors, the ABA hired former DePaul University and Minneapolis Lakers six-foot-ten white star George Mikan, "Mr. Basketball," to be commissioner. Now forty-two years old and bespectacled, Mikan had been first-team All-NBA for six consecutive seasons in the late 1940s and early 1950s.[34] Because he refused to move to New York City, the ABA's league office was originally located in Minneapolis, where he was an established attorney and owner of a travel agency.[35]

By the beginning of its first season, in fall 1967, the ABA boasted eleven teams: the Indiana Pacers, Kentucky Colonels, Minnesota Muskies, New Jersey Americans, and Pittsburgh Pipers in the Eastern Division, and the Anaheim Amigos, Dallas Chaparrals, Denver Rockets, Houston Mavericks, New Orleans Buccaneers, and Oakland Oaks in the Western Division. Although most teams were in markets previously overlooked by the NBA, the ABA set out to challenge the established league head-on in three major metropolitan areas: New York, San Francisco, and Los Angeles.[36]

Now the dilemma was to stock the new clubs with talent. "Our biggest job was to find players," recalled Max Williams, former coach and general manager of the Dallas Chaparrals. "I got a lot of letters and calls. One guy wrote me from the state penitentiary in Oklahoma. He said if he could produce a contract, they'd let him out to play ball for Dallas. I passed on that one. We had an open tryout and drew about 100 guys. That was just a zoo, people killing each other, but we didn't find anyone of significance." Most ABA players initially came from the Amateur Athletic Union leagues and the Eastern League. Bob Bass, then coach of the Denver Rockets, had scoured NBA rosters for the names of players no longer in the league and attempted to track them down.[37]

For the ABA to draw fans, however, it needed stars, so team owners initially hoped to pluck them from the NBA. Although Commissioner Mikan assured sportswriters that there would be no deliberate raids of NBA teams, he acknowledged, "We would be stupid . . . not to ask players if they are not tied down." With the new league, Mikan predicted that player salaries would increase, spiraling costs and inducing expansion in the NBA.[38] Indeed, rumors of the ABA's impending arrival had prompted the NBA to grant franchises to San Diego and Seattle.[39] Unaccustomed to having any serious competition for talent and spectators, NBA club owners were in for a rude awakening. The ABA now threatened its hallowed draft and reserve systems, which for years had kept players underpaid and under the thumbs of the team owners.

In challenging the established league, the ABA also helped to transform the character and pace of the professional game. Billing itself as "a movement to bring excitement back to pro basketball," the ABA instituted four key changes to the pro game: the 3-point shot, the 30-second rule, the 12-foot lane, and the multicolored ball.[40] The ABA believed that the 3-point shot, taken 25 feet from the basket, would reward the skillful shooter and challenge the defense by forcing it to guard the perimeter. With the 30-second rule, ABA players would have 6 more seconds than their NBA counterparts to take a shot before having to give up possession. The extra time would open up the game, giving players more time to maneuver. The ABA also decided to use a 12-foot lane—the same size as the NCAA lane, but 4 feet narrower than the NBA lane.

ABA games would feature a red, white, and blue ball, reminiscent of the one used by the Harlem Globetrotters. Mikan was not a fan of the brown ball used by the NBA. "The arenas were darker then than they are now, and the ball just sort of blended into the background," he later explained.[41] Rather than sporting the typical black-and-white uniforms, the referees would also be jazzed up, dressed in red shirts, white trousers, blue belts, and blue shoes. Mikan hoped that these splashes of color on the court would appeal to spectators in the arena while also being immediately recognizable to TV viewers at home. However, little did Mikan and the ABA team owners realize that their upstart league would change the color of the game in more ways than one. It would soon become an incubator for a new style of pro ball—Black ball—and its existence would help spur Black players to lead a more forceful push for higher compensation, better contract terms, and more control over their careers.

As THE ABA CAME TOGETHER IN THE SPRING OF 1967, THE NOW twenty-four-year-old Hawkins was still living in a rundown rowhouse on Charles Street in Pittsburgh's Black North Side neighborhood, unable to support his family on his meager earnings. "He was playing in an industrial league at the Young Men's and Women's Hebrew Association (*a team called the Porky Chedwicks*) and admission was 50 cents a night," local sportswriter Jim O'Brien recalled.[42] The Hawk supplemented his paltry income from the Porky Chedwicks by cobbling together a number of side gigs. He played with a comedic basketball troupe called the Harlem Wizards, and he participated in playground tournaments for charity in New York City.[43]

The ABA's Oakland Oaks were the first team to express interest in signing the still disgraced and unemployed Black player.[44] Fearful of doing anything that might hurt his lawsuit against the NBA, Hawkins discussed the opportunity with David Litman. Litman thought that an ABA contract would only help the Hawk's cause, proving that he was a player of professional caliber. But Litman also worried that a cross-country move would throw a wrench in his plans to keep Hawkins's trial based in Pennsylvania, where the judge and jury would likely be more sympathetic to the longtime resident's plight. The NBA's chief counsel, George C. Gallantz, was attempting to get Hawkins's suit thrown out, arguing that western Pennsylvania was an improper venue because the NBA did no business there and had no team in the district.[45] If Pittsburgh remained Hawkins's place of employment, however, it would strengthen his case, so Litman put feelers out to Gabe Rubin, owner of the ABA's Pittsburgh Pipers.

Rubin was a "portly, dapper little man" with a "gravelly voice" who owned a local movie theater called the Nixon.[46] "You could say that the Nixon Theatre featured 'adult art films,'" O'Brien reminisced. "I knew the Nixon as a place I wasn't allowed to go as a teenager."[47] The Nixon had made Rubin a small fortune—the operative word being *small*. Although he claimed to have very deep pockets, Rubin had nowhere near enough money to sustain a franchise through a long-term fight against the NBA. Like many of the other initial investors in the ABA, Rubin hoped to profit from a quick merger. "He talked an opulent game and operated on half a shoestring," David Wolf

observed. Notoriously stingy, Rubin was the master of getting people to work for him for free. O'Brien, who at the time edited a small
paper called *Pittsburgh Weekly Sports*, crafted numerous press releases
for Rubin. "I put in a lot of work for him," O'Brien recounted. "Then
he'd phone me and pick my brain for hours. But when I mentioned
money, Gabe always said, 'We'll discuss it later.' Finally, after I'd
bugged him for two months, he paid me $200. It came out to about
two dollars an hour."[48]

Rubin had negotiated with the Oakland Oaks for the rights to sign
Hawkins. Although Litman was still concerned about his client's eligibility to play in the ABA, Rubin assured him that Commissioner
Mikan would give the green light for Hawkins to enter the league.
Sure enough, in April 1967, Mikan announced that he was allowing Hawkins, Roger Brown, Tony Jackson, and Doug Moe to play
in the ABA. All four players had been passed over by the NBA for
their alleged ties to Molinas's gambling ring, but none of them had
been charged with anything.[49] "The thing I was concerned about was,
Would he do it *again*? We investigated and found he's totally a reha-
bilitated family man," Mikan later told Wolf.[50] In truth, the ABA had
never done any serious investigation. They were not particularly interested in clearing Hawkins's name. Their "forgiveness" was strategic,
for the fledgling league was desperate for talented ballplayers.

Litman then set his sights on negotiating a flexible contract with
Pittsburgh: "The ABA was only a hiatus and a tool that we were using
to get into the NBA. My major concern wasn't money, it was getting a
clause in the contract that would permit Connie to go to the NBA in
the event the case was settled."[51] Because he had not done much legal
work in the sports industry, Litman was unaware of the significance of
his unconventional requests. Although the pro basketball leagues did
not have as draconian a reserve system as Major League Baseball, they
kept players bound to teams through the option clause. When a player
signed a contract, this clause gave the team an option to his services
for the next season. Unless the team decided to trade or release him,

the player could attempt to gain his freedom to move only by refusing to sign a contract and sitting out the season. Somehow Litman convinced the Pipers owner to delete the option clause *and* add a no-trade clause in Hawkins's contract.

Because Rubin, also a neophyte in the business of pro sports, was more concerned about getting Hawkins for cheap, he had agreed to the unorthodox terms. Commissioner Mikan had likewise approved the deal, skeptical that the NBA would ever lift its ban of the blacklisted player.[52] Hawkins's contract with Pittsburgh included a $5,000 bonus, with a $15,000 salary for the first year and a $25,000 salary for the second, with the option of becoming a completely free agent at the end of the second season.[53] Still, his salary was a pittance compared to those of his contemporaries in the NBA, with the 76ers star center Wilt Chamberlain making around $250,000 per year and veteran Cincinnati Royals guard Oscar Robertson earning about $100,000.[54]

Despite being woefully underpaid, Hawkins's access to top-flight representation and the flexible terms of his contract foreshadowed the changing power relationship between the players and the owners in professional basketball. As the players became more savvy in their business dealings, the club owners no longer held all the cards. And as they began to find common cause, the players would soon launch a more frontal assault on the NBA's option clause.

Even though publicly the ABA claimed it would not go after NBA players still under contract, behind the scenes the team owners planned to poach talent from the established league. "All the owners got together one day and we drafted all the NBA players. It was like dealing baseball cards," Dick Tinkham recalled. "We hadn't played a game, but we were deluding ourselves into thinking that all these NBA guys would jump leagues."[55] There were initially rumors that Chamberlain might make the jump, but he chose to stay with the 76ers, as did most other NBA players reportedly mulling over a move.[56] Unable to lure more than a few NBA players to the new league, ABA team owners soon set their sights on the NCAA as potentially the best source of rising stars. "The college crop is immense," *Basketball News* noted, "and a lot less of a legal problem."[57]

One exception to this trend was Rick Barry, the first NBA superstar to announce he was jumping to the ABA. When Barry, the San Francisco Warriors' talented white forward, decided to sign with the ABA's Oakland Oaks in June 1967, he quickly became the centerpiece of the new league's marketing campaign. Thanks to his skills and the color of his skin, Barry graced the covers of early ABA media guides and pictorials and became the most reported-on player in the league. If the outsized promotion of Barry is any indication, the ABA, though now popularly remembered as a "Black league," was by no means trying to position or sell itself as such in its early years.

Signing Barry was definitely a coup for the ABA. He had been the NBA's leading scorer in the 1966–1967 season, knocking the bombastic Chamberlain out of the top spot after seven consecutive wins.[58] Under the leadership of the Oaks' majority owner, the popular singer Pat Boone, the new team had privately plotted to steal Barry from its rivals across the bay. Hiring Bruce Hale as head coach was the first step. Hale just happened to be Barry's father-in-law, and he had also coached the young star at the University of Miami.[59]

Knowing that the Oaks were interested in signing him, Barry told both Oakland and San Francisco to submit their best and final contract offers. The Oaks offered him $75,000 per year for three years and an unprecedented 15 percent stake in the team. He would also receive 5 percent of the gate receipts once $600,000 was reached.[60] In contrast, Frank Mieuli, the Warriors team owner, tried to lowball Barry, offering $45,000 per season with *potential* bonuses of $30,000. Mieuli's offer felt like a slap in the face. Hobbled by a sprained ankle and shot up with Carbocaine to dull the pain, Barry had still managed to carry San Francisco through the 1967 playoffs after center Nate Thurmond had broken his hand. He had more than paid his dues.

Although the Warriors still retained the rights to Barry for another season because of the option clause in his contract, the young star's lawyers advised him to sign with the Oaks. They did not think the option clause would hold up if tested in court. Neither did the Oaks majority owner and his attorneys. "We would never have been interested in signing Rick Barry if we didn't feel he was legally free to sign with us," Boone told reporters.[61] For his part, Barry hoped he could jump leagues without ever having to miss a season. On January 20, he announced his three-year deal with the Oaks to the press: "The offer Oakland made me was one I simply couldn't turn down."[62]

Barry's potential departure from the NBA threatened the entrenched system of player recruitment and retention that had long favored the interests of professional sports team owners. "I feel the whole structure of sports as we know them have been shaken by Barry's move," Mieuli cautioned. "If it can happen to the Warriors what's to prevent it from happening to any other pro team?"[63] The Warriors sued Barry for breach of contract, hoping that the courts would find in their favor.[64] Mieuli could not fathom a professional sports system in which athletes had an actual voice in where they wanted to play.

For now, pro basketball's option clause would remain intact. In August 1967 the Warriors won in court to keep Barry from jumping to the Oakland Oaks. Judge Robert J. Drewes ruled in San Francisco that the option clause in Barry's contract with the Warriors was binding. Therefore, he was not legally free to play with the Oaks. "There is no vindictiveness on our part against Barry," Mieuli claimed on the heels of the court's decision. "We just did what we thought we had to do and felt right along the NBA option clause was legal."[65]

Still, Judge Drewes's decision presented Barry with a choice. He could play for the Warriors for the season or not play for anyone until his contract with San Francisco expired on September 30, 1968. Ever the iconoclast, Barry snubbed his nose at the NBA and chose instead to sit out his option year and then join the ABA in the 1968–1969 season. Rather than playing ball, he would work with the Oaks as a commentator for the team's televised games. His choice was certainly made easier by the fact that he would still receive his guaranteed

$75,000 salary with the Oaks whether he played or not.[66] The NBA might have won this battle, but there was a much bigger talent war brewing on the horizon.

Even though Barry was forced to sit on the sidelines, Oakland and the ABA continued to lean on the white superstar for publicity. He traveled to ABA cities to boost ticket sales and court corporate sponsors.[67] At the Oaks' home opener in October, Barry wore a mustard jacket and fawn slacks and hobnobbed with Boone's Hollywood friends. "Bench those nothing bums," the fans yelled, "we want Barry!"[68] Mieuli and the Warriors could only look on with regret and contempt, for Barry seemed to be having the last laugh.

Despite his controversial challenge to pro basketball's option clause and benching for the season, Barry did not seem to be hurting for fans or financial opportunities. He received invitations to play at celebrity golf games and to make appearances at basketball schools across the country. He was reportedly courted by Hollywood producers for possible film projects, asked to judge a beauty contest, invited to be a color commentator for university games, and offered $5,000 to pose for a series of national magazine ads. Sales of the Rick Barry Basketball Shoe and Spalding's Rick Barry outdoor basketball boomed, and businesses offered to sponsor his Rick Barry Youth Basketball Clinics. With his Porsche and his convertible Chevrolet Stingray, his natty wardrobe, and his luxury apartment overlooking Oakland's Lake Merritt, Barry was living well.[69] If Barry had been Black, both his determined defection to the ABA and his unabashed life of luxury would have been cause for harsh public criticism. Instead, he was a celebrated and sought-after figurehead for the new league. Black players who dared to defy the system in the same ways as Barry would not be so lucky.

"I REGARD IT AS A HANDSOME CONTRACT. I FEEL AS THOUGH I'VE gotten a new life," Hawkins said in June 1967 of his newly minted deal with the ABA's Pittsburgh Pipers. He was relieved. Playing for peanuts with second-rate teams had left him exhausted, depressed, and unfulfilled. "This kind of (barnstorming) basketball hurts me," Hawkins told Seymour Smith of the *Baltimore Sun*. "It's been hurting me for the last four years." Litman saw the ABA contract as a chance to emphasize his client's innocence and pro-level talent. "He never had any connection with point-shaving," Litman averred. "As far as his basketball ability is concerned, the worst thing I ever heard anyone say is that he could make any team in the N.B.A."[70]

In its first season the ABA's claims of burgeoning success were still more hype than reality. Although it had two strong franchises from the start—Indiana and Denver—the ABA was, in many respects, a bush-league operation in its early years. When Pittsburgh played New Orleans in Memphis on October 30, the game was delayed thirty minutes after the power went out, plummeting the arena into darkness. Apparently, an opossum had gotten caught in the building's wiring, and by the time the lights came back on, most of the small crowd of four hundred had already left.[71]

Pittsburgh, despite Rubin's bluster, was one of the least stable franchises in the ABA. There was frequent turnover in his front office. Cheap and dictatorial in his management of the team, Rubin insisted on personally approving all expenditures, no matter how small. At the same time, the attendance at the Pipers' home games was initially abysmal, with often far fewer than a thousand spectators in the stands. Ever the cheerleader, Commissioner Mikan still maintained that the league was in good financial shape, with a "healthy and substantial" network television proposal on the table—yet no ABA games appeared on network TV for the next three years. Even with these hurdles, the ABA was leaps and bounds ahead of the short-lived ABL experiment of the early 1960s. "Schedules were met, players were paid, and nobody traveled by station wagon," Hawkins's biographer Wolf noted. "Salaries were generally reasonable."[72] If the new league could attract more fans, it seemed as if it might actually be able to challenge the NBA's monopoly on pro ball.

While Pittsburgh struggled financially, the Hawk's flashes of brilliance on the court helped to resuscitate his stalled career. After he scored 34 points against the New Jersey Americans in his first ABA game on October 23, fans eagerly anticipated his appearance at the Pipers' home opener against the Minnesota Muskies the next night.[73] "Probably the ablest of the Pipers," the local Black newspaper, the *New Pittsburgh Courier*, declared, "Connie will be a fulcrum, both ways, for the coming season."[74] The twenty-five-year-old rookie was under a lot of pressure to perform. But he was rusty and inconsistent at first, having been away from serious competition for the better part of four years. "Much of the time, he seemed in a daze—listless, almost aloof," Wolf recalled. After a particularly sluggish first half against the Denver Rockets on November 1, in which he scored just two points, Hawkins confided in Coach Vince Cazzetta in the locker room: "I can't get going . . . I feel lost out there."[75] Hoping to jolt Hawkins into action, team trainer Alex Medich gave him a green Dexamyl pill, a popular amphetamine among pro ballplayers at the time. It seemed to do the trick. In the second half, Hawkins scored 27 points, leading the Pipers to an overtime victory of 112–103.

However, Dexamyl was no quick fix for Hawkins's uneven play. Although most agreed that at his best the Hawk was "the most dangerous player in the league," his somewhat spotty performance also gained him a reputation for being, in the words of New Jersey coach Max Zaslofsky, "a lazy player who just plays when he wants to."[76] Early on, he became a target of local white sportswriters, who assumed he was a coddled and entitled prima donna—a common critique of talented Black players at the time. They expected him to instantly perform on command, regardless of the fact that he had been publicly shamed and shut out of top-level professional play since 1961.[77] Hawkins tried to ignore it, but the criticism stung. What did they expect? In the first five games of the season he averaged 26 points per game.[78] He *was* working hard. He *did* care. Hawkins felt entirely misunderstood. His calm persona on the court did not do him any favors. "With his placid demeanor and graceful loping stride," Wolf noted, "he makes things look so easy, some wonder if he's trying."[79]

After a short period of adjustment, the African American star settled in and became a dominant force in the ABA. However, thanks to the league's lack of network TV presence and the small crowds at Pittsburgh home games, few hoops fans actually saw Hawkins play. Still, his legend grew, especially among Black basketball fans, thanks to regular coverage in the Black press. He became a kind of underdog hero for the Black community—a hardworking, long-suffering man who finally had his chance to shine. By December 1967, Hawkins ranked in the top ten in five of six ABA statistical categories: he was first in field-goal percentage (52.5 percent), third in scoring (25.1 points per game), fifth in both rebounding and assists, and eighth in free-throw accuracy.[80] As *Chicago Defender* sports columnist Lawrence Casey declared, "Connie can dribble like a guard, play in the hold like

Connie Hawkins with the American Basketball Association Most Valuable Player award for the 1967–1968 season.

a pivot man and has the size, strength, moves and shots to go with any forward alive."[81] Dubbed "Mr. Versatility," he was already playing the kind of "positionless basketball" that would come to dominate the modern pro game.

Hawkins led the Pipers all the way to the first ABA Championship Finals, where they faced the New Orleans Buccaneers. Led by Doug Moe, a talented white player also blacklisted by the NBA for his alleged ties to Molinas, the Buccaneers put Hawkins and the Pipers to the test. It was a punishing series that went all the way to seven games. Although the Hawk's heroic performance in the championship helped to cement his reputation as a bona fide superstar, he suffered the first of two serious knee injuries sustained while in the ABA—injuries that would haunt him for the rest of his career. The Pipers took the first game, with Hawkins scoring 39 points, whereas New Orleans won the next two.[82] In game 4 the Pipers eked out a come-from-behind win in New Orleans thanks in part to his 47 points; however, Hawkins tore a ligament in his right knee.[83] With Hawkins injured on the bench in game 5, the Buccaneers won 111–108 in Pittsburgh. The Pipers worried that their star might be out for the rest of the series. "When you lose a player that averages 30 points a game it's going to hurt," said Coach Cazzetta.[84] With the championship on the line, Hawkins steeled himself to return in game 6. Although his heavily bandaged knee was still stiff and excruciatingly painful, he somehow managed to score 41 points, securing a Piper victory in front of 7,200 hostile Buccaneers fans, some of whom taunted him with racial epithets.[85]

With the series tied at three games apiece, the Pipers returned home for the seventh and deciding game. Much to the team's surprise, droves of Pittsburgh's hoops fans—11,475 of them to be exact—showed up for the game. Still injured, the Hawk put up 20 points, 16 rebounds, and 9 assists, leading the Pipers to a 122–113 victory and the first-ever ABA championship title. It may not have been the NBA, but it was a major triumph for the long-disgraced Hawkins.[86]

It is no wonder that he later looked back on the 1967–1968 season as one of the "most enjoyable and exciting of his career."[87] Not only had his team won the championship, but he had also led the league in scoring (1,875 points in 70 games, averaging 26.8 points per game) and two-point field-goal accuracy (52.1 percent), finished second in rebounds (13.5 per game), and posted 76.4 percent at the free-throw line. He won both the ABA's regular season and playoff Most Valuable Player awards and was unanimously voted an ABA first-team All-Star.[88] Maybe his luck was finally changing.

In August 1968 the Hawk's good fortune continued—Judge Rabe Ferguson Marsh Jr., of the US District Court of the Western District of Pennsylvania, decided in his favor. After NBA attorney George Gallantz filed a motion to have Hawkins's lawsuit thrown out of court "for lack of proper venue," the Litmans had spent several months investigating the NBA's dealings and preparing a response. In reviewing the Litmans' evidence, Judge Marsh concluded that Hawkins's suit could proceed in Pennsylvania's Western District because the NBA, and several of its teams and team owners, did, in fact, do business there.[89]

Hoping to stall things again, Gallantz filed another motion to transfer the case to New York City, citing a federal rule that the "convenience" of witnesses and parties to the case and "the interest of justice" should be considered when setting the venue for a trial. He contended that New York City was an ideal location because it was the site of both the 1961 gambling scandal and the NBA's corporate offices.[90]

Worried that a move to New York would allow the NBA to outfinance them and continue to postpone the case, the Litmans pushed back. They asserted that most of the key witnesses would be NBA team owners and general managers, and they would be coming to trial from all over the country. Again, Judge Marsh ruled in Hawkins's favor, arguing that the NBA had failed to prove that more people would be inconvenienced by coming to Pittsburgh rather than to New York City.

As the legal wrangling continued, Hawkins decided to play out his option with Pittsburgh. He still desperately hoped that the NBA would give him a chance, especially because the Pipers seemed to be on shaky financial ground. Before the start of the ABA's second season, the team changed majority ownership, prompting a move to Minneapolis. Thanks to chronically low attendance, Rubin had been losing money from the start. Unable to find a radio station or sponsor to broadcast the games for the upcoming season, he decided to sell 85 percent of his stock in the Pipers to a thirty-eight-year-old Minnesota attorney named Bill Erickson, who also happened to be the ABA's general counsel. Commissioner Mikan encouraged Erickson to move the Pipers to Minneapolis because the Muskies' recent departure to Miami had left the home of the ABA's league offices with no team.[91]

Hawkins showed up to the Pipers' training camp a week late. He had held out while Litman worked to get him a $5,000 bonus to help cover his extra living costs now that the team was based in Minneapolis. At first, Erickson had been unwilling to negotiate and even wanted to add another year to Hawkins's contract. However, Litman warned him that because Hawkins had signed a nontransferable contract with the "Pittsburgh Basketball Club" and Erickson had formed a new corporation with his purchase of the team, his client's contract might actually be void, making the Hawk a free agent. Erickson quickly backed down on the extra year and agreed to the bonus.

Even with the extra $5,000 in hand, Hawkins had reservations about returning to the Pipers. Cazzetta was no longer coach, having resigned after Erickson had refused to give him a raise to help cover the costs of relocating his large family to Minneapolis. In Cazzetta's place the Pipers brought in Jim Harding, an autocratic disciplinarian who had racked up a number of NCAA violations in his years as a college coach at Loyola (New Orleans) and LaSalle (Philadelphia).[92]

Yet, Harding was in for a challenge. It was fall 1968. In the midst of Black urban uprisings and the rise of Black Power activism, Black ballplayers were no longer willing to sit back and take abuse from a white man like Harding. Hawkins and his African American teammates were convinced the new coach was a racist. Harding was not only extra harsh with them but also quick to fire them for flimsy reasons. He cut Black center Ted Campbell based on rumors of marijuana use and Black forward Richie Parks because he thought Parks was giving him defiant looks.[93] Harding even showed little respect for Hawkins, the league's MVP.

In his own quiet way, Hawkins rebelled against Harding. When Harding tried to correct his jump shot, Hawkins just ignored him, which only riled up Harding even more. Hawkins also refused to comply when Harding tried to introduce a more rigid dress code: a white shirt and tie were to be worn on the road at all times. This was not how Hawkins dressed. Much like other young Black men of the time, he had a closet full of turtlenecks, Ban-Lon shirts, sweaters, slacks, and dashikis, and when he wore a suit, he usually paired it with a brightly colored shirt. The Hawk's embrace of "soul style"—a mix of African American and African-inspired modes of dress—was not just a fashion statement; it was a political act. As the rallying cry of "Black is beautiful" grew louder in the late sixties, dressing on one's own terms became an important expression of Black manhood and, by extension, Black Power.[94] Because of their public visibility, Black pro ballplayers were at the forefront of this stylistic transformation, challenging the respectability politics of their parents' generation and showcasing new modes of rebellious Black masculinity. "This ain't no college. I ain't no college guy," Hawkins told Harding. "Why do you want me to dress like one?"[95]

Perhaps Harding thought that if he could make Hawkins and his teammates dress like college guys, he could control them like college players. Yet even college athletes were becoming harder for coaches to discipline. Although the Hawk never had a chance to play NCAA ball, he took his personal stand against Harding's racism right around the same time that Tommie Smith and John Carlos raised their black-gloved fists on the podium at the Mexico City Olympics in October 1968. "My raised right hand stood for the power in black America. Carlos's raised left hand stood for the unity of black America," Smith later explained to sportscaster Howard Cosell. "The black scarf around my neck stood for black pride. The black socks with no shoes stood for black poverty in racist America. The totality of our effort was the regaining of black dignity."[96] Their now iconic stand helped amplify a wave of Black athletic protest against white authorities at colleges across the nation—a surge of activism that African American sociologist and activist Harry Edwards dubbed "the revolt of the black athlete." Black amateur and professional athletes alike no longer wanted to be used as triumphant symbols of white American racial tolerance while they and their communities still faced injustices in sports and beyond.

In the meantime, celebrated white forward Rick Barry was finally free of his NBA contract with the San Francisco Warriors and was allowed to play for the Oakland Oaks. While African American athletes struggled for basic respect, Barry dominated the mainstream sports news coverage of the ABA and drew big gates wherever he played. In his first three games, Barry scored a total of 114 points in front of 24,984 fans. Hawkins, in contrast, continued to play in relative obscurity. Moving to Minnesota proved disastrous for the Pipers. Some nights they had fewer than 2,000 fans in the stands.[97]

The Hawk's rocky sophomore season continued to be full of both ups and downs. In early January 1969 he met a young journalist whose reporting would change the trajectory of his basketball career. Tenacious Manhattan native David Wolf began working on a story about him for *Life* magazine. The stocky, twenty-five-year-old sportswriter had grown up in New York City at the same time as Hawkins and recalled watching the high school phenom play at Madison Square Garden. Following the 1961 game-fixing scandal,

Wolf became fixated on the ballplayer's ill-fated career. When he first started interviewing Hawkins, he had no real inclination that the rumors about the Hawk's involvement with Molinas were false. Wolf had simply intended to write a short piece on Hawkins's feelings about his ongoing exile from the NBA.[98]

Fateful as Hawkins's meeting with Wolf would soon prove, there were already signs that the ABA star's best playing days might be behind him. During a practice, he tore a piece of cartilage in his knee just days before an upcoming home game against the Oakland Oaks on January 18. Minnesota's front office had tried to promote the game as a battle between two superstars—Hawkins and Barry—and the two best teams in the league. However, when Barry injured himself and pulled out of the game, their plans to draw a large crowd seemed to be in jeopardy. Hawkins felt immense pressure to play. "If I wear a brace and they wrap the leg real tight, I could do it," he told Wolf. "What the hell for?" Wolf asked. "Wait till the whole leg is a little stronger."[99] On game day, they tightly bandaged his knee, and with six minutes remaining in the first quarter, Hawkins took to the floor in front of 4,722 fans, a large crowd by Minnesota standards. Although he hobbled, unable to run or pivot, dragging his injured leg around the court, he still managed to score 14 points.

During halftime, with the Oaks up 55–49, trainer Medich removed part of the tape around Hawkins's knee to give him a bit more mobility. Hyped up, adrenaline pumping, the Hawk scored another seven points in the third quarter. But after going up for a rebound, he crashed back down to reality. Hawkins landed hard on his leg, locking up his knee. Curled up on the floor and squirming in pain, the Pipers' star had to be carried to the bench. Although his knee unlocked, he never returned to the game, and Oakland won 111–108. Hawkins had tried his best to avoid going under the knife, but he now had to have an operation to repair his knee.[100] When he returned on March 19 to play against Oakland, some eight weeks after surgery, he was a shadow of his former self.

MEANWHILE, THE LITMANS CONTINUED TO BUILD THEIR CLIENT'S case against the NBA. Wolf also began to interview Hawkins and compile his own research on the lawsuit. Thanks to the Hawk's brilliant record in the ABA, his professional-level talent was no longer in question, so his antitrust case now hinged on the Litmans' ability to prove two main contentions. The first was that the NBA and its member teams had conspired to arbitrarily blacklist him. Because the league had a virtual monopoly on professional basketball during the time in question, the suit alleged that it was in violation of the Sherman Act, which prohibited restraint of trade. The second was that Hawkins had no involvement in the 1961 game-fixing scandal.[101]

As Wolf crisscrossed the country to conduct his own investigation, often bumping into the Litmans as they prepared for trial, he uncovered evidence in support of both contentions. Witness after witness told Wolf that Hawkins had no involvement in the scheme: he had never knowingly associated with gamblers and had never introduced a player to a fixer. Wolf even spoke with Molinas and Hacken, who both attested to Hawkins's innocence. It turned out that the only damaging statements about Hawkins's involvement in the scandal were his own—statements he had made, under duress, as part of a false confession. Hawkins was no gambler, no criminal. He had never been in trouble with the law, let alone charged with anything. He had certainly done nothing to justify being banned by the NBA.[102]

Wolf also discovered that the NBA had barred Hawkins without any concern for the ballplayer's right to due process or presumption of innocence. The league never bothered to seriously investigate whether or not Hawkins was actually involved in the 1961 scandal. Instead, it had banned him based on rumors and accusations in the press and unsubstantiated statements from the district attorney's office. In 1965, the year after Hawkins became eligible for the NBA draft, the New York Knicks, St. Louis Hawks, and Los Angeles Lakers had asked Commissioner Kennedy for permission to negotiate with Hawkins, but Kennedy had denied their request. By the time the Litmans received the commissioner's letter in May 1966, in which he stated that he had no control over the draft picks of individual teams, the NBA board of governors had voted to officially bar the Hawk, pending an investigation by Kennedy.[103]

With this plan to ban Hawkins already in place, Kennedy had invited Hawkins and David Litman to his office, where Hawkins was to be questioned by Kennedy and the NBA's attorney. After the questioning, Hawkins would be permitted to make a statement, and then Kennedy would make his final ruling. Litman had, at first, agreed to the hearing, but he insisted that the process be amended for the sake of fairness and impartiality. Either the league had to inform him of the specific charges against his client and give him time to investigate them before the hearing, or the NBA had to allow him to cross-examine the Hawk's accusers and then let him investigate and present a defense.[104] When the league refused both of Litman's proposals, he had no choice but to advise Hawkins against meeting with Kennedy.

On May 16, 1969, *Life* published Wolf's findings in a nine-page feature article on Hawkins titled "The Unjust Exile of a Superstar." Perhaps anticipating the concerns of the magazine's mostly white middle-class readers, Wolf was careful to make the case that Hawkins was not a "Black Power guy." He described the player as "a warm, gentle man of simple tastes"—one who still spent his off-seasons on Pittsburgh's North Side because he felt most comfortable there.[105] Wolf's was a sympathetic, if paternalistic, portrait of a naive young Black man who grew up in poverty and was wronged by the system.

Although Wolf's damning exposé went out on the wire services, bringing the Hawk's hard-luck story to a national audience, there was no immediate response from NBA executives. However, many NBA players telephoned him to volunteer their help. Senator Edward Kennedy (D–Massachusetts) was one of the first public figures to contact Hawkins, inviting the ballplayer to the athletes' memorial dedication of the Robert F. Kennedy Stadium in Washington, DC. At the dedication Hawkins spoke with more NBA players, including his former Iowa teammate Don Nelson, who now played for the Boston Celtics, and Ray Scott of the Detroit Pistons. He was touched as they expressed their support and offered to testify at his trial about his basketball talent.[106]

For three weeks the NBA said nothing. Then, out of the blue, on Friday, June 6, David Stern, who was helping NBA counsel Gallantz with the Hawkins case, called the Litmans' office. Roz Litman was at work prepping for another round of depositions on the West Coast when she answered the phone. Stern, then a twenty-six-year-old lawyer for Proskauer, Rose, Goetz, and Mendelsohn, told her to expect a call on Monday from Gallantz about a possible settlement. She could barely believe her ears. Stern advised her that a league meeting was taking place in Detroit over the weekend where Hawkins's case would be discussed. "I almost dropped dead," Roz Litman remembered. "But I had to act as though I wasn't impressed. I said I wanted to proceed with the depositions because it was hardly likely that one telephone call would result in a settlement."[107] She hung up and ran into her husband's office jumping and shouting.

Sure enough, at 10:50 a.m. on Monday, June 9, Gallantz called to talk about the possibility of a settlement. Right off the bat, Roz Litman asked if the settlement would include a contract for Hawkins to play in the NBA. This was, after all, the main thing that her client wanted. She held her breath. For a moment Gallantz was silent. "A contract," he said, "is feasible." She shook with excitement. "The rights to Hawkins have been assigned to Phoenix," Gallantz added. Roz Litman called Hawkins to tell him the news, but she warned him not to get his hopes up just in case the negotiations went south. "I had no feelings," Hawkins later recalled. "I'd formed a mental block in my head. I didn't believe it could ever happen, so I sort of shrugged my shoulders and forgot about it."[108] He had become very accustomed to disappointment over the past eight years.

The Phoenix Suns were a new expansion franchise still struggling to gain their footing in the NBA. In the 1968–1969 season, their first in the league, they had posted a paltry 16 wins in 82 games. At the same meeting where NBA executives and team owners discussed a possible settlement for Hawkins, they had held a coin toss to decide whether the Phoenix Suns or the Seattle SuperSonics would have the rights to the ABA star. Still smarting over losing Lew Alcindor— UCLA's towering three-time All-American center, who had dominated the college game—to the Milwaukee Bucks, the Suns were ecstatic when they won the toss. But the Detroit meeting had been a heated one, with some NBA executives strongly against any kind of settlement. In the end, however, the league voted to settle. Wolf's exposé had done its damage. "It was damn clear we were going to lose if we went to court," one NBA general manager later told Wolf.[109]

After several nail-biting weeks of haggling over the terms of the settlement, both parties finally came to an agreement. Hawkins would receive a five-year, no-cut contract for $410,000; a $600,000 annuity starting at age forty-five; $250,000 in damages (50 percent at signing and the rest over five years); and an option to purchase a percentage of the Suns. The Litmans would receive $35,000 for their firm's legal expenses and a cut of the damages for their legal fees. The total value of the package minus the option was $1,295,000. As the significance of his victory began to sink in, Hawkins was overcome with emotion. "Oh thank you. God, oh thank you Father, oh Jesus, oh God thank you," he wept.[110] His long and arduous journey to the NBA was over. He no longer had to worry about money. His family was set for life.

As confirmation of the Hawkins settlement spread, the NBA went into damage-control mode. Commissioner Kennedy issued an official statement through his New York office. Blaming circumstances supposedly beyond his control, he tried to sidestep any responsibility for unfairly barring Hawkins from the league. "Shortly after I became commissioner, I attempted to look into the serious charges against Hawkins," Kennedy wrote. "I was unable to complete that

investigation." Ironically, the lawsuit's "depositions and other procedures" had brought those facts to light, proving Hawkins's innocence.[111]

For Sam Lacy of the *Baltimore Afro-American*, Kennedy's terse,
unapologetic statement rang hollow: "There was so much milk and
honey emanating from the mouths of National Basketball Association
officials last weekend, it's a wonder to me they didn't choke on it." It
was too little too late, for the league had failed to provide Hawkins
with anything resembling due process—until he sued them. "B-r-o-
t-h-e-r! . . . Kennedy should be sentenced to seven years of looking in
a mirror at himself," Lacy wrote. "It took the NBA that long (seven
years) to decide that Connie Hawkins was guilty of no wrongdo-
ing. . . . Anyone with common sense would agree that the commissioner is being a little fuzzy when he implies the same 'depositions and
other procedures' which have been produced today weren't available
over the seven years of the player's disbarment."[112]

The Hawk's triumph was historic. It was the first time that an
American athlete had won an antitrust battle against a major professional sports league. With the support of the Litmans and Wolf, he
had put league executives and team owners on notice. This new generation of Black ballplayers would no longer accept unjust treatment
at the hands of monopolistic team owners without a fight—in the
courts, if necessary. Taking advantage of the openings created by the
formation of the ABA, they brought the defiant spirit of the revolt of
the Black athlete with them into the pro ranks, exposing more cracks
in the armor of the white basketball establishment.

Chapter 2

Hardship

Spencer Haywood vs. the White Basketball Establishment

They pat us on the back when we win and kick us in the teeth when we lose. They don't want to know why something is happening, only what's happening. They just care about the score. They're front-runners. We're like tenant-farmers harvesting a crop for their table.

—Spencer Haywood, *Stand Up for Something:*
The Spencer Haywood Story, 1972

RECOGNIZING THE FINANCIAL IMPORTANCE OF THE 1970 ALL-STAR Game to ABA team owners, the players seized the opportunity to stage a protest in the hours before the 2:00 p.m. tip-off in Indianapolis. Commissioner Jack Dolph had managed to secure a contract with CBS to televise the game live and in color. It would be the league's first national exposure, and the deal included an option for CBS to broadcast future games if the ratings proved attractive.[1] Huddling together in Room 802 of Stouffer's Inn at 2820 North

Meridian Street, the determined athletes, including six-foot-nine Denver Rockets rookie Spencer Haywood, threatened to sit out the game if the league did not recognize their players association. As the negotiations dragged on, the dozen or so sportswriters gathered outside the room began to joke that CBS might have to put on *Heidi* if the negotiations fell through.[2] Just forty-five minutes before the scheduled start, the ABA relented, and the players got their union. The game went on as planned in front of 11,931 spectators at the Indiana State Fairgrounds Coliseum.[3]

With fans none the wiser, the ABA did its best to put on an entertaining showcase, hoping that its brand of free-flowing, high-flying play would help bring the league new converts. Eight thousand dollars' worth of extra lights brightened up the dingy arena for the color TV cameras. The ABA's signature red, white, and blue basketball and performances by Indiana State University's women's dance and drill team added even more flair to the game.[4] If the ABA proved its ability to produce a lively television spectacle on a shoestring, Haywood also showed that he more than belonged in the ranks of professional basketball. "He looked head and shoulders better—literally, when jumping—than many of the more experienced players," the *Gettysburg Times* reported.[5] Going head-to-head against Eastern Division center Mel Daniels, he scored 23 points, pulled down 19 rebounds, and blocked 7 shots, leading the West to a 128–98 blowout. In his first ABA All-Star appearance, the twenty-year-old sensation was voted Most Valuable Player and took home a five-foot trophy, color television, and new car.[6]

RIDING A WAVE OF NATIONAL PUBLICITY THANKS TO HIS STAR PERformance at the 1968 Olympics in Mexico City, Haywood had been a hot recruiting prospect in early 1969. The dynamic, 225-pound center was a dominating force for the University of Detroit (UD) Titans, averaging 32.1 points and 22.1 rebounds per game. In a time of heightened Black athletic activism, Haywood was also a seemingly safe and apolitical prospect.[7] The only reason he had made the Olympic squad in the first place was because other Black collegians, most notably Lew Alcindor (University of California, Los Angeles), Wes Unseld (University of Louisville), and Elvin Hayes (University of Houston), had decided not to try out for the team amid calls for an African American boycott of the games by the Olympic Project for Human Rights (OPHR). Although Unseld cited fatigue and Hayes said he needed to train for his pro debut, Alcindor stayed home to denounce racism in America.[8] The OPHR, an outgrowth of the revolt of the Black athlete that was happening on college campuses across the nation, condemned the anti-Blackness of the games, demanding, among other things, the banning of apartheid South Africa from Olympic competition and the removal of the openly racist Avery Brundage as head of the US Olympic Committee. Although a collective boycott never got off the ground, the OPHR's public criticism did manage to get South Africa barred, and many African American athletes performed symbolic protests in front of the international media in Mexico City.[9]

Amid this swell of activism, Haywood remained largely agnostic. A junior college player for Trinidad State in Colorado at the time of the Olympic tryouts, Haywood rose to the occasion, and his inspired play helped the US team win the gold medal. The nineteen-year-old phenom was not only the youngest player to ever make the squad, but he also led the team in scoring at the games with 145 points and set a US team record by shooting 71.9 percent. However, unlike African American sprinters Tommie Smith and John Carlos, with their raised Black Power fists on the podium, Haywood made no protest at the medal ceremony. The decorated Black track athletes Wilma Rudolph and Willye White, the latter Haywood's girlfriend at the time, had convinced him that he had too much to lose.[10] Both Rudolph and White had grown up in the South, in Clarksville, Tennessee, and Greenwood, Mississippi, respectively. They understood what

Haywood had on the line. "Three years ago you were picking cotton, Spencer," Rudolph reminded Haywood.[11]

After the games, Haywood joined the UD Titans in fall 1968, where he played on a team of five dynamic African American starters, still a rarity in the NCAA. Despite his Olympic fame, he was beginning to develop a reputation as a hothead and troublemaker. With his teammates, he brought the aggressive and flamboyant style of Black playground ball to the college game. "On the court," Haywood recalled, "we feared no one, and we were making our own sweet music."[12] Although the NCAA's "Lew Alcindor Rule" (enacted in 1967 to thwart the dominance of UCLA's star Black center) made dunking illegal, Haywood jammed at every opportunity.[13] He even tore down a rim and shattered a backboard in honor of Tommie Smith after hearing that the Black Olympian was in the stands. (He now sympathized with Smith and Carlos after having personally witnessed the racist backlash against their podium protest in Mexico City.[14]) In a game against the University of Toledo, Haywood punched white player Steve Mix after Mix had fouled him repeatedly with no calls, and then took a swing at the referee. This offense got him kicked out of the game, and he received a one-game suspension.

Off the court, Haywood stood his ground when UD's athletic department tried to stack his schedule with easy classes like the Theory of Basketball, Beginning Badminton, and Square Dance, demanding that he be allowed to study radio and television production. When UD head coach Bob Calihan inexplicably put two mediocre white players into the starting lineup midseason, precipitating an eight-game losing streak, Haywood lashed out publicly. "We lost to Notre Dame on national TV," he recalled, "and in a postgame interview I told my national audience that I didn't like college ball, that it was too political, that I was looking forward to pro ball."[15]

Haywood had begun to test just how much leverage his star power gave him. As part of the deal for coming to play at UD, he had been under the impression that the university would hire his mentor and former high school coach, Will Robinson, to replace Calihan upon retirement. He envisioned that with five Black starters and a Black coach, the team would be well on its way to becoming a Black dynasty. However, UD passed over Robinson and eventually hired white coach Jim Harding, the same tyrannical disciplinarian who had tormented Connie Hawkins and other Black players on the ABA's Pittsburgh Pipers. Haywood suspected that Harding was brought in to tame him and his African American teammates. "He was a drill sergeant, the kind of coach who rules by fear, anger, and intimidation," Haywood recounted. "Apparently the administration felt that we had a renegade-type team and what we needed was a militaristic coach."[16] Needless to say, Haywood did not take well to Harding, and he made it known that he was unhappy. "I could see their word meant nothing," he later told sportswriter Bill Libby.[17]

All the while, the ABA continued to search for creative ways to combat the NBA in the war for basketball talent. It was still largely unsuccessful in convincing well-known NBA players to jump leagues, with the exception of Rick Barry. The next step was to scour the college ranks. But even in their quest for star seniors, ABA teams had mixed success, having lost UCLA center Alcindor to the NBA's Milwaukee Bucks in spring 1969.[18] Now, improvising on the fly, the ABA proposed a controversial amendment to its bylaws in order to snag talented underclassmen, and Spencer Haywood would become its test case.

As the battle over Haywood became a proxy war in the interleague competition for talent, the young player was catapulted into the spotlight. Over the next two years, his struggles to garner a fair contract laid bare the exploitative practices of the white basketball establishment, whose interlocking monopolies controlled both the amateur and professional game. But Haywood was by no means unique in his challenges to "business as usual" in big-time basketball. Empowered by the revolt of the Black athlete and Black Power currents beyond basketball, in the early 1970s Haywood and his contemporaries intensified their efforts to gain greater compensation, more control over their careers, and, ultimately, greater respect as workers, athletes, and men.

AT THE TIME, THE ABA, LIKE THE NBA, HAD A "FOUR-YEAR RULE" that prohibited teams from signing young players until four years after high school graduation. The addition of the so-called hardship clause to the ABA's bylaws in 1969 allowed teams to draft a player before his years of college eligibility were over, as long as he could demonstrate urgent financial need.[19] "There was no legal research or anything, we just invented the term," recalled Mike Storen, then part-owner of the ABA's Indiana Pacers. "So we came out and said that Spencer was a special case, he had to take care of his mother and his nine brothers and sisters."[20] Though framed as a racially progressive measure steeped in the Great Society logic of equal opportunity, this was a strategic, rather than humanitarian, move.

Hearing that the disgruntled star was contemplating leaving UD, the ABA dispatched sports agent Steve Arnold to meet with Haywood and his mentor, Robinson. Arnold, who helped the league to procure college players at arm's length, showed them what the NBA was paying first-round draft picks out of college versus what the ABA could offer Haywood for the next season.[21] At the time, Haywood's only spending money was the $15 per month he made working at a clothing store called Jack's Place for $1.75 per hour. "When suddenly someone says you can make $100,000 a year, you start listening," he explained to sportswriter Bill Libby. "They [the ABA] weren't prepared to pay me $100,000 a year straight salary. But they said they'd give me money for my old age, and it would amount to around $300,000 for three years. They put out the line and they had me hooked."[22]

To a young Black man who was born in 1949 and came of age in Silver City, Mississippi, a small town on the Yazoo River, this was an astronomical amount of money. Haywood's father, a carpenter, had died a month before he was born, leaving his mother, Eunice, to raise ten children on her own. Like many Black southern women of her generation, she labored long days both in the cotton fields and as a domestic servant. As children, Haywood and his siblings spent half the year in the cotton fields toiling alongside her, yet the family still lived in abject poverty. "We had no indoor plumbing, no telephone, no television," he recalled.[23] Haywood had also worked as a caddie at the local all-white country club, further exposing him to the stark and demeaning racial inequality of the Jim Crow South. Although this job helped him escape backbreaking work in the cotton fields, it had its own indignities: golfers often used him and his fellow Black caddies as live targets on the driving range.[24]

When Haywood started his freshman year at McNair High School in the nearby city of Belzoni, he was already six feet six. Coach Charles Wilson spotted the lanky youngster in the hallway and recruited him to play for the team.[25] Though initially awkward and clumsy, Haywood came into his own during his sophomore year. "The dunk and the block, the two plays that symbolized power and domination, became the heart of my game," Haywood later recounted.[26] Such brashness, even if contained on the court, was a liability in rural Mississippi. Several years earlier, in 1955, African American teenager Emmett Till had been brutally lynched for allegedly whistling at a white woman named Carolyn Bryant. As civil rights protests picked up speed across the South in the late 1950s and 1960s, "Mississippi whites stood out as the most obstinate and violent in their protection of segregation."[27] Becoming a high school basketball star did little to shield Haywood from the ever-present threats of racist violence and incarceration in his home state.

Eager to escape, after tenth grade Haywood joined the Second Great Migration north to live with older siblings in Chicago. Then, after a brief stay in Ohio with his brother Leroy, he moved to Detroit. There he played for Coach Robinson at Pershing High School and was taken in by James and Ida Bell, the parents of his teammate

Will. In some respects, he was like the young man in Stevie Wonder's iconic R & B song "Living for the City" (1973), his early life in "hard time Mississippi" marked by scarcity, itinerancy, and instability.[28] As he sought greater opportunity in the North, a lucrative professional contract, like the one Arnold was now dangling before him, was too much to pass up.

The potential of an NBA-ABA merger and its impact on Haywood's future market power also influenced his thinking. Robinson advised Haywood to go to the ABA early rather than wait another two years to enter the NBA draft. "I said this was war, between the NBA and ABA," Robinson told sportswriter Libby, "and he could take advantage of it by signing with the ABA for the sort of money he couldn't command if there was peace by the time he graduated."[29] The Rockets also lured Haywood into the fold with their newly hired African American coach, John McLendon, whom Haywood knew from his days on the US Olympic team.

Robinson and his protégé headed to Denver, prepared to negotiate a contract with the Rockets' owners, trucking magnate J. W. (Bill) Ringsby and his son Don, who was then team president and general manager. No stranger to the bargaining table, Bill Ringsby had started out as a coal-truck driver in Denver in the 1930s and went into business for himself in 1940. By the early 1970s, Bill and his sons had built Ringsby-United into a transcontinental trucking line that grossed around 100 million dollars annually.[30] Like many other ABA owners, he was new to the sports industry and more than willing to break a few rules and gentlemanly agreements to get what he wanted.

The Ringsbys' initial offer to Haywood was $50,000 per year for three seasons and an annuity of $15,000 to be paid from age forty to sixty. Haywood then asked for living expenses, so they raised his salary to $51,800 to cover rent for an apartment in Denver during the season. They also gave him a $10,000 advance. Although much of

Haywood's compensation was deferred and therefore not guaranteed if the Rockets or the ABA went out of business, the press reported that his multiyear contract was worth around $250,000.[31]

After twelve hours of tough negotiations, Haywood signed with the Denver Rockets on August 16, 1969. Because Haywood was only twenty, Robinson also signed the contract as his legal guardian. At a press conference to announce the agreement, Haywood told journalists that he had decided to turn pro early so that his sixty-one-year-old mother would no longer "have to be scrubbing floors for $10 a week." He explained: "This is a thing anyone who loved his mother would do."[32] Don Ringsby characterized Haywood's signing as a charitable project of sorts. "Spencer called me on the phone and told me he wanted to play professional basketball because of overwhelming family responsibilities," the Rockets' GM maintained.[33] In taking on this hardship case, Ringsby implied, the team was helping to uplift a fatherless Black family. Although Ringsby tapped into prevailing stereotypes popularized by the Moynihan Report (1965) about the connections among poverty, pathology, and Black female-headed households, Haywood saw through the propaganda. "The hardship rule was born not because pro teams felt sorry for my poor mother scrubbing floors back in Silver City," he later recounted, "but because I could tear down backboards and draw fans."[34]

The reaction among the white basketball establishment was swift and scathing. At the college level, UD announced plans to launch a formal protest to the NCAA against the ABA's "illegal" signing of their star player. "I don't think there is any possibility of getting him back," Bob Calihan, now UD's athletic director, complained.[35] But, he argued, they were making this protest "with an eye to the future," hoping that the NCAA would step in to broker an agreement with the ABA to bar the signing of underclassmen until after their four years of college eligibility were up. Meanwhile, Johnny Dee, head coach at Notre Dame, urged the National Association of Basketball

Coaches to ban ABA scouts from all college games, practices, and locker rooms.[36]

For the mainstream sports media and NBA team owners, Haywood's premature jump to the ABA seemed to portend disaster for the entire sports industry. "When Haywood turned pro, . . . we thought it was un-American, that it would tear down the structure of sports and would lead to chaos," sportswriter Bob Ryan later reflected. "The sports world was a simple, uncomplicated place until the ABA came along and screwed things up. That was the prevailing view and it was mine for a long time." Haywood's talent was not in question, nor were Ryan and others particularly concerned about his right to earn a living. Rather, it was his challenge to the system that they found so threatening.[37] What made matters even worse was what Edgar "Doc" Greene of the *Detroit News* saw as the growing leverage of African Americans in sport. Greene blamed UD for making a "tactical error" in not hiring Robinson as head coach, thus opening the door for Haywood's exit to the pros. Together, Haywood and Robinson had upended the rules governing the interconnected system of big-time amateur and professional basketball. "This was a case where the White establishment ran into . . . Black Athletic Power," Greene wrote. "And, Black Athletic Power won."[38]

African American sportswriters tended to be more sympathetic to Haywood's plight. Sheep Jackson of Cleveland's *Call and Post* urged readers to put themselves in Haywood's position: "Can you, or anyone else, in his right mind turn down such an offer when they are living in poverty?"[39] Jackson was also skeptical of the various doomsday predictions for college ball, which he considered "bunk." Haywood had the right to make decisions about his career and future without the paternalistic interference of the white basketball establishment. "Don't tell me how I screwed Detroit. They treated me like a black stud," Haywood once complained to sportswriter Libby. "You ask the players. . . . Not while they're in college, afraid to talk. Ask the pros. Or any of the guys after they've left college. Find out how many graduated. Find out how many feel they were treated right. Ok, I wasn't happy, so I left. That's my business, right? That's my right. Right?"[40]

All the while, the ABA and NBA had been embroiled in preliminary merger talks. In the immediate wake of Haywood's signing, however, NBA commissioner Walter Kennedy called a press conference in New York City to announce that he was halting the discussions because of the ABA's disturbing "breach of faith." He told reporters that the NBA would not deal "with any professional entity" that insisted on "raiding" college campuses for talent.[41] Undeterred, the ABA supposedly made overtures to Black underclassmen Calvin Murphy and Bob Lanier.

Although Murphy and Lanier opted to remain in college, Black players' frequent combination of incredible talent and financial hardship put them right at the center of this interleague clash. As the *Baltimore Afro-American* observed, "It seems fairly obvious that the American Basketball Association is bent on using topflight colored players as weapons in its full-scale war with the older National Basketball Association."[42] Although Black players possessed a new kind of leverage in this escalating conflict, as Haywood would soon discover, they often got caught in the cross fire, criticized by team owners, sportswriters, and fans alike for their supposed lack of morality, loyalty, and maturity. New to the business of sport, they also frequently found themselves entangled in dubious contracts filled with loopholes.

IN FALL 1969, HAYWOOD EAGERLY STEPPED INTO HIS ROLE IN DENver, where he transitioned to playing power forward. Before long, he proved he was not just a talented athlete but also a showman. "The Denver fans loved it, and I could control the crowd," he later recounted. "I could make them shriek and scream by throwing down power dunks that shook the backboard." Even as a rookie, he had no shortage of confidence, having challenged various pros, from Dave

Bing to Cazzie Russell, as a high schooler on the playground courts of Detroit. His background in streetball turned out to be good training for the ABA. As Haywood recalled, "The ABA game was fast and wide open, and that suited my style perfectly." Still, given that he was the youngest, highest paid, and most publicized athlete in the league, he knew that other players would most certainly test him. He was fined $200 for duking it out with Rick Barry and ejected from a game against the Miami Floridians for knocking out white center George Sutor. Haywood was no pushover. "If they're going to give it to me, I'm going to give it back," he told reporters.[43]

Haywood may have been a college dropout, but he was living a crash course in the rigors and responsibilities of professional ball. "I'm really getting an education," he told Dan Hafner of the *Los Angeles Times* before a game against the LA Stars in October 1969. "I learn something every game. . . . The time spent in airports and hotel lobbies, playing in strange arenas—all those things have been a revelation."[44] The Rockets traveled to faraway games in Bill Ringsby's clunky DC-3, a World War II–era fixed-wing, propeller-driven plane. The Ringsbys were too cheap to remodel the interior, so the towering players sat in the original seats with their knees up to their chins. "When you fly a DC-3, you always know what the weather is outside without looking out the window. You feel every cloud, every drop of rain, every gust of wind. You are at one with nature, and scared as hell," Haywood later joked.[45] Still, Haywood was just happy to be able to provide for his family, and he sent money back to his mother in Mississippi. He talked about continuing his college education, hoping to enroll in the UCLA drama school and become an actor.[46] He was a young Black man on the rise who saw an open future ahead of him, and NBA scouts and representatives were already swarming.

Nervous that they might lose their star player, the Ringsbys invited Haywood and Robinson to attend a presentation by accountant Ralph Dolgoff about a financial opportunity he had devised for their players. The Dolgoff Plan, as it came to be known, was supposed to provide ABA teams and players alike with greater returns and tax shelters; it promised to save the Rockets cash up front and earn Haywood more money in the long run. Organized around "the investment of contracted sums in a combination of mutual funds and life insurance in the form of a variable annuity," the Dolgoff Plan allowed the fledgling ABA teams to offer what looked like big-money contracts to players, even though much of the projected value of these contracts came in the form of deferred and unguaranteed compensation.[47]

In October 1969, Haywood and Robinson signed a second, preemptive contract with the Rockets. Haywood was to receive $50,000 per season for three years and have $3,000 per year invested for him for ten years in the Dolgoff Plan. The Ringsbys claimed that this investment would generate about $300,000 for Haywood by the time he reached sixty years of age. The total value of the three-year contract was supposed to be around $450,000.[48] Driven by competition and self-preservation, rather than altruism, the Ringsbys had employed the Dolgoff Plan to exert a firm grip on their blue-chip rookie, and it would become a weapon cleverly wielded by the ABA to hit NBA team owners financially in the war over talent. "The ABA paid in paper money," attorney and player agent Ron Grinker recalled, "but the NBA responded to that by paying in real dollars."[49] This interleague rivalry would touch off the exponential increases in player salaries over the course of the seventies.

With a new contract in hand and emboldened by his success on the boards, Haywood carried himself like a celebrity off the court. Having escaped small-town Mississippi, he felt he was long overdue for a bit of flash. The twenty-year-old had no interest in acting with humility, seriousness, or restraint after enduring so many years of poverty and emasculation at the hands of white racism. Freelance sportswriter Bill Libby, who had shadowed the young star during his rookie season, described the scene as Haywood donned what he proudly called his "Chicago Gangster suit" to head to a home game against the Indiana Pacers on February 27, 1970: "He took the suit from a closet packed with fancy clothes. It was raspberry shaded, striped and double-breasted. He hummed a jazz tune as he pulled it on over silk underwear. . . . He knotted the laces of shiny black shoes, pulled a large feathered hat down over one eye, admired himself briefly in the mirror, and cut out of his large, lavish apartment." Haywood's ample wardrobe was not only colorful, but he bragged that much of it was self-designed.[50] The talented rookie with an infectious smile and perfectly groomed facial hair was always flamboyantly styled.

That night, in front of a capacity crowd of more than seven thousand Denver fans, Haywood gave an athletic and impassioned performance against the Pacers. For a big man, his skill and agility with the ball were impressive, allowing him to shape-shift into different roles on the court. "Spencer Haywood does things men his size rarely attempt," Libby noted. "He is perhaps the finest dribbler for his size ever to come along."[51] When the Pacers' defense put pressure on the Rockets' guards, the power forward brought the ball up court. He took advantage of his unusually large hands and long arms. Haywood could hit jump shots from anywhere. "One time he cradled the ball in his hand, drove toward the basket, took off, flew ten feet through the air and violently stuffed the ball down into the hoop," Libby described. Haywood played with an intensity that was felt by both the players and referees. At one point, he hit Mel Daniels so hard that he tore the athletic tape off the Indiana star center's wrist. Daniels retaliated by knocking him into the courtside spectators. Haywood yelled at the officials for not disciplining Daniels, offering a glimpse into why he led the league in technical fouls. However, he was more than just "muscle and rage," for he blocked shots with a "panther's grace," forcing the Pacers to play a perimeter game.[52] His 35 points helped Denver beat the Eastern Division champs 132–100, and for his virtuosity, Haywood received a standing ovation from the packed house. After the game, he worked his way through a crowd of admiring kids waiting outside the arena and walked the block home to his apartment at Brooks Towers.

In his off-time, Haywood was known to frequent Denver's jazz clubs, and he often played host to late-night parties in his twelfth-floor pad in a doorman building in the heart of the city.[53] Although he had initially rented a modest $150-a-month flat on East Colfax Avenue, he had moved to the more expensive Brooks Towers early on in the season.[54] "I like my privacy," Haywood told Libby, "but women are my real hangup. I love 'em, I really go after 'em. I kind of have my long-time lady picked out, but she'll have to be patient and wait till I love all the rest."[55] In addition to money, his access to women was a hallmark of his status as a star Black male athlete.

His penchant for luxury and conspicuous consumption also extended to his choice of cars. "Spencer was very cocky," Gene Littles, then a guard for the Carolina Cougars, recounted. "He drove a big black custom-made Caddy, and that was in 1969 when guys in the ABA drove Chevies and Buicks."[56] Having disposable income was a tangible sign that he had made it, and he unapologetically flaunted his ability to spend it. "I have money in my pocket now for the first time in my life," he told Libby. "I have a closet full of clothes. I have a nice big car. I can buy all the jazz records I want. I can get me almost anything I want."[57]

Some sportswriters equated Haywood's flamboyance with ignorance, immaturity, and irresponsibility, but he was the embodiment of Black urban cool. No longer confined by the austere aesthetics of respectability politics, Haywood and other pro ballplayers of his generation expressed their masculine power through extravagance. One cannot help but see Haywood's influence in the pages of *Black Sports*, the first major sports magazine dedicated to covering Black athletes and targeted at Black men in the seventies.[58] Alongside regular travel, car, and business features, *Black Sports* began publishing a style series called "Peacock Alley" in August 1973. "To the Brother, fashion is a feeling, an expression of pride," *Black Sports* explained.

"It's just as much a style of manner as it is a style of dress."[59] Rather than following the trends or attempting to appease white folks, the fashionable Black man was his own authority.

In April 1970, with the announcement of Haywood's newly re-negotiated contract with Denver—his third in less than a year—it seemed as if his money problems would now be permanently a thing of the past. Amid circulating reports that as many as five NBA teams had expressed interest in him, the Rockets had come back to the table, even though he still had two years left on his contract. By threatening to leave the ABA, Haywood had managed to garner a reported six-year, $1.9 million package that supposedly made him the highest paid player in the history of professional basketball.[60]

In a press conference to announce the new contract, Rockets owner Bill Ringsby smiled for the cameras as he sat next to Haywood, yet his words betrayed an undercurrent of anger. "All I can say is Spencer is the greatest player in the world and this is the best contract in the world," Ringsby asserted. "It is unheard of to renegotiate a contract in the middle of a season."[61] In not so many words, Ringsby let everyone know that Haywood should consider himself lucky to be getting such a generous package. However, the contract was not actually as lucrative as Ringsby claimed. Haywood was to receive $50,000 for the first two seasons and then $75,000 for the next four, making up a total of $400,000. The Rockets would also invest $10,000 per year into the Dolgoff Plan, which they claimed would generate around $1.5 million to be paid to Haywood from age forty to sixty.[62] As with Haywood's previous deal, most of the reported compensation was deferred and therefore not guaranteed if the Rockets or the ABA folded.

Regardless of the actual value of the contract, by the end of the 1969–1970 season Haywood had shown that he was more than worth his big-money billing. As the league leader in scoring (30 points per game) and rebounding (19.5 rebounds per game), he won both Rookie of the Year and Most Valuable Player. Beyond his individual stats, he had also helped the Rockets move from last to first place in the ABA's Western Division, and he had brought sellout crowds to the Denver arena twenty-one times.[63] In the opening round of the playoffs, Haywood and company beat out the defending ABA champions, the Washington Capitols, in a grueling seven-game series. Even though the Rockets then suffered an embarrassing second-round elimination at the hands of the lightly regarded Los Angeles Stars, Haywood had played well, averaging 37 points and 20 rebounds.[64]

Nevertheless, longtime NBA players worried about the possible fallout from the lucrative deals awarded to Haywood and other rookies in both leagues. Haywood was just one of several young players who had received million-dollar contracts in spring 1970. In the NBA, white college star "Pistol" Pete Maravich had signed with the Atlanta Hawks for $1.5 million, and All-American Black center Bob Lanier was able to command a $1.5 million contract with the Detroit Pistons from his hospital bed, where he was recovering from knee surgery.[65] This must have seemed almost unbelievable to veteran players used to more modest compensation and little leverage in dealing with team owners. As Claude Harrison Jr. of the African American *Philadelphia Tribune* reported, "The NBA-ABA feud, which is producing instant millionaires, is of major concern [to] veteran NBA performers, many of whom may find themselves unemployed next season due to the no-cut clauses in contracts being signed by the current crop of seniors."[66] In particular, Black journeymen were concerned that they would be the first to be released from teams in order to make room for these high-priced and often untested rookies. Even NBA superstars were taking notice of the escalating rookie contracts. Together, they put the team owners on notice, announcing that they planned to fight a merger of the two leagues, which would eliminate their ability to bargain with multiple teams for higher salaries. They also wanted a piece of the action in the ongoing talent war.

Thanks to the advice of older players, Haywood started to question the terms of his deal with Denver. In summer 1970 he played on a team of American professional basketball stars in a series of seven exhibition games in Panama. "We drank, smoked, and partied our way through Panama, and had a great time," Haywood recounted. One night when they were sitting around, the topic of contracts came up. When Haywood bragged about his $1.9 million package with Denver, veterans Archie Clark (Philadelphia 76ers) and Lloyd "Sonny" Dove (New York Nets) decided to school the rookie. "Wood, we hate to say this, but your contract ain't that great. In fact, it's lousy," they told him. They encouraged him to read the fine print; contract terms were never as good as the newspapers reported. When Haywood returned home, he followed their advice. What he found was startling. "There were clauses I didn't understand. For one, I would have to play for the Rockets for ten years, not six, to get all of the future returns from the investments made for me," he recalled. "And there was no indication of how much, if anything, I would be paid to work those additional four years."[67]

With all of his awards and his supposed million-dollar contract, he had become "a valuable piece of propaganda" in the battle between the NBA and ABA. Yet his yearly salary was only $50,000—less than what players of inferior talent were earning. The ABA and especially the Rockets had taken advantage of his ignorance about the financial side of sport: "I realized I should have had expert legal advice and business counseling before I ever signed anything, and it pissed me off that the Ringsbys had never suggested that."[68] With this new insight, he asked the Ringsbys to explain the terms of his contract again, but they simply stonewalled him.

The young star no longer trusted the Ringsbys and even began to question whether or not his mentor, Robinson, had his best interests in mind. That same summer, Haywood had met up with player agent Al Ross and signed a deal with Ross's All-Pro Management firm to help secure him commercials, endorsements, and appearances. In return for handling his affairs, All-Pro would receive 25 percent of any new business it brought him.[69] But Ross was not necessarily the most scrupulous character himself. "The other agents called Ross 'The Pirate,'" player agent and attorney Ron Grinker recounted. "He came out of nowhere and all of a sudden he had all these clients—other people's clients."[70] Nonetheless, young and inexperienced, Haywood wanted help, and Ross stepped into the breach.

EARLY IN THE 1970–1971 SEASON, EMBATTLED AND UNENTHUSIAStic, Haywood seemed almost relieved when he was sidelined with a broken hand because it gave him time to regroup and think about the trajectory of his career. He needed someone more knowledgeable to take a closer look at his contract with Denver, and he asked Ross, who was managing other aspects of his business, for help. Much to Haywood's dismay, Ross confirmed that he had signed on to a terrible deal. "If I ever got hurt, cut, or traded, or if the team folded, I had no guarantees or protection," Haywood realized. "I could not withdraw any of the money until thirty years after signing the contract. And there were no guarantees that the investments would yield that $1.5 million."[71] Ross even questioned the validity of the contract itself, noting that Haywood had still been a minor when he signed his third deal with Denver on April 1, 1970, without the benefit of proper legal advice. In October, Haywood went AWOL, flying to Los Angeles to meet with Ross about his next move.

In LA, Haywood signed a new contract with Ross to handle all of his affairs for 10 percent of all his income, a deal that superseded his previous pact with All-Pro. He also moved into Ross's home in Beverly Hills. Rather than threatening to go to court right away, Ross first attempted to negotiate with the Ringsbys, asking that Haywood's contract be restructured so that he would receive $1.9 million after six seasons of play. The Ringsbys' response? "A contract is a contract."[72] They saw both Haywood's use of an agent and his request to renegotiate his deal as clear affronts to their authority as team owners. "All these clubs have high-powered legal advice, yet they resent the athlete who comes to them with a lawyer," Haywood later complained.[73] Perhaps more significantly, the young star was openly defying the mores of white paternalism and possession that had long structured the asymmetrical relationship between white club owners and their African American players.

Ross and Haywood made little headway in their tumultuous negotiations with the Ringsbys, flying back and forth between Denver and Los Angeles. After a particularly turbulent meeting, Haywood returned to his hotel room, which happened to adjoin with Bill Ringsby's room. Through the wall the beleaguered star heard Ringsby say that "he wasn't going to let 'that Black nigger' push him around." Another time, Haywood overheard the Rockets' owner tell ABA Commissioner Dolph that he was not a "good nigger" and that they would not be able to deal with him "like they could with a white man."[74]

Haywood decided to go public about his contract dispute with the Ringsbys in early November. Ross launched the opening salvo in criticizing Haywood's deal with Denver, arguing that the Rockets' initial cash outlay in the Dolgoff Program was insufficient to make the overall package worth $1.9 million, and the investment account was not even in Haywood's name. Bill Ringsby shot back in the press. "If control of the money is taken over by the boy," he said, "then you pay the taxes and then it goes down the drain." He kept calling Haywood "the boy." Much as he had in the past, Ringsby framed the Rockets' treatment of Haywood as both benevolent and protective. "It's what is known as a forced savings program," Ringsby stated, implying that Haywood was incapable of managing his money on his own terms.[75] By deferring the young star's compensation, they were ensuring that he would end up earning more in the long run. Frustrated with the Rockets' intransigence, Ross threatened to leak the contract to the press and find another team for Haywood. In response, the Rockets slapped Haywood with a suspension and refused to negotiate any further with their unruly player until he returned to Denver.

Spencer Haywood of the Denver Rockets before entering a US district court hearing room in Los Angeles on November 25, 1970, where he attempted to iron out his contract differences with the team. (AP Photo)

A few weeks later, Don Ringsby and his two attorneys, William C. Barnard and Frederick P. Furth, held a press conference to announce the filing of a $1 million lawsuit in the US District Court for the Central District of California in Los Angeles against All-Pro Management, Inc., and its executives Al Ross and Marshall Boyer for slander and inducing breach of contract. Despite his hostile behavior behind closed doors, Ringsby played it cool in the public eye, claiming that he had no personal conflict with Haywood and that he hoped they could settle their dispute amicably. Ringsby maintained that Haywood had been satisfied with his contract until Ross and All-Pro came on the scene as outside agitators, filling the star's head with unreasonable expectations.[76] Attorney Furth added, "We really can't determine what Haywood wants."[77] The suit reeked of condescension, as if Haywood was not only unable to think for himself but also had no legitimate grievances of his own.

Adding insult to injury, public sentiment against the Rockets' star appeared to be growing with each twist and turn in his dispute with the Ringsbys. In an open letter to Haywood, Jim Graham of the *Denver Post* questioned the integrity and maturity of the greedy Black malcontent: "Just because things don't turn out exactly the way you thought they would, does not give you the right to run out on them. A man does not welsh on a written agreement bearing his signature. His word has to mean something if he is to call himself a man."[78]

In the meantime, the Ringsbys' strategy was to keep Haywood isolated. They asked district court judge Warren J. Ferguson for a temporary restraining order to enjoin Ross and All-Pro from "interfering" with their contract negotiations with Haywood and from negotiating with any other professional clubs on his behalf. Judge Ferguson granted the temporary restraining order but modified it, giving Ross permission to speak with Commissioner Dolph on Haywood's behalf about the possibility of playing with another ABA team.[79] The battle also continued to play out in the media. In a taped segment on a Denver radio station, Haywood declared, "I will not play basketball for

Denver . . . under the Ringsbys."[80] He had put his trust in the Rings-bys, and they had taken advantage of him. Now they were trying to smear his reputation and turn his teammates against him.

In interviews Haywood spoke openly about the Ringsbys' racism: "You can tell by some of the quotes from them calling me 'boy,' and black people don't want to be called 'boy' anymore. I know there is a quota on the team as far as black players are concerned. Some good ones were cut because of race—too many of them."[81] Haywood was airing pro basketball's dirty laundry, exposing how white team own-ers continued to treat African American players with disrespect. "The Ringsbys made me look like an ass and I'm saying this, not Al Ross," he told the *Denver Post*, "and if it takes six years I'll fight this. It's that important to me and to my people."[82] He demanded to be treated like a man.

Haywood decided to take legal action of his own. In late November, he filed a $1 million countersuit against the Denver Rockets, charging them with fraud. The suit claimed that he had signed the contract when he was twenty and although he signed a ratification of it at age twenty-one, he had not understood its terms. Instead, he had been in-duced to sign the deal with Denver on the basis of "misrepresentation and undue influence."[83]

With all of these suits and countersuits alongside various small acts of resistance, it appeared as if the NBA-ABA talent war had made Hay-wood and other Black players more rebellious and entitled. When the Rockets suspended Haywood, he became the third Black player pushed off the payroll in the first few months of the season. Rookie Mike Maloy, who had put on fifty pounds during the summer, was suspended by the Pittsburgh Condors and then traded to the Virginia Squires. Mean-while, Warren Armstrong of the Kentucky Colonels found himself in hot water when, reportedly, he had refused to take the team bus to an exhibition game and tried to organize the Colonels' Black players. The "independently minded" Armstrong, who scoffed at the latter accusa-tion, was suspended and then traded to the Indiana Pacers. A number of African American players on the Utah Stars had also recently made waves by noting how hard it was to navigate being Black in Salt Lake City after the team had moved from Los Angeles. Dave Overpeck of *Basketball Weekly* summarily dismissed their complaints, denying the likelihood that they experienced racism in their daily lives off the court. "A visit to Salt Lake City makes it hard to believe the black members of the Utah Stars were as discontented as earlier reports had it," Overpeck wrote. "There seems to be an almost small town recognition, even adulation, of the players—black and white."[84]

Even at the college level, Black players were exercising their power. At Haywood's alma mater, UD, the majority-Black team revolted against Coach Harding, calling for him to be fired. Harding found support among politically conservative, white basketball writers such as Roger Stanton of *Basketball Weekly*, who argued that the UD players' protest against Harding showed that American society had become too permissive: "We are a nation of law and order—in the streets and on the athletic fields. Let us never forget that."[85]

These concerns about the rising defiance of Black ballplayers dovetailed with broader concerns about the growing ungovernability of young Black men and calls for greater policing and punishment in the War on Crime. In the aftermath of the urban uprisings of the late 1960s, politicians increasingly recast ongoing African American discontent as a crime problem rather than evidence of persistent racial inequality. And their prescribed solution was more discipline, rather than social reform. They ramped up foot patrols in urban Black neighborhoods to contain Black violence and disorder, effectively criminalizing a generation of Black youths.[86] Thus, the disobedient behavior of African American athletes seemed to foreshadow anarchy, on the court and in the streets. Yet the white basketball establishment could no longer survive without the talents of Black players, no matter how troublesome they were.

Without Haywood, the Rockets struggled on the court, and their game attendance lagged. Through the first twelve home games of

Haywood's rookie season, the Rockets had drawn a total of 57,042 spectators; this season, however, the number dropped to 47,599. Bill Ringsby lashed out at Denver's fair-weather fans. In his eyes, they were encouraging Haywood's bad behavior, and he intimated that he might move the team to Kansas City or Omaha, Nebraska. "They want to see Haywood and I can't say if they'll see Haywood. I just don't know."[87]

DURING HAYWOOD'S DISPUTE WITH THE ROCKETS, ROSS HAD ADvised him to contact Sam Schulman, the maverick owner of the Seattle SuperSonics, one of several NBA teams that previously had expressed interest in signing him. Haywood called Schulman and had a good feeling about their conversation. Unlike the Ringsbys, Schulman "seemed calm and rational, and not condescending." Schulman had his lawyers look at Haywood's deal with Denver, and he came to the conclusion that Haywood "was a decent guy with a bad contract."[88] At a meeting in San Diego, Schulman asked NBA Commissioner Kennedy and the league front office for permission to go after a contract with Haywood. The request was denied; signing Haywood would violate the NBA's four-year rule.[89]

But Schulman pressed ahead in his discussions with the ABA star, offering Haywood $1.5 million for playing six seasons, to be spread over fifteen years, with Haywood receiving $100,000 cash per year. Perhaps even more importantly, he also promised to pay all of Haywood's legal fees in the athlete's fight to play in the NBA. On December 30 the SuperSonics went public about their multiyear deal with Haywood just as a new development in the embattled player's case was announced: Judge Ferguson had issued a temporary restraining order prohibiting the NBA from imposing its four-year rule on Haywood and the Sonics, pending a scheduled hearing about his contract dispute with Denver in early January 1971.[90]

Commissioner Kennedy was not at all impressed with the district court's interference in the NBA's internal dealings. "For the first time

I can recall in the history of sports," he said, "a court has superseded a commissioner or organization in a conduct of its affairs."[91] In the meantime, Bill Ringsby threatened to do everything in his power to hold onto Haywood and keep him from playing for Seattle. "As far as I'm concerned, we'll have him sitting for six years," Ringsby declared.[92]

Amid this tense legal battle, Haywood made his first appearance on the basketball court with the Seattle SuperSonics on January 4, against the Milwaukee Bucks. Looking out of shape, he did not play much, but he still managed to score 14 points and grab 9 rebounds. Afterward, Milwaukee president Ray Patterson called for Seattle's expulsion from the league.[93] Other NBA teams, even those that had tried to sign Haywood, filed official protests against his presence at games. When the Sonics played in Chicago on February 2, All-Star forward Chet Walker twisted his ankle during the pregame warm-up, and the Bulls filed a $600,000 lawsuit against the Sonics. Although it was later withdrawn, the suit claimed that Haywood's presence had created a "distractive and disruptive atmosphere which was a direct cause of an injury" to Walker.[94] Haywood even suspected that the team owners were encouraging veteran NBA players to take cheap shots against him on the court.[95] At away games, programs listed Haywood as "No. 24, Ineligible Player," and announcers pointed out that an illegal player was on the floor. This only stoked the white-hot ire of fans. They booed and spewed racial epithets reminiscent of Haywood's youth in Mississippi. They threw programs, paper cups, ice, beer, and whatever else they had on hand at the defiant star. A couple of times the home team walked off the court and went to the locker room, refusing to play if Haywood remained in uniform on the floor. Even Haywood's Seattle teammates were suspicious of him because of the controversy swirling around the ABA transplant.

White sportswriters criticized Haywood, arguing that his conduct was ruining professional basketball. They also blamed team owners for enabling his bad behavior from the moment he had left college under the ABA's hardship clause. "Haywood became an immediate star, but he has been a problem child ever since," Roger Stanton of *Basketball Weekly* complained.[96] Unlike the pro football leagues, which had the foresight and discipline to avoid raiding the college ranks, professional basketball's permissiveness had created a mess. "There are many like him in pro sports today," Stanton contended. "They can play. But they have a hard time reacting to life and early success. They squander their money, give nothing to society and lead the fast life." The chaos caused by the Haywood affair was "bad for the image of the game" and set "a bad example for American youth." Pro athletes, especially Black players like Haywood, were promoting the worst impulses of the 1970s "Me Generation."

With his future as a professional ballplayer hanging in the balance, Haywood had become listless and depressed. He was worried that the NBA might blacklist him, thereby ending his career before it had even started. He became a hermit, holing himself up in his Seattle hotel room. "I'm tired," he told reporter Libby. "I'm bone-tired physically. I feel all used up mentally. I can't think straight any more. I have been pulled this way and that way until I feel like I'm just going to come apart." He knew his reputation had taken a hit. "I'm supposed to be a bad man. Greedy Gus." His bucking of the system, from his early jump to the ABA to his recent move to the NBA, had angered hoops fans and the white basketball establishment. "Detroit and the NCAA and the public still haven't forgiven me for turning pro before I graduated from college. Why? Isn't it my business? If the man wants to pay me to play, why shouldn't I be free to make a buck?" he asked.[97]

He began to see that the entire sports system—from college athletics to the professional leagues—was set up to extract his labor without granting him much in the way of self-determination or financial security: "Ain't I free? Are all athletes slaves to the system? . . . Who the hell was going to give me a buck, a nice place to live, some decent clothes, a nice car to drive? Who the hell was going to give my mom a few bucks so she could start living decent? How does the system protect me?"[98] Tempered by his own experience of heady success and bitter critique, Haywood had come to realize that he had to stand up for himself.

On January 8, 1971, at a hearing in Haywood's continuing legal fight with Denver, Judge Ferguson refused to issue the preliminary injunction sought by the Rockets to bar Haywood from playing with any other team. In a second action, he added ten days to the temporary restraining order barring the NBA from enforcing its four-year rule and preventing Haywood from playing with Seattle, pending a hearing on the matter. Judge Ferguson also noted that there was a "strong probability" that Haywood's legal team could effectively challenge the four-year rule as a violation of antitrust laws. "If that's what we have to do to keep Haywood on the basketball court, that is what we're going to do," the young star's attorney Morris P. Pfaelzer declared.[99]

Meanwhile, the swirl of controversy surrounding Haywood cast a shadow over the NBA All-Star gathering in San Diego on January 12, dominating official meetings and casual conversations and garnering more press than the game itself. Lenny Wilkens, Seattle's Black player-coach, was named the All-Star Game's Most Valuable Player, yet he spent most of his time defending his team's signing of Haywood. "The ABA made him a pro and there is no way he is going back to college now," Wilkens said. "I get tired of teams suing us because we signed him. They wanted to sign him, too."[100] NBA team officials admitted as much to reporters, although they still chastised team owner Sam Schulman and wanted Commissioner Kennedy to punish him for going rogue.

On January 14, Haywood, with Schulman's financial backing, turned around and sued the NBA in Ferguson's court, alleging the league, through its threatened sanctions against him and Seattle for noncompliance with its player draft rules, was violating Section 1 of the Sherman Antitrust Act, which prohibits restraint of trade.[101] In other words, Haywood's case claimed that "the NBA was excluding an entire class of people (a group boycott) who were not four years beyond high school and that the group boycott was illegal *per se* and should be overturned by the courts."[102]

Professional sports leagues had long argued that they were not like other businesses and should be exempt from the Sherman Act. But Haywood's battle against the NBA's four-year rule highlighted the intertwined monopolies of big-time sport that stripped young athletes of their autonomy and kept their compensation artificially low. Leonard Koppett of the *New York Times* argued that the NCAA and the NBA had a "gentleman's agreement" that helped them maintain control of the sport at the college ranks and the pro ranks, respectively. Outwardly, the white basketball establishment claimed that the four-year rule was guided by ethical considerations. "'The boy' must not be 'enticed' away from his invaluable college education by fabulous financial offers while he is still 'immature,' college coaches often say," Koppett wrote. "And even the pros, who don't really have to, tend to discuss the rule as some sort of moral obligation."[103] Given the fact that many of the top college players were poor or working-class African Americans, the NCAA and NBA often cloaked themselves in a mantle of racial uplift.

In reality, economics, not idealism, undergirded their commitment to the four-year rule. "For colleges, it means protecting the supply of cheap labor," Koppett explained. "For professionals, it makes possible the draft system, which reduces bidding for talent, and it helps maintain the free farm system the college teams constitute." The real reason that other NBA teams were attempting to block Haywood from playing with Seattle was because Schulman had bypassed the league's hallowed draft system, which required a "common starting point" in order to work. If there were no four-year rule, "All the pro clubs would have to compete with each other all through a college player's career," Koppett noted. "That would be expensive, and it would antagonize the free farm system."[104]

The NCAA was no more principled in its support of the four-year rule. Many college athletes in revenue-generating sports struggled

academically or failed to graduate. "By openly providing athletic schol-
arships and other benefits, and by collecting large sums in gate receipts,
colleges create an employee-employer relationship in practice no matter how much they deny it in theory," Koppett charged. He understood
that as businesses, NBA teams wanted to keep their labor costs down
in order to expand their profit margins. But the college player alone
bore the risk of seeing his future earnings as a professional evaporate
in the case of injury. Despite the benevolent stance of the NCAA and
NBA, the four-year rule was not there to nurture and "protect" young
players. Their rules were designed "to control and diminish bidding
for the services of talented athletes."[105] Now, Haywood threatened
this mutually supportive arrangement between two profit-motivated
businesses.

Much to the NBA's chagrin, on January 18, Judge Ferguson denied the league's motion to suspend the district court's injunction.[106]
"If Haywood is unable to continue to play professional basketball for
Seattle," Ferguson ruled, "he will suffer irreparable injury in that a
substantial part of his playing career will have been dissipated, his
physical condition, skills and coordination will deteriorate from lack
of high-level competition, his public acceptance as a super star will
diminish to the detriment of his career, his self-esteem and his pride
will have been injured and a great injustice will be perpetrated on
him." The NBA immediately filed an appeal.[107] It realized that its
fight with Haywood was not simply about the legality of the four-year
rule. The NBA's iron-fisted control over the entire system of player
recruitment and movement was at stake.

Just when it seemed as if the courts were on Haywood's side, a
panel of three federal judges in San Francisco reversed course. On
February 15 the Ninth Circuit Court of Appeals heard the NBA's appeal and stayed Judge Ferguson's injunction, which barred the league
from taking any action against Seattle to stop Haywood from playing,
pending the outcome of his legal battles with Denver and the NBA.[108]
The federal judges sided with the NBA, citing "the public interest in

the institution of professional basketball" and the need for "the orderly regulation of its affairs."[109] Once again, Haywood was prohibited from playing for Seattle.

Forced to sit on the sidelines, all Haywood could do was wait while his lawyers appealed the stay of the injunction to the US Supreme Court. This legal tug-of-war continued to take its toll on him. He worried that Seattle might release him or that the district court would rule he had to return to Denver: "It's a big mental strain on me. It's impossible to drive the thing out of my mind. You're always thinking that at any time you might not be here to play. I wanna play."[110]

Yet there was little public sympathy for Haywood. Even the Black press criticized him for being too greedy too soon. He was just twenty-one years old, with a life story that already had the makings of an intriguing novel, but he had ruined it by trying to skip ahead in the plot. "His motives were good and pure when he sought to help his mother working in Mississippi. You can't blame any boy for that, but Haywood was looking out for himself at the same time," the *Chicago Defender* maintained.[111] His former mentor Will Robinson had also turned on him. "The more money he got, the more he wanted. He wanted to see it in piles around his feet. He got greedy," Robinson argued.[112] At a moment when everyone else, particularly Black America, was suffering economically, Haywood's demands seemed excessive and out of touch. Robinson and others feared that the young ballplayer's arrogance and lack of gratitude would be his downfall.

Nevertheless, Haywood persisted in his fight. After all that he had gone through, it was about more than just money; it was a matter of principle. Over the next month, his crusade against the Ringsbys and the NBA would take him all the way to the highest court in the nation.

WITH THE NBA PLAYOFFS SET TO BEGIN IN A FEW WEEKS, TIME WAS of the essence. Because it can take years for cases to get in front of the entire Supreme Court, each member serves as a circuit court justice, deciding on urgent appeals. In spring 1971 Justice William O. Douglas was the jurist assigned to review the cases coming from the Ninth Circuit Court of Appeals. Douglas was, in some respects, the ideal Supreme Court justice to evaluate Haywood's appeal of the stay of the injunction that kept him from playing for the Sonics. He was an ardent proponent of legal realism, which "argued that law should be based less on formalistic legal doctrines (like precedent) and that judges instead should base their decisions on the real world effects of the laws themselves." Appointed to the US Supreme Court by President Franklin Roosevelt in 1939 at the age of forty, he spent thirty-six years on the bench and became one of the most liberal justices of his era.[113]

On March 1, 1971, Judge Douglas released his three-page decision in the case of *Haywood v. NBA*. He began by briefly recapping the history of Haywood's suit. Although Douglas did not tackle head-on the broader antitrust concerns raised by the case, he noted that basketball, unlike baseball, was not exempt from antitrust laws, and he acknowledged that "this group boycott issue in professional sports is a significant one." Douglas then called for the reinstatement of the district court's preliminary injunction against the NBA, thereby permitting Haywood to play for Seattle. Noting the impending start of the playoffs on March 23, he claimed that the action would preserve "the integrity of the playoff system." Ever the legal realist, he laid out succinctly the stakes of his decision. Douglas reasoned that if Haywood was unable to play, most likely Seattle would not make the playoffs. Therefore, if the stay of the injunction remained in effect and Haywood went on to win his suits against Denver and the NBA, the young star and the Sonics would be irreparably harmed. If, however, the injunction was reinstated, allowing Haywood to play for the Sonics, there were three possible outcomes. If Seattle was eliminated before the playoffs, then no one would be harmed. If Seattle made the playoffs and Haywood lost his suits, then the district court could decide whether "the NBA could disregard the Seattle victories in all games in which he participated and recompute who should be in the playoffs."[114] Finally, if Seattle made the playoffs before a ruling on Haywood's suits, the district court could then determine a fair solution for the NBA.

If Haywood was back in the game thanks to Douglas's ruling, his fight continued nonetheless. While the NBA appealed Judge Douglas's order, the Atlanta Hawks, slated to play the Sonics on March 2, announced that they would take the court under protest.[115] Then, on March 9, the entire Supreme Court upheld Douglas's decision without comment. As the legal battle returned to the lower courts and Haywood awaited Judge Ferguson's decision about the validity of his contract with Denver and the legality of the NBA's four-year rule, he told his side of the story in the March issue of *Sport* magazine. He did not mince words in describing what it felt like to play for the Ringsbys: "At best, it was like we were hired slaves, circus freaks who had to perform on command."[116] They had swindled him. Because he was a minor at the time, the Rockets had found him a new guardian when his longtime mentor Robinson was unavailable—a banker named Ben Gibson who was in cahoots with the team. Gibson never bothered to explain the terms of the deal to his young charge. Haywood had signed a ratification of the contract after he turned twenty-one, still believing that it was worth $1.9 million for six years of service.[117]

Despite everything that the Ringsbys had done to mislead him, Haywood still felt it necessary to defend his position: "I am not a militant black. I belong to no radical groups. I feel I've suffered from prejudice but you can't find the man, white or black, who will tell you I've ever acted with prejudice. Still I am black and I do have pride." Regardless of the district court's looming decision, he had already decided that he would never play for the Ringsbys again. They had tried to deny him control over his own career: "A salesman can shift from one firm to another freely, but an athlete seems bound in slavery."[118] Haywood had drawn a line in the sand, and now he had to suffer the consequences.

Even though the Supreme Court had decided in his favor, Haywood found little support in the court of public opinion. "Writers, fans, even some players are putting me down," Haywood complained. "I don't care if they don't like me, but I do want them to respect me. All I've tried to do is live by a rule I learned on the Chicago streets: Man, if you don't stand up for something, you'll fall for everything."[119] Roger Stanton of *Basketball Weekly* went out of his way to refute Haywood's version of events in *Sport* magazine. Stanton had zero sympathy for the Black star: "He has acted like a spoiled child who doesn't know right from wrong. He is ungrateful, misguided, un-educated and irresponsible."[120] For Stanton, Haywood's fall from grace was symbolic of everything that was wrong with young African Americans of the 1970s.

As Haywood's district court date approached, his legal team filed a motion requesting a summary judgment rather than jury trial, on the grounds that there was no dispute over the material facts of the case. Judge Ferguson agreed. On March 22 he announced his decision, and two days later he released his written opinion. In finding in Haywood's favor, he reaffirmed that the NBA was not exempt from antitrust laws and struck down the NBA's four-year rule as illegal under Section 1 of the Sherman Act. He argued that with member teams in seventeen different cities with games and media contracts in various states, the NBA was clearly engaged in interstate commerce. He also maintained the preliminary injunction enjoining the NBA from preventing the young star from playing with Seattle.[121]

In analyzing the facts of the case alongside antitrust laws, Ferguson argued that the NBA bylaws that prohibited a qualified player from negotiating with any member team until four years after his high school class graduation constituted a "group boycott." Indeed, the bylaws had no provisions for considering any exceptions to the rule, making them an illegal restraint of trade. Ferguson contended that this group boycott was illegal per se and that the "reasonableness of it" was "no defense to its illegality." Countering the typical justifications cited for the NBA's four-year rule, he argued that it was illegal even if (1) it was necessary for the economic survival of professional basketball and (2) it protected the educational opportunities of collegiate players.[122] He maintained that legislators, not the courts, would have to determine if any of these considerations should override the antitrust issue.

Ferguson's written opinion also revealed some of the more shocking aspects of Haywood's alleged six-year $1.9 million pact with Denver, confirming what the young star and Ross had been saying for months about its deferred-compensation structure. It turned out that Haywood had no control over the investment fund in the Dolgoff Plan—the one that was supposed to pay him around $1.5 million from age forty to sixty. The fund was not registered in his name but remained the property of the Ringsbys and could be used as collateral for loans. Any time after the payment of the final installment on October 1, 1979, Haywood would have the right to direct annual payments to himself in the amount of 10 percent of the value of the fund, until the fund was exhausted. However, in order to receive those payments, he would have to work for the Ringsbys from October 1, 1970, to October 1, 1979. And as long as he was receiving these payments, he was required to "render advisory and consulting services" to the Ringsbys. "The contract does not provide for compensation for Haywood's services for six years in the amount of $1,900,000," Ferguson concluded. "Compensation in excess of $394,000 is illusory and indefinite."[123] Not only did Haywood have no control over "his" money, but the contract also required more than six years of service in exchange for far less compensation than the Ringsbys claimed.

The NBA's conduct was no more upstanding, Ferguson noted, as it had tried to bully Haywood and the Sonics into abiding by the four-year rule. Commissioner Kennedy had made statements to the news media that were meant to intimidate Haywood and Seattle, and the NBA board of governors had threatened Seattle with "drastic penalties," including possible expulsion, fines, and suspension of draft picks.[124]

Ferguson's ruling had potentially far-reaching consequences. Even though his summary judgment considered only the legality of the four-year rule, Ferguson acknowledged that Haywood's suit against the NBA also challenged the reserve system and the college draft "as being similarly violative of the antitrust laws." In particular, it claimed that the college draft was essentially anticompetitive because once one team acquired the exclusive right to contract a new player, no other club could compete for his services.[125] In what had started out as a personal struggle for better compensation and more control over his career, Haywood had managed to publicly expose the tangle of racism, exploitation, and monopoly that fueled the growing enterprise of professional basketball.

Reaction to the district court's summary judgment was overwhelmingly critical. White sportswriters continued to argue that the four-year rule was a matter of morals rather than money. College players needed "protection," particularly from the unscrupulous practices of the rival ABA. "This is an open invitation for more ABA teams to perform the dastardly deed of depriving a boy of his college education so that he can play pro sports immediately," Gar Yarbro of *Basketball Weekly* warned. Yarbro took special aim at the ABA's latest hardship case, seven-foot-two center Artis Gilmore, who had been signed by the Kentucky Colonels to a multiyear, multimillion-dollar contract. "He has a bad attitude and lacks that inner drive to succeed," Yarbro declared. Gilmore's Afro only made matters worse: "If I were [team owner] Mr. Cherry, I would demand that Mr. Gilmore get a new hair stylist before he starts playing for the Colonels so that his hair won't get in his eyes next season."[126] A new generation of players—unschooled, entitled, and unapologetically Black—were threatening to flood the ranks of professional ball.

Still hoping that somehow the district court's ruling would be overturned, on March 29 the Buffalo Braves selected Haywood in the second round of the 1971 NBA draft. Commissioner Kennedy told them they were wasting a draft pick.[127] He had ruled that the Sonics could keep Haywood if they agreed to pay a $200,000 fine. The Sonics had also settled out of court with the Rockets for an undisclosed sum. After months of living in basketball limbo, Haywood was finally free to play with Seattle. And with the Haywood affair wrapped up, the two leagues could now revisit their merger talks.[128]

When sportswriter Sam Lacy of the *Baltimore Afro-American* was asked by a white counterpart if it wasn't "a shame that an irresponsible fellow like that can cause all of this trouble because he's greedy and wants to play wherever they're paying the most money," the implications of the question angered him.[129] Black players, not the team owners, were the ones getting a raw deal. "No matter how much the professional owner contends that his empire will crumble if he doesn't have the protection of a legitimate contract, it doesn't seem at all equitable to me that such a contract should give the owner the privilege of dispensing with the services of a player, while denying that same player the opportunity to better his position," Lacy wrote. The NBA's "holier-than-thou" claims about not wanting to lure young players out of college were complete "hogwash."

The NBA and NCAA worked in concert to control ballplayers' careers. "While they are scratching each other's back, the player is hanging around the campus, waiting for injury or a poor season that will virtually wreck his bargaining power," Lacy maintained. Unlike white stars Pete Maravich or Rick Barry, who were from middle-class or wealthy families, most African American ballplayers came from poor or working-class backgrounds. Moreover, there were few fringe benefits for Black players in the form of endorsements, personal appearances, or stock in a team. Maravich had managed to snag a shoe deal after one season, whereas it took eleven years of pro basketball stardom for Oscar Robertson to land an endorsement deal from a razor-blade company. It was their time now, and Black players needed to seize the opportunity.

Chapter 3

Bondage

Overthrowing the Option Clause

Was sports a form of business or a kind of slavery?
Were the players free laborers or chattel? Were owners
feudal lords or modern entrepreneurs?

—Lewis Cole, on the NBPA's fight against the
option clause, in *A Loose Game*, 1978

ON WEDNESDAY, SEPTEMBER 22, 1971, NBPA PRESIDENT OSCAR Robertson, otherwise known as "the Big O," sat in room 318 of the Old Senate Office Building, ready to give his testimony in front of the Senate Subcommittee on Antitrust and Monopoly. The stakes were high, for this subcommittee was charged with helping lawmakers decide if they should grant an antitrust waiver to the NBA and ABA, thereby opening the door to a merger. Despite Robertson's outsized contribution to the players' campaign against the consolidation, his speech that day was relatively short. Back in August, while the veteran Milwaukee Bucks point guard should have been readying himself for training camp, he spent the last part of his off-season working with NBPA attorney Larry Fleisher in preparation for his appearance in Washington, DC. At the time, they had no idea what questions the senators would ask, so they role-played various scenarios. Robertson was determined to effectively represent the players' concerns.[1]

Accompanied by Fleisher, and fashionably dressed in a patterned suit jacket, blue shirt, and striped tie, the thirty-two-year-old greeted the imposing half-circle of subcommittee members. After introducing himself, he read from his prepared remarks:

> I speak here today on behalf of the players in the National Basketball Association. Our opposition to the proposed merger is total. Every player supports our stand and the positions as indicated by our counsel in prior testimony. The players recognize the unfairness of a system of professional basketball which allows them to negotiate with only one team. They have gone through the experience of no competition prior to the ABA's existence and of great competition since 1967. They understand that every player has been dramatically helped by the competitive aspects of a second league. All of their salaries have increased, from the last man on the team to the superstars.[2]

He had personally witnessed "the terrible hardships" faced by NBA players of the early 1960s: "the men who played for $5,000 or $6,000 a year, the men who were not able to bargain effectively for increases, the men who retired and were finished with their careers at age 30 without any benefits."[3]

Yet for Robertson and the members of the NBPA, this fight was about far more than money. As a superstar, he already had a lucrative, long-term contract. "I do not stand to benefit financially by having the leagues continue to compete for my services," he said, "but I do stand to benefit as a man. I do stand to benefit by seeing that the 300 some-odd ball players in professional basketball have an opportunity to be treated as other people in American life; that they can truly negotiate for their services."[4] This fight was about the players' dignity as workers, their desire to be recognized as men, and their right to have the same economic freedoms as other US citizens. Building on the antitrust battles of Connie Hawkins and Spencer Haywood, the NBPA would now take aim at pro basketball's reserve system.

ROBERTSON'S OWN EXPERIENCES IN THE SIXTIES, AS A BLACK STAR IN a white-controlled league, had prepared him to head the players' push for free agency. He had been part of the NBPA leadership that organized the near boycott of the 1964 All-Star Game in Boston, which was called off at the last minute when the team owners agreed to establish a pension plan for the players. In the summer of 1965, Robertson took over as president of the NBPA when the Celtics' white forward Tommy Heinsohn retired. The association leaders reasoned that the new president needed to be a premier player with the gravitas to command respect from front-office executives. And because of the increasing number of African Americans in the league, it needed to be a Black player. Robertson fit both of these criteria.[5]

When the Big O took the helm, the character of the NBPA changed. Before, it had been largely the province of star players. He helped to democratize and integrate the union, recruiting the league's journeymen, especially Black journeymen, to the cause. Black players infused the NBPA's labor fights with the ethos and strategies of the African American freedom movement beyond basketball. They could not help but see their struggles against the all-white team owners as part of the wider push for Black economic equality and self-determination in the post–civil rights era. They were not alone: Black-led labor activism was the rule rather than the exception in professional sports. On January 16, 1970, star center fielder Curt Flood, with the support of the Major League Baseball Players Association, lodged an antitrust lawsuit that challenged the MLB's reserve clause. A similar fight was brewing in the NFL. Two years after leading a successful strike in 1970, star Baltimore Colts tight end and National Football League

Players Association (NFLPA) president John Mackey became the
lead plaintiff in a suit against the "Rozelle Rule," a league bylaw that
restricted player movement.[6]

The work of Robertson and Black members of the NBPA also coincided with the energetic push for unionization across the United States
in the late 1960s and 1970s—a push largely led by those previously
left out of organized labor, particularly Black men and women. As
increasing numbers of African Americans gained work in the public
sector, they engaged in illegal strikes to combat poverty wages and to
gain union recognition and collective bargaining rights in everything
from garbage collection to mail delivery. In the private sector they
borrowed lessons from the civil rights movement to win economic
power in the manufacturing, construction, and service industries.[7]

Meanwhile, Robertson's own contract battles with the Cincinnati
Royals had convinced him that NBA regulations gave white team
owners undue power over the league's now majority-Black athletes.
He had played for the University of Cincinnati, and the Royals had
snapped him up as a "territorial pick" in 1960. In existence from 1950
to 1966, the territorial draft helped to keep professional players geo-
graphically close to their college fan bases at a time when NCAA
basketball was more popular than the NBA. It also meant that the
Royals had full control over his career, thanks to the reserve clause,
which effectively bound a player to a team for life. As Robertson explained, "The only way a player could leave was if he was traded; when
a contract was up, the only team he could negotiate with was the team
that held his contract."[8] Under this exploitative system, players were
not only labor but also a form of property.

When Robertson's first contract ended in 1965, the Royals refused
to give him a raise. They offered him the exact same amount of money
he was earning (around $33,000 per year in base pay, plus a percent-
age of the gate receipts), despite the fact that he had been a first-team
All-Pro for five years and had won the 1964 league MVP award. Because of the reserve clause, his only move was to withhold his labor. In

spite of all he had done for the Royals, the team owners still treated him with disrespect. They refused to negotiate with him and began to smear him in local newspapers, exaggerating his contract demands, implying that he was an ingrate. In response, he bluffed in the press, threatening to leave Cincinnati and go on a barnstorming tour. Just five days before the start of the season, the two sides finally came to an agreement: Robertson was to receive around $70,000 per year, along with a percentage of the gate receipts and the use of a car.[9]

A year later, Robertson began to publicly criticize the reserve system—a fairly radical stance for the time. Appearing before the team owners at the league's annual meeting in June 1966, he announced the NBPA's call "for the elimination of the present contractual arrangement under which [players] are not able to negotiate with other teams in the league."[10] The following year, Robertson presided over a threatened strike of the playoffs. Since the NBPA's last strike threat at the 1964 All-Star Game, the team owners had failed to keep their promise of a satisfactory pension plan. Now the players set a date for a league-wide walkout unless the owners met their demands. Although an agreement was reached at the eleventh hour, thus averting a strike, it was the first time that any players organization had dared to set such a deadline.[11]

Despite this truce, a few months later Robertson found himself embroiled in yet another contract fight with the Royals. Again, he chose to hold out, skipping the Royals' training camp and preseason exhibition games. Cincinnati sportswriters, who aligned themselves with the Royals' front office, attacked his character, calling him greedy. When he met with Royals general manager Pepper Wilson, the Big O retorted, "If I am greedy, I learned from you."[12] In an interview with George Vecsey of *Sport* magazine, Robertson said he might not return to Cincinnati, and the recent establishment of the ABA made this threat all the more real.[13] His standoff with the Royals continued into October 1967.

Known around the league as a fierce competitor, the Big O brought that same determination to his contract negotiations. "They expect a lot from me," he complained to Vecsey. "When I get 30 points, ten assists and ten rebounds [a triple double], . . . they say, 'Oscar Robertson played his usual game. . . .' What else could I do for them? Sell popcorn? Sweep the floor? Do handstands?"[14] They were already extracting their pound of flesh from him, jeopardizing the longevity of his career by playing him 46 minutes per game. This time around, his dispute with the Royals was about more than just a raise. He was demanding money owed to him. The Royals had yet to pay Robertson his designated percentage of the gate receipts, at least $33,000. He did not want the matter to go to arbitration because the decision maker would be Commissioner Walter Kennedy, whose salary the team owners paid.

Robertson was also frustrated that he had no freedom of mobility. "If a man is not happy with his salary or anything else, they ought to trade him," he complained.[15] He saw the Royals' refusal to pay him what he was worth as part of a broader pattern of front-office racism against the team's African American players. After seeing the team mistreat and discard Bob Boozer, Wayne Embry, and Tom Thacker in recent years, Robertson had begun to wonder if the Royals were operating under an unspoken racial quota designed to keep the number of Black players from becoming a majority on the team.

It was not just the Royals who undervalued him. White-owned businesses in Cincinnati expected Robertson to endorse them for next to nothing. With personal appearances, it was more of the same. He had no problem speaking with kids for free, but when people were making money from his presence, he expected to be paid appropriately for his time. It was more than a matter of money for Robertson; it was a matter of dignity and pride. The Royals' disrespect was also part and parcel of the broader white backlash against racial integration. He had chosen to live in a Black section of Cincinnati, and still there were always rumors that he might move into a white neighborhood. The local white resistance to busing had spurred him to speak out more forcefully against racism: "They were bussing [Black] kids from our neighborhood to another school . . . but the white people didn't want their kids bussed into our neighborhood. . . . 'What's wrong with our school?' I asked them."[16]

Robertson's prolonged and ugly contract battle with the Royals in early 1970 proved to be the final straw. In January he had heard from a reporter, rather than from the front office, that he had been traded to the Baltimore Bullets. However, as Robertson and his lawyer reminded the Royals, according to his contract he had the right of refusal over any trade. *He* would tell them where *he* wanted to be traded. Once again, the Royals set out to undermine him in the press, exaggerating his demands. They threatened to take legal action against him if he decided to jump to the ABA.[17] The Big O demanded a trade to the Milwaukee Bucks, and news of his move became public in April 1970.[18]

The fact that the Royals had tried to dispose of him without honoring the terms of his contract had not only angered him but also inspired him to fight back more systematically: "It reinforced everything I believed about owner arrogance, the need for players' rights, and the importance of getting rid of . . . [the] reserve clause."[19] With the Royals out of the playoffs and his time with the team coming to an end, Robertson turned to organizing. Together with NBPA lawyer Larry Fleisher and players John Havlicek, Paul Silas, and Dave DeBusschere, he began planning a challenge to the team owners' monopolistic power over pro ball. Enough was enough.

On April 16, 1970, Robertson and other player leaders filed a class-action antitrust lawsuit against the two leagues. All but 1 of the 166 players in the NBA authorized the suit, the first time in the history of professional sport that players had brought such a concerted action against their club owners. There was some speculation that the lone dissenter was Connie Hawkins because his contract was said to prohibit him from suing the league again.[20] The named plaintiffs in the lawsuit included Robertson and the player representatives from the NBA's teams.[21] As NBPA president, Robertson's name appeared first and became identified with the suit. Even though the plaintiffs included both white and Black players, the fact that the suit had a Black face attached to it was significant. *Oscar Robertson et al. v. NBA* came to represent the shifting racial and labor politics of professional basketball in the seventies.

Although the lawsuit went right to the heart of the team owners' monopolistic practices, it was filed during the NBA playoffs, so it initially garnered little public attention. It charged the NBA with "conspiring to restrain competition for the services and skills of professional basketball players through such devices as the college draft, the reserve clause . . . and various boycott and blacklisting techniques." It also argued that the NBA and ABA sought "to effectuate a non-competition agreement, merger or consolidation."[22] A merger would limit their competitive bargaining powers and bind the players involuntarily to one team for their entire pro career. Therefore, the leagues were in violation of sections 1 and 2 of the Sherman Antitrust Act. In addition to opposing the merger, the players sought damages for past salary losses resulting from the reserve clause.[23]

Several weeks later, Judge Charles H. Tenney for the Southern District Court of New York granted the NBA players' request for an injunction prohibiting the NBA and ABA from merging until the players' lawsuit was heard. But the injunction still permitted the two leagues "to negotiate a proposed merger for the sole purpose of petitioning Congress for antitrust exemption legislation."[24] NBA players had managed to block the attempted consolidation for the time being, forcing the team owners to justify their business practices in front of federal lawmakers and the American public in Washington, DC.

Those actually paying attention to the emerging legal battle offered little encouragement to Robertson and other Black players. Even African American sportswriter Howie Evans of the *New York Amsterdam News* had no sympathy for their claims of economic bondage under the reserve clause. Echoing larger debates about the shifting trajectories of African American politics in the post–civil rights era, he argued that it mattered little that a few Black athletes had found relative financial success and fame when the majority of African Americans were still suffering. Making matters worse, white Americans pointed to Black athletes' integration into professional sports as evidence that the struggle for racial justice was over. Why were Black players fighting so hard for a bigger piece of the sporting industry's pie when Black communities were crumbling under the weight of poverty and drug addiction? In other words, Black professional athletes were being used against their own people, and their silence about the ongoing ravages of white racism in the rest of America seemed to mark their consent. "This is the hour to speak out loud and clear," Evans entreated. "Where are you, oh! million dollar Black athletes? Why are your voices not being raised in protest?"[25] Now that they had achieved a degree of prosperity, Black athletes seemed to shun their own communities in favor of assimilation and self-promotion. "Are you ashamed to be seen in Harlem—Bed Stuy—Watts, etc?" Evans asked. "We don't want to see your faces on bill boards, we don't want to hear your voices on the radio. We want you back home to help us in the fight to save your Black Brothers."

Because Black basketball players had chosen to integrate into the NBA rather than forming a separate Black-run league, Evans saw little point in their antitrust fight. In his eyes they had taken the easy way out, seeking inclusion into the white basketball establishment rather than pursuing the more radical goals of Black ownership and control. Now they were merely pawns of the system. Evans urged them to look outside their own legal battles. Black players needed to remember that their fates were still linked with those of everyday African Americans. They had the power to make change both on and off the court.

For white sportswriters, however, the majority-Black NBPA and its lawsuit seemed to encapsulate everything that was wrong with

the revolt of the Black athlete and the broader Black Power movement. The new generation of Black players entering the professional
ranks were by far the most entitled. No longer did they simply want
to be treated as fellow Americans; they wanted special consideration
as well. "Many blacks feel hatred against whites, and many feel that
being black is more important than anything else," Roger Stanton of
Basketball Weekly complained.[26] Stanton insisted that sport, far more
than any other aspect of American life, was a level playing field where
color did not matter, so why were Black athletes trying to destroy it?
He argued that African American players now had a racial persecu-
tion complex, whether they be ballplayers blocking a merger or the
University of Wyoming's "Black 14" protesting the racist practices of
the Mormon Church. Stanton and others opined that Black athletes
should serve as upstanding role models and help to restore order in
their crime-ridden communities, rather than demand more autonomy
or fair compensation for playing a game.

In the meantime, both the NBA and the ABA sought to dis-
solve the district court's injunction and filed motions for a summary
judgment on all the players' charges. They claimed that the business
practices cited in the suit were issues to be dealt with in collective bargaining under the jurisdiction of the National Labor Relations Board,
not in the courts. In short, this was a labor issue, not a legal matter.
However, Judge Robert Carter rejected their reasoning, noting that
the draft, reserve clause, and other league rules had never been the
subject of serious collective bargaining. The leagues were simply trying to sidestep these charges and had no intention of actually having
good-faith negotiations about these issues with the players. Carter
ruled that there was no "labor exemption" protecting the leagues from
the players' allegations of antitrust violations.[27]

Now tied up in a fight against a common enemy, the warring leagues
called the first of several cease-fires. In June 1970, the NBA and ABA
announced that they had reached an agreement on a merger plan and
would go about seeking congressional approval. They hired Covington

and Burling, the same law firm that had handled the successful NFL–AFL merger in 1966.[28] Robertson and company were quick to respond. "We're going to fight a merger in every way we know how," the NBPA president declared. "We think it's a violation of the antitrust laws and it clearly eliminates competition."[29] Robertson warned that the players planned to lobby in Washington against the merger. They would remain a united front.

As the battle heated up, white sports columnists expressed their nostalgia for a mythical NBA of the past, when the league was supposedly unencumbered by racial conflict and labor strife. "There was a time in the early days when $6000 was a top salary, and the payroll of any club did not go over the $60,000 mark," Bill Mokray of *Basketball News* recalled.[30] It was a simpler time, when white players such as Bob Cousy and Frank Ramsey purportedly signed blank contracts and let the Celtics' management fill in their salaries. Now, troublesome NBA players, represented by high-powered agents, demanded astronomical, no-cut contracts.[31] The payroll of the NBA champion Knicks had apparently expanded to $700,000 for the upcoming season. "Not so long ago that would have been enough to cover the complete expenses of a team, including travel, salaries, rent—and still leave a profit," Mokray reminisced. Even when compared to other US professional sports leagues, the majority-Black NBA seemed to be totally out of line. The Philadelphia 76ers had a reported payroll of $842,000 for twelve players, he noted, but the Philadelphia Flyers of the NHL had a payroll of just $450,000 for twenty-one players.[32]

Bob Maisel, sports editor of the *Baltimore Sun*, agreed: "They are already easily the highest paid of any team in pro sports."[33] There no longer seemed to be any honor or loyalty among ballplayers. "Obviously, what they seek is to force the two leagues to keep going to ridiculous figures to acquire their services while they continue to jump back and forth offering themselves to the highest bidder." This "burden" was hurting both the profitability and stability of professional basketball. For Maisel and most mainstream sportswriters at the time, the white team owners were the victims, whereas the majority-Black players held all the cards. Of course, the players saw things differently, claiming that the owners' greed and speculation were to blame for their teams' financial distress. They maintained that the leagues had expanded too quickly, "watering down the talent, going into questionable towns with poor facilities."

These struggles made it clear that professional sports were more than just play. Teams were not just cultural institutions; they were also profit-oriented businesses that had their own share of conflicts between management and employees. Because of the players' defiance, hardworking fans (for the most part, assumed to be white and male) could no longer use sports as a mental escape from work and life's other troubles. During a time of economic hardship and inflation, they also faced rising ticket prices purportedly thanks to the players' massive contracts.[34] Much like the team owners, many fans saw themselves as casualties in this unfolding conflict. Gone were the good old days when professional athletes would just shut up and play, no matter the pay or conditions.

IN APRIL 1971, ROBERTSON FULFILLED A LIFELONG DREAM. ALONGside rising star Lew Alcindor, the Big O led the Milwaukee Bucks to their first NBA Finals. Coming off an incredible upset of the New York Knicks in a grueling seven-game series, the Baltimore Bullets were the underdogs, despite having their own Black stars: center Wes Unseld and guard Earl "the Pearl" Monroe. The Bucks used Alcindor's size advantage and Robertson's relentless defense to disrupt the Bullets' half-court offense. They quickly went up 3–0, but game 4 was back in Baltimore, where the Bullets would have home-court advantage. The Bucks kept the pressure on and were up 60–47 with two minutes remaining in the first half. In the second half, the Big O smothered Monroe defensively, frustrating his spin moves and preventing him from posting up. On offense, Robertson hit shots from the outside, pulling Baltimore's attention away from Alcindor, opening up

Fans of the Milwaukee Bucks reach out for superstar Oscar Robertson at the airport in Milwaukee on May 1, 1971. Some twenty-thousand people came to the airport to welcome the NBA champions after they defeated the Baltimore Bullets in four straight games. (AP Photo/Paul Shane)

the big man for a scoring run. By late in the third quarter, the Bucks had a commanding 82–64 lead, and at the final buzzer, Robertson and company claimed a 118–106 victory over the beleaguered Bullets to become NBA champions.[35]

Having achieved this monumental triumph on the court, the NBPA president turned his attention back to union matters. Sam Lacy of the *Baltimore Afro-American* noted that Robertson was now the third Black player "to be put on the hot spot in the three major sports," joining John Mackey and Curt Flood in the "uncomfortable position of leading the fight against the professional establishment."[36] As Black athletes led the struggle for player rights in the seventies, the white sports media, white team owners, and white fans found common ground on the terrain of race. Black ballplayers—especially the outspoken ones—became the villains responsible for all of the ills associated with the increasing corporatization and commercialization of pro ball.

After several more twists and turns in their contentious merger talks, the NBA and ABA finally reconciled in early May 1971 and began planning to present their case for consolidation to federal lawmakers. Much as the NFL and AFL had in 1966, the two pro basketball leagues sought an antitrust exemption that would clear the way for a merger. "It may take two years before we can get Congressional approval," Commissioner Kennedy told reporters, "but at least we're on the right road."[37]

The leagues did not have to wait long for a response from Washington. On July 29, bills that would grant the leagues a Sherman waiver allowing them to merge were introduced into both houses of Congress. Senators Roman L. Hruska and John Tunney introduced the Senate bill (S. 2373), and Representative Jack Brooks introduced a bill in the House. The team owners hoped to get the lawmakers' blessing by Christmas.

Meanwhile, to counter all of the one-sided coverage of the merger, the players did their best to explain their side of the story. African American players were by far the most outspoken, and for them, this meant going to the Black press. Robertson found a particularly sympathetic platform in the newly established *Black Sports* magazine. Publisher Allan P. Barron hired mainly Black journalists and had an all-Black editorial staff because he wanted "articles written, or at least edited, with a sensitivity to Black problems."[38]

In the August 1971 issue, a rap session on the draft, salaries, contracts, and the merger in professional basketball revealed the magazine's commitment to exposing the questionable aspects of the sporting industry.[39] Whereas the mainstream sports media tended to side with white team owners and league executives and pander to white fans, *Black Sports* went out of its way to amplify Black voices. Robertson and Joe Caldwell, a Black NBA veteran who jumped to the ABA in 1970, represented the players' side of the debate. Two Black basketball coaches—Marshall Emery of Howard University and Sam Jones of Federal City College—spoke about how the existence of two pro leagues affected their athletes. Finally, Ned Doyle was the lone white participant, offering his take as the owner of the ABA's Miami Floridians. This frank conversation was, in some respects, a dress rehearsal for the upcoming Senate subcommittee hearings on the NBA-ABA merger in September 1971, as Robertson and Caldwell picked apart the team owners' typical arguments in favor of existing regulations.

Black Sports gave the veterans a chance to share their candid opinions about the current draft system in professional basketball. "The draft system hinders a lot of ballplayers," Caldwell contended. "Like Curt Flood said in his law case, and I am forced to believe it, this is 20th century slavery. Whether he is white or brown or whatever, once a ballplayer is drafted, he has no other means of making money for himself other than playing for that club and if they don't want to give him the money, he's still got to play." Robertson agreed. The existence of two leagues had not only opened up more opportunities for players but had also exposed the anticompetitive nature of the college draft: "I feel that as long as we have the NBA and ABA opposite each other . . . the kids coming out of school have a good chance to earn some money they should be making." Yet even with two leagues, team owners still figured out ways to collude with one another to keep players in check. "If you're drafted by a certain ball club, you are tied in, because there are certain things like 'blackballing' that we're aware of that goes on," Robertson explained. "If a ballplayer wants to work for a certain team, and the owners don't want him to go, they can keep him from the sport forever."[40]

For his part, Doyle said he did not blame the players for taking advantage of the interleague talent war. However, his claim that "the owners are going broke" elicited much laughter in the room. Doyle suggested that veterans like Caldwell and Robertson should be offended that untested rookies were now garnering million-dollar contracts: "You have proven yourselves. Then some youngster comes along who happens to be seven feet tall, or wears a band around his head, and all of a sudden he's worth two million dollars. This is ridiculous!"

Robertson refused to take the bait, quipping, "I feel that a player is only worth what you're paying him. If you don't think he's worth two million bucks, why pay him?" Doyle responded, "If you don't pay him, you don't get him and—," but Robertson cut him off. "Well, then, don't get him! There are other good ballplayers around the country." In the years before the ABA was established, NBA team owners had proven that without the threat of competition, they did not negotiate fairly with the players—something Robertson knew from personal experience.[41]

Doyle was in the minority of team owners who thought that the NBA's reserve system needed to go. He encouraged the players to fight against the option clause, perhaps because its existence made it harder for him to woo NBA veterans to his ABA squad. Under the NBA's option clause, Article 22 in its uniform player contract, a ball-player had to take a 25 percent pay cut and sit out a year if he wanted to move to a new team. Although seemingly less restrictive, basket-ball's option clause had the same effect as baseball's more draconian reserve system because teams informally conspired to blacklist players who decided to exercise their right to move.[42]

Robertson and Caldwell argued that a merger would, in effect, take away all of the players' current bargaining power and serve to rein-stitute the NBA's monopoly. "For the owners to say that they want one league where they can control who's going in . . . and how much money they're going to pay them; I think, is totally wrong. And it is against the Sherman Anti-Trust Act," Robertson maintained.[43] Even though some ABA players reportedly supported a merger, Caldwell disagreed with them. His contract dispute with the Atlanta Hawks had convinced him that having only one league would be bad for the players, especially African American players. When Atlanta had signed the white college star Pete Maravich to a million-dollar pact in 1970, Caldwell had tried to renegotiate his own contract. Atlanta refused. "Consequently, I ended up in Carolina. They paid me a few dollars more than they were going to in Atlanta," he recounted. If there had been only one league, he would have had to settle for the Hawks' lowball offer while watching Maravich rake in all the money. The players' revelations about the team owners' array of racist and repressive tactics were damning. But *Black Sports* was hopeful that better communication could help mend the labor strife in professional basketball: "Possibly many of the overly defensive owners, offended players and overlooked coaches could work out many of the problems in pro ball by having sessions like this."[44] But this point of view naively assumed that league executives and team owners would willingly relinquish some of their power over the players.

At a meeting between a group of team owners and players that very same month, the owners had offered the NBPA a one-year option clause similar to that of pro football. According to the NFL's Rozelle Rule, a player received the same compensation during his option year, and once it was completed, he was supposedly a free agent. However, there was a catch. The team that signed him would have to compensate the team he left. In practice, not many teams were willing to take on this expense to procure new talent. The NBPA rebuffed the team owners' offer, instead demanding the elimination of the NBA's reserve system. "That's ridiculous," said Richie Guerin, coach of the Atlanta Hawks.[45] With no reserve clause, Guerin predicted that players would be jumping from club to club, sowing chaos and destroying the competitive balance of the league. And from the team owners' perspective, the potential fall of this system imperiled both their coercive labor practices and their capital investment in player contracts.

As the opening of training camps approached, the NBPA threatened to boycott upcoming exhibition games, especially those against ABA clubs. The union believed that acquiescing to interleague play would only weaken its stance in opposition to the merger. In light of the recent failed negotiations, front-office personnel saw the players' "no exhibitions" stand as "a power play move" against the league's reserve system.[46]

In addition to threats of fines and suspensions, the NBA responded with a letter containing proposed amendments to Article 22 of the uniform player contract. It was a last-ditch effort to water down the option clause in order to convince the players to drop their lawsuit and allow the merger to proceed. But the letter once again outlined an option clause akin to that of the NFL, a proposal that the players had previously refused: (1) the term of a rookie contract was to be one year with an option to renew for a single additional year at no reduction of compensation; (2) there would be no option clause in future contracts with veterans; (3) the option clause would remain in existing contracts; (4) a player would not be permitted to negotiate with another team until he had played the last game (playoffs included) covered by his contract (and the option year, if any), and before he could sign with another club, his former club would have the right to meet the highest offer to retain him and sign him to a new contract; and (5) if a free agent signed with another club, the signing club would have to compensate his former club in the form of money, draft choices, and/ or the assignment of player contracts.[47] The NBA claimed that this revision of the option clause would address the players' concerns about mobility while still maintaining the league's competitive balance for the sake of the fans.

The NBPA summarily rejected the league's offer. Team owners and general managers then visited their training camps, hoping to change their players' minds, but to no avail.[48] They would have to make their case for the merger in Washington against a very well-organized and unified foe.

ON THE MORNING OF TUESDAY, SEPTEMBER 21, 1971, FOUR MEMBERS of the Senate Subcommittee on Antitrust and Monopoly took their places in Room 318 of the Old Senate Office Building, ready to hear testimony from both sides of the merger debate.[49] They would help determine whether or not the Senate should grant the leagues their requested Sherman waiver. Philip A. Hart, the subcommittee chair, had put Sam J. Ervin, a longtime Democratic senator from North

Carolina, in charge of the proceedings. The sponsors of Bill S.2373, senators Hruska and Tunney, were also present.

The appointment of Ervin as acting chair of the hearings proved opportune for Robertson and the NBPA: he became an unlikely yet staunch supporter of their cause. Ervin had opposed almost all of the civil rights legislation brought to the Senate floor, arguing that such laws restricted the individual rights of citizens to hire whom they wanted, to do business with whom they wanted, and to send their children to school where they wanted. A member of the Senate's Southern Caucus, he had helped to write the Southern Manifesto of 1956, which called on white Southerners to "use all lawful means" to resist court-mandated school desegregation.[50] Ervin was also not a fan of labor unions. In 1965 he had opposed the repeal of Section 14(b) of the Taft-Hartley Act in order to "keep the labor unions from putting people under subjection and requiring them to pay dues."[51] A strict constitutionalist, he believed in the freedom of the individual above all and sought to reduce government interference in the private affairs of US citizens.[52] Most remember him as the folksy chair of the Select Committee on Presidential Campaign Activities, popularly known as the Watergate Committee, which held hearings about the scandal in 1973. For now, Ervin was the only senator of the four-man panel who spoke out, rather vociferously, against Bill S.2373.

Given his libertarian views, it is perhaps not so surprising that Ervin found common cause with the members of the NBPA. Despite his disapproval of labor unions, he saw the merger as an assault on the basketball players' constitutional right to freedom of contract. Ervin kicked off the hearings with a forceful yet freewheeling thirty-minute statement in opposition to Bill S.2373, evoking the history of slavery and linking it to the autocratic power of modern-day team owners in professional sports. "Many years ago the term chattel was used to denote the legal status of slaves," Ervin began. "That is, they were considered a type of chattel which was owned as a piece of furniture or livestock was owned. This use of the term chattel applied to human beings and the condition it stands for are so abhorrent that we don't even like to acknowledge that they ever existed. Yet, in a real sense that is what these hearings are about today—modern peonage and the giant sports trusts."[53] Given that the team owners were all white and a majority of the players were Black, the racial overtones of Ervin's analogy would have been hard to miss. Club owners might not literally own their players' bodies, but the terms of the NBA's uniform player contract gave the teams undue control over their labor.

Ervin suspected that the NBA and ABA were hoping for Congress to simply rubber-stamp legislation authorizing a merger, just as it had for the NFL and AFL back in 1966. However, he warned his fellow lawmakers about the danger of repeating this precedent. The football merger bill had passed through the Senate without any hearings or debate. The same thing had happened in the House, where the bill had slipped through as a rider on a revenue measure. Ervin cautioned his peers that this legislation was about more than a simple consolidation: "The common draft and the option clause which will result from the merger are issues concerning the economic enslavement of professional basketball players, and are too important for such ephemeral treatment as was accorded the football merger."[54]

At stake was the players' fundamental right to participate in a free market. Under the college draft system, rookies were assigned to teams without their input or consent. Once drafted, they could negotiate a contract with only one team. Thus, the draft had the effect of keeping salaries and bonuses artificially low. "The only reason for the institution of the common draft and the passage of this bill is the pocketbooks of the owners," Ervin charged.[55]

With the merger, the earning potential of veteran players would also be reduced because of the option clause. Even though the NBA had made some small concessions in its recent revision of Article 22, it had not gone far enough. The case of the post-merger NFL showed that the threat of mandatory compensation had the effect of deterring teams from signing free agents. The ongoing practice of blacklisting only made matters worse. This was a situation unique to professional sports. "In no other work in this country is this practice of selling souls allowed," he maintained. "If a salesman or any businessman is transferred to another city by his owner, he can still quite [*sic*] and bargain with other companies in his home area and practice his trade if he secures employment."[56] At issue then, was the very future of player rights in professional sports writ large.

Ervin saw S.2373 as a form of corporate subsidy. If the NBA and other professional sports leagues wanted to operate like monopolies akin to public utilities companies, they should be subject to federal regulation. At the same time, players should have the right to shop their talents to the highest bidder, for team owners would pay only what the market would bear. He granted that basketball players' salaries were higher than those of other professional players, but this simply confirmed his belief that "the monopolistic conditions which exist in other sports keep the salaries of professional athletes below what they should be." In general, athletes deserved high salaries because of the brevity of their careers. Team owners were cognizant of this reality, regardless of what they said publicly. "Nowhere is the short duration of an athlete's playing life given colder and more clinical treatment than in the owner's income statement," Ervin noted. "They are treated as capital assets and depreciated as a car or a machine with a useful life of 5 years."[57]

Given the tax benefits associated with depreciation and the fact that the leagues were reluctant to share their full financial information with lawmakers, he was skeptical of their current claims of insolvency. And even if they were losing money, he did not believe it was the government's job to bail them out.[58] They should be subject to the risks and rewards of the free market, just like any other business in America. The NBA wanted lawmakers' compassion because the players' demands were supposedly bankrupting them. However, Ervin noted that they had treated their fellow ABA team owners with a lack of compassion in their most recent merger agreement, charging them an exorbitant indemnity and refusing to share any of their television money or gate receipts. Ervin believed there were other modes of achieving financial stability and competitive balance in the leagues, with revenue sharing being the most obvious one. He could not see the merger as anything more than a cash grab by a small interest group of well-monied team owners.

After more opening remarks, the NBA and ABA had the rest of day to lay out their rationale for the merger. Much of the testimony simply rehashed the well-worn narratives of economic crisis propagated in the mainstream sports media. Economist Robert R. Nathan did his best to counter Ervin's criticisms of the merger. Ironically, Nathan, who ran an eponymous DC-based economics consulting firm, had previously testified for Curt Flood in the players' antitrust suit against baseball's reserve clause. This time, Nathan found himself on the other side, arguing that pro sports leagues were not like other businesses. They needed their own set of internal rules, he claimed, to maintain order and competition among the teams. Nathan had analyzed four seasons of financial information—from 1967 to 1971—from eleven ABA teams. He found "not one single year of profit for any ABA team," and many had experienced substantial losses. He did the same analysis for the NBA, looking at seven seasons of financial records—from 1964 to 1971—from seventeen teams. His data were spotty, but he found that only twenty-five team seasons showed profits, whereas forty-two showed losses.[59] He argued that this level of financial risk would inhibit future investment in professional basketball, for no businessman enjoyed taking losses, even if those losses could provide substantial tax advantages.

What was causing these losses? Nathan noted that game attendance was up, so the problem was not a lack of demand. Teams could raise ticket prices to try to recoup their losses, but this would ultimately limit the accessibility of the sport to regular fans. He pointed to various charts in his formal report to illustrate that the real problem was rising rookie salaries. They were growing out of proportion to both team revenues and veteran salaries, pushing owners into financial distress and causing internal strife among the players. Continuing on with two leagues would not only hurt the owners but would also have adverse consequences for both the players and the fans. If teams went bankrupt, jobs and opportunities to see games would disappear.[60]

But looking for profits in the early years of the ABA's existence presupposed that the team owners were actually trying to be profitable. ABA franchise owners had deliberately engaged in a talent war with the NBA, driving up contract values in order to force a merger with the more established league. Ervin pointed to the hypocrisy of the leagues in their efforts to push through Bill S.2373: "The queer thing about this proposition . . . is here are some men who are unwilling to restrain themselves in their competition for new players, so they ask Congress to pass a law so as to restrain somebody else, namely, the players."[61] The team owners had manufactured this crisis, not the players. They had no business asking Congress to clean up their mess.

On the second day, the players had their chance to present their case against the merger. NBPA attorney Larry Fleisher was the first to testify, laying out the basic contours of their argument. They would refute the leagues' central claim: that the majority of teams were losing money because of rising rookie contracts caused by the talent war. And, beyond just financial considerations, they would show that the proposed legislation had clear racial stakes. "Pro basketball, a sport in which over 65 percent of the players are black, has a unique place in the lives of hundreds of thousands of black children," Fleisher declared. "How Congress treats the economic rights of black basketball players who have escaped the ghetto by hard work will be noted by all black Americans."[62] If famous Black athletes had no rights that Congress respected, then why should the average Black citizen have any faith in the system? Black America was watching.

Oscar Robertson (foreground) of the Milwaukee Bucks and Dave DeBusschere of the New York Knicks sit in the hearing room as they wait to testify at a Senate Antitrust and Monopoly subcommittee hearing in Washington, DC, on September 22, 1971. (AP Photo/Henry Griffin)

Oscar Robertson then outlined the players' position. After his statement, the NBPA president stayed for questions. Ervin was the first to speak. Through his strategic questioning of Robertson, Ervin bolstered his contention that the proposed consolidation was an assault on the players' constitutional rights:

> **Senator ERVIN:** And you are satisfied that if this exemption from the antitrust laws were passed it would disable basketball players in the future to negotiate for the sale of their skills for the highest price. . . .

> **Mr. ROBERTSON:** Yes, sir; that is correct.

> **Senator ERVIN:** And for that reason, you do not wish to see a group of Americans who have skills in basketball placed under what is essentially economic bondage in that it deprives them of

the freedom of contract and the power to obtain by fair negotiation what their skills are actually worth.

Mr. ROBERTSON: Yes; that is correct.[63]

Together, the improbable allies landed a one-two punch.

Robertson then faced the more hostile members of the subcommittee. Senator Hruska went on the attack, peppering the star guard with questions about the details of his compensation, pension, and fringe benefits with the Milwaukee Bucks, hoping to rile him up and break his concentration. But the Big O maintained his composure. Hruska changed tack, shifting his focus to the draft, as he tried to make a case about its necessity for preserving order and competitive balance in professional basketball. Robertson stood his ground, picking apart Hruska's reasoning:

Senator HRUSKA: It is wrong to limit the amount of money that a man can earn?

Mr. ROBERTSON: I think in America it is.

Senator HRUSKA: Does the draft system do that?

Mr. ROBERTSON: I think if you only had one league that is true. As long as there are two leagues there is no telling what a person can earn.

Senator HRUSKA: You seem to have done pretty well. Do you think you are worth more than [the] $100,000 you are getting?[64]

Fleisher, realizing that Hruska was just trying to get a rise out of Robertson, leaned over and cautioned him to keep his cool. Robertson took a beat to think and sip some water, and then calmly responded,

"To be honest and frank, I think so." His answer evoked laughter in the room.[65]

Hruska continued to harp on the details of Robertson's salary, but the labor leader remained unflappable. "No owner will pay you any more than he thinks you are worth," Robertson said. "So no use talking about my making $700,000 or a million dollars. If the owner does not think a player is worth it he should not pay him." Still, Hruska seemed bent on getting Robertson to express his gratitude to the NBA for his financial success as a basketball player. Instead, Robertson insisted that he had earned his lucrative contract because of his record of strong performance on the court. His salary was no gift, nor was the NBA a charitable organization.[66] All of that preparation with Fleisher had come in handy, for Robertson more than held his own in the hot seat.

Next, Robertson's counterpart, ABA Players Association president Zelmo Beaty, confirmed his members' opposition to the merger. Beaty noted that he had used the existence of the two leagues to his advantage, jumping from the NBA's Atlanta Hawks to the ABA's Utah Stars in 1970 for a five-fold salary increase: "Prior to the time that the ABA came into existence, I, like every other player in the NBA, had only one team to negotiate my salary with, namely the club that had drafted me." Because of this, for years the Hawks were able to pay him far less than what he was worth. "It is interesting to note that the day I signed a contract with the ABA, the Atlanta Hawks instituted a lawsuit to stop me from playing in the ABA," Beaty added. "They claimed that the loss of my services entitled them to compensation of $4 million." Clearly, the team owners had no real interest in relinquishing their control over the players. They could not be trusted to merge and then negotiate in good faith about the option clause: "Anything less than the total elimination of the restrictions on the player to freely sell his services is unacceptable."[67]

On the third and final day, the bulk of the testimony came from two economists whose independent research, funded by the Ford

Foundation, challenged the leagues' claims of impending financial disaster. But Roger G. Noll and Benjamin A. Okner, both senior Fellows in the Economic Studies Division of the Brookings Institution, were there by invitation of the subcommittee and not at the behest of the players. They were at work on a larger research project about the financial health of the sports industry, including professional basketball. Noll specialized in the government regulation of business, and Okner was an expert in taxation and public finance. In addressing the senators, Noll outlined their six main findings. First, they found that the finances of even the weakest professional basketball teams were not as dire as the leagues claimed. Federal tax laws allowed for a team owner to take losses incurred by running a basketball team and use them to offset gains in other sectors. This helped them to balance the books in their personal finances, even when their basketball teams generated substantial losses. Additionally, local governments often reduced expenses by providing playing facilities that were either free or substantially below standard rates.[68]

Second, despite all of the public uproar over rising player salaries, Noll and Okner found that even the so-called superstars were not being overpaid. They were worth their salaries (or even more) because they helped to raise their teams' gate receipts. Noll and Okner estimated that Lew Alcindor, for instance, was worth at least $500,000 to $1 million annually to the Milwaukee Bucks, yet the star center's reported salary was no more than half of the former amount. Third, Noll argued that "ticket prices reflect[ed] the monopoly position that exclusive franchise rights confer[red] on a team." Simply put, contrary to media reports, rising player salaries were *not* to blame for rising ticket prices.

The economists' last three findings were, perhaps, the most damning to the leagues' case for a merger. Moving down the list to number four, Noll declared, "The principal purpose of the merger is to permit teams to pay lower salaries to players, especially rookies." Noll and Okner thus confirmed Ervin's and the players' suspicion that the merger was, at heart, a cost-cutting measure. "The merger as presently planned," Noll continued, "will not contribute to equalizing competition within the leagues." This fifth finding directly challenged the NBA and ABA's claim that a merger was necessary to maintain adequate competition among the teams. As Noll noted, the proposed consolidation would do nothing to help the teams on shakier financial ground: it included no revenue-sharing plan. Gate receipts would still go to the home teams, meaning that the richer teams in bigger markets would still have more money than their small-market counterparts to acquire the most talented players. Ironically, Noll and Okner concluded, "The merger per se is not the key issue that the merger bill raises." Instead, the critical policy issues at play included the legality of the rules binding players to teams (the option clause and team compensation), "the exclusivity of franchise rights," and "the revenue-sharing arrangement of the new league." Although the two economists were not in total opposition to the merger, they recommended that the above issues be addressed before lawmakers granted the leagues a Sherman waiver.

After laying out their main findings, Noll also offered some more detailed insights from their research into the finances of professional basketball teams from both leagues. He drilled down into the question of profitability: "Conventional wisdom has it that professional basketball is only one step from philanthropy since only three of the 28 ABA and NBA teams are said to be operating in the black." However, he and Okner had found that this was not necessarily true, even for relatively new NBA expansion teams located in smaller markets, such as the Milwaukee Bucks. After accounting for the Bucks' losses, they discovered that Milwaukee had an after-tax profit of 20 percent annually, well above the average of 10 percent annually for US industry. Moreover, in looking at the Bucks' bookkeeping, they found that administrative costs had roughly doubled over the past two years, and they suspected that the officers of the corporation had given themselves substantial raises.[69] Yet the Bucks were not even the most profitable franchise in the NBA. The Lakers and the Knicks made far more money. It certainly helped that each played in an arena owned by the same corporation as the team. In the case of the Knicks, their ticket revenues alone were estimated at twice their costs. This figure did not even take into account the team's revenues from concession rights and television rights.[70]

As for the ABA, Noll and Okner found that three teams (Indiana, Kentucky, and Utah) were likely making money or at least breaking even. According to their calculations, to be profitable an NBA team needed roughly 325,000 spectators during the regular season, whereas an ABA team needed 300,000.[71] The size of a team's fan base, not its rookie salaries, largely determined its financial health. And, given the favorable tax situation for team owners, it was difficult to discern their actual losses versus their paper losses.

Noll and Okner contended that the two leagues had effectively created this so-called financial crisis. The NBA had driven up rookie salaries in an effort to put the ABA out of business, and the ABA had done the same, hoping to push the NBA to seek a merger. Now, in order to prove the need for antitrust immunity from Congress, the "crisis" had to continue. One outgrowth of this manufactured crisis was the widespread demonization of the majority-Black players and their supposed greed. "People look at a high salary of a star and say, gee, these people make a lot of money. They play instead of work," Noll noted. However, this was just a distraction from the real issue. "The issue is not, are these men paid a lot, but are they paid substantially less than they would be if they were in a competitive system," Noll argued. "The relevant issue is: is a lot of their worth being captured by someone else, other than themselves, because of restraints on competition, and the answer to that is obviously 'yes.'"[72]

The players had presented compelling evidence, and after the first round of Senate hearings, they appeared to be gaining the upper hand. Not only did they have a champion in Senator Ervin, but they also had the potential to ally with powerful special interests in what one journalist observed was a burgeoning "War on Sports."[73] With its overwhelmingly African American membership, the NBPA could appeal to traditional civil rights groups such as the National Association for the Advancement of Colored People (NAACP). And thanks to rising numbers of Black elected officials across the nation, they also had new allies in government. At the federal level, Black political power coalesced in the formation of the Congressional Black Caucus (CBC) in 1971.[74] In turn, organized labor and consumer advocates, such as Ralph Nader, who opposed corporate corruption, could also enter the fray on behalf of the players.[75] With these constituencies involved, the balance of political power could easily shift against the merger bills.

With various delays to the start of the second session of Senate hearings, the team owners' hope for a quick Sherman exemption began to fade.[76] On November 15, 1971, the leagues finally had another opportunity to make their case for a merger. Back in room 318 in the Old Senate Office Building, the verbose Wendell Cherry, principal owner of the ABA's Kentucky Colonels, took center stage, making a fervent speech about the urgent need for consolidation: "If we don't have a merger by next season, you've signed the death knell of the ABA."[77] Pointing to a balance sheet covering the past three years, Cherry claimed that the Colonels had lost around $500,000 per year.

Senator Ervin, however, was not convinced that the Colonels' balance sheet told the entire story. He noted that the team owners had refused his request for their personal income tax records and other financial data, claiming it was an invasion of privacy: "Attempting to hide behind the defense that Congress only looks at income tax returns of racketeers is laughable . . . when you consider that the basketball owners are asking for control over the lives of human beings that would make a racketeer green with envy that he hadn't thought of the scheme first." Throughout the day he traded sharp barbs with the pro-merger advocates as he questioned them exhaustively about their financial claims. When Ervin adjourned the hearings until January

1972, it looked as if the leagues' struggle for a merger would continue for the foreseeable future.

NBA team owners were starting to feel the heat of the public spotlight. Harry Glickman, executive vice president of the Portland Trail Blazers, said that it was time that "someone stood up and defended the men who operate professional sports franchises in this country." He complained to reporters, "I have never accepted it as my duty that for an average career of five years, a player should be so rewarded that never agains [*sic*] in his lifetime will he face the necessity of seeking gainful employment."[78] It was as if Glickman felt he was paying welfare to his ballplayers rather than fair compensation for their talents based on market demand.

When the Senate hearings resumed in the new year, the main attraction of the day was the testimony of the two league commissioners. A young Bryant Gumbel covered this session for *Black Sports*. He had taken over the editorship of the magazine in 1971 at the age of twenty-three, just a year after his graduation from Bates College, and would soon after continue his career as a sportscaster for KNBC-TV in Los Angeles.[79] Gumbel wondered how the leagues could expect to win this fight when the letter of the law seemed to be against them. In 1956 a federal district court had ruled that professional basketball, unlike baseball, was not exempt from the Sherman Act on the grounds that it was interstate commerce. Nevertheless, NBA commissioner Walter Kennedy insisted that they had precedent on their side, citing the NFL-AFL merger in 1966: "We are asking for nothing more, or less, than football got five years ago."[80]

ABA commissioner Jack Dolph went one step further. He argued that sports leagues should not be treated as businesses because they were more akin to trade associations than conventional corporations.[81] They were not against competition; instead, competition was their business, and the leagues needed to set their own internal regulations, from the college draft to the option clause, in order to maintain it. For professional basketball, the merger was an existential matter of survival. The commissioners were taking this benevolent stand in Washington to save the sport from ruin.

The players' turn to respond came on March 6, and this time they did not come alone: new political allies took up their cause.[82] Representative Louis Stokes testified that Black federal lawmakers in the CBC stood with the players in opposition to Bill S.2373. They could not help but see it as a legislative assault on the bargaining power of the leagues' majority-Black workforce.[83] Clarence Mitchell, the director of the Washington bureau of the NAACP, also expressed his disapproval of the bill in a written statement entered into the record. The racial significance of the ballplayers' struggle for freedom of mobility and freedom of contract was not lost on the NAACP. With the college draft and the option clause, professional players labored under an "arrangement [that] was just a little bit better than the status of a valuable race horse or a prize bull. . . . The system was the same old type of low pay for hard work status that black people have been mired in for generations."[84] No longer was the merger just an issue affecting a few hundred pro ballplayers; it was a fundamental question of Black economic rights.

A few weeks after the hearings were over, the Antitrust and Monopoly Subcommittee held a forty-five-minute closed executive session, during which Ervin managed to persuade the other senators in attendance to postpone any action on the bill. For now, S.2373 would not be sent to the full Judiciary Committee for further consideration.[85] Still, Commissioner Kennedy remained hopeful that the bill would eventually come to a vote on the Senate floor.[86]

THE NBA BEGAN CRACKING DOWN ON ANY EFFORTS OF THE PLAYERS to organize independent of league oversight. Robertson and other NBA stars, defying Commissioner Kennedy's warnings, participated in the second annual NBA-ABA All-Star Game at Nassau Coliseum on May 25, a nationally televised event arranged by the respective players associations to raise money for charity.[87] There were 14,086 spectators on hand to witness this clash of titans. Taking advantage of the NBA's initially sluggish play, the ABA went ahead 49–30. At one point, rookie Julius Erving of the ABA's Virginia Squires impressed fans with a gravity-defying move, flying ten feet through the air before dunking the ball. Stepping up its defense, the NBA battled back with a fifteen-point scoring run, but at the end of the first half the ABA still led 56–50. After halftime, the NBA began to gain the upper hand. With 3:13 left in the third quarter, the Boston Celtics' John Havlicek hit a jump shot to put the NBA ahead 75–74. But the ABA continued to push, and by the fourth quarter the NBA clung to a narrow lead. With just thirteen seconds remaining, Rick Barry, now of the New York Nets, hit a spectacular three-point shot, bringing the ABA within one point. At four seconds to go, the NBA had a chance to cement its win when Archie Clark went to the free-throw line, but after making the first shot, he missed the second. In the ensuing scramble under the basket, Barry came out with the ball. Dribbling to just inside the mid-court line, he launched a last-ditch forty-footer as the buzzer was about to sound—but it fell short of the basket. The NBA clinched the game 106–104.[88]

NBA team owners responded by fining the players who participated $3,300 each for making "unauthorized appearances" in the charity game. The NBPA announced that it would stand by its members and ensure that they did not have to pay the penalties. By July, the NBPA was threatening to strike or refuse to report to training camp if the fines were not lifted.[89]

Despite the NBA's attempt to strong-arm its players, the political opposition to a blanket approval of an NBA-ABA merger seemed to be growing. In June 1972 the Senate Committee on Commerce held hearings about the creation of a federal sports commission to regulate professional sports. And even if the merger bill eventually made it to the Senate floor, it would still have to be approved in the House, where it would face another hostile opponent, Judiciary Committee chair Emanuel Celler. From July to September the House subcommittee hearings on the merger mostly rehashed the information revealed in the Senate hearings.[90]

On September 7 the Senate Antitrust and Monopoly Subcommittee unanimously approved legislation allowing an NBA-ABA merger but with several key amendments—one of which would virtually eliminate the reserve clause.[91] This amendment would permit drafted players to be signed for only two years—a one-year contract plus a one-year option—after which a player would become a free agent, able to negotiate with any team. There would be no compensation for the team losing the player.[92] A *New York Times* special report speculated that this amendment could have the effect of killing the merger and potentially opening the door to similar legislation involving other professional sports, including Major League Baseball.[93] The approved merger legislation also contained provisions stipulating the sharing of gate receipts (a 70–30 split with visiting teams) and prohibiting the NBA from charging ABA teams an indemnity fee. Even though the amended merger legislation left the college draft system intact, it was a clear victory for the players.[94]

A week later, the full Senate Judiciary Committee approved the amended bill; however, it died without ever coming to the Senate floor for a vote, and it never even got out of committee in the House of Representatives.[95] In November, NBA club owners met to discuss how to proceed. Their only option at this point was to propose a new bill when a new Congress convened in January 1973. But a bill would, again, have to go through the same Senate subcommittee, of which Ervin was still a member. Although Ervin's amendments were good for the players and satisfactory for the ABA, the clubs in the NBA remained vigorously opposed to gate sharing and any weakening of the option clause. They were not yet ready to let go of the reins of power.

For their part, Robertson and the players were prepared to continue their fight against the merger and the reserve clause. There was simply too much at stake, not just for them, but for the rest of Black America as well. They knew, after all, that they were role models for thousands of Black children across the nation. As some of the most famous and highest-paid Black men in America, they could not simply roll over and accept this unjust state of affairs while their people looked on. They had to fight for their autonomy and their economic rights.

Part 2
The Black Tide

Chapter 4

Troubled

Black Players Flood the Leagues

People have a feeling that I'm a nasty nigger, you know. See, now I don't mind that. . . . That, to me, is a compliment.

—Kareem Abdul-Jabbar, on *Black Journal* (WNET), 1972

"HOW IT IS FOR A 22-YEAR-OLD ROOKIE THRUST INTO A PRESSURE-cooker; how it is to be rich and talented and black and troubled." That is how Roger Kahn of *Sport* magazine had summed up "Lew Alcindor's Life as a Pro" back in February 1970. The Milwaukee Bucks' seven-foot-two center seemed emblematic of the growing power of Black pro athletes, chafing against the rigid expectations of the white basketball establishment, the white sports media, and white fans. Kahn had interviewed Alcindor in a dingy room at the Quality Courts Motel in St. Louis on November 25, 1969. It was 4:00 p.m., just hours before the Bucks were to play a game against the Atlanta Hawks to benefit a local charity and honor some of the retired Hawks stars from the franchise's days in St. Louis.[1] Alcindor was lying under a brown blanket trying to clear his "hyperactive" mind of all the noise and clutter. The drapes were drawn, the only light emanating from a reading lamp on the night table.

It had been difficult for Kahn to get an appointment with the NBA's newest superstar. Not wanting to antagonize its franchise player, the Milwaukee Bucks' front office did little to help the writer connect with Alcindor. Kahn, not surprisingly, had come to the meeting chock-full of nerves and with very low expectations. Even before his difficulties in reaching the enigmatic Black center, he had already had a bad impression of Alcindor thanks to the sports pages. Alcindor was reportedly "mercenary, rude, possibly anti-white," and "he had an unnerving recent record of aggressiveness toward opponents: one broken jaw, one knockout and one foiled attack in a few months." As Kahn joked, "You go into this kind of interview carefully, preparing all the questions, gauging your subject, wondering about your own jaw." Despite his fears, what he discovered instead in that dreary motel room was "a bright, sensitive, and esthetic young man." It made Kahn wonder. What did this misunderstanding say about the status of Alcindor and other Black people in America? What did it say about US society— "the society that had made him both millionaire and nigger"?[2]

Admittedly, it was hard for Kahn to describe Alcindor for readers. His was not a simple *Reader's Digest* story: "The Alcindor phenomenon is a mix of rough edges, and incompleteness and immaturity and wisdom and misinterpretations and rages and regrets."[3] Yet, love him or hate him, there was no denying the big man's talent. How white sportswriters and fans wrestled with Alcindor's dominance on the court and surliness off the court was a microcosm of their reaction to the rising tide of Black professional ballplayers throughout the 1970s.

In the wake of the civil rights victories of the sixties and in the midst of surging Black Power activism and a deepening "urban crisis," which disproportionately affected African Americans, the racial politics that greeted Alcindor and his generation of Black ballplayers were complicated. "How do you see your role in the black movement?"

Kahn asked. Emotionless, Alcindor simply blinked. Born on April 16, 1947, one day after Jackie Robinson officially desegregated Major League Baseball, Alcindor understood that what was expected of him as a Black athlete was much different than what had been expected of Robinson and other pioneering African American pros.[4] All Robinson had to do was make base hits "because white people thought he wasn't good enough to do it," Alcindor noted. But that was not enough anymore. "It's fragmented, man," Alcindor said of the wider Black movement. "Some go to church. Some go to school. Some do nothing. Some want revolt." Although some members of a budding Black middle class had begun to make strides, the Black poor and working class found themselves largely left behind in a changing economy. For the young Alcindor, figuring out where he fit into this complex picture was no easy task, especially because his own ideas about Black activism were still evolving. "Try to get change as quickly and painlessly as possibly," Alcindor said of his political vision. "Try to stand for something positive. Be something positive."[5]

For many white sportswriters and fans, Alcindor seemed to be anything but positive. He and the new wave of Black players inundating the pro ranks appeared threatening, even violent. On Halloween night in 1969, the Bucks had played against the 76ers in Philadelphia. Alcindor was matched up against veteran white center Darrall Imhoff, who shoved and elbowed the rookie under the basket. Early in the second quarter, as they both scrambled for a loose ball, Alcindor's frustration reached a boiling point. He swung his right elbow full force into the back of Imhoff's head. "Imhoff fell on all fours, the way fighters sometimes do, and stayed there on knees and elbows too dazed to move," Kahn recalled. The Philly crowd hooted. Alcindor walked to mid-court and stood with his hands on his hips, watching calmly. When Imhoff came to, he took a run at Alcindor, but 76ers forward Jim Washington and one of the referees stopped him and ushered him off court. He was so out of it that he did not return until the second half. When Alcindor later fouled out, the fans booed him. Alcindor gave the peace sign, but the boos continued, so he clenched his fist and held it high in a Black Power salute. After the game, journalists swarmed him with questions, but he said, "I have no comment."[6]

There was no love lost between Alcindor and white sportswriters. He had antagonized Evans Kirby, a local reporter charged with interviewing him for a magazine feature in the *Milwaukee Journal*. To Kirby, the rookie was supposedly "aloof in speech and habit."[7] He was not only late but brusque, and at the end of the interview he left without even saying good-bye. Perhaps Alcindor's abruptness stemmed, in part, from the fact that he had already sold the exclusive rights to his life story to *Sports Illustrated* for a reported $20,000.[8] Nevertheless, he had managed to alienate the local media, for he often declined to answer questions or replied with grunts and one-word answers. Alcindor refused to play by the typical rules of etiquette that white reporters and fans alike expected of African American athletes: be humble, be grateful, be cheerful, be accessible, and, above all, be apolitical. Instead, the quiet, brooding rookie kept white sportswriters and fans off balance.

Shy and introverted, Alcindor desperately wanted to maintain his privacy, but this was proving hard in a small market like Milwaukee. A seven-foot-two Black man in a majority-white Midwestern city, Alcindor could not help but stand out. Bucks fans mobbed him, and reporters wanted a piece of him at all times.

"You better get used to it," Kahn warned him.

Alcindor looked off into the distance.

"You're going to play for a while, maybe 15 years," Kahn continued. "Well, you better be ready for 15 years of interviewing. That's part of what all the money is for."

"I don't have to give up my privacy," Alcindor replied. "I'm not peddling that."[9]

Although he worked hard on the court, he felt in no way compelled to go out of his way to please or placate the NBA's majority-white fan base. At a game against the Seattle SuperSonics in late November

1969, Alcindor fouled out in the final seconds of the fourth quarter after lunging at Black center Bob Rule. As the capacity crowd of 13,000 in the Seattle Center Coliseum jeered at him, Alcindor responded by spitting on the court. The game ended with a narrow 117–115 victory for the Bucks. As the teams walked to the locker rooms, a white teenager ran toward Alcindor and yelled, "You big bum!" With one swing of his long arm, Alcindor knocked the teen to the floor.[10] "It gets me," he told Kahn, "the way people say now you've got the money, you've got contentment. The money makes for a stability, but there are pressures, man. Out there you're a vector for all the hostility in the stands. It all comes and they're shouting that I'm not hustling and that I stink and I'm a bum."[11]

Unlike some African American athletes from previous generations who sought crossover acceptance from white fans, Alcindor was unapologetically Black. His family background and his experiences growing up in New York City likely colored his approach to the game. Although his parents had met in North Carolina, when his father, Ferdinand L. Alcindor Sr., was stationed at Fort Bragg during World War II, they later settled in Harlem. His family took great pride in their Black diasporic roots. Alcindor's paternal grandfather had migrated from Trinidad to New York and spoke the West African language of Yoruba. "Around my house, there was no speaking shamefully about our ancestors," Alcindor recalled.[12] When Alcindor's father graduated from the prestigious Julliard School of Music in 1952, symphony orchestras were still racially segregated. With no prospects for a career in classical music, he held on to his job as a bill collector for a furniture company and then took a post in the Transit Authority Police Department. Part of a rising African American middle class, the Alcindors left Harlem, moving further north to the racially mixed Dyckman housing project in the neighborhood of Inwood. "He carries all that heritage within him, a sense of black aristocracy and black dignity and how the Moors were warriors and how his uprooted family was supposedly free in a society which condemned a Julliard man to work in subways," Kahn observed.[13] Alcindor carried a heavy chip on his shoulder, carved from generations of injustices.

Back in spring 1969, he had brought that sense of pride into his initial contract negotiations with the pros. Accompanied by his father and two UCLA alumni acting as his pro bono financial advisers, Alcindor had met with representatives from the NBA's Bucks and the ABA's Nets in his home city of New York.[14] To avoid a nasty and protracted bidding war, his negotiating team had asked Milwaukee and New Jersey to submit their best and final offers. Alcindor had wanted to return to the New York area to play professionally, but the Bucks made the strongest offer. He and his advisers were shocked: they had expected the ABA to offer more money in place of stability and prestige. Despite Alcindor's misgivings about moving to the Midwest, he signed with Milwaukee for around $1.4 million over five years, reportedly the highest contract ever paid to any athlete.[15] "I had wanted to sign with the Nets," he later explained, "but I was offended to be taken so lightly. If they hadn't taken me seriously when I was calling the shots, how would they treat me once I was under contract?"[16] From the very start, Alcindor wanted to exercise his power and gain control over his career.

Kahn's time with the Bucks' star rookie had revealed as much about the racial tenor of the times as it had about the man. "The pressure is enormous," Kahn explained. "He is potentially *the* black athlete of his era, as Jackie Robinson was the black athlete of another. His role is not more difficult than Robinson's—after all, the Klan is not threatening to shoot Alcindor. . . . But it is more complex. The black movement has become more complex." Alcindor, in many respects, embodied the intricacy of African American politics in the post–civil rights era. His favorite book was the *Autobiography of Malcolm X.* He listened to the jazz music of Miles Davis, converted to Islam, and studied African languages. Although he called out white racism, he was not a militant in the same vein as the Black Panthers or Kwame Ture.[17] He simply

Kareem Abdul-Jabbar poses for a portrait at his home in Los Angeles, 1973. (Photo by
Walter Iooss Jr./NBAE/Getty Images)

endeavored to be his own man, to explore and define his evolving
sense of Blackness on his own terms.

In June 1971 Alcindor stood in front of the US State Department,
flanked by teammate Oscar Robertson and Coach Larry Costello, for
a press conference announcing their upcoming government-sponsored
tour of the African continent. The trio were to spend three weeks
abroad, visiting Algeria, Senegal, Mali, Nigeria, Tanzania, and the
Somali Republic. At each stop along the way they would conduct basketball clinics, give exhibitions, and meet with the respective national
teams.[18] Basketball and Black American athletes had long been tools
of US soft power in the region, deployed to court the favor of African people and their politicians during the Cold War.[19] For Alcindor,
however, this was an opportunity to fulfill a lifelong dream. "For me
this is a return to the fountainhead," he told reporters.[20] He had studied African history at UCLA and now looked forward to visiting the
original home of his forebears.

Alcindor then introduced Habiba, his wife of just a few weeks,
who would also accompany them on the trip. And he insisted that

reporters call him by his new name, Kareem Abdul-Jabbar. "I first used the name in 1969," he said, "but now that I am going overseas to represent my country, I would appreciate that courtesy." He explained that Kareem translated to "noble or generous," Abdul meant "servant of Allah," and Jabbar meant "powerful."[21] As his faith had deepened, it no longer felt authentic to keep it hidden from public view. "I had lived two lives too long," he recalled. "I knew I was going to take some heat for it, but Muhammad Ali had established a precedent and borne some of the brunt of the attack."[22] To dispel any confusion between his religion and that of the controversial heavyweight boxer, however, Jabbar clarified that he was not a member of the Nation of Islam. He practiced Sunni Islam under the mentorship of Hamaas Abdul Khaalis, the leader of a Black American sect known as the Hanafi Muslims.[23]

Stunned, reporters asked about the logistics of using his new name. Jabbar said that he did not expect the Bucks to immediately change his name in their programs or advertising because the fans knew him as Alcindor. But, he insisted, "I do expect people to use my Islamic name when they're talking to me."[24] Anytime that reporters addressed him as "Lew" or "Mr. Alcindor," he respectfully but resolutely replied "My name is Kareem" or "My name is Jabbar" before answering their questions. Later on, he signed autographs as "Kareem."[25]

Though exceptional in size and talent, Jabbar was by no means singular in his desire to push back against white Americans' rigid expectations of Black athletes. As African American ballplayers gained strength in numbers and greater financial clout in the early 1970s, they were no longer content to abide by the rules and customs of the white basketball establishment, whether on or off the court. Some even refused to be bound by Black leaders' ideas of what it meant to be respectable role models for Black youths. Diverse expressions of Black identity and Black Power from political and cultural currents outside sport seemed to be seeping into professional basketball.

"Basketball is merely the most natural channel of a black tide that has been flooding professional sports," remarked journalist Terry Bledsoe.[26] There were murmurs that this "Black tide" could be bad for business. By 1972, Black players made up around 60 percent of professional basketball's workforce (up from 55 percent in 1970), and both leagues' players associations had outspoken Black presidents.[27] Could the leagues survive what appeared to be a mounting mismatch between the athletes and the fans? African American ballplayers seemed to be making all the money and having all the fun, at the very same moment that white working stiffs were losing financial ground and spending their days doing increasingly monotonous jobs. Although 1972 marked the apex of earnings for white male workers in the United States, from 1973 on their real earnings began to stagnate and then continued to fall over the course of the next two decades. It was a sharp turn away from the prosperity to which they had grown accustomed. Since 1960, their incomes had risen an astounding 42 percent. But the ensuing oil shocks and inflation, coupled with deindustrialization, globalization, plant closings, and the dismantling of unions, had ushered in a time of austerity and uncertainty. With diminished salaries and job security, some white workers found the tedium of the assembly line more and more unbearable.[28] They had been willing to trade monotony for stability, but now corporations were refusing to hold up their end of the bargain.

Making matters worse, this economic downturn occurred just as Black Americans were ramping up their demands for more access to jobs and trades formerly reserved for white workers. But despite white complaints to the contrary, when urban labor markets collapsed in the early 1970s, it was Black workers who bore the brunt of the crisis. New manufacturing jobs that opened up were generally located in the suburbs. Housing policies continued to encourage white flight. As jobs and the tax base left, many African Americans found themselves trapped in decaying city neighborhoods and increasingly blamed for their own misfortune.[29]

Some white hoops fans were part of the continuing out-migration to the suburbs, but most basketball arenas were still located in the downtown core. Even these more affluent fans expressed their annoyance at the expense and trouble involved in going to watch a bunch of Black men play ball. "It costs me a bundle of dough to attend a sporting event in the city. Baby-sitter, drive in, dinner for four, parking, tickets," one white Philadelphian told author James Michener for his tome titled *Sports in America*. "I don't intend to lay out that dough to be insulted by some black agitator or get mugged on the way home."[30] Black basketball came to represent the so-called urban crisis in more ways than one.

Given African American professional ballplayers' growing celebrity, wealth, and power, it is hardly surprising that they became objects of intense public scrutiny amid the decade's economic and urban decline. Worth a reputed $1.6 million over four years, Jabbar's 1972 contract was one of the richest in the history of US sports.[31] By 1973, just as the recession really hit, sixteen out of the twenty-three NBA players with million-dollar, multiyear contracts were Black, and fifty out of the sixty-seven making more than $100,000 per year were Black.[32] Reports set the average NBA salary at around $90,000 and the ABA's average at about $37,000, when the median family income in the United States was just $12,050.[33]

Even so, it was not just about the money or the fact that they "played" for a living. It was the *way* they played that rubbed some white fans wrong. With Afros waving in the breeze, players such as Earl "the Pearl" Monroe (NBA) and Julius "Dr. J" Erving (ABA) were remaking the professional game by infusing it with the aesthetics and ethics of Black streetball. Nurtured on the playground courts of Black neighborhoods, this aggressive, aerial, and fast-paced brand of basketball emphasized feats of individual athleticism, creative deception, and stylish improvisation, from trash talking and in-your-face shot blocking, to behind-the-back or no-look passes, to nimble jump shots and sometimes backboard-shattering slam dunks. It was hard to deny that this influx of Black players brought something new to professional basketball. Exciting to watch, they were at once objects of white fascination and resentment, as playground ball and the Black city attitude that went along with it became popular targets of white disdain. Deemed "selfish," unnecessarily flamboyant, and hostile to the "fundamentals" of the game, playground ball was initially a racial smear rather than a celebrated style.

In February 1972, *Black Sports* spoke with Monroe about his artistic influence on the professional game. As he sat in front of the microphone sporting a four-inch Afro, metal-framed aviator glasses, a large gold chain, and tight sweater, Earl the Pearl looked smooth. The interview offered a rare glimpse into the mind of the New York Knicks' six-foot-three guard. Monroe was relatively quiet off the court. He did most of his "talking" through his playing. But he was by no means a pushover. The year before, he had stood his ground against the Baltimore Bullets, refusing to play until team owner Abe Pollin acquiesced to his demand for a trade, dealing him to the Knicks. There had already been bad blood between Monroe and the Bullets' front office. The night before the 1967 draft, they had pushed him into signing a two-year contract for $20,000 per year, without the benefit of proper representation, and when it came time to negotiate a new deal in 1971, they tried to shortchange him. No wonder he was an opponent of the ABA-NBA merger. Without the threat of competition from the ABA, he might have been stuck playing for the Bullets for much less than his worth.[34]

Earl the Pearl's contributions to the game far outweighed his initial earnings. Placing Monroe next to the likes of former greats Bill Russell and Elgin Baylor, *Black Sports* asked, "How do you feel when you realize that you've changed the style of playing basketball?" However, Monroe was reluctant to claim such a central role in spurring this shift: "I think my style of play is basically just the style of about every Black player in America today. As you know, most Black players are, more or less, playground players and this is just about the basic style that I play."[35]

Although for many white sportswriters, playground play suggested a lack of sophistication or even a kind of Black moral failing, Monroe saw its development at the intersection of persistent racial and class discrimination in the United States. "If you come from a white middle-class environment, for instance, quite naturally you're going to have the type of coaching and facilities to teach how to play basketball on a certain level," he explained. "But being in a Black ghetto area, you have to use the facilities available. And, of course, this changes the style because here you're playing on places with cracks in the cement, you're playing on half-moon backboards, basket rims that are bent and what not. So you kind of deviate the style of play and you kind of compensate for the different things."[36] For Monroe, playground ball was an inherited style born of the collective Black struggle, of making a creative way out of no way: "Before me, it was someone else. It's just that *I've* had the exposure; people have gotten to see the way that I play." Still, thanks in part to Monroe, this approach to the game had leaped from African American playgrounds to the professional leagues. His own life story, in many respects, resembled the conditions of urban deprivation that he described to *Black Sports*.

Born on November 21, 1944, Monroe had grown up in a rough part of South Philadelphia, learning the hoop game on the Black playground court at 30th and Oakford. Sometimes he and his friends went to the court at 30th and Tasker, where the white boys played, hoping to pick up a game. "If we black guys won," he reminisced, "we'd have to fight our way out of there going home."[37] Thanks to his inventive moves, he became a playground legend and a star player at John Bartram High School. He found his way out of South Philly through a scholarship to the small Black college of Winston-Salem State in North Carolina, where he played ball under the mentorship of famed coach Clarence "Big House" Gaines. Alternately known as "Slick," "Black Magic," "Einstein," and "Black Jesus" because of his inspired play, as a senior Monroe picked up the nickname "Earl the Pearl" after local Black sportswriter Luix Overbea described his

high-scoring games as "Earl's pearls." Monroe also helped lead the
Rams to an NCAA Division II basketball championship in 1967, the
first time a Black college had ever won an NCAA basketball title.
The Baltimore Bullets then drafted him second overall.[38]

Monroe's transition to pro ball was far from seamless. The Bullets'
head coach, Gene Shue, a Baltimore native and former NBA player,
helped teach him the ropes. Sensing that Monroe's creative style would
help put fans in the stands at the Civic Center, Shue gave the rookie a
lot of space to play, reining him in only when necessary. His behind-
the-back and no-look passes initially caught his white teammates off
guard, creating turnovers. "They were missing passes even when they
were wide open because they were used to traditional passes from
their teammates," Monroe recounted, "not these razzle-dazzle dishes
that were coming from me." Coach Shue asked him to tone things
down a bit until they got used to his style of play. Meanwhile, the
referees kept calling Monroe for palming the ball when he made his
signature spin move. As Knicks guard Bill Bradley described it, "He
drove toward the defensive man only to turn his back on him at the
last possible second before collision, pivot with his left foot, and head
away at a forty-five-degree angle." What made Monroe's spin move
unique was his "one-handed control; it was as if the ball were attached
by a short string to his fingers." Shue ended up having to pull the refs
aside and give them films of Monroe so that they could see that he
was not palming the ball.[39] The way that he moved seemed to defy the
laws of nature.

After Monroe scored an incredible 56 points against the Los Angeles Lakers in February 1968, a Baltimore sportswriter had started
using the nickname "Earl the Pearl" in his columns. "It quickly spread
to the national media and stuck in a way that 'Black Magic' and 'Black
Jesus' hadn't, except in the Black community," Monroe recollected. It
probably helped that "Earl the Pearl" was race neutral and appealed
to a broader fan base. As Monroe's confidence grew, he became even
bolder on the court: "I started to make the crowds go wild."[40] He

The Baltimore Bullets' guard Earl Monroe scrambles after the ball while guarded by the New York Knicks' Walt Frazier in the first quarter of an NBA Eastern Division semifinal playoff game in Baltimore, April 5, 1970. New York's Bill Bradley watches in the background. (AP Photo/Bob Schutz)

became a significant drawing card, attracting fans to the Civic Center and other NBA arenas across the country.

Monroe's inspired play won him the NBA's Rookie of the Year award in 1968. For him, it was not just an individual triumph. The award affirmed "a black approach to the way basketball should be played: with a whole lot of music up in the moves, a lot of rhythm like James Brown's music or Miles Davis's approach to jazz."[41] Trickery, improvisation, innovation, and mastery were central to his style of play. Black sportswriter Clayton Riley perhaps delineated it best: "Monroe's attack, as an offensive ballplayer, was really the sports version of the sound that bop era musicians in America had certified as the brilliant message of gifted men, a song based on themes of personal expression emerging from a structured, collective effort."[42] Monroe saw himself as both an artist and a competitor: "I was consciously trying to embarrass the guys I was playing against."⁴³ It was as if he was playing the dozens with the ball.

In the off-seasons, Earl the Pearl continued to refine his moves by playing in Philadelphia's legendary Charles Baker Memorial Summer League, founded in 1960 by William Randolph "Sonny" Hill. The Baker League attracted top-notch street and professional players hoping to develop and sharpen their skills. Monroe felt free when playing in the Baker League: "In those games, I could always be creative, imaginative, take risks not only with the shots I took but also with my ball handling, my razzle-dazzle passes, and the fans loved it."⁴⁴ There was no money involved. Instead, the athletes played for reputation.

Monroe's playing style thrilled spectators, but it also drew criticism from white sportswriters. When he was traded to the New York Knicks in 1971, reporters predicted that he would struggle to play next to Walt Frazier and company. He was a great one-on-one player, but could he adjust to the Knicks' brand of team ball? Monroe pushed back against their doubts, arguing that he was, above all, committed to winning. "I don't just go out to play, just to be there," he told *Black Sports.* "I take pride in myself and the things that I do. And regardless of who has the ball, I'm out there to win; I'm not concerned about scoring. I know if we win, I'm going to reap benefits from it anyway, regardless of what I do."⁴⁵ For Monroe, individual creativity and team play were entirely compatible. It was not a zero-sum game. Amid the murmurs of disapproval, he was helping to transform the guard position from a supporting role charged with feeding the ball to the upcourt big men to being a central part of the team's point production, scoring off improvisational drives to the hoop.⁴⁶

Over in the ABA, Julius Erving was also making waves. "Erving represents the very soul of a subculture," *Black Sports* contributor Eric Lincoln observed in March 1973.⁴⁷ Although Dr. J still played in the relative obscurity of the upstart league, Black kids could be found emulating his free-flowing, aerial style in the schoolyards of Harlem. Born on February 22, 1950, Erving was not that far removed from them, having grown up in Hempstead, Long Island. After his parents divorced when he was three, his mother was left to raise three children on her own.[48] "It was just my mother and the kids," Erving told Lincoln. "We were on welfare. We lived in the projects. . . . And most of the kids I played basketball with lived on pride. You know, didn't have much at all. My mother did domestic work on the side from the time I was 3 on up to 13. I guess you could say that I saw the darker side of life."[49] Like many of his young African American fans, he first honed his basketball craft in local schoolyards. At age twelve, he began playing organized ball with a Salvation Army team that traveled around Long Island for games, giving him a glimpse of how the other half lived. From this experience, he learned that a college education was the key to upward mobility, so he set his mind to take that path.

After his mother remarried, his family's fortunes improved. They bought a home in the Long Island hamlet of Roosevelt, where he played varsity ball for the local high school. But his aerial game was incubated on the outdoor courts in nearby parks. Erving was part of a broader transformation of the game taking place on Black playgrounds across New York City in the mid-to-late 1960s. The game he and his friends played outside was much more fluid, flashy, and improvisational than the one they played in organized ball. It was also a rougher, more in-your-face game, where disputes and scuffles were not uncommon. "I'm developing a game and a style that is very different from what we are doing inside the gym," he recalled of his teen years. "I'm dunking backward on eight-foot and nine-foot baskets, able to dunk one-handed with ease on ten-foot rims. I'm jumping over guys ten years older and five inches taller on courts all over town. Some of the dunks are so spectacular that the games almost come to a halt after I throw down."[50] Erving and other Black youths looked to Elgin Baylor and Connie Hawkins for inspiration as they experimented with new moves.

What they learned on the playground through trial and error often countered what their high school coaches were teaching them:

"Indoors, the coaches tell us never to leave the ground without knowing what you are going to do with the ball. Indoors, the coach always tells me to go up with two hands and secure the rebound, bringing the ball down to chest level before making an outlet pass to a guard." Outdoors, however, they routinely improvised in the air, and one-handed moves were commonplace. The playground was like a "laboratory for new experiments in scoring."[51]

Their approach to the game was grounded in their social reality as young Black men coming of age in the sixties. "That kind of improvisation on the basketball court is a form of expression," Erving recounted, "and I come to see it as a response to what is going on in the world around us, where the politics of race, the turmoil of riots, the drug culture, and rock music are transforming how everyone looks and dresses and acts." Off the court, Erving was relatively conservative, with a fondness for rules and order. He did not mess with drugs and was somewhat skeptical of the Black Power militancy rising up around him. He was trying to work within the system, not burn it down, to make his way to college, to better himself. The basketball court was the one place he felt he could rebel and express himself without restraint.[52]

Erving also knew that an athletic scholarship would be his only route to higher education. He received offers from a number of colleges, but New England's charm ultimately convinced him to attend the University of Massachusetts, Amherst, in 1969. Although he struggled academically at first, he seemed to adjust well to college play. Other than being chastised by his coaches for doing playground moves, the only difficult thing for him was "resisting the urge to dunk."[53]

Erving was still relatively unsung when he decided to leave college after his junior year, signing with the Virginia Squires of the ABA in the spring of 1971. That summer he readied himself for the pros by playing in New York City's Rucker Pro League. At the time, playground legends competed alongside NBA and ABA All-Stars in free-flowing games held at Holcombe Rucker Park in Harlem at the corner of 155th Street and Frederick Douglass Boulevard. Released from the strictures of college ball, Erving was free to dunk as much as he wanted. He could play without the fear of a coach taking him out of the game if he made a bad decision or threw the ball away. It proved to be an eye-opening experience: "I'm discovering that some of my playground moves, the dunks and spins and finger rolls, will not only work against this professional-level competition, they are actually more effective than some of the methodical zone-busting, outside-in, pass-and-cut offensive moves that my coaches taught me back at UMass."[54] An important meeting ground, the Rucker was central to Black basketball culture in New York City. The games were not televised; you had to witness them in person or hear about them from your friends. Though surrounded by the impact of urban disinvestment, the Rucker was Black New York's outlet, their park, their experience.

With one summer at the Rucker under his belt, Erving quickly distinguished himself as an ABA star in his rookie season, averaging nearly 28 points per game and 16 rebounds. When he turned pro, he decided to let his Afro grow another three inches, which made him seem even taller than his lanky six-foot-seven-inch frame. His hair became part of his image: fans came to see the wind pushing it back as he flew through the air toward the basket.[55] Although he had been known by the nickname "Doctor" since his youth in Long Island, his Squires teammate Willie Sojourner shortened it to "Dr. J," and the moniker stuck. Dr. J's moves were "at once, explosive, mysterious and bewildering."[56] His playing style epitomized Black freedom. He was Black joy personified. "When his body writhes, jukes, floats, feints, it is, in essence, the release of expression from bondage," Lincoln wrote. Erving seemed to offer a glimpse of African American men's limitless potential as he soared over obstacles with grace and determination. In bringing his freewheeling playground moves to indoor ball, he was helping to transform a once-horizontal game into one of vertical virtuosity.[57] Unsurprisingly, he emerged as the new face of the ABA. By the early 1970s, the ABA, even more so than the NBA, had become known as a "Black league."

EARLY IN THE MORNING ON OCTOBER 6, 1972, MILWAUKEE BUCKS general manager Wayne Embry was woken up by a phone call in his hotel room in Denver. "Do you have any comment on Kareem and Lucius getting arrested last night for possession of drugs?" the voice on the other end of the line asked. Thinking it was a prank call, the bleary-eyed Embry slammed the phone down and turned over to go back to sleep. The night before, he had drunk his fair share of beer while out celebrating the Bucks' easy 130–92 victory in their pre-season exhibition game against the ABA's Denver Rockets. Perhaps, Embry thought, he was just having a nightmare.[58]

A few minutes later, the phone rang again. This time it was Bucks coach Larry Costello. He confirmed that Jabbar and Lucius Allen had been arrested on drug charges and were sitting in the county jail. This was a nightmare, all right. The hotel phone started ringing off the hook: news of the arrests had traveled back to Milwaukee, and reporters wanted more information. Embry let the phone ring and headed to the jail.[59]

This was hardly how he imagined his first season as GM would unfold. Earlier that year, in March, the Milwaukee Bucks had promoted Embry from assistant to the president to general manager, making him the first-ever Black GM in North American professional sports. "This was 1972 in Milwaukee, which had a reputation as one of the most segregated cities in the country," Embry recalled. "The city was only a few years removed from the race riots. As much as I grew to love it there, it was hardly the most progressive of communities, and this was a ground-breaking move."[60] The six-foot-eight former front-court enforcer had played college ball at Miami University of Ohio and then had a distinguished eleven-year NBA career as a five-time All-Star who played with the Cincinnati Royals, the Boston Celtics, and finally the Bucks.[61] Embry felt a lot of pressure to excel in his new front-office position. How would it look for the league's first Black GM to be running a team with two Black drug criminals? As he drove to the jail, he hoped that he was not walking into a public relations disaster.

After all, sportswriters were quick to report on anything involving Jabbar that smacked of controversy. The Bucks' star center had been traveling in a car with Allen—they had known each other for years, having been teammates and roommates at UCLA—and two of Allen's college-aged friends, Stephen E. Duncan and Mordecai C. Cooke. Cooke was at the wheel when the four were arrested outside their downtown hotel at around 3:30 a.m.[62] Police from the city's vice squad claimed that during a routine traffic stop they had detected the smell of burning marijuana and subsequently found small amounts of suspected marijuana, amphetamines, and LSD in the car. When tested, the samples proved positive for drugs.[63] Even so, this seemed out of character for Jabbar. He had never been in trouble with the law before, and his Muslim religion prohibited smoking.

Allen, however, had more of a checkered past, with two previous marijuana-related brushes with the law. One set of charges was dismissed for lack of evidence in 1967, but a year later he pled guilty to a misdemeanor and received probation, a suspended sentence, and a fine. Although Allen's connection to UCLA basketball likely shielded him from the worst consequences of his drug infraction, he ended up dropping out of school after the second drug case and not playing his senior year.[64] He had been talented enough, though, to land on his feet in the NBA.

Back in Denver, Embry had made it to the jail at 5:00 a.m. When he asked to see Jabbar and Allen, the front-desk clerk pointed to a metal cell door with a small barred window. Embry looked through the bars: "Both of them were wide awake, sitting with their chins in their hands, staring into space. I stood there dumbfounded. . . . Even though I was angry, I had to keep cool and try to be sympathetic. I kept reminding myself that people are innocent until proven guilty."[65] They needed to be bailed out, but neither they nor Embry had enough money on them to spring them from jail. After calling around, Embry finally found someone to pay the players' bond. It took a couple of hours for Arlen Preblood, a Denver attorney and executive director of the ABA Players Association, to arrive with the money. Cooke and Duncan were left to find their own way out.

The police released Jabbar and Allen on bond after a five-hour stint in jail. Later in the day, District Attorney Jarvis Seccombe announced that he was dropping the charges against Jabbar and Cooke and releasing their bonds because of insufficient evidence. However, the cases against Allen, for marijuana possession (half an ounce or less), and Duncan, for possession of marijuana, amphetamines, and LSD, remained open. Although the charge against Allen was a misdemeanor in Colorado, it still came with a maximum penalty of one year in jail and a $500 fine.[66]

Now the challenge was how to get the two players back home without creating too much of a media circus. They could disguise Allen, but there was no way to hide Jabbar. To cut down on the commotion, Embry decided to fly them into Chicago, instead of going directly to Milwaukee. Hoping to control the narrative, the Bucks had scheduled a press conference for Jabbar and Allen's arrival by bus at the Milwaukee airport. However, by the time they got to the Denver airport, it was mobbed with reporters and television trucks. Airport security and police held the media at bay, and the two players were able to board their plane with only a minor scuffle. After landing in Chicago, they headed back to Milwaukee. As the bus approached the airport, it slowed. To Embry's surprise, Jabbar and Allen opened the front door of the bus, jumped out, ran to their parked cars, and immediately fled the scene.[67]

Furious with his two stars, Embry was left to face the media alone. "Kareem and Lucius chose not to appear at this news conference because of the way they had been hassled all day by the press at the

Denver airport," the Bucks' GM told reporters. He then read a prepared statement on behalf of Jabbar and Allen, attesting to their innocence. They were just passengers in the car. They had not been doing
drugs, nor did they have any knowledge of the drugs found in the
car. As instructed by Preblood, Embry answered most questions with
"No comment." But the reporters continued to press him for information. "What were Jabbar and Allen doing out after 3 am?" one
asked. Embry said the players had no curfew that night because the
Bucks did not have another game for a week. He added that the team
did not plan to take any action against the two athletes. "Because it
was Jabbar it was magnified," Embry complained.[68] What seemed like
a nonissue—young men allegedly using marijuana—somehow made
the national television news.[69]

Although the charges against Allen were eventually dropped a few
months later, the specter of Black criminality hung over the Bucks
and professional basketball more generally. It appeared as if Black
players were not only bringing streetball but also urban crime to the
professional leagues, and all against the backdrop of increasingly strident calls for "law and order." Capitalizing on white perceptions of the
connection between civil rights legislation and Black disorder, especially amid the urban uprisings of the late 1960s, conservative politicians appealed to white voters with promises of stepped-up policing
and punishment.[70] But the expansion of the criminal-justice system
in the name of taming Black lawlessness had long been a bipartisan
effort. Although President Richard Nixon certainly intensified the
War on Crime in the early 1970s, he built on an "already-vibrant law
enforcement infrastructure" created by the Johnson Administration.
Many of the social programs aimed at African American communities as part of President Lyndon B. Johnson's Great Society "centered
on crime control, surveillance, and incarceration."[71]

When Nixon declared his "War on Drugs" in June 1971, it was
based on a pernicious racial double standard. On the one hand, it
offered second chances and rehabilitation for white drug users in the

suburbs. On the other, it encouraged increased policing and punishment for Black drug pushers. And, in practice, drug possession could be easily spun into an attempt to distribute if the offender was African American. Protecting white people and white spaces from Black drug crime was the war's organizing principle.[72]

Black basketball players became lightning rods in this context. They were the highest-paid athletes in all of North American professional sports, and many were now using their wealth to buy large homes in the predominantly white suburbs.[73] At the same time, they retained strong ties—both actual and metaphorical—to Black neighborhoods through their friends and families, their fashion sense, and their style of play. As they and their images moved between these worlds, they threatened to contaminate professional ball and other heretofore white domains.

The early 1970s marked the first murmurs about a possible "drug crisis" in professional basketball. As more and more newspaper reports featured African American ballplayers being arrested for drug charges (albeit mostly minor possession charges), to the casual observer it must have appeared to be a "Black crisis." However, alcohol and drugs were hardly new to the NBA. After-game beers in the locker room were a long-standing tradition, and most players had gone to colleges where marijuana and other counterculture drugs were easily accessible and generally not policed.[74] What was different in this moment was the color of the players and the stepped-up calls for law enforcement targeting Black youths in particular.

Jabbar recalled that pro athletes worked hard and played hard, and alcohol and drugs were often in the mix during their time off. They were, after all, young, fit, attractive, and often unmarried guys with disposable income. This was not just a Black thing. Jabbar's white teammate Mickey Davis had once taken him to a party at a friend's house where he saw "bales of marijuana." So how did white players remain under the radar while Black players found themselves stopped by police? It was likely because they lived in separate social worlds off the court. "If white guys haven't hung with blacks before, they rarely start in the pros," Jabbar later explained. "Even on the team bus the coaches and press sit up front while the black players go to the rear. White players are often left somewhere in between."[75] Connie Hawkins had similar observations about the lack of interracial socializing on the Phoenix Suns: "At night, we were never with the white guys. . . . They don't eat soul food. They don't dance. We don't drink beer. There was nothing in common."[76]

As young Black men who drove nice cars, pro ballplayers became easy targets in Nixon's War on Drugs. Jabbar and Allen had fallen victim to a "pretext stop": when police officers use minor traffic violations as an excuse to pull over a vehicle and search for illegal narcotics. Such stops of Black Americans became more commonplace as the drug war eroded Fourth Amendment protections against unreasonable search and seizure.[77]

Jabbar and Allen were far from the only Black ballplayers hassled by law enforcement. Wali Jones, a recent trade from the Philadelphia 76ers, may have been the newest member of the Milwaukee Bucks, but he was no stranger to getting pulled over by police. "I used to get stopped two or three times a week in Philly," the seven-year veteran NBA guard said, shortly after he arrived in Milwaukee. "It's a police state. The Philly cops are like the Gestapo."[78] So far, the twenty-nine-year-old Philadelphia native and Villanova graduate felt more at ease in his new city. "Here I don't have to look for the cops like I did in Philly," he said. Jones looked forward to starting a new chapter of his life with his wife and two sons.

While playing for the 76ers, Jones had created a service group called African American Athletes in Action, which then became Concerned Athletes in Action (CAIA). Made up of professional athletes with ties to Philadelphia, its mission was to mentor Black youths and keep them on the straight and narrow.[79] Jones made no secret of his past experiences on the tough streets of Philly, where he came of age playing basketball, fighting in a gang, and experimenting with alcohol and marijuana. He was one of the lucky ones who had managed to escape without a criminal record.[80] Through CAIA, he hoped to help other Black teens avoid the pitfalls of gangs, drugs, and crime: "The only thing these guys can create is better ways of fighting. If they have any creative energy, that's where it goes. . . . What we did was try and get them involved in other things. Music and drama and black history and making dashikis. Anything to give them new things to experience."[81] He had even coauthored a book, *Black Champions Challenge American Sports*, to teach young people about the historical importance of African American athletes.[82] When Jones arrived in Milwaukee, he continued this work, establishing another CAIA branch with fellow teammate Bill Dinwiddie (Rashid Kareem Shabazz). They put on exhibitions at local playgrounds and visited boys' institutions, using these opportunities to educate kids about the dangers of drugs. They also worked with drug users, helping them through the rehabilitation process.[83]

It was therefore ironic that Jones soon found himself at the center of the NBA's most prominent and perplexing drug scandal of the

Wali Jones, #24 of the Milwaukee Bucks, poses for an action portrait circa 1971 in Milwaukee. (Photo by NBA Photo Library/NBAE via Getty Images)

early 1970s. On December 12, just two months after the arrests of Jabbar and Allen, the Bucks put Jones on indefinite medical suspension without pay for allegedly losing weight and stamina. Milwaukee's front-office management did not elaborate any further on the reasons for Jones's suspension, so rumors began to fly about him being on drugs.[84] Jones felt unfairly defamed. Although he did not initially seek out the NBPA's support, he decided to fight back. He flew to Philadelphia to consult with his lawyer, Richard G. Phillips, and underwent a physical examination by several local doctors. Moose Detty, the trainer for the NFL's Philadelphia Eagles, also pronounced him in good shape.[85] Phillips announced to the press that the doctors had given his client a clean bill of health and that, contrary to the Bucks' accusations, the six-foot-two guard was still 170 pounds—the same weight as the year before. However, the NBA stated that Jones would remain on suspension until its doctors had a chance to examine him.[86]

Jones suspected that the Bucks were attempting to invalidate his contract and dispense with him. It was common knowledge among players at the time that the taint of possible drug abuse provided a good excuse for management to get rid of "troublesome" ballplayers who were not performing up to expectations on the court.[87] Jones had a reputation for being a firebrand when it came to contract negotiations. The Bucks had acquired him in December 1971 after he sat out the first few weeks of his season with the 76ers because of a dispute over money. When Philadelphia suspended him for refusing to play, he filed a $5 million federal lawsuit against the NBA for "depriving him of making a living."[88] Although Jones later dropped the suit, his reputation as a troublemaker stuck. He was also relatively expensive. He had reportedly signed a four-year, no-cut contract with the Bucks worth around $350,000.[89]

Perhaps even more concerning, Jones was a bit of a wild card when it came to his behavior on and off the court. He boldly asserted his Blackness, both in terms of his style of play and his community service. Jones had recently changed his name from Wally (né Walter) to

Wali, and he sported a tall, bushy Afro and Black liberation wrist-
bands on his elbows. Known for his signature "jackknife" jump shot,
he brought an aggressive Black streetball sensibility to the NBA. "You
like to make it personal, like a boxer saying 'take that,'" Jones once
told *Washington Post* sportswriter Thomas Boswell.[90]

Jones also used his access to the media to raise awareness about the
plight of urban Black communities facing grinding poverty and unjust
criminalization. For him, this crusade was both personal and political.
His older brother's suffering had left a deep imprint on him. After
spending two years in jail on a case of mistaken identity, Bobby Jones
struggled with depression and drug addiction. Jones saw his brother's
predicament as connected to white America's ongoing abandonment
of poor Black communities. He lamented the lack of educational and
recreational opportunities for Black teens in Philadelphia. "All the
graffiti on the walls tells you the history of that city," he said of his
hometown. "Thousands of kids who need to create something, and
they write on the walls."[91] Stepping into the gaping breach left behind by deepening cuts to government programs, the veteran guard
spent his spare time and summers running youth camps and drug-
prevention clinics in the African American neighborhoods of Milwaukee and Philadelphia. Although Jones's work mentoring young
people was hardly controversial, his strong connection to the inner
city remained problematic for a league attempting to make its Black
players more palatable to its still majority-white fan base.

On December 29, attorney Phillips, acting on Jones's behalf, filed
an official grievance with NBA commissioner Walter Kennedy. The
complaint protested both Jones's suspension and Milwaukee's refusal
to pay Jones for the games he had missed since it was invoked. Phillips
had also reached out to Larry Fleisher, the NBPA's general counsel,
to apprise him of the situation.[92] "Even if tests show he is not able to
play, according to his contract it is our contention that he is entitled to
his salary," Phillips told reporters. "But we feel so confident about his
condition that we have made an offer to the Milwaukee *Journal . . .* to

have Wali examined by a physician of their choice." Phillips charged that the Bucks had unjustly suspended Jones without a proper medical consultation.[93]

A few days later, Phillips disclosed to the *Milwaukee Journal* that in addition to the medical suspension, the Bucks had also slapped Jones with a thirty-day suspension for "curfew violations and other conduct detrimental to basketball."[94] Phillips's revelation forced the Bucks to publicly concede that they had suspended Jones for both medical and disciplinary reasons; however, the team remained mum about the specific allegations against Jones. Although the Bucks' cryptic announcement of purported "disciplinary problems" helped to explain why the team refused to pay Jones while he was on suspension, it only further fueled the circulating rumors of the player's drug abuse. Seeking help for his embattled client, Phillips referred the matter to the NBPA for arbitration.[95]

Before the end of the thirty-day disciplinary suspension and before any arbitration came to pass, the Bucks announced that they had lifted Jones's medical suspension. After examining him, their team physician, Parks LeTellier, reported that he could find no cause for the guard's alleged physical decline. "Under the circumstances," Milwaukee GM Embry said, "we see no reasonable prospect of Jones returning to the level of performance which we expected of him."[96] The Bucks then cut Jones and placed him on waivers on January 9, hoping that another NBA team would pick him up within the forty-eight-hour window and assume his contract. If no club claimed him within that time for the $1,000 waiver price, he would become a free agent. If a team signed Jones after the waiver period expired, Milwaukee would have to make up the difference between his new salary and the amount guaranteed in his Bucks contract.[97] Meanwhile, Phillips declared that they would appeal Milwaukee's decision to put Jones on irrevocable waivers. He argued that his client had the right to remain a Buck for at least the remainder of the season and was entitled to his salary for the remainder of his guaranteed four-year contract.[98]

Jones was one of the more talented guards in the league, yet no other team claimed him within the waiver period. The cloud of drug-related rumors surrounding his dismissal from the Bucks was apparently enough to scare them off. But even though Jones had no team to play for and his appeal was still in process, he refused to go away quietly. The veteran guard, accompanied by Phillips, held his own press conference in Milwaukee on January 13. Wearing a knitted kufi over his Afro, he pulled thoughtfully at his beard as he addressed reporters. "The Bucks have offered me as a sacrifice—a sacrificial lamb," Jones declared. "I have been spit upon and I have been defamed. . . . I am positive about my own well-being, physically and mentally, and about my integrity and honor."[99] For now, he would have to wait for a resolution to his predicament.

In the meantime, sportswriters were also starting to take notice of the recent spate of drug arrests involving pro ballplayers. Sandy Padwe of *Newsday* investigated the seeming uptick in drug problems that threatened professional basketball's public image. In December 1972, right around the time that the Bucks suspended Jones, suburban Buffalo police arrested rookie guard Harold Fox and his teammate Dick Garrett of the NBA's Braves on drug-related charges. The two were in an apartment in the white suburb of Amherst, New York, where the police reportedly found marijuana. Although a local judge later dropped the case because of insufficient evidence, the Braves still cut Fox, suspended his four-year contract, and stopped paying him. Because of the taint of suspected drug use, no other team picked him up. Although Garrett remained on the Braves, he admitted to feeling less than secure because his contract was set to expire: "The way they're doing Harold, I don't know. . . . I don't know if the team is trying to make an example of him or trying to get rid of a big contract. . . . Ever since I was arrested, I'm trying to stay out of trouble. . . . But drugs are everywhere . . . they're all over in society." By the middle of the 1972–1973 season, rumors of increasing drug use in the league were troubling enough to cause

NBPA attorney Fleisher to contact all of the player representatives: "I told them that there was too much at stake, that we've worked too hard, too long to suffer any scandal."[100] The collective reputation of the NBA's majority-Black players was at stake.

It did not help that the archetypal image of the Black drug pusher had already made its way into broader currents of American popular culture. *Super Fly*, a film about a character named Youngblood Priest (Ron O'Neal), a Harlem cocaine dealer who tries to make one last score before retiring, hit theaters in 1972. It became a runaway success, grossing more than $12 million as part of the growing Blaxploitation genre, and Curtis Mayfield's soulful single "Pusherman" helped the soundtrack to gross even more than the movie itself.[101] Although Black audiences viewed Priest as a suave folk hero who "stuck it to the Man," for white viewers the movie seemed to confirm prevailing stereotypes about rampant Black crime in US urban centers.[102]

Meanwhile, Padwe's interviews with several NBA and ABA players revealed that drug use in professional ball was not just a simple case of Black criminality or moral failing. "Much of it results from the grueling schedule in both professional basketball leagues," he concluded.[103] Nate Archibald, the Kansas City Kings' star Black guard, denied that the NBA had a problem with hard drugs; instead, he argued that marijuana was popular among players for relieving the stress of their hectic, high-pressure careers.

The Denver Rockets' African American guard Warren Jabali noted that the ABA's drug scene had changed considerably since he had entered the league in 1968: "When I first started, you could get uppers from trainers. Now you can't anymore."[104] Professional sports leagues had all clamped down on drugs in the locker room after Houston Ridge sued the National Football League and the San Diego Chargers for conspiracy and malpractice in April 1970. Hobbled by hip problems since October 1969, the Black former defensive end claimed that he was disabled, in part, because the Chargers had given him a mix of amphetamines, barbiturates, and methandrostenolone to get him back on the field quickly after an injury, without warning him of the possible long-term consequences.[105] Now that athletes could no longer go to team trainers for drugs, they had to find their own supply of uppers and downers to help them cope with the strain and pain of pro ball.

Instead of acknowledging the impact of both the demanding season and the recent changes in drug policy, the NBA and ABA responded with surveillance. The players all knew that team and league officials were keeping tabs on them. "They bring in FBI guys, police," Jabali told Padwe, "and tell you that they're going to be checking." One unnamed ABA coach even admitted that he had started having the trainer search his players' luggage without their knowledge. Bucks coach Larry Costello conceded that he had no idea how to effectively police the players' drug use: "Who do you watch? The people in the lobbies? Have you seen the number of people who hang around a basketball team in the hotel lobbies? How do you know who they all are?"[106]

Shortly after the arrest of Jabbar and Allen, in November 1972 the NBA quietly established its first security office, run by ex-FBI agent Jack Joyce. And by June 1973, Joyce claimed to have a network of security men in each NBA city who reported to him on a weekly basis.[107] Most were retired FBI agents and police officers—some of whom had likely spent their careers policing Black activists and Black youths. "They are paid by us," Joyce explained, "and handle any matter pertaining to security, be it drugs, gambling, anything like that." Likewise, the ABA hired Fidelifacts, a New York–based private-security firm staffed largely by ex-FBI agents and with offices in most ABA cities.[108] Both leagues felt compelled to take these measures to protect their brands and their investments. Black players getting arrested for drugs meant bad publicity for pro ball, and given the value of their contracts, teams also saw this as a way to safeguard their assets. Fears about illegal narcotics opened the door not only to the heightened scrutiny of professional athletes but also to racial profiling.

In late May 1973, the season now finished, Commissioner Kennedy announced from his New York office that the Bucks and Jones had settled their dispute. For their part, Milwaukee refused to comment any further about the suspension and the settlement, leaving the entire affair shrouded in mystery. Back in Philadelphia, attorney Richard Phillips confirmed that his client had received a cash settlement valued at "nearly 100 percent of his $95,000 annual salary for the next four years."[109] Now a free agent, Jones looked forward to playing for another team, and Phillips contended that he had already received inquiries from several clubs in the NBA and ABA.[110]

Hoping to get some clarity about the scandal, the United Press International (UPI) and the *Milwaukee Journal* had conducted their own independent investigations of the circumstances surrounding Jones's suspensions.[111] Reportedly, several sources had told the Bucks that they believed Jones was using illegal drugs. The Bucks had then asked Milwaukee lawyer and former assistant district attorney Frank Croak to help them find private investigators to follow up on these rumors. Croak hired Merle Parker and Associates, a Los Angeles detective agency, to carry out a sting on Jones when the Bucks were in town to play the Lakers. On December 4, while the Bucks practiced for their upcoming game, two private investigators entered Jones's room at the Airport Marina Hotel, where they allegedly "found approximately half an ounce of white crystalline powder wrapped in tin foil inside a pocket of a pair of pants lying on the bed."[112] A week later, they reputedly took the powder to a lab technician with the Los Angeles Police Department who was moonlighting for the detective agency. The technician claimed to have tested the substance in a private lab, confirming that it was cocaine. The Bucks suspended Jones the next day; however, roughly two weeks passed before the investigators took the case to the Los Angeles district attorney. As a result of the time delay and the detective agency's dubious practices, the DA's office declined to prosecute Jones. "Too many questions would have been raised about the evidence: whether it (the cocaine) belonged to Jones, how it was obtained," a spokesperson for the DA claimed. "The ownership was not duly determined and the whole thing was very badly handled by whoever set it up."[113]

Jones continued to assert his innocence, categorically denying all allegations of illegal drug possession and use. "There is no evidence against me, just hearsay and conjecture," he told UPI reporter Dave Begel. The veteran guard maintained that the whole affair had been a setup that the Bucks engineered in order to nullify his contract. They had used his involvement in urban antidrug efforts against him. "I have worked on the streets and playgrounds in my fight against drugs," Jones explained. "On the streets and in the playgrounds there are drugs and that's where we had to go to get the message across. Of course people saw me where drugs were present."[114] He hoped to eventually put these lies to rest.

Still, Jones refused to let the persistent rumors silence or stop him as he pushed ahead with his community work. In early June he held a press conference in Milwaukee to announce a fund-raising drive for CAIA's youth programs. When the topic of his alleged drug use came up, Jones refused to talk about it. "I don't have to defend anything," he told reporters. "My life and my endeavors have always been to save youngsters from drugs and gangs."[115] By this time, CAIA had grown to involve both active and retired NBA and NFL players, along with several staff members, including a doctor, drug experts, former drug users, teachers, and coaches. The organization's footprint had also expanded beyond just Philadelphia and Milwaukee to include chapters in Muncie, Indiana; Norfolk, Virginia; Washington, DC; and Boston, Massachusetts.[116]

Jones's success with CAIA had caught the attention of Senator Birch Bayh (D–Indiana), the head of the Senate Judiciary Committee's Subcommittee to Investigate Juvenile Delinquency. On June 18, Bayh called on Jones and several members of CAIA to testify at the first of a series of investigative hearings on the "Proper and Improper Use of Drugs by Athletes."[117] In light of the recent string of drug scandals involving high-profile athletes, Bayh and his colleagues wanted to assess the nature and extent of drug use in both amateur and professional sports. Even though the senators were primarily concerned about the problem of performance-enhancing drugs (PEDs: amphetamines, steroids, etc.), Jones came in with his own agenda. Here was his chance to rehabilitate his public image and promote his organization's antidrug work in urban Black neighborhoods.

Jones provided a Black, albeit decidedly male, perspective on the issue. He argued that for both Black athletes and urban Black communities, drug use ultimately stemmed from the enduring effects of racial and economic inequality. Describing his childhood neighborhood in Philadelphia as "a disaster area," Jones indicted white America for sitting by idly as Black youths suffered, locked in spaces of concentrated poverty, with no access to quality education, jobs, or recreation. As young people looked for a momentary escape from the harsh realities of African American life in the city, many turned to illegal drugs. "They say we shouldn't be hysterical, but we are hysterical about the drug situation," he declared. "Young people are dying in some of these areas."[118] He called on the subcommittee and society at large to take notice and take action.

For Jones, it was impossible to separate the experiences of Black athletes from those of Black teens more generally. He claimed that some Black athletes, even those as young as high school age, took drugs not only to deal with the stress of, but to also gain an edge in, the hypercompetitive arena of sports. With so few educational and economic opportunities available, many young African American boys set their sights on becoming professional athletes. Other than entertainers and drug pushers, athletes were their communities' most visible symbols of success.

As a college athlete at Villanova, Jones recalled feeling "the pressure of having to produce" even while injured, no matter the long-term consequences. "Whether it was the gung ho attitude or just the pressure of an athlete who is black who wants to keep advancing, I don't know but I played a whole year with a torn cartilage and my leg would rock periodically," Jones testified. The team trainer had given him various drugs and treatments so he could play through the pain. He saw the NCAA as "an industry of thousands and thousands of basketball players all over the United States trying to become professional."[119] In this cutthroat industry, African American athletes had the most to lose if they could not perform at their peak ability. They played with the heavy burden of knowing that making it to the pros might be their (and their family's) only chance of escaping poverty.

Jones experienced more of the same in the NBA. He quickly discovered that team personnel did not have the best interests of the athletes at heart but would push them to play with injuries: "I had a torn muscle in my back and the pressures were put on, like, you know, this won't hurt you and this will only help the pain stop. But I was shot in the back with Novocain [by the team trainer] and my whole side, I couldn't move it for a couple of days."[120] Jones later went to his personal physician, who said that the trainer had endangered his health by shooting him up and putting him back on the court. Even at the professional level, the pressure to return after an injury was especially intense for Black athletes, particularly for those who were not star players. Not only were they disposable, but they also typically had few other career prospects. As Jones described it, the entire US athletic system, from college to the pros, took advantage of the poverty and marginalization of young African American men. These were the very same conditions that also put them at risk for abusing drugs.

Jones believed that Black professional athletes had an important role to play in the antidrug work of their communities. He presented CAIA as a model, giving the example of a "marathon" session that the organization had recently hosted in Milwaukee. They had kept a gym open for forty-eight hours straight, inviting everyone in the community, young and old, to drop in for basketball games and "rap sessions" with CAIA members. "It gave a chance for the kids who were idle—and as we say, idle minds are the devil's workshop—to come in and participate," Jones explained. "We felt the marathon was a positive force because while they were playing, they got a chance to sit around and talk with us about drugs."[121] With programs that focused on male mentorship and behavioral modification, CAIA was by no means revolutionary in its approach to reducing drug abuse in Black neighborhoods. But it offered an important alternative to the increasingly strident calls for "law and order" in the form of greater policing and punishment.

Through his testimony, Jones had managed to take the issue of PEDs in sports and spin it out into a broader argument about the need for greater investment in social programs for poor Black communities. A return to the principles of the Great Society—with the help of Black athlete role models—would help keep the next generation away from drugs and crime, he asserted. Yet despite his best efforts to clear his name and promote his antidrug work, the specter of Black criminality still haunted professional basketball.

Although this rising tide of African American ballplayers was often criminalized and scorned, their talent and skill were undeniable. The preeminence of Kareem Abdul-Jabbar and his peers was, in the words of Black sportswriter Sam Lacy, like "Jim Crow in Reverse."[122] By the end of the 1973–1974 season, the controversial center had won the honor of NBA MVP three times in five years, and by mid-decade, Black players composed 71 percent of the NBA players who logged a thousand minutes or more in a season. African Americans were taking over and reshaping professional basketball whether white fans liked it or not. And, adding insult to injury, they were taking over not only on the court but also increasingly off the court, in the executive suites and front offices of the NBA.

Chapter 5

Professional

Simon Gourdine and the NBA's White Ceiling

Until we reach the point where competent Blacks can expect to be appointed or elected to important policy-making positions within the N.B.A., then we really haven't gotten our share.

—New York state senator Carl McCall, 1975

ON THE EVE OF LONGTIME COMMISSIONER WALTER KENNEDY'S RE-tirement in 1975, there appeared to be a dark cloud on the NBA's horizon. Whoever replaced Kennedy would surely step into a thunderstorm of problems. Alongside the merger issue and the *Robertson* suit, the constant infighting between team owners, the now uncontestable dominance of Black players, and shrinking gates amid economic stagnation all seemed to threaten the NBA's stability and success. Sportswriters began to wonder if a Black league could realistically remain popular among the mostly white fans who bought the tickets. As *Ebony* magazine noted, out of the 215 players in the NBA at the start of the 1974–1975 season, 132 (61 percent) of them were African

163

American.[1] The NBA All-Star Game in January 1975 featured only three white players out of ten starters, with John Havlicek (Boston Celtics) for the East and Gail Goodrich (Los Angeles Lakers) and Rick Barry (Golden State Warriors) for the West. And for the first time ever, both teams had Black coaches, with K. C. Jones for the East and Al Attles for the West.[2]

Meanwhile, behind the scenes, one African American attorney had managed to gain entrance to the NBA's inner sanctum of power. In June 1970, at just twenty-nine years of age, Simon Gourdine had snagged an executive post in the league's New York City headquarters. Following in the footsteps of Buddy Young and Monte Irvin, Gourdine worked in the office of Commissioner Kennedy as the NBA's legal counsel. Reportedly, former pro player Young had become the first Black executive hired by the NFL in 1964. Then, in 1968, Monte Irvin, who started out in the Negro Leagues and jumped to the majors in the wake of Jackie Robinson, became assistant director of promotions and public relations in MLB commissioner William D. Eckert's office, making him the first Black executive in professional baseball.[3] But these three men were the exception rather than the rule. The administrative ranks of the major US professional sports leagues remained nearly all white, even as their players became increasingly Black. White sportswriters and fans often decried African American athletes' rising salaries, yet they said little about the fact that a tiny group of wealthy white men still controlled the leagues' purse strings and owned all of the franchises.

ONE EVENING, DURING HIS FIRST YEAR ON THE JOB, GOURDINE HAD sat with Kennedy in their offices at 2 Penn Plaza as they tried to cool down after a heated discussion with a rather contentious club owner. The fifty-eight-year-old Kennedy looked tired. The stress of being commissioner was starting to affect his health, and he had begun to contemplate his exit:

"Play your cards right and you might have my job some day."

"I'd love that," Gourdine said.

"Are you kidding?" Kennedy asked.

"Not at all," Gourdine said. "I don't mean tomorrow or the next day but maybe some day."[4]

Gourdine *was* serious. Over the next four years, he did everything he could to prepare himself to take over from his ailing mentor. Unlike the handful of African Americans who had put cracks in the NBA's white ceiling by moving into coaching positions, Gourdine was not a former player. Instead, he was emblematic of a rising Black professional class in the post–civil rights United States—one that was beginning to gain a foothold in the offices of corporate America through educational attainment and business savvy.

Despite Gourdine's groundbreaking success, very few Americans, Black or white, had heard of him in 1970. That began to change

Simon Gourdine, the NBA's first Black league executive, circa 1972. (Photo by NBA Photos/NBAE via Getty Images)

in 1972, when Kennedy promoted his now thirty-one-year-old protégé to be the NBA's vice president for administration. To celebrate Gourdine's achievement, *Black Sports* published a feature about the still relatively unknown attorney. As one of two vice presidents, Gourdine was in charge of all of the NBA's legal affairs. "He inspects and puts his seal of approval on everything that says more than hello and good-bye," *Black Sports* boasted.[5] Although Gourdine worked largely out of sight and in the shadow of Commissioner Kennedy, he was gregarious and dynamic: "Put me in a stadium of 20,000 people and let me make a speech. That's what makes me tick. I love to talk. The larger the crowd, the better I will perform." That confidence did not come off as cockiness. With his short Afro, black horn-rimmed glasses, and signature mustache, Gourdine was also respectable and likable. Everyone called him "Si." He was not only right at home in the NBA's headquarters but was also a family man, with a wife named Patricia and a young son named David. Like many other Black professionals of the time, he sometimes struggled to reconcile a desire for upward mobility in the still white-controlled white-collar world with a sense of racial responsibility. As he and his peers climbed the corporate ladder, they hoped to find ways to make change from within.

Gourdine had entered the NBA's executive suites amid a surge of action on the part of African American shareholders, consumers, and government officials, calling for an end to racial discrimination in some of the United States' largest corporations. In May 1970, five Black members of Congress—including Shirley Chisholm (New York), William Clay (Missouri), Charles C. Diggs Jr. (Michigan), Augustus F. Hawkins (California), and Louis Stokes (Ohio)—had criticized General Motors for its poor record of minority hiring. "For too long black men have been systematically excluded from decision-making in American corporations," their joint statement declared.[6] In response to such pressure, over the next decade, US corporations appointed Black managers and directors in record numbers, yet these numbers were relatively small. By 1972, there were still only fifty-four Black directors in *Fortune* 500 companies.[7]

In the NBA's administration, Gourdine had few Black peers. At the time, the next-highest-ranking African American in the league was former player Wayne Embry. In early March 1972, the Milwaukee Bucks had made Embry the first Black GM in North American professional sports. As Bucks GM, Embry stood to make between $27,000 and $32,000 per year. "I was sure my [white] colleagues in similar positions made more," he recounted, "but I was not going to make an issue of it."[8] He did not have to. Embry was also the owner of a highly profitable McDonald's franchise in Milwaukee and part of a new wave of Black entrepreneurs who, much like Gourdine, embraced the ethos of "Black capitalism," viewing business as an important site for Black progress.[9]

At the Bucks' press conference announcing Embry's appointment to GM, the news sent shock waves through the room. Some sportswriters ran out in search of available phones while others stayed behind to ask questions. "How does it feel to be the first black general manager in professional sports, and do you think that it is significant?" one reporter shouted. "It is significant, only if others think it is significant," Embry replied modestly. The media coverage of his achievement was widespread, with headlines from around the country calling him a pioneer. "In almost every interview I did, I was asked if I felt added pressure because of my color," Embry later noted. "I always said I did not, and I would bring up my grandparents and parents raising families when the racial climate was much more tense. That was pressure."[10]

The public response to Embry's promotion was varied. Some accused the Bucks team owner, Wes Pavalon, of appointing Embry as "window dressing in response to the civil rights movement." Pavalon tried to refute these claims by pointing to Embry's extensive pro basketball credentials and experience. Embry himself was inundated with mail, some of it laudatory but much of it rabidly racist and hateful. At the time, Embry worried that white season-ticket holders and sponsors might start abandoning the team; however, Pavalon pledged to back him even if they did. "Whenever doubt started to creep in, I would think about what Jackie Robinson or Dr. Martin Luther King had experienced," Embry recalled. "I could not allow their struggles, nor those of so many blacks, to go to waste."[11]

Although Gourdine's path to the NBA's management ranks was quite different from that of Embry, he, too, was determined to make the most of his new position as vice president of administration. Like many other Black professionals of the seventies, Gourdine's success and self-assurance belied his humble origins. Born in Jersey City on July 30, 1940, Gourdine spent his formative years on the Upper West Side of Manhattan and in the Bronx. Gourdine's father worked in a chemical plant to support him and his six siblings. "It was kind of taxing growing up, but I don't complain," Gourdine recalled. "I remember that moving to the Bronx River Projects was moving up economically, because where I had lived, I had seen my fair share of rats and roaches." From a young age, Gourdine was observant and perceptive, searching not only for a way out but for a way to help his community. He went to rough schools where he had to fight for respect, and he saw many of his peers getting swept up in the criminal-justice system. He began to think about becoming a lawyer.[12] Notwithstanding the many obstacles he faced, he gained admission to the City College of New York (CCNY) in 1958, where he majored in political science.

Gourdine was part of a new generation of college-educated African Americans, many of whom hoped to garner white-collar jobs and make racial change. The number of Black students going to college increased by 370 percent from 1960 to 1973, although they were more likely to attend public and junior (two-year) colleges and to attend part-time.[13] And Gourdine's time at CCNY was transformative, only strengthening his commitment to racial justice. As a junior, he met his hero Malcolm X at a Harlem restaurant and interviewed him for a term paper.[14] Yet over the years, he became even more convinced that legal strategies presented the best route for Black advancement. While serving as president of the City College chapter of the NAACP, he had invited noted Black civil rights lawyer Paul B. Zuber to give a talk. Gourdine felt buoyed by Zuber's speech about his experiences fighting against the segregated and inferior schools for Black children in Harlem: "He said, in effect, anytime he saw something wrong, he could file a complaint. That's all it cost to start the necessary legal steps toward changing it." But if the cost of legal change seemed relatively low, the cost of school was a constant burden for Gourdine. With other children to feed, his family had no spare funds to put toward his college expenses, so he paid for school by borrowing money through the New York State Scholar Incentive Program.[15]

After graduating from CCNY, Gourdine attended Fordham Law School, where he was one of only two Black full-time day students.[16] Money remained an ever-present issue, but relatively low tuition rates, continued access to public student loans, and the support of his wife, Patricia, who was a teacher in the Bronx, made his legal education possible. To supplement his loans, in the summers he worked as a law clerk in the office of US Attorney Robert Morgenthau, where he had his first exposure to criminal law. After Gourdine graduated, he served as an army captain in Vietnam doing investigative work and later scored a job as an assistant to US Attorney Morgenthau.[17]

Although he found the prospect of practicing criminal law exciting, Gourdine left the attorney general's office when he received an offer to work at a large private chemical company called the Celanese Corporation. "I did a lot of work on questions rising around antitrust," he remembered of his time at Celanese. "It was tough, challenging work, but I learned a lot and thoroughly enjoyed every moment."[18] His corporate law experience would later make him highly attractive to the NBA: the league faced antitrust challenges from both its players and its rival, the ABA. However, after six months at Celanese, Gourdine took a leave of absence to work for his old boss when Morgenthau sought the

Democratic nomination for governor in 1970. Although Morgenthau qualified for the primaries, he dropped out a few weeks into the race.

The campaign proved to be Gourdine's launching point into the world of sports management. While he was working for Morgenthau, a friend asked him if he would be interested in a position as the NBA's in-house counsel.[19] He jumped at the chance to submit his résumé for consideration. As Gourdine recalled, the NBA's hiring process was rather unorthodox, which likely helped him get his foot in the door. After several interviews with Commissioner Kennedy, Gourdine agreed to take the job, hoping to gain a wide range of experience that would set the foundation for future advancement within the NBA organization.

Gourdine's hiring and subsequent promotion coincided with heated public debates over affirmative action that gave rise to false narratives about Black advantage and "racial quotas" in an already depressed job market. The recently passed Equal Employment Opportunity Act of 1972, which prohibited job discrimination for reasons of race, religion, color, national origin, and sex, only added to white perceptions of African Americans' upper hand. Although affirmative action and antidiscrimination legislation did help Black Americans move up in the world, their impact tended to be exaggerated. The biggest gains for African Americans came at the lower end of the labor market, for many moved out of unskilled labor and farm work and into semi-skilled operative and clerical jobs. Even with the push for more Black managers, they still accounted for only 1.7 percent of such workers in the private sector. Most remained excluded from the highest-paying management positions, yet cries of "reverse discrimination" and calls for "colorblindness" in hiring and other aspects of American life became louder as the decade progressed.[20]

In this context, men like Gourdine became beacons of hope for African Americans eager to integrate into the professional ranks. They also represented a threat to the customary power and status of white men in corporate America. "Did being Black have any bearing in being selected over other candidates?" *Black Sports* asked Gourdine of his recent promotion. "I asked the commissioner that question once I got here, but he said they were not looking for a Black person," Gourdine replied. "He did say that 'it wouldn't be bad to have a Black person.' So it's kind of difficult to say whether they were looking principally for a Black person." On the surface, the magazine's question seemed simple enough; however, it pointed to mounting anxieties about the NBA's changing racial dynamics. Did the NBA hire Gourdine as a way to placate its majority-Black players? Was the league actually committed to increasing Black representation in the boardroom, or was it just using him as a token of supposed racial progressiveness? After all, in addition to his administrative responsibilities, Gourdine was also the league's primary liaison with the Black-led and Black-dominated NBPA. He believed that being Black *was* an advantage in his position. But the racial politics of being the lone African American voice in the NBA's headquarters remained fraught. "One would have to be conscious of the implications of hiring me to the job," he admitted.[21] On the one hand, he represented the commissioner and the league, but on the other, he was a Black man committed to racial justice.

Gourdine believed that what he achieved in the boardroom, even beyond the NBA, was linked to the fate of the wider Black community. Over the years, he had spent much of his free time helping local organizations in the Bronx. After finishing his army service, he had worked with the Morrisania Community Corporation, an antipoverty program funded through the Office of Economic Opportunity (OEO) as part of President Lyndon Johnson's Great Society. As a board member, Gourdine put his education to good use, advising on legal matters. He saw himself as more of a facilitator than a savior. "The real strength of the anti-poverty program is in the fact that it gives ordinary people a voice in what will happen in their community," he told *Black Sports*.[22] Gourdine also volunteered with the National Legal Services Program, serving four years on the board of directors, with the last two as chair. Another OEO-funded, war-on-poverty initiative with offices in the Bronx, this organization provided free legal advice and other services to the local community.

Gourdine ultimately hoped that he could use his legal skills to reshape the NBA from within. And although he emphasized that he was not simply "after the commissioner's job," it was clear that he could eventually see himself in the NBA's top spot. "I would not fool you or myself and say I wouldn't want that job if it came available," he admitted. In fact, he had a lot of optimism about the future of Black men in sports management: "This is a key time for Blacks. As professional basketball expands, there has to be more administrative jobs for Blacks." There was a lot riding on Gourdine's success as a trailblazing African American executive. "What he does will have a great bearing on the future hiring of Blacks in sports administration," *Black Sports* declared. "He knows this, and is going about his job as only we could expect from one we call—*the Man*."[23]

IN SUMMER 1973, COMMISSIONER KENNEDY DECIDED THAT HE would retire at the end of his contract in June 1975. A year later, speculations about his possible successor began to circulate with the approach of his final season. Many Black sportswriters believed that Gourdine was poised to make history as the first Black commissioner of a major US professional sports league. A high-level aide to Kennedy, Gourdine was certainly qualified for the job. The NBA also seemed ready. "Basketball, a slow starter in professional sports integration, has jumped ahead of the heap and has been setting a fast pace," the *New York Amsterdam News* noted.[24] In 1966 Boston Celtics star Bill Russell had made history when he became the first Black player-coach in the league. At the time, some white journalists had worried about the effect that his promotion would have "upon the structure of American sport."[25] Eight years later, that effect was most visible in the NBA. As vice president of NBA administration, Gourdine was part of a growing cohort of Black leaders in the league, including Lenny Wilkens (coach of the Portland Trail Blazers), Al Attles (coach of the Golden State Warriors), K. C. Jones (coach of the Washington Bullets), Ray Scott (coach of the Detroit Pistons), Bill Russell (coach and general manager of the Seattle SuperSonics), and Wayne Embry (general manager of the Milwaukee Bucks).

Despite the hopes of African American sportswriters, the NBA's all-white board of governors had other ideas. Although Gourdine made it to a short list of six candidates, by May 1974 only two finalists remained: West Coast lawyers Allen Rothenberg and Henry Steinman. A graduate of University of Michigan's law school, the thirty-five-year-old Rothenberg had learned the inner workings of the NBA through his close relationship with the Los Angeles Lakers' owner, Jack Kent Cooke. Rothenberg advised Cooke and had been his representative at NBA board meetings for the past three years. Steinman, who was forty-one, had played ball for UCLA in the early 1950s and had also served as law clerk to Chief Justice Earl Warren.[26] Neither of them were more qualified or distinguished than Gourdine, but they were both white and well connected to power players in the white basketball establishment and beyond.

The NBA's board of governors met at New York's Hotel Americana in June 1974, determined to decide on the new commissioner. The league's constitution required that a nominee win the support of fourteen out of the eighteen board members in order to be appointed. However, the governors could not seem to agree on anything. They appeared rudderless, having lost all regard for Kennedy. "I urge you," Kennedy declared, "to elect a new commissioner today and have him take office on Oct. 1, 1974." He continued: "One you respect. One you won't bad-mouth."[27]

Kennedy recommended Gourdine as his replacement. But when he left the room, the board members considered Gourdine for only a moment before returning to their bickering over Rothenberg and Steinman. After nine hours of debate and several votes, they remained hopelessly deadlocked. Having failed to accomplish their main order of business, they disbanded the meeting in dissension. "This disunity will tear us apart for months, if not for several years," one owner predicted, and another warned, "We are in a state of peril."[28] The NBA could hardly afford this type of schism at a moment when it faced legal challenges from the players and the ABA, and a brewing image crisis in the eyes of the public.

A few months later, there was renewed hope that Gourdine would eventually succeed Kennedy. When the NBA announced the election of Gourdine to the post of deputy commissioner on November 8, it made national news. The board of governors had voted unanimously in favor of Gourdine's promotion, which reportedly came with a three-year contract worth $60,000 per year, or roughly $350,000 in today's dollars.[29] He was now the highest-ranking Black executive in all of US professional sports. And if the young attorney proved he could handle the deputy job, perhaps the board would be more inclined to appoint him as commissioner.

Having so far experienced one letdown, Gourdine was cautious in his public comments. "I want to make it clear that my election as deputy commissioner does not automatically give me the position of commissioner," Gourdine told reporters. "However, I am hopeful that I will become commissioner sometime in the future. My new position gives me a forum to show my skills, and I think that I have the ability to compete for the job."[30] If he were to become commissioner, it would be based on his merit, not his skin color. In an effort to counteract any charges of Black chauvinism, he emphasized his impartiality. "I don't think being black has helped me as much as some people think it has," he told Dave Anderson of the *New York Times.* "Some people think that just because so many players and so many coaches are black, a black commissioner would be important. But the coaches and players just want you to be fair."[31] Still, Gourdine understood that his latest promotion was both historic and symbolic. His success would help show the nation that Black professionals were more than qualified to hold top-level management positions in the sports world. It had already gotten the attention of the White House. An avid basketball fan, President Gerald Ford phoned the NBA's headquarters to congratulate the new deputy commissioner.[32]

Ignoring Gourdine's own words of caution, some African American sportswriters reported that he was more or less "guaranteed" the commissioner post when Kennedy retired.[33] Sam Lacy of the *Baltimore Afro-American* argued that Gourdine's promotion proved that professional basketball was moving beyond both baseball and football "in pushing for racial progress."[34] Some Black NBA players expressed a similar optimism about Gourdine's appointment. "Pro basketball has again proven it doesn't care what color a man is as long as he can do the job," said Walt Frazier, star guard and captain of the New York Knicks.[35]

Upon closer inspection, that optimism clashed with several hard realities. When it came to the financial and administrative side of the sports business, the racial hierarchy was still alive and well in all of the major leagues. "While black athletes snatch glamour, glory and sky high salaries, the really big money remains firmly grasped in white hands," *Black Enterprise* magazine noted. "Of the 120 major league teams on the scene right now, in eight leagues in four sports, no more than five teams are known to have blacks sharing a piece of gate receipts, or who have assumed an ownership stance in a major sport franchise."[36] In the case of the NBA, all of the owners and the vast majority of the men in management positions remained white.

With the league still in the throes of the *Robertson* suit and hoping to effect a merger with the ABA, NBA team owners saw Gourdine's racial connection with the majority-Black players as a potential liability. They questioned whether an African American commissioner could help them regain control over mounting labor costs in the face of growing labor power. Back in early October, with the start of the 1974 season fast approaching, discontent had appeared to be spreading among the NBA's Black players. In Detroit, guard Dave Bing and forward Don Adams had not yet shown up to the Pistons' camp. In

Boston, Celtics guard Don Chaney had made a salary demand that General Manager Red Auerbach rejected. Instead of sticking around, Chaney had jumped to the ABA's Spirits of St. Louis. Meanwhile, in Chicago, small forward Bob Love and point guard Norman Van Lier had both decided to hold out in an attempt to renegotiate their contracts with the Bulls.[37]

Love and Van Lier argued that the Bulls' front office had broken its promises to pay them more money. Nevertheless, local fans and sportswriters sided with team owner Arthur Wirtz and GM Dick Motta, casting the Black players as greedy ingrates whose selfish actions were hurting the Bulls' chances at an NBA championship.[38] The Bulls slapped the two holdouts with indefinite suspensions and fined them 1/82nd of their salary for each game missed. By late October, Love owed almost $10,000 in accumulated penalties. Some white Chicagoans took the players' protest as a personal affront. "We fans are tired of paying the freight," one wrote. "Let these freeloaders sit out for a season, or get a job like the rest of us working stiffs."[39] How dare these highly paid Black athletes complain when real working people were footing the bill for their enormous salaries?

NBA team owners realized that they needed to get tough with the players. The racial optics were bad. With ten of the league's seventeen franchises reporting falling attendance figures and the rival ABA still cutting into its market share, the NBA could ill afford to further alienate its majority-white fan base in this time of economic recession. The biggest downswings in attendance were in some of the NBA's major cities, including Atlanta, Los Angeles, Washington, and Detroit, all places hit hard by unemployment.[40] "They're really planning to make an example of Love and Van Lier," an inside NBA source told the *Chicago Tribune*. In addition to suspending and fining the two holdouts, the league threatened to sue them for breach of contract.[41] "Fans and writers alike are considerably weary of such interminable hassles, present company included," columnist Bob Logan opined in *Basketball Weekly*.[42] As Chicago owner Wirtz held the line, Love and Van Lier eventually rejoined the team. "All the newspapermen were against me," Love later complained. "They only printed the Bulls' side of the story."[43] Wirtz's toughness had pulled the wayward Black players back in line. Could a Black commissioner do that too?

As Commissioner Kennedy's retirement date approached, Gourdine sat down with *Black Sports* magazine in spring 1975 to talk about his responsibilities and experiences as the highest-ranking Black executive in professional sports. He remained guarded yet hopeful about his prospects for attaining the top spot. "Part of the motivation in the owners selecting me was to have a safety valve," Gourdine explained. "They figured I knew a lot about the operation of the NBA and obviously I felt confident that I could run the NBA if the Commissioner were not here. However, they didn't say that I was going to wither on that vine, nor did they promise me that I was going to be elevated to Commissioner."[44] Could it be that Gourdine was chosen to be a "safety valve" in other ways? The *Robertson* suit still had yet to be settled, and the current collective-bargaining agreement with the players was soon to expire. Perhaps the team owners hoped that appointing Gourdine as deputy would help them gain more goodwill from the league's increasingly restive African American players.

Although Gourdine had a good rapport with the NBPA, as *Black Sports* noted, league commissioners were, at the end of the day, both appointed and paid by the team owners. Even if Gourdine managed to snag the NBA's top job, would he be any different from a white commissioner? Or would he simply become yet another front man for the all-white owners, doing their bidding and making decisions favorable to their interests? Gourdine disagreed with this one-sided characterization of the commissioner's role: "True, his prime responsibility is to the people who hire him. . . . [W]hile the players do not hire and cannot fire him, at the same time he certainly should make an effort to have a degree of credibility with the people who play the game."[45] In the NBA, Gourdine pointed out, the commissioner was not all-powerful; he did not have the final say in disputes between labor and management. Players could choose to take their complaints to arbitration.

Despite his own struggles to prove his worthiness to be commissioner, Gourdine retained a deep faith in the ability to bring about meaningful change through negotiation within existing institutional structures. "Other than court action, how are rules changes effected in the NBA?" *Black Sports* asked, alluding to the *Robertson* lawsuit. "It happens a number of ways and the least desirable obviously is for someone to go to court and challenge our league but that is obviously one way to change when you're directed to change," Gourdine replied. "But we think we're a little more flexible than that. We periodically amend the bylaws." Not satisfied with Gourdine's answer, *Black Sports* pressed him further: "Do the players have a part in that input?" They did, Gourdine noted, but within certain bounds: "We will listen but the final decision is made by the owners."[46] From his vantage point in the NBA's headquarters, Gourdine had much more confidence in the fairness of the owners than the players did.

It did seem as if the NBA was at least making steps to incorporate more Black executives into its administrative structure. Gourdine saw two possible reasons for the league's relative racial progressiveness. As a comparatively young league that had expanded significantly over the last decade, the NBA had attracted a different breed of investors. Caring more about the bottom line, Gourdine argued, they made decisions based on what was best for business rather than clinging to outmoded social mores. They were not the fusty traditionalists who dominated the ownership ranks of pro baseball and football: "That's why I've been happy in the NBA because I felt that if I'm good—and I'm not being naive—but if I'm good, there's a better chance of it being recognized in the NBA." Perhaps interrelated, the second reason for

the NBA's apparent enlightenment had to do with the racial dem-
ographics of the players: "All you have to do is look at the product
and the product that we sell is basketball and it's two-thirds Black."[47]
Gourdine was pointing to a recent trend in corporate America. By the
1970s, it had become more commonplace for US companies to hire
Black professionals to court the loyalty of the burgeoning African
American consumer market.[48]

But, as *Black Sports* questioned, was the NBA's Black product actually one consumed by Black fans? Although the league had yet to
conduct a more scientific survey, Gourdine claimed that anecdotal
evidence from various franchises suggested that African Americans
made up about 5–10 percent of the NBA's total audience. He further
speculated that in a market like Detroit, Black consumers formed
closer to 25–30 percent of the ticket-buying audience.[49] Gourdine
believed that attracting the entertainment dollars of the growing
Black middle class would have to form part of the league's strategy
going forward. Debuting in January 1975, the CBS television sitcom
The Jeffersons, which features the experiences of a Black dry-cleaning
entrepreneur and his family on Manhattan's Upper East Side, was a
recognition of this growing class of African Americans with disposable income to spend on entertainment. Hollywood's Blaxploitation
craze was also proving that African Americans were a significant
enough market to help revive the flagging movie business.[50] For now,
however, the NBA was still largely consumed by white spectators.

The Blackness of the league's players also made the whiteness of
the team owners all the more conspicuous. So far, only a few prominent Black men had managed to invest in NBA teams. For example, real-estate company owner Judson Robinson Jr. and entertainer
Bill Cosby had made small investments in the Houston Rockets and
San Francisco Warriors, respectively. Robinson had already sold his
$10,000 stake after the Rockets struggled to make a profit in their first
few seasons.[51] Gourdine speculated that the dearth of Black ownership in the NBA had more to do with economics than outright racism.

"It has not been discouraged by the league," he told *Black Sports*. "Unless it's our purchase price for expansion ($6 million). I think a group of Blacks possibly could come up with that kind of money but I don't know of any Black group that has made out an application."[52] African American entrepreneurs had trouble raising enough capital to become majority team owners. And even if they managed to purchase a small stake in an expansion franchise, they were less likely to weather the short-term risks, even if the long-term profits were potentially huge.

For the foreseeable future, Gourdine was on his own in the NBA's executive suites. He, like many other Black professionals of his generation, struggled with how to be a racially conscious Black man in the still white-dominated business world. He seemed caught between his desire to acknowledge his Blackness and, at the same time, remain neutral and trust the fairness of the NBA's existing rules and procedures. When talking about the prospect of becoming the league's first African American commissioner, he shied away from saying that race would be a factor in his decision-making: "I'm a Black man but I wouldn't be a Black man's commissioner. If anyone infers that I would reject all the claims of white players and accept all the claims of Black players, that's absurd. But I have a Black perspective and I guess a white man has a white perspective."[53]

Gourdine knew that all eyes were on him. Any mistake he made could easily be spun into a tale of Black men's inability to excel in leadership positions. He spoke more about this racial "burden" in subsequent interviews with Black-oriented media. Host Roscoe C. Brown interviewed him for the talk-radio show *Soul of Reason* in April 1975. The half-hour program, produced from 1971 to 1986, features interviews with Black leaders in politics, education, medicine, the arts, and sports. "Do you feel any particular pressures and/or responsibility as a Black in this particular position?" Brown asked Gourdine of his job as the NBA's deputy commissioner. "Well, I certainly do," Gourdine replied. "I recognize that we do not live in a color-blind society. So as a result, I feel very strongly that my actions might possibly affect those who might want to pursue the same interests after me."[54]

It was tough for Brown to see the fight over the reserve clause as anything other than a racial fight—one that was tied to African Americans' long-standing struggle to gain greater self-determination and mobility. But when he evoked the history of slavery, using the phrase "human chattel" to describe the players' status under the NBA's reserve system, Gourdine corrected him: "I mean, the men are not chattel to the extent that they are basketball players who are playing the game."[55] Careful semantics helped the deputy commissioner sidestep any echoes of racial slavery. He preferred to speak of trading "contracts" rather than trading "players." "The option clause that exists in the NBA protects an owner for one additional year," he added. "It's not a reserve system where a player is bound to his team in perpetuity." Although, as a Black man, he was cognizant of the option clause's racial symbolism, he still sided with the owners, repeating their well-worn defense of it. Gourdine faced an impossible situation. Try as he might to gloss over the thornier issues of race and labor in the NBA, in the eyes of the owners he was still a Black man, but from the players' perspective he could only ever be the owners' front man.

Finally, after two years of speculation and debate, the wait for Kennedy's replacement was over. At a special meeting of the NBA board of governors on Friday, April 25, the league chose its new commissioner by unanimous vote. Despite Gourdine's best efforts to prove his mettle for the job, he was passed over in favor of a white successor: ex–postmaster general and former Democratic National Committee (DNC) chair Lawrence Francis O'Brien.[56] O'Brien's appointment initially took sportswriters by surprise, for he had no background in sports, let alone basketball. When the NBA had first approached him about the position, he had turned it down. "I had never even envisioned myself in the role of sports," O'Brien confessed to Stephen Isaacs of the *Washington Post*.[57]

Yet whatever O'Brien may have lacked in basketball experience, he more than made up for with his deep political connections in Washington, DC. A native of Springfield, Massachusetts, the fifty-seven-year-old O'Brien had first gained prominence as director of John F. Kennedy's two Senate campaigns in the 1950s and his presidential campaign in 1960. After Kennedy's assassination, O'Brien served as a lead political adviser for Lyndon B. Johnson's 1964 presidential bid and then as US postmaster general from 1965 to 1968. From 1968 to 1969 and 1970 to 1973, he was chair of the DNC. (It was O'Brien's office that was burglarized by prowlers connected to President Nixon's reelection campaign, spawning the infamous Watergate scandal that led to Nixon's impeachment and resignation.) The NBA hoped that their new commissioner's clout with federal lawmakers would help the league score an antitrust exemption. Maybe O'Brien could finally get the stalled merger with the ABA back on track, on terms that were more favorable to the interests of NBA team owners.

The NBA formally announced O'Brien's appointment to commissioner at the plush 21 Club in New York City. For his Rolodex and his efforts, the gray-haired, chain-smoking O'Brien would be paid handsomely, with a three-year contract worth $150,000 per year, around $800,000 in today's dollars.[58] Though clearly disappointed that his deputy had been passed over, Kennedy insisted that there was nothing sinister about the league's decision. "You know I wanted Simon," he said during a visit to the Capital Centre in Landover, Maryland. "I know people will be inclined to make a racial issue out of it, but I feel that will be a mistake in judgment. Simon was well-qualified, but the owners felt he was too young for the job."[59] This was a flimsy defense. The previous two finalists, Rothenberg and Steinman, were not much older than Gourdine. Moreover, Pete Rozelle had been just thirty-four when he became NFL commissioner in 1960, and the ABA had recently hired a relatively inexperienced Dave DeBusschere, also thirty-four years old, as league commissioner.

Regardless of why, for Gourdine the news of O'Brien's appointment must have stung. He had already been doing much of the work to run the league—and for less than half of O'Brien's salary. As deputy commissioner, he wore many hats in the organization. He advised the commissioner on legal matters and reviewed all player contracts, recommending approval or denial. He handled arbitration and grievances and liaised with the NBPA on labor matters. He also oversaw trades, ran the NBA college draft, and handled the hardship cases.[60] Despite his best efforts on behalf of the league, he would continue to play second fiddle, serving as O'Brien's chief adviser.

Although Gourdine chose not to express any outrage publicly, Black sportswriters, ballplayers, and politicians did so for him. "That paint job still matters," Brad Pye Jr. of the *Los Angeles Sentinel* declared. "And Gourdine apparently had the wrong paint job for the positions [*sic*]."[61] For David DuPree of the *Washington Post*, one of the few African American sportswriters working for a mainstream national newspaper in the mid-1970s, the NBA's decision was "mind-boggling" and infuriatingly hypocritical. "Blacks have been told ever since Jackie Robinson made it to the Brooklyn Dodgers that hard work will be rewarded," he wrote. "That does not seem to apply if the prize is something as influential as a commissioner's job."[62] Meanwhile, Howie Evans of the *Amsterdam News* tried to put the situation in basketball terms that his New York readers would understand: "To think that Gourdine at this time, could not represent the owners in a highly professional and skillful fashion, is to say that a healthy Willis Reed would be a hindrance to the Knicks."[63] Evans warned that in hiring O'Brien, the league might now face a more recalcitrant players association.

True to form, the Black-led NBPA was quick to register its discontent. "The players are upset that Gourdine didn't get it," said Larry Fleisher, the union's general counsel. "We felt he was extremely qualified." They were upset, not just by the team owners' choice of commissioner but by the selection process itself. "Unfortunately, the owners never discussed with the players the choice of commissioner," Fleisher noted. "I would hope Mr. O'Brien has not been chosen because some of the owners thought he could help persuade Congress to pass new legislation against the interest of the players."[64] The NBPA worried about the real impetus behind O'Brien's appointment at such a critical juncture in their fight against the option clause. But they were hardly surprised. As DuPree reported, "More than just a few NBA players said they felt Gourdine was not chosen because he is black. Others said they knew he would never be chosen in the first place, because they think whites don't want to be ruled by blacks, period."[65]

By early May, New York state senator Carl McCall had also jumped into the fray. A Black political pioneer in his own right, he criticized the NBA's decision to bypass Gourdine and called for a boycott of the league by Black players and ticket buyers: "The N.B.A. became a multimillion-dollar super-agency because Black athletes, who make up the majority of the association's superstars used their talent to make money for the N.B.A. and themselves. However, when it comes around to selecting the people responsible for directing the N.B.A. the picture changes and the administration, at the highest level, remains lily white."[66] William Alverson, president of the Milwaukee Bucks and chair of the NBA's board of governors, dismissed these charges of racism: "Our league doesn't have to prove itself in our dealings with blacks. It's all on the record and a good one."[67]

Yet not much had changed in the upper echelons of league management. The all-white team owners were happy to profit on the backs of Black ballplayers, but they had little desire to stand face-to-face with Black executives in the boardroom. In an interview with *Black Sports*, civil rights leader Rev. Jesse Jackson noted that the sports industry in general was still characterized by what he called "vertical segregation": "Horizontal participation is Blacks running up and down the

ballfield. Vertical is once you move up to the coaches, general managers and sportswriters and that gets progressively white, almost lily
white." This racial division of labor funneled all the profits into white
hands and also served to reinforce long-standing white perceptions of
Black inferiority: "For white people to control the money, to control
the management and to control the image apparatus is to really have
us in slavery and limit us to the state of gladiators."[68]

Ever the diplomat, Gourdine said that he appreciated all of the
support but added that "I'm kind of put in the middle of this."[69] When
speaking with the press, he made sure to keep any bitterness or rancor
from infiltrating his voice. Although he was admittedly disappointed
that he did not get the job, he confirmed his intention to remain with
the league as O'Brien's deputy: "I'm still young. . . . Maybe next time
around it'll be my turn."[70] Gourdine's personal fight against vertical
segregation in the NBA had implications that reached far beyond the
basketball court.

ALTHOUGH GOURDINE'S INABILITY TO BREAK THE WHITE CEILING IN
sports administration cast doubt on the NBA's commitment to Black
equality, the 1975 finals seemed to mark a racial tipping point in the
league. It would be the first professional league championship series
in North America to feature two Black head coaches, Al Attles and
K. C. Jones, leading two majority-Black teams, the Golden State
Warriors and the Washington Bullets, respectively.[71]

But before the NBA Finals even got started, African American basketball fans had yet another reason to be miffed. Despite the momen-
tous nature of their achievements, both Attles and Jones were passed
over for the honor of "Coach of the Year."[72] On April 22, Kennedy, in
one of his last acts as commissioner, announced that Phil Johnson, the
white rookie head coach of the Kansas City–Omaha Kings, had won
the award. The thirty-three-year-old Johnson had finished first in the
balloting with twenty-one votes from the panel of fifty-four writers

and broadcasters (three from each NBA city). Although considered by many to be a shoo-in for the honor, Attles, who had coached Golden State to its first Pacific Division title, came in second with ten votes, and Jones finished third with only five votes. True, the Kings, under Johnson, had posted a respectable 44–38 regular season record, second best in the Midwest Division, and had qualified for the playoffs for the first time since 1967; however, even Johnson was a bit taken aback by the honor.[73] Perhaps pro basketball's press corps could not stomach giving the award to two Black coaches in a row. Detroit's Ray Scott had won the honor the previous season for leading his team to a franchise record of fifty-three victories and unprecedented game attendance at Cobo Arena (more than 300,000 spectators).[74]

In mid-May, as game 1 of the NBA Finals approached, Jones's Bullets were 3–1 favorites to win over Attles's underdog Warriors. Washington had finished the regular season atop the standings in the Central Division with an impressive 60–22 record. The team was talent-rich with star players. It also had more recent championship experience, having made it to the finals in 1971, although the Bullets lost in four straight games to the Milwaukee Bucks. The last time that Golden State had vied for the NBA title was all the way back in 1967, when they lost 4–2 to the 76ers. And this season the Warriors had barely made it to the finals. They had posted an unremarkable record of 48–34 and had been forced to come from behind to eliminate the Chicago Bulls in a grueling seven-game Western Conference semifinal series. The Warriors were a bit of a ragtag squad, and thanks to various trades and injuries, they were a virtually all-Black team. Rick Barry, the Warriors' only white player and only real superstar, headed up a Black corps of rookies and journeymen. Many doubted whether this lopsided matchup would produce an exciting championship series.[75]

Nevertheless, Black sportswriters were much more interested in discussing the significance of both teams' Black coaches. "The presence of Jones and Attles in the top jobs of the league's best teams, helps

enhance the image of the NBA," declared Sam Lacy.[76] Both Jones and
Attles had compelling rags-to-riches stories, having come from poor
backgrounds to make it big, first as professional point guards and then
as pathbreaking Black coaches in the NBA. For some African Americans they came to represent the success of racial integration, but for
others they became an argument for self-determination, one of the core
tenets of the Black Power movement. And for African Americans of
all political stripes, they proved that Black people, if given the chance,
could rise to the occasion in important leadership roles.

Jones, born in 1932, the oldest of six children, had spent his early
years moving around Texas, from Taylor, to Corpus Christi, to Dallas, to MacGregor. After separating from Jones's father, his mother,
Eula, took Jones and his siblings to San Francisco when he was nine
years old. The Bay Area was a big change from the strict segregation
of Texas, yet it was far from a racial panacea. Jones and his family lived in the predominantly Black housing projects in the Double
Rock section of San Francisco. During World War II, Eula had found
work at the nearby Hunter's Point Naval Shipyard, but after the war
ended, she lost her job and the family was forced to go on welfare. As
a teen in Double Rock, Jones spent much of his time at the local recreation center, where he not only honed his basketball moves but also
learned perseverance and how to be cool under pressure. Although he
excelled in basketball at Commerce High School, attending college
had not really entered his mind. A teacher had helped to get him an
athletic scholarship at the University of San Francisco in 1952, where
he roomed with and played alongside Bill Russell. Together, they
led the Dons to two NCAA championships and developed unique
defensive plays.[77]

Russell went directly into the NBA in 1956, whereas Jones served
two years in the army and tried out for the NFL's Los Angeles Rams
before joining the Celtics in 1958. Jones barely made the roster. The
six-foot-one guard was not a particularly great shooter—he averaged 7.4 points per game during his career—but he proved to be a

solid defensive player and playmaker. In 1967, after nine years in the league, he retired at the age of thirty-four and became head coach of the basketball team at nearby Brandeis University. After three years at Brandeis, he worked as an assistant coach at Harvard for one year. He then served as Bill Sharman's assistant coach for one season, helping lead the Los Angeles Lakers to an NBA championship in 1972. Next, the ABA's brand-new expansion team, the San Diego Conquistadors, hired him to be head coach. Although Jones brought the Conquistadors to a respectable 30–54 record and a spot in the playoffs, he left after one season because the front office had shown little faith in his abilities, constantly second-guessing and backbiting him. Then Jones got his chance to return to the NBA. When Baltimore Bullets owner Abe Pollin announced he was moving the team to Washington, the head coach, Gene Shue, quit. Pollin hired Jones to take over. By 1973, Jones appeared to have it all: a head coaching job in the NBA, a beautiful family—his wife, Beverly, and five children—and a nice home in the quiet, leafy suburb of Columbia, Maryland.[78]

Born on November 7, 1936, Newark native Attles had never really envisioned himself becoming a professional basketball player, let alone a pioneering Black coach in the NBA. "Sure, as a kid I grew to love basketball, but only as a means to an end—to get a college education," he had told *Black Sports* back in 1972. "Coaching was even further removed. . . . In those days, who could envision me being a professional coach? So it never really entered my mind."[79] Attles had been a multi-sport athlete at Weequahic High School in Newark, playing baseball, football, and basketball. Although he was good enough at football to garner a scholarship offer from Tennessee State University to play fullback, by graduation, basketball had become his real passion. Attles received only one basketball scholarship offer, from North Carolina A&T, a small Black college located in Greensboro.[80]

Attles made the most of his time at college, both on the court and in the classroom. He was named to a few all-America teams and twice made the dean's list.[81] At the time, NBA clubs did not regularly scout the talent at Black colleges. But Attles's college teammate Vince Miller had told his friend Wilt Chamberlain, then playing for the Warriors in Philadelphia, that Attles was a good prospect. In 1960 the Warriors selected Attles in the fifth round of the NBA draft, and he ended up making the cut.[82]

Despite his rather inauspicious start, Attles played eleven seasons in the NBA. Much like Jones, Attles was just six feet tall and not much of a shooter, averaging 8.9 points per game as a point guard for the Warriors. Nicknamed "The Destroyer," Attles made his mark as a fast and formidable defender, and on occasion, when the need to protect one of his teammates arose, as one of the NBA's best fighters.[83] While still a player for the Warriors, he had been serving as assistant coach when team owner Frank Mieuli fired George Lee and asked Attles to take over in January 1970. The next season, he officially took on the head coaching job.[84]

Both Jones and Attles continually downplayed the significance of race in their role as head coach. However, as Black men leading majority-Black teams, they embodied aspects of Black Power culture and politics, for they challenged many of the established norms of NBA coaching. Not too far removed from the players in age—Jones was forty-three and Attles was thirty-eight—they both epitomized a crisp and polished sense of Black masculine cool. From the sidelines, their visual presence was striking. They both sported thick, well-groomed Afros and wore the latest fashions: brightly colored leisure suits and bold, wide-collared shirts; printed sport coats with shirts and ties in coordinating patterns; and turtlenecks, leather jackets, and shaded glasses.

Defying stereotypes about African American men's inability to command respect, they carried themselves with quiet aplomb. Their low-key demeanor was all the more striking when placed against the backdrop of rising calls for a return to harsh discipline and law and order in pro basketball and beyond. Sportswriters often praised loud, irascible, and authoritarian white coaches, such as Dick Motta of the

Chicago Bulls, as examples of old-school character and leadership. They were supposedly the ones who could bring the increasingly lazy and overpaid Black players back in line.[85] But Jones and Attles took a markedly different approach to the role of head coach.

Their more egalitarian coaching styles resonated with broader shifts in Black Power politics. In the early seventies, African American leaders attempted to forge a national Black political bloc with the help of the Modern Black Convention Movement (MBCM). Through this series of mass meetings involving thousands of activists, elected officials, and everyday people, they created a more democratic process of agenda building that gave local communities a greater say in determining the issues that mattered to them most.[86] The MBCM fostered the development of Black leadership among youths and helped an increasingly diverse (in terms of region, class, political persuasion, etc.) set of African American activists figure out a collective way forward. Community control replaced charismatic leadership as the movement's organizing principle.

Jones embodied this ethos. During games, he maintained an understated presence. "On the bench, he's cool, calculating and intensely involved in the action," observed Rudy Langlais of *Black Sports*. "Seldom does he jump off the bench to protest a call."[87] Jones excelled as a coach because he understood his players. As a Black man and former pro, he could relate to their experiences and emotions. Leading them required a certain amount of psychology. "The pro mind is super sensitive; it's egotistical," Jones told Langlais. "So a pro coach has to take five egomaniacs and make them play as a totally unselfish group. It's a real job but I know it can happen because I was part of it in Boston." Red Auerbach's emphasis on teamwork certainly influenced Jones's coaching style. He was committed to mentoring his players in the nuances of the game.

Jones was not one to rant and rave from the sidelines. "He's honest in a quiet sort of way," said Bullets point guard Kevin Porter. "If K.C. pulls you out of the game, it's straightforward and honest—you know

Washington Bullets head coach K. C. Jones instructs his team during a 1975 NBA game at the Capital Centre in Landover, Maryland. (Photo by NBA Photo Library/NBAE via Getty Images)

he's pulling you because you're not helping the team; you don't have to worry about his embarrassing you and you don't have to worry about being pulled for personal reasons. That's important to an athlete."[88] Porter was not the only Bullet to praise Jones's candor and composure. "He doesn't yell or scream or curse at us," said veteran point guard Clem Haskins. "He still has the respect of everybody on this team, which is the one thing a coach must have."[89] Jones understood the value of treating his players with dignity rather than distrust and derision. "These men are professionals," he said. "If they win, fine, but if they lose, how can anybody knock them? They're trying to win as hard as they can. . . . The best thing to do is congratulate them when they win and don't say much of anything when they lose."[90] He saw himself as more of a mentor than a dictator. As head coach, his job was to help them to work together as a team and to foster their own leadership on the floor, rather than commanding their every move.[91]

This collaborative approach seemed to be common among Black coaches of the time, from Ray Scott to Lenny Wilkens.[92] Attles also believed that mutual trust and regard were paramount in the coach-player partnership. "He has no obsessive compulsion to dominate or rule his employees," *Black Sports* said of Attles's coaching style. "He is, most of the time, a portrait of studied cool on the bench, a man considered by most of his players to be a player's coach."[93] Attles concluded practices with team meetings rather than mindless pep talks. Although he allowed a certain playfulness among his squad, he still garnered their respect. A sportswriter once asked what he desired most from his players: love, fear, respect, or admiration. "Respect!" Attles replied without pause. "I don't want them to love me; I certainly don't want to frighten anybody, and they don't have to admire me. As long as they respect me, that's enough." He, in turn, gave as much respect as he demanded, vowing never to embarrass any of his players in public.[94] He did not yell and swear at them; instead, he was generous with his praise when they did well.[95] Attles believed that at the professional level, it was the players, not the coaches, who ultimately made the game. "I have a rule that I don't overcoach. . . . I try not to get involved with running plays. I think my job is getting the right team together and getting everyone into the right attitude," he told *Black Sports*.[96]

For Attles, the "right attitude" was all about fostering a sense of collective endeavor among the players. "We lose as a team, we win as a team," said Warriors center Clifford Ray. "This is the philosophy handed down from coach (Al) Attles. It's paying off when you don't have to worry about dissention and ego tripping."[97] Ironically, Attles's concept of team basketball went even further than that of the former Celtic Jones. Because of the Warriors' motley crew of rookies and journeymen, throughout the season Attles had implemented a novel strategy of "free substitution," making liberal use of his entire bench, whereas Jones had relied mostly on his top seven players. The upcoming championship series would test the two coaches' respective strategies.[98]

Because of their superior regular-season record, the Bullets held home-court advantage. On Sunday, May 18, a crowd of 19,035 fans packed the Capital Centre, located in Landover, Maryland, just a few miles outside Washington. A national television audience also tuned in to see the two teams battle it out for the NBA championship. The Bullets initially pulled out in front, leading 54–40 at the end of the first half. Hoping to get his team back on track, Attles changed the Warriors' lineup at halftime, taking out the veteran guards and replacing them with the rookies. His gamble seemed to pay off. The underdog Warriors stunned everyone with a 101–95 victory over the home team.[99]

As they headed back to the Bay Area for game 2 of the series, the Warriors were riding high on a wave of optimism. Yet their home-court advantage was compromised. Because no one had expected them to make the playoffs, let alone the NBA Finals, their regular arena, the more modern Oakland–Alameda County Coliseum, was already booked for a run of the Ice Follies, a touring figure-skating show. The NBA was not a big enough draw in 1975 to supplant the ice show. Instead, the Warriors' championship games were relegated to the franchise's previous home arena for most of the 1960s, the antiquated Cow Palace in Daly City, located on the northern edge of San Francisco. Despite these unfavorable conditions, Golden State managed to pull off a come-from-behind, 92–91 squeaker over the Bullets, jumping ahead 2–0 in the series.[100]

Game 3 was also played in the outmoded Cow Palace. Buoyed by the support of their fans, for the first time in the series Golden State pulled out in front with an early 22–14 lead. The Bullets battled back, chipping away at the Warriors' advantage. However, when the final buzzer sounded, the Warriors were victorious over the Bullets with a score of 109–101.[101]

As game 4 approached, the Bullets took stock of their situation. No team had ever dug their way out of a three-game deficit to win the NBA championship before, but the Bullets were not yet ready to give up.[102] They returned to Landover, where they hoped that a sellout crowd in their home arena would help to lift their spirits and push them to victory. It was an intense, physical game, as the Bullets fought with the ferocity of a team on the verge of being swept out of an NBA championship—for the second time. Although it was a close contest, with the lead changing hands numerous times, Golden State bested Washington by one point (96–95) to become the 1975 NBA champions.[103]

The Bullets were dejected. It was only the third four-game sweep in the twenty-six-year history of the league playoffs, the most recent being Milwaukee's rout of the Bullets in 1971. Even in defeat, Coach Jones remained a man of few words: "We tried, but they played better." When pushed for more detail, he added, "They took the middle away from our offense and we didn't adjust to that fully enough or soon enough."[104] The Washington Bullets were more like the Washington Blanks.

As Black sportswriters noted, the series still proved otherwise historic for Black coaches. "All of that talk about blacks not being able to manage men and whites not taking orders from blacks should have gone out the window with the final whistle in Landover, Md. last week," argued Rick Booker of San Francisco's *Sun Reporter*.[105] Although not much was made of it in the mainstream media, both teams had not only Black head coaches but also Black assistant coaches. Joe Roberts, a former NBA player for the old Syracuse Nationals, was Attles's second in command. Jones was also backed up by a Black assistant coach, Bernie Bickerstaff, a former player, then coach, at the University of San Diego. According to Black sports columnist Brad Pye Jr., many African American fans had been rooting for Attles's underdog Warriors to upset Jones's heavily favored Bullets all along. They reasoned that a win for Attles and his nearly all-Black Warriors would help to further explode the long-standing myth that Black men were ineffective leaders. Golden State's victory made Attles the second Black head coach in NBA history to lead his team to a league championship. The first had been former Boston Celtics player-coach Bill Russell in 1969.[106]

There was still some question about whether this nearly all-Black championship was a good sign for the future financial health of the NBA. Would white fans continue to support a league dominated by Black athletes, and with rising numbers of Black coaches and front-office staff? Booker believed that the Warriors' victory celebrations proved that Black ball could appeal to mainstream America: "If there are still some who think white youngsters can't relate to black heroes, let them look at some of the camera footage shot at San Francisco airport Sunday night. For a club with two black coaches, ten black players and two white players over 8,000 people turned out, ninety-five percent of them were white youngsters."[107] And if television ratings were any indication, white fans from across the country seemed willing to support, or at least watch, Black ball. The Warriors-Bullets finals drew a Nielsen TV rating of 10.1, nearly a full point better than the 2014 finals and better than any NBA finals between 2005 and 2009.[108]

Yet African American sportswriter Ulish Carter remained skeptical about how much of a watershed moment the series actually was. "Professional basketball is just not like it used to be. Everybody, both Blacks and whites, knows that Black folks aren't ready yet to be leaders," Carter wrote sarcastically, as if channeling a disgruntled white basketball fan. The white basketball establishment appeared intransigent to change, unwilling to even acknowledge its racism. "We all know there's no such word in sports," Carter scoffed. "Sports is the leader in racial harmony."[109]

Attles continued as head coach of the Warriors until 1983, but Jones's fortunes seemed to take a turn for the worse after the Bullets' defeat in the championship. Jones suspected that television footage of a timeout during the finals had hurt his public image and his credibility with the Bullets' management. In an effort to give its television audience a more immersive experience of the series, CBS had wired both coaches for sound to pick up their comments. At the time, sportswriters had commended both Jones and Attles for their remarkable restraint, as they refrained from cursing and verbally attacking the referees. CBS cameras had also covered both teams' huddles during their timeouts in the closing minutes.[110] During one such timeout, Jones had called the play and let Bickerstaff diagram it for the players. Coming back from commercial, the screen had cut to the Bullets' huddle, where Bickerstaff was outlining the play while Jones watched.

Although it seemed harmless enough at the time, this footage haunted Jones in the years to come. After the Bullets were eliminated in the first round of the playoffs in the following season, Jones was fired and replaced by Dick Motta. Jones was not the only Black coach to get the axe that year. Lenny Wilkens also lost his head coaching job with the Portland Trail Blazers, replaced by Jack Ramsay, a white coach formerly with the Buffalo Braves. *Black Sports* was alarmed enough to call Black coaches an "endangered species."[111] By the start of the 1976–1977 season, only two African American head coaches remained standing in the NBA: Attles at Golden State and Russell at Seattle. "If Attles and Russell don't win big this season," Ulish Carter warned, "they may be on the unemployment line."[112]

Given that Jones had the third-best coaching record in NBA history (155–91) at the time, he thought he would have no trouble finding work with another team. But he struggled to find a head coaching job. In his case, the behavior that had made him respectable as a pioneering Black coach—his quiet demeanor on the bench—had somehow transformed into a liability when his team was losing.[113] With no other prospects, in 1978 he took a post as an assistant coach with his old team, the Boston Celtics. He watched as white coaches with inferior records, including Larry Costello, Kevin Loughery, Gene Shue, and Doug Moe, were fired and then quickly rehired by other teams, some even moving into management positions.

In the meantime, Gourdine's failed bid at becoming NBA commissioner highlighted the persistence of vertical segregation in professional basketball. His promotion to deputy commissioner turned out to be his last within the organization. African Americans may have been welcome as entertainers on the court but not as white-collar professionals in the boardroom. And they remained completely shut out of the inner circle of all-white team owners. For now, the NBA's racial ceiling remained more or less intact.

Part 3
Backlash

Chapter 6

Criminal

Kermit Washington's Infamous Punch

Criminals have no rights and Kermit Washington is a criminal. . . . I don't know Kermit personally. But some guy broke the law and he belongs behind bars. If he did to me what he did to Rudy, I'd go out and get the biggest gun possible and shoot him.

—Mike Newlin, Houston Rockets
guard, *Basketball Weekly*, 1978

ON THE NIGHT OF DECEMBER 9, 1977, THE LOS ANGELES LAKERS' African American power forward Kermit Washington became the face of the league's descent into its so-called Dark Ages. As David Stern, who was then the NBA's outside counsel, recalled, "We were looked upon as a league that was too black, too violent, and too drug-involved during the late seventies."[1] In front of a packed crowd at the Los Angeles Forum, the known enforcer had punched white Houston Rockets star guard Rudy Tomjanovich with enough force to knock him out, resulting in serious injuries to his head and face.

As television footage of the incident played again and again, not just on sports shows but on news and entertainment programs (including *Saturday Night Live*), the NBA's top brass went into damage-control mode. Commissioner Larry O'Brien quickly slapped Washington with a $10,000 fine (equivalent to about $47,400 in today's dollars) and a sixty-day suspension without pay (which one journalist estimated at a $53,560 loss, equivalent to about $254,100 in today's dollars)—the harshest punishment for fighting that had ever been given in a professional sport to date.[2] Washington became a scapegoat in the league's "get-tough" approach to restoring law and order—one that seemed to parallel the efforts to punish Black crime and quell the chaos in America's deteriorating cities.

No one was more shocked by the incredible backlash than Washington. The flurry of national newspaper reports and the wide dissemination of his punch via broadcast television were quite exceptional for the time. Even in the late 1970s, most NBA games were not televised nationally. Most fans still heard about their favorite teams through their local sports pages and radio stations, and even taped highlights were somewhat rare and often delayed.[3] "We played in privacy," Washington recollected. "You'd hit somebody, maybe get fined $250 and that was it."[4]

The uproar over Washington's punch seemed to mark a turning point in professional basketball. As Black players became even more numerous and more dominant in the NBA, they came under heightened scrutiny. For the white sports media, they represented the league's imagined decline. They threatened its future. "I knew I was in a lot of trouble—not because what I did was right or wrong, but because of how it was portrayed in the newspapers," Washington later recalled. "I was on the front page everywhere. I was like Public Enemy No. 1. They kept making me taller and heavier so I would look more like a bad guy. I was the 'enforcer.'"[5] As footage of the punch played repeatedly on television, it fueled public discussions among white commentators and fans alike about the inherent violence, ungovernability, and

Los Angeles Lakers forward Kermit Washington was fined an NBA league-maximum $10,000 and suspended for sixty days by NBA commissioner Lawrence O'Brien for punching Houston's Rudy Tomjanovich at the Inglewood Forum on December 9, 1977. The picture from NBC television tape shows Tomjanovich going down at right. (Bettmann/Getty Images)

delinquency of Black ballplayers—and by extension Black America. Much like the nation as a whole, the NBA appeared to be mired in its own crisis of Black criminality.

Despite all the hype and repetition, the extant television clip of the punch provides a notably incomplete representation of the fight. The camera joins the action at center court belatedly, meaning that any reconstruction of what initially provoked the incident relies on the memories of those involved and those who witnessed it live. In the second half of the game, Washington and the Rockets' white center Kevin Kunnert had gone up for a rebound. The two ended up in a skirmish under the basket that continued as they moved to center court. Reputedly, Kunnert had elbowed and hit Washington, and Washington had punched Kunnert in response. The Lakers' star center Kareem Abdul-Jabbar had stepped in to break up the fight, and Tomjanovich had rushed back to center court to help Kunnert. Seeing Tomjanovich approaching out of the corner of his eye, Washington suddenly turned around and punched the white guard, landing a solid right hand under Tomjanovich's nose. It was an impulsive, split-second reaction. Tomjanovich was knocked out cold and landed smack on the back of his head. It took him several minutes to come to, and he was escorted off the court and into an ambulance. At the hospital, X-rays revealed that Tomjanovich had a broken nose, fractured skull and concussion, cracked eye socket, and leaking spinal fluid, and he ended up in the intensive-care unit, his season over.[6] Certainly the physical consequences of the punch were dire, but had Washington committed a crime—a deliberate assault? Was the NBA becoming a den of Black delinquency?

WITH THE APPROACH OF THE 1976–1977 SEASON, THERE HAD BEEN A sense of renewed optimism about the future of professional basketball. The civil war between the NBA and ABA was finally over. Although the leagues had been battling each other since the ABA's establishment in 1967, by 1975 the stalemate had started to unlock. With an unsympathetic judge and a trial most certainly on the horizon, in March the NBA began to consider settling the *Robertson* suit to make way for a merger. "It is no exaggeration to say that an adverse result in the case . . . threatens the very existence of the NBA," the league's outside counsel George Gallantz warned then Commissioner Walter Kennedy.[7] Later that fall, the ABA's Denver Rockets and New York Nets went rogue, attempting to jump to the NBA on their own. Both teams hoped that their dynamic Black stars—Rockets guard David "Skywalker" Thompson and Nets forward Julius "Dr. J" Erving—would make them especially attractive to the NBA. Meanwhile, CBS also dangled a $5 million television contract in front of the leagues if they could settle their differences with the players and come to an agreement about a merger.[8]

Floundering financially because of its continuing fight against the NBA, the ABA needed a merger—and quick. Although it had started out the season with ten teams, by the time of its All-Star Game on January 27, 1976, it was down to just seven, after three struggling franchises, the Baltimore Claws, the San Diego Sails, and the Utah Stars, folded.[9] There were no longer enough teams to do an East-West matchup, so the Denver Rockets played against a squad made up of the top players from the six remaining clubs. Not confident that it could fill Denver's brand-new McNichol's Sports Arena with ABA fans alone, the league booked country music stars Glen Campbell and Charlie Rich to give a two-hour pregame concert. It was a bit of an incongruous choice for a nearly all-Black league steeped in urban Black culture, but this was Denver in the late 1970s. The ABA's gamble paid off, for more than seventeen thousand spectators packed the arena. Beyond McNichol's, however, few saw the game that night because it played on only five independent TV stations in the ABA cities of Denver, San Antonio, Indianapolis, St. Louis, and Louisville.

Still, ABA officials wanted to make the most of this chance to promote the league's first-class talent. They needed more than just country singers to spice things up. That night the Slam Dunk Contest was born. This innovative marketing stunt was designed to showcase the league's exciting, high-flying style and, hopefully, help accelerate merger talks with the NBA. "We had no idea about rules or anything like that," recalled ABA public relations man Jim Bukata. "So we simply made it up as we went along."[10] During halftime, each of the five Black competitors—Artis Gilmore (Kentucky Colonels), George Gervin, Larry Kenon (both of the San Antonio Spurs), Thompson, and Erving—had two minutes to attempt five dunks. In the end, it came down to a battle between the upstart Skywalker and the already legendary Dr. J, the league's two most exceptional leapers. Thompson, who at six-foot-four was explosive and quick, with phenomenal jumping ability, put up a good fight. After missing his fourth dunk, he finished with a twisting 360-degree jam from the baseline. But Dr. J was simply magical that night. In what has become an iconic moment in basketball history, he ran from the other end of the court, his Afro blowing in the wind, and took off flying from the foul line to execute a gravity-defying dunk that helped seal his victory.[11] Yet Dr. J's iconic moment proved to be the last hurrah of the outlaw league. Less than a month later the *Robertson* suit was settled, opening the way for the long-awaited NBA-ABA merger.

The timing of the settlement in early February could not have been more opportune. The year 1976 marked the bicentennial of US independence, so it was fitting that pro ballplayers were beginning to break free from the imperious rule of the team owners. The *Robertson* settlement was part of a wider movement in professional sports, as players in the three major US professional leagues fought to remove the option or reserve clause from their contracts. Back in December 1975, the NFL had lost a battle in the courts when a Minnesota judge struck down its option compensation clause, also known as the Rozelle Rule. And in the days after the *Robertson* settlement, a federal judge in Kansas City upheld an arbitration ruling that granted free-agent status to MLB pitchers Andy Messersmith and Dave McNally, much to the chagrin of baseball's establishment.[12] Although it had once seemed like an invulnerable fortress, the old order was beginning to topple.

With legal expenses mounting—the dispute was reputedly costing the NBA more than a million dollars per year—Commissioner Larry O'Brien helped to broker a deal between the team owners and the players. The process had taken so long that Robertson himself was now retired. Another Black player, veteran forward Paul Silas of the Boston Celtics, had taken over the helm of the NBPA in 1975. Despite Robertson's absence, the settlement virtually swept away the option clause, moving the players one step closer to unrestricted free agency. Under the original rules, a team that signed a player who had played out his option had to compensate his former team. The agreement

American Basketball Association Slam Dunk Contest, the New York Nets' Julius "Dr. J" Erving (32) in action in Denver on January 27, 1976. (Photo by Carl Iwasaki/Sports Illustrated via Getty Images/Getty Images)

eliminated this mandatory compensation, replacing it with the "right of first refusal," an opportunity to match any offers from other teams.[13] But it would be a gradual emancipation, for this amendment would not take effect until 1980.

The *Robertson* settlement also changed the college draft rules, giving incoming players more choices. A drafted player could sign either a one-year contract with a one-year option or a multiyear contract with no option. Or he could refuse to sign at all, sit out a season, and then put his name back on the list of draft-eligible players the following year. If he was still unsatisfied after his second time in the draft, he could sit out another year and then become a free agent able to sell his services to the highest bidder.[14] Moreover, the owners had to pay the NBPA's legal fees and a $4.3 million cash settlement to be distributed among the players.[15] The *Los Angeles Times* called the historic settlement "a near-total victory by the players."[16]

Many fans worried that this settlement might just spell the end of pro basketball. Now players could more easily sell their talents to the highest bidder, thereby raising their salaries. This would bankrupt the team owners and raise ticket prices, some reasoned, causing the NBA to fold. Had the pendulum swung too far in the favor of the players? Black sportswriter Ulish Carter said no: "If total chaos occurs because of the [*Robertson*] agreements, it will be because of the greed of the owners trying to buy championship teams rather than drafting for it and thinking about the overall good of the league rather than their team."[17]

Unfortunately, one of the biggest losers in all of this seemed to be the very man for whom the lawsuit was named. Six days after his retirement in 1974, Oscar Robertson had signed a multiyear contract to be a color commentator on CBS—but he survived only one season before being fired. Yes, he was a rookie announcer, and it showed, but no one seemed interested in helping him improve his craft. He got the sense that the NBA was not too keen on having a Black commentator. CBS producers tried to censor him. "Whenever I criticized officials, I was told to be quiet," Robertson recalled. However, there appeared to be more at play in his firing than just his lack of training, his Blackness, and his candor. Immediately after hearing of Robertson's new gig on CBS, in September 1974, Paul Snyder, the outspoken owner of the Buffalo Braves, had sent a cautionary letter to then commissioner Walter Kennedy: "It is my opinion that Robertson is presently an adversary of the NBA and should be treated accordingly."[18] With the *Robertson* suit unresolved, Snyder was concerned about the retired player's continued visibility on NBA broadcasts.

Even after the settlement, the league still seemed to be arrayed against Robertson. Despite the fact that he was one of the greatest NBA players of all time, no team owners had yet approached him about a coaching position. "While Robertson hasn't openly sought a coaching job, you'd think someone would at least ask him," *Black Sports* complained.[19]

Although Robertson's labor fight may have hurt his future career prospects in pro basketball, thanks to the settlement the players had gained limited free agency and the two leagues were now free to consolidate. Merger negotiations had started up again at the end of May 1976, and both sides knew that time was of the essence.[20] The ABA's latest antitrust suit against the NBA would go to trial in federal court on July 1 if no progress was shown toward a merger agreement by June 18.[21]

On that very date, some five years after merger talks first began, Commissioner O'Brien announced that the NBA and ABA had finally come to an agreement, albeit one lopsided in favor of the established league. Only the four most financially stable ABA franchises—the Denver Nuggets (formerly the Rockets), Indiana Pacers, New York Nets, and San Antonio Spurs—were allowed to enter the NBA, bringing the total number of teams to twenty-two. For the privilege of joining, each team had to pay the NBA a $3.2 million fee, yet they were to receive no revenue from the NBA's national television contracts for the first three seasons. The New York Nets would also have to pay the New York Knicks $6 million over twenty years for infringing on their territory. Any remaining ABA players would become part of the NBA through a special dispersal draft.[22]

African American sportswriters took a special interest in the potential impact of the merger on pro ball and its majority-Black players. "A sad day for basketball," lamented Lester Carson of *Black Sports*. The merger had been the plan of the ABA's "corporate rulers" all along as "the only sure route to making a buck." Although Carson acknowledged that NBA fans would benefit from being able to see the likes of Erving and Thompson on a regular basis, the consolidation ultimately threatened the power of the players. "In the long run . . . it's probably not so good, especially for youngsters who someday hope to make a living in pro basketball," he warned. "Players hoping to sell their talents to the merged league will discover it's like selling something to the phone company; you do business their way, or you don't do business."[23] Carson's prediction proved true for the ABA's average players, for they were ultimately the biggest losers in the merger. Many failed to garner positions in the consolidated league, and even those who did found that their years served in the ABA would not count toward any of their future NBA benefits. At the same time, the guarantees in their ABA contracts were routinely and illegally ignored.[24]

After a drawn-out duel, the NBA had finally managed to fend off its vexing rival and regain its monopoly. But even though the ABA was no more, its imprint remained, for it had helped to foster the growing dominance of Black players and Black style in professional ball.

NOW THAT THE TEAM OWNERS WERE NO LONGER ENGAGED IN INternecine battles, they could shift their focus to regaining control over the newly merged league and turning it into the profit-making machine that they had long envisioned. Perhaps pro basketball would finally have a chance to live up to its billing as the "sport of the seventies." However, one major obstacle stood in their way. The majority-Black players, having flexed their collective power, were not so easily pushed back into silence or submission.

Hardened from years of dealing with disrespectful and inept management, NBA veteran Charles "Chet" Walker vented his grievances in the June 1976 issue of *Black Sports*. The Chicago Bulls had recently rebuffed the thirty-five-year-old forward's request for a trade, effectively forcing him out of the league. Though now a man without a team, Walker refused to go down quietly: "The Bulls took the stand that either I'd play for them or I would not play for anybody." In response, he had filed a $2 million lawsuit in January 1976, charging the Chicago Bulls with depriving him of his right to play basketball.[25] As the Bulls' former team captain and player representative, and one of the named plaintiffs in the *Robertson* suit, Walker had grown tired of Chicago's front-office chaos: "I think the biggest fault now in professional basketball is incompetency on the management level."[26] Walker had sat down repeatedly with Bulls owner Arthur Wirtz to talk about the problems he saw. But Wirtz, like most NBA team owners and general managers, underestimated the intelligence of his players and showed little regard for their opinions.

Walker's experience was indicative of the league's continued disdain for Black ballplayers and their contributions to the game. At the time of his forced retirement, he was one of the best forwards in the NBA, earning around $200,000 per year. He had been a loyal team player, performing even when injured. Yet he was ultimately disposable. "If you're a Black player—when you get a certain age, owners start playing a game with you. They play a game with you to try and keep from giving you a raise," Walker explained. "They try to convince you that you're no longer of value to the team, and that they can function without you." And after African American players retired, the white basketball establishment, from the NCAA to the NBA, had no interest in hiring more than a token few as coaches, administrators, and commentators: "There are a lot of people who complain behind closed doors, but we have players who have to bring these things out into the open, and make these people aware of what they are doing to the Black player in the sport."[27]

And there was something perhaps even more troubling than Black players' willingness to speak truth to power. They no longer seemed concerned about catering to the whims of the league's still largely white fan base. They were going to play Black ball, like it or not. NBA purists, accustomed to the more plodding, half-court style of days gone by, were particularly alarmed by what they saw as an increase in "dirty play." Was the game, now dominated by Black athletes, many of them trained on the rough and tough playground courts of African American neighborhoods, becoming too violent?

"The NBA: Where It's Legal to Mug a Fellow Worker," a *Los Angeles Times* headline declared. Sportswriter Ted Green dubbed professional basketball "the roughest game in sneakers." "The style has evolved to where just about anything goes, short of aggravated assault," he wrote. "Holding. Grabbing. Shoving. Elbowing."[28] The woes of the newly merged NBA appeared to be an omen of sorts—a disturbing microcosm of America's declining cities at a time when media reports focused on the dangers of Black youth crime. By the mid-to-late 1970s, the national panic over armed violence involving gangs had reached a fever pitch. In Detroit, reporters likened it to "urban terrorism," and in the South Bronx, the local police precinct was nicknamed "Fort Apache." And popular films such as *Precinct Thirteen* (1976) and *The Warriors* (1979) sensationalized the threat of gangs populated by vicious Black male teens.[29]

Professional basketball seemed to be straying further and further from the sport's supposedly wholesome, white roots. "It has become more of a physical, muscle game than ever," said Bill Sharman, coach of the Los Angeles Lakers. "The players are so big and so strong and so tricky, and the court is so small, that it's taken away a lot of the finesse." Moreover, the referees had lost control. "It must drive officials crazy," one NBA coach told Green, "because often they'll call a lot of fouls early, telling the players, in effect, to cut out the rough stuff. But the players keep it up and the officials have to be reluctant to keep blowing their whistles because the fans start to get restless." As the refs allowed the players to foul with relative impunity, violence became normalized on the court, and serious injuries were now more commonplace. Pro ball was apparently so rough that it no longer resembled the more staid and systematic college game—a game whose popularity was only growing. "So if players have their own rulebook in a game where emotions run high," Green surmised, "it follows that pro basketball is next to impossible to police."[30] His proposed solution? Referees needed to crack down on the majority-Black players, call more fouls, and regain control. The NBA, like America's cities, needed a healthy dose of law and order.

Although white and Black NBAers alike played this aggressive brand of basketball, over the course of the late 1970s on-court violence became increasingly perceived as a "Black problem." Worried about the league's public image in the aftermath of the merger, Commissioner O'Brien announced a crackdown. In February 1977 he sent a memo to all NBA teams: "During the last several weeks, there has been a disturbing increase in the number of league rule violations, involving unprovoked punching and other flagrant fouls, player movement from the vicinity of the bench during fights on the playing floor and abusive behavior directed at officials." It cautioned, "Any player who without provocation intentionally engages in punching or fighting or commits any form of flagrant foul, will be met with stern measures from the commissioner's office." It also prohibited any player or coach from leaving the bench during fights, expressing "excessive demonstrative behavior" upon ejection from a game, and engaging in "intentional physical contact with an official."[31] Although the commissioner's warning was posted in all NBA locker rooms, the teams seemed impervious to its message.

What was causing this apparent crisis of violence on the court? Golden State's outspoken white forward Rick Barry blamed it on a lack of fundamentals: "There are too many players in the league now who don't know how to play basketball. I'll bet . . . that if you gave a test to all the players in the league on the basic concepts of the game, 60 per cent would fail."[32] Given that 75 percent of the league's players were Black and most teams fielded starting lineups that were 80 percent Black, the racial implications of Barry's statement were clear.

Although to the average white fan it may have seemed that urban Black violence was taking over the league, some coaches and players traced its roots elsewhere. Herb Brown, coach of the Detroit Pistons, one of the most combative teams in the league, blamed the NBA's lax officiating: "They seem to allow so much hand-checking and have an inconsistent approach to how they call it. There are also a lot of people who condone banging people with forearms off the ball. . . . Many of the fights are caused by the frustration of being constantly pushed around."[33]

Others claimed that the increase in fisticuffs was a function of the merger itself. In the now-consolidated NBA, competition—for players and teams alike—was even more fierce. "A lot of teams are under pressure to be successful and [a] lot of guys are fighting for their jobs," said New York Nets assistant coach Bill Melchionni. Jim McMillian, African American forward and player representative for the New York Knicks, agreed: "With one league now, there are more pressures on the individual players."[34] Because profits came before the athletes' well-being, the NBA expected them to shoulder the brunt of its quest for greater reach and market share.

The league's increasingly grueling schedule only added more fuel to the fire. "With 22 teams, we're all over the map," noted one general manager, who wished to remain anonymous. "The players are getting wearly [sic] of the constant travel, and so are the officials."[35] So frustrated were the referees with their working conditions and the league's reticence to recognize their union that they threatened to strike with the approach of the 1977 playoffs.[36]

Regardless of these more deep-rooted concerns, the NBA pushed ahead with its clampdown on fighting. On March 7 the team owners voted to give the commissioner sweeping powers to levy large fines and place players under long suspensions.[37] Under the old rules, the commissioner could fine a player a maximum of $500 and suspend him for up to five days without pay for fighting. Under the new rules, the commissioner could fine a player up to $10,000 and suspend him indefinitely.[38] In announcing these new measures, Commissioner O'Brien used the language of crime and punishment. Noting the recent rash of fights, he maintained, "While such incidents represent a small percentage of the total of N.B.A. games they pointed [out] the need for stiffer penalties for offenders. I want the new measure to act as a deterrent to fighting."[39] Not only did the league toughen the penalties, but it also concentrated the power to punish without due process in the hands of a commissioner appointed by and beholden to the team owners, both troubling precedents in the eyes of the NBPA.[40]

The NBA was uniquely severe in its punishment of fighting. At the time, the maximum fine for fighting that the NHL and MLB could impose on a player remained $500.[41] Because of the NBA's overwhelming Blackness, front-office executives, team owners, sportswriters, and fans alike saw player violence as a real threat to the integrity of the sport and the league. Would the NBA become nothing more than a glorified Black streetball league? If so, they worried that its popularity and profitability would suffer.

In contrast, violence during NHL games had a different significance for the league's white spectators. Walter Menninger, a psychiatrist and former member of President Lyndon Johnson's National Commission on the Causes and Prevention of Violence (1968), explained the appeal of fighting in hockey: "Many of the 'silent majority' who feel frustrated, angry and helpless today can readily identify with the beleaguered, assaulted hero of the 'war on ice.' They experience a vicarious satisfaction from the open aggression and mayhem on the ice."[42] Bench-clearing brawls and the aggressive play of "goons" became a celebrated part of pro hockey, most notably with the popularity of the 1970s Philadelphia Flyers, otherwise known as the "Broad Street Bullies." NHL president John Ziegler even argued that fighting acted as a safety valve, helping to prevent "really dirty tactics like spearing, slashing, high-sticking."[43]

However, in the social and political context of the late 1970s, on-court violence involving Black professional basketball players simply could not hold the same meanings for the sport's majority-white fans. Although aggressive players in the NBA were called "enforcers" (with all of the word's criminal connotations), in hockey they were sometimes called "policemen."[44] Violence among white hockey players could somehow represent law and order, but among African American ballplayers it came to symbolize the growing ungovernability of Black communities and the need for greater discipline and punishment in the post–civil rights era.

Despite the NBA's attempt to curb fighting, altercations continued, and over the course of the 1976–1977 season there were forty-one fights that led to the ejection of at least one player.[45] One of the most notorious scuffles happened during game 2 of the 1977 NBA Finals, in front of a capacity crowd of 18,276 fans at the Philadelphia Spectrum and 40 million television viewers at home. It was the highest-rated NBA Finals to date.[46] The fourth-quarter clash between two Black players, 76ers center Darryl Dawkins and Portland Trail Blazers power forward Maurice Lucas, had spun out into a chaotic free-for-all. They had squared off at mid-court after the six-foot-eleven, 260-pound Dawkins had tried to punch Lucas's white teammate, the wiry six-foot-six forward Bob Gross. This spectacle of Black violence, what one sportswriter called "a savage brawl that almost became a riot," was hardly what the NBA needed at such a critical point in its rebuilding phase.[47]

From the opening tip-off, it was a rough game. Dawkins made his presence felt in the middle, clogging up the lane and neutralizing the Trail Blazers' white star, center Bill Walton. Frustrated and hoping to knock the 76ers off their rhythm, the Blazers responded with physical play, but with 4:52 remaining, Philadelphia retained a comfortable 96–76 lead.[48]

Then all hell broke loose. Gross and Dawkins fell to the ground as they fought for a rebound from a shot by the Blazers' Herm Gilliam. Dawkins ripped the ball away from Gross, and both players jumped to their feet, trading obscenities.[49]

Portland coach Jack Ramsey ran onto the court to confront Dawkins while Philadelphia guard Doug Collins tried to hold back Gross. Dawkins charged at Gross and threw a wild, looping punch that glanced off of Gross and hit Collins in the eye. (Collins ended up with four stitches to close up the cut.) As Dawkins backed away, Lucas ran up from behind and punched him in the back of the neck. Dawkins lost his footing, but he got back up and squared off against Lucas at mid-court. "They danced and head-faked as if in a boxing ring," wrote Dave DuPree of the *Washington Post*.[50]

Both benches emptied as the teams tried to hold back the two combatants. Even Fitz Eugene Dixon Jr., the 76ers' owner, and Dawkins's brother Mitch jumped out of their seats and ran into the fray.[51] Only Lucas managed to land a punch before he and Dawkins were finally pulled apart. Lucas was no slouch. He had come to Portland from the ABA "with a street-fighter's reputation."[52] The fisticuffs helped to seal his notoriety as a pugnacious player, nicknamed "The Enforcer."

Meanwhile, about a hundred 76ers fans had flooded the court, getting into skirmishes with Portland players and coaches. Security guards and police went about breaking up fights and pushing fans off the floor. In the end, however, only Dawkins and Lucas were ejected from the game. Back in the locker room, an enraged Dawkins continued on a tear, ripping a toilet out of its moorings, causing water to gush out of the hole in the floor. In spite of all of the commotion, Philadelphia still managed to breeze past Portland 107–89 to gain a 2–0 lead in the championship series.[53]

The very next day NBA commissioner O'Brien announced that he was fining Dawkins and Lucas $2,500 each—an unprecedented amount—for their part in the free-for-all. "Your conduct could have resulted in a serious injury to another player and it created the potential for a violent crowd reaction that might have led to a serious injury to innocent spectators," O'Brien chastised the two players in a telegram. "You are hereby informed that any similar action on your part during the remainder of the series will be dealt with even more severely."[54] Despite the size of the melee, Dawkins and Lucas were to shoulder all of the blame.

Fans likely saw this stiff punishment as necessary, if not fair. By the time of the fight, Dawkins was known for being raw, rough, and immature, in part because he was the first high school player drafted directly into the NBA, in 1975. The ABA had led the way in 1974, drafting the gangly, six-foot-ten, 215-pound Moses Malone out of Petersburg High School in Virginia. The first player in nearly thirty years to be drafted into the pros directly out of high school, Malone had inked a multiyear deal worth a reputed $3 million with the Utah Stars. He had been enticed to sign with the Stars just days before he was scheduled to start his freshman year at the University of Maryland, and not without cause. He grew up in a ramshackle home in Petersburg, raised by his single mother, Mary, a supermarket packer by day and nurse's aide by night.[55] Nevertheless, many decried his signing as a bad omen for basketball.[56]

A year later, fans and sportswriters saw Dawkins's premature entry into the NBA as a harbinger of the more-established league's decline. "How low will the pros go in their quest for talent?" scoffed Rob Sieb of *Basketball Weekly*. "If a college degree is superfluous, then might not a high school diploma also be considered unnecessary?"[57] It seemed as if the NBA was in a race to the bottom in its talent war with the ABA. As scouts scoured high school gyms and playground courts for athletic African American youngsters, professional basketball was moving further and further away from being a white college men's game.

The 76ers drafted Dawkins in the first round out of Maynard Evans High School in Orlando. He was one of two high schoolers and eighteen college players on the NBA's hardship list in 1975.[58] Though still a teenager, Dawkins already had the size to turn pro. He was also an aggressive, physical player who could shoot, slam-dunk, block shots, and make rebounds. Hundreds of college recruiters had tried to woo him over the years. "I was offered a car (a Cadillac)," Dawkins told the *Chicago Defender.* "I was offered money, $60 a week. Then $150 a week. One of them even offered me a new outfit (street clothes) every game."[59] In spite of these overtures, Dawkins decided to turn pro: "I've got a family to support, there are six of us."[60] The high school star lived with his mother, Harriet, and four siblings in Orlando's Ivey Lane housing projects.[61] Basketball was their ticket out of poverty. Faced with the prospect of an impending NBA-ABA merger in the middle of a deepening economic recession, Dawkins and other young Black players worried about losing millions of dollars if they delayed entering the draft.[62]

The 76ers announced the signing of Dawkins on May 29, 1975. His first multiyear contract, at the tender age of eighteen, was worth a reported $1 million (in 1975 the median annual household income in the United States was $13,720).[63] Wearing a white suit and black velvet bow tie at the news conference, the newest 76er said that his first priority was to get his mom out of the projects and buy her a nice home.[64] Despite Dawkins's best efforts to improve his family's circumstances, white sportswriters cast him as an undeserving boy who had been given too much too soon. And they nicknamed him "Baby Gorilla," conjuring up a long history of anti-Black stereotypes.[65]

By the 1977 NBA Finals, the now sophomore center was regularly ridiculed in the press. Curry Kirkpatrick of *Sports Illustrated* mockingly portrayed Dawkins as a savage animal "roaming unchained," whose only job was to "get the colors on the uniforms right" and "take names and blast bodies."[66] Ted Green of the *Los Angeles Times* was equally derisive of the "20-year-old boy in a he-man's body." "When he isn't out with the ladies or trying on another outrageous outfit or pretending he's a disc jockey or dunking like his teammate, Julius Erving," Green joked, "Dawkins probably will be in his Cadillac, rollin' down Highway 295, playing with his favorite toy, a CB radio."[67] Rather than strike back, Dawkins poked fun at and played into this image. His eccentric yet warm and outspoken personality had made him one of the most popular athletes in Philadelphia.

It did not help that many fans and commentators also envisioned the championship series as a racial battle. The Trail Blazers, an expansion team based in Portland, a small majority-white city in the Pacific Northwest, squared off against the legendary 76ers, located in the northeastern city of Philadelphia, with its large African American community. Which would be basketball's future? The series was a contest between white (Bill Walton and the Trail Blazers) and Black (Julius "Dr. J" Erving and the 76ers) basketball styles—one that emphasized "Blazer calculation vs. 76er creativity" and "Portland discipline vs. Philly anarchy."[68] "Can the Doctor and his often disorganized staff known as the Philadelphia 76ers do in the Mountain Man, or will Portland and the Family Trail Blazers once again prove that a good team can beat five good individuals?" asked sportswriter David DuPree. Referencing the popular television show *The Waltons*, a nostalgic tribute to hardworking, family-oriented rural white America in the 1930s and 1940s, DuPree characterized the NBA Finals as a "classic matchup of team versus individual."[69]

Others took the disparaging metaphors even further. Kirkpatrick of *Sports Illustrated* noted that the 76ers' Black stars had a reputation for being "wealthy, spoiled, egocentric, selfish monsters." He and other white sportswriters described their practices as chaotic, with players sneaking cigarettes, playing with teammates' children, reading newspapers, and horsing around.[70] Although Portland had "orderly, disciplined workouts," Philly's training sessions were "a coach's nightmare."[71] These derogatory depictions of the 76ers were hardly unique: white sportswriters of the time tended to characterize African American players as childish, lazy, and overpaid. Green of the *Los Angeles Times* even described the 76ers as the "world's most colorful zillion-dollar playground team," in contrast to the "unselfish, high-on-basketball Portland Trail Blazers."[72] The Trail Blazers represented wholesome white morality, whereas the 76ers embodied urban Black pathology.

The white-dominated sports media, not surprisingly, saw the Dawkins-Lucas fight through the lens of racialized images of civil unrest and Black male criminality. CBS sportscaster Brent Musburger had feared that "a full-scale riot was going to break out."[73] In what was supposed to be the ultimate advertisement for the newly merged NBA, on prime-time national TV, this display of Black violence threatened the league's ongoing attempt to connect with and grow its majority-white fan base.

Thankfully, from the NBA's perspective at least, the Trail Blazers emerged victorious in the end. Buoyed by the "Blazermania" of the noisy, capacity crowds at Portland's Memorial Coliseum, Walton and company turned things around.[74] They clawed their way back from a two-game deficit, winning the next four games to take the series 4–2.[75] Though shaky at first, Walton gained momentum and won the finals' MVP. Given his counterculture style, progressive politics, and numerous injuries, Walton was hardly an ideal White Hope for the league. However, his victory seemed to prove that a white center could still be triumphant in a Black game.[76]

DESPITE THE NBA'S EFFORTS TO ELIMINATE FIGHTING, ON OCTOBER 18, the opening night of the 1977–1978 season, the Los Angeles Lakers' star Black center Kareem Abdul-Jabbar exchanged blows with the Milwaukee Bucks' white rookie center Kent Benson. The two players had been jockeying for position in the opening minutes of the game when Benson elbowed Jabbar in the midsection. Jabbar doubled over in pain and then a few seconds later wheeled around and hit Benson in the face, dropping him to the floor. Jabbar broke his right hand, and Benson suffered a mild concussion and two-stitch cut over his blackened right eye. This incident only added to the Laker star's notoriety as "basketball's big, black villain," for TV news reports painted him as the aggressor.[77] Although usually aloof on the court, he was known for having a volatile temper. He had been ejected from a game for throwing a ball at a referee, he had been fined several times for making derogatory comments about officials, and three years earlier he had broken his hand when he punched a backboard support after getting a finger in the eye. But Jabbar claimed that he was justified in his anger. Because of his size, referees routinely allowed other players to foul him with impunity.[78]

In response to the fight, Commissioner O'Brien released a statement: "Conduct of this nature will not be tolerated and will be punished accordingly. Every player in the N.B.A. is on notice that I oppose fighting during games, no matter what the provocation." Even though O'Brien acknowledged that Benson had instigated the fight by elbowing Jabbar, he maintained that "unfortunately, the violation took place far from the ball and game action, and therefore escaped detection by the referees. . . . Whether or not Abdul-Jabbar was fouled, however, there is no excuse for a premeditated punch from the side."[79] Commissioner O'Brien fined the Black star $5,000, the largest amount in the league's history to date. Because Jabbar's broken hand meant that he would be out for six weeks, O'Brien chose not to slap him with an additional unpaid suspension, perhaps a measure of leniency in recognition of the dominant center's importance to the league.[80] Nevertheless, Jabbar was so incensed about being singled out, with Benson receiving no punishment, that he requested a face-to-face meeting with O'Brien a few weeks later to complain about the league's obvious "double standard." Dismayed that the referees failed to protect him from cheap shots in the paint, he vowed to "take care of himself in his own way."[81]

Although the NBA outwardly maintained a punitive stance toward fighting, some believed that O'Brien and the club owners were not actually all that committed to ending on-court violence. Jack Scott, the white sports activist and author of *The Athletic Revolution* (1971), argued that they were more concerned about profits and victories than about player safety: "Violence . . . seems to contribute to crowd appeal. The men in authority don't seem prepared to take steps that could immediately eliminate violence." The league appeared to be playing both sides, in other words—they would tolerate some violence to draw in fans yet also punish the players involved, especially Black players, to demonstrate their control over the game. Scott even argued that some club owners were actively fomenting fights. "I talked to one player on a team in the NBA playoffs," he told the *Chicago Tribune*. "In a playoff game, he got into a big fight. He took out the star player on the other team—KOd the other guy. And his owner said to him, 'I'll give you a thousand bucks if you do that again.'"[82] Black players were just doing what they had to do in the increasingly dog-eat-dog NBA.

A few weeks after the clash between Jabbar and Benson, *Sports Illustrated* sought to capitalize on the uproar over fighting in the league by making a feature on "enforcers" the centerpiece of their NBA preview issue. None other than Maurice Lucas graced the cover. Of the six players featured—Lucas, Bob Lanier, Calvin Murphy, Kermit Washington, Darryl Dawkins, and Dennis Awtrey—only Awtrey was white. (Awtrey's sole claim to fame was having once slugged Jabbar in the jaw.[83]) Although the story's visual imagery was rife with anti-Black stereotypes, white sportswriter John Papanek presented a surprisingly nuanced take on the league's "top enforcers." He claimed that bench-clearing brawls were not actually commonplace in the league and that enforcers rarely had to fight: "Sometimes a glance is all it takes, sometimes a word or two, sometimes an elbow or an extra-hard pick." The coaches he spoke to admitted that their teams relied on the presence of enforcers to "keep order," and he argued that the refinement of the professional game over the past decade meant that most enforcers were "also highly skilled finesse players." Papanek noted that this was not the case with enforcers from the NBA's "Golden Age" of the 1950s and early 1960s: "In those days, enforcers were more crudely known as 'hatchet men.'"[84] There were plenty of fights, but the typical punishments of the era were much more lenient, ranging from ejection from the game to a small fine.

Photographer Harry Benson's accompanying "portfolio of the NBA's Most Wanted Enforcers" told a much different story, playing on popular associations between African American men, anger, physicality, violence, hypersexuality, and criminality.[85] Although these anti-Black images embodied contemporary discourses of Black masculinity in the midst of racial integration and the so-called urban crisis, they also echoed historical constructions stretching back to slavery and reconstruction, such as the dandified zip coon, the animalistic Black brute, and the lecherous Black buck. Shot from below to accentuate his height, Lucas's full-page photo references urban violence and decay. "He plays even meaner than he looks in a Portland alley," the caption declares. Lucas stands defiantly, arms crossed, chin up, and looking down at the camera. Garbed in a patchwork denim suit, his imposing body fills the narrow, littered space between two derelict buildings. On the opposite page, the portrait of veteran Detroit Piston Lanier evokes two Black male archetypes: the jungle savage and the urban pimp. As the caption jokes, "Lanier has been intimidating big cats for seven years." Holding a basketball while wearing a black fedora at a rakish angle and a cream-colored trench with a raised collar, Lanier stares intently into the camera. He stands in front of two caged tigers in what appears to be an abandoned industrial space.

The next three photos emphasize the intimidating physical power and dominant sexuality of Murphy and Washington. Shown from both the front and back, the Houston Rockets' five-foot-nine guard Murphy grimaces as he flexes his chiseled upper body. Beside Murphy, a shirtless Washington looks back over his muscular shoulder, glaring at the camera. Similarly, Dawkins's portrait epitomizes the archetypal angry Black inner-city youth. In a full-page close-up, he sports his Sixers jersey, gold jewelry, and a sullen expression. Given the pictorial's visual narrative of threatening Black masculinity, the photo of the Phoenix Suns' white center Awtrey seems entirely out of place. Wearing a Phoenix tank top, Awtrey is submerged in shallow water, his eyes nearly closed, and his face and body obscured by shadows and refracted light.

Knowing that the special issue could negatively affect his public image, Washington had hesitated to participate, let alone pose for a photo, but eventually agreed to at the behest of the Lakers' top brass. "They pay my salary, so I did what they said," he told Paul Attner of the *Washington Post*. "But I know people will get the wrong impression. I'm not like that at all."[86] During the photo shoot Washington had at first refused to give a "mean look," even though the photographer, Benson, had pleaded with him to do so. He ended up complying with Benson's request, and the shot of him glowering at the camera is the one that appeared in the magazine.[87] But Washington challenged his violent reputation. "I'm not a policeman," he told Papanek. "I'm not a fighter. I'm just trying to make a living for myself and my family. If I think someone is going to be taking food off my table away from my family, I get mean. . . . They will push you around if you can be pushed around." He was a solid but not star forward trying to maintain his position and ensure his livelihood in an increasingly skilled and competitive league: "Some of us don't have the talent of the Dr. J's and the Kareem Abdul-Jabbars, so we have to do our jobs the best way we can. I'm just an aggressive guy trying to survive."[88] He may not have had the skill of Jabbar, but he understood that it was his job to protect the Lakers' marquee player.

Notwithstanding his enforcer role, Washington was by no means a violent brute. Before his rise to more prominence in the NBA, he was the kind of prototypical "safe Black man" whom the white basketball establishment celebrated. A native of Washington, DC, he overcame a troubled childhood to earn a basketball scholarship at the predominantly white American University in 1969. He was a hardworking student and athlete who adjusted well to life at AU and was popular on campus. Washington emerged as a star player in college—one of

the few to average 20 points and 20 rebounds per game during his career at AU. He was also a two-time Academic All-American.[89] In the
1973 NBA draft he was the fifth pick overall for the Lakers, but after
riding the bench for his first few seasons, Washington hit the weight
room, training hard and bulking up. This strategy paid off, and he
earned a coveted starting position. However, the events of December
9 changed the trajectory of his career. Even his clean-cut image off the
court could not save him from vilification in the media.

Just four days before Washington's infamous punch, the
NBA's new committee on violence convened its first meeting as part of
Commissioner O'Brien's continued crusade against fighting. O'Brien
instructed the committee to "review rules, procedures and conduct of
the game to determine what the root causes of this (violent) nature
might ultimately be."[90] O'Brien's framing of the problem in terms of
"root causes" seemed promising. It hearkened back to an earlier moment in Democratic politics, when President Lyndon Johnson formed
the Kerner Commission to study the underlying conditions that had
led to a wave of urban uprisings in the late 1960s. Rather than blaming Black criminality, the resulting report cited persistent poverty and
institutional racism as the key forces behind the unrest.[91] O'Brien's
words revealed both his long history as a Democratic operative and
the growing power of the NBPA.

Given the NBPA's clout, the commissioner had to walk the line
between appeasing team officials, placating NBA fans, and seeking
input from the players. Consequently, the committee was fairly representative of the league's racial makeup and its various constituencies,
including Black deputy commissioner Simon Gourdine, coaches, and
players. The committee later approved three recommendations, calling on the NBA to implement a program for training better officials,
to add a third official on the floor, and to institute a new rule against
unnecessary fouls such as elbowing, tripping, and tackling.[92]

The NBPA overwhelmingly supported the addition of a third official as a possible solution to the uptick in fighting. But the team owners rejected this measure because the estimated cost would cut into their annual profits.[93] "The players are getting bigger, better and stronger, and if that is happening, then the officiating has to be upgraded," committee member Earl Monroe told Baltimore sportswriter Seymour Smith. Detroit pivotman Lanier agreed: "If there were three officials, and the third had more responsibility than just watching the lines, it would keep guys from unnecessarily abusing each other. . . . Flagrant things just do not happen. They build up."[94] Both the NFL and MLB had added officials to improve the game experience; it was time for the NBA to follow suit.

Any changes would come too late to help Washington out of his bind. When Commissioner O'Brien notified the disgraced Black player of his $10,000 fine and sixty-day, unpaid suspension, he had little recourse to challenge the ruling. Washington was left to fend for himself. "No hearing, no appeal, no grievances," he later recalled. "If the Lakers could have dropped me off at the end of the earth, they would have." At the time, Washington had been keenly aware of the fight's racial optics: "Let's be realistic, the NBA was worried about the image of the black athlete. . . . They thought they were doing what was best for the league, so they were willing to sacrifice me. . . . People threw things at me, they cursed me. And the league didn't care. I knew that."[95] He recognized that he had become not only a convenient scapegoat in the NBA's crackdown on fighting but also the violent Black bogeyman of white basketball fans' imaginations.

Adding fuel to the fiery opposition against Washington, Tomjanovich was one of a shrinking number of white players in the Black-dominated NBA—a White Hope on the court whose life story resonated with the league's majority-white fan base. Although he was not a household name like other prominent white players of the era, such as Bill Walton and Pete Maravich, Tomjanovich was a working-class everyman of sorts—a player on the margins of celebrity known for his diligence and strong basketball fundamentals.[96] Of Croatian descent, he had a hardscrabble childhood in Hamtramck, Michigan, a blue-collar town that bordered on Detroit. His alcoholic father, Rudy Sr., was in and out of his life. The elder Rudy worked as a shoemaker and a garbage collector, but he also experienced stretches of unemployment that forced the family to go on welfare. Despite these obstacles, Tomjanovich had managed to make his way out of Hamtramck to play basketball for the University of Michigan in the late 1960s, and at the time of the fight, he was the Houston Rockets' top scorer.[97] He was a quintessential white bootstraps success story, an emblem of the silent majority who had been unjustly attacked by a vicious Black adversary. Whether through the story of Tomjanovich or that of the fictional Rocky Balboa of the silver screen, white men increasingly embraced an "underdog" status.[98]

Most mainstream sportswriters sensationalized the fight, calling it a "basketball bloodbath," a "violent brawl," a "spectacular fight," and an "assault."[99] Still shots from the television footage of the punch— showing Washington's swing or Tomjanovich lying on the court— accompanied articles on the incident. Descriptions of the fight tended to cast Washington as a criminal and the white players Kunnert and Tomjanovich as his blameless victims. They described Kunnert as a "skinny" center (even though he was seven feet tall and 230 pounds) who was just trying to pull free when he accidentally elbowed Washington. They also characterized Tomjanovich as a "mild-mannered" peacemaker and team player who was simply trying to help his "fallen team-mate."[100] Comments from Houston Rockets coach Tom Nissalke supported this narrative of white victimization. "It was the most malicious thing I've ever seen in basketball," he told reporters. "It was a sucker punch."[101]

Footage of Washington's punch also played repeatedly on broadcast television. Black sportswriter Clayton Riley observed that none of the action that precipitated the punch made the cut in the endless TV replays of the fight: "The Kunnert phase of things wasn't shown, but over and over again we saw Tomjanovich getting wasted in his role of peacemaker."[102] Earl Gustkey of the *Los Angeles Times* even went so far as to blame the harshness of the penalty on "the magnifying effect of repeated TV replays."[103]

The unprecedented severity of the NBA's punishment of Washington became a central part of this unfolding morality tale of Black criminality and white innocence. In a statement released to the press, Commissioner O'Brien announced, "The suspension will keep Washington out at least 26 games. It is the longest in memory and the fine is the highest provided for by the rules of the NBA."[104] In a piece on the history of punishment in professional sport, Sam Goldaper of the *New York Times* noted that Washington's ranked among the harshest. Penalties of similar severity were usually reserved for players who gambled on games, or teams and players caught using performance-enhancing drugs. Before Washington, the highest penalty ever levied for fighting was Jabbar's $5,000 fine in October 1977.[105] Writing to the *Los Angeles Times*, some fans (presumably Lakers fans) expressed their support for O'Brien's strict sanctioning of Washington. One fan from Gardena, California, declared that "Kermit Washington got what he deserved from NBA commissioner O'Brien. In fact, he's lucky he wasn't banned for life," and another from Torrance maintained that "it was a flagrant crime."[106] In taking a punitive posture, O'Brien tried to reassure the NBA's majority-white fan base that the league would restore order and make basketball great again.

Tomjanovich's struggle to recover also became an important chapter in this story of white suffering in the face of Black violence. With his face swollen and his jaw wired shut, Tomjanovich was unable to speak publicly in the month after the fight; however, national newspapers regularly reported on the severity of his injuries and the progress of his treatment.[107] Eight days after being admitted to Centinela Hospital Medical Center in Los Angeles, Tomjanovich underwent surgery to repair his battered face. During the three-hour operation, doctors placed his upper jaw back into proper alignment with his lower jaw and wired them shut.[108] Although successful, this procedure was just the first of many. By late December, Tomjanovich was stable enough to return home to spend Christmas with his family in Houston.[109]

Faced with all of this negative publicity about his supposed criminality, Washington tried his best to convey his side of the story through the press. He expressed his remorse to reporters, arguing that he had not punched Tomjanovich intentionally. He merely reacted to seeing the Rockets' forward running toward him out of the corner of his eye: "It was an honest, unfortunate mistake."[110]

Washington was sleepless, wracked with anxiety about how the negative publicity would impact his future. "This is terrible for my image. What if I want to get a job when I'm out of basketball?" Washington asked. "[O'Brien] doesn't know me as a person: he doesn't see me for what I really am." The league and the public saw him only as a bully. Searching for a bright side to his situation, he joked, "At least, the people who always ask me for money won't anymore. I won't have any."[111] Although Washington felt abandoned, some of his friends came to his defense, characterizing him as a "gentle giant." A publicist who knew him from his college days said that he was the epitome of the "American Dream," without a "malicious bone in his body." Washington's supporters feared that he would be unfairly "cast in an image for the rest of his pro career that [was] completely opposite to his true personality."[112]

Black newspapers tended to present a more sympathetic portrait of Washington and question mainstream interpretations of the incident. The *Black Panther* (the official newspaper of the Black Panther Party) called Washington's punishment "blatantly racist." In the case of both Washington's and Jabbar's fights, the Black players were the only ones to receive disciplinary action, "while their White adversaries were regarded as martyrs."[113] Their plight mirrored the punitive treatment of Black men in the larger US criminal-justice system.

Rather than interviewing NBA officials, Thomas Giles of the African American *Bay State Banner* turned to Black players for their point of view. "This was a tragic and regrettable incident, but it wasn't a fight," Wes Unseld of the Washington Bullets argued. "The NBA has created a monster out of fighting. Now, let them live with it." Likewise, Celtics guard Don Chaney attested, "Anybody who knows Washington knows that he's not the type who goes out looking for fights. He's not a villain, but they want to write about it, and they want to talk about it on TV, and there's nothing you can do about it."[114] Washington did not deserve to be the NBA's scapegoat.

Yet the demonization and punishment of Washington was not simply about eradicating on-court violence; it was an attack on the changing racial makeup of the league. "If Kareem Abdul-Jabbar and Kermit Washington were playing in the National Hockey League—and they were white—there would be little fuss made about their fisticuffs," Carl Nesfield of the *New York Amsterdam News* contended. League executives and the media were exaggerating the extent of fighting in the NBA, he wrote: "The hue and cry about violence makes one think it's a race riot. And maybe that's the point."[115] The campaign against violence was working to discredit the rising influence of African American players and coaches in the league. Nesfield's colleague, Howie Evans, went one step further, arguing that the scapegoating of Washington shone a spotlight on the racial double standard at the heart of the US justice system:

> You know, to be Black in this world is a bitch. Our dramas so often end in tragedy or in the case of [Kareem] Abdul[-Jabbar] and Kermit, misjustice. . . . How in the world can anyone in this country justify Kermit Washington being suspended from his chosen employment and fined all of that money. [John] Dean, [Richard] Nixon, [H. R.] Haldeman, [John] Mitchell and all the rest, took this country to task with their Gestapo-like tactics and inner-espionage activities, and yet, they are given the red-carpet treatment.[116]

The Black-dominated NBPA understood that this maligning of Washington threatened its reputation and had real implications for its leverage as a labor union. NBA executives and team owners had already publicly disparaged the NBPA in its fight for higher compensation and free agency; now they were painting its members as violent criminals.

Many veteran players continued to challenge the very premise that violence in the league was at "crisis" levels. Black NBPA president Paul Silas claimed that the game was actually rougher when he first came into the league in 1964. "We had whole teams going at it then," he recalled, and the referees allowed more contact under the boards. Silas saw no clear or easy solution to the problem of violence in professional basketball: "It's a physical game and tempers are going to flare." Even though both Jabbar and Washington had mixed it up with white players in recent months, Silas denied that NBA fights were "racially motivated."[117] Black players were not bent on attacking white players. Physical contact was just part of the game.

Carey McWilliams of the left-leaning *Nation* magazine was one of the few white journalists to offer a structural critique of Washington's punch and its punishment. Rather than treating the fight as a sign of Washington's personal failure or inherent pathology, he viewed it as part of the broader societal shift toward hyperindividualism, privatization, and the worship of free-market capitalism: "Individual incentives have become detached from social incentives. The violence is 'structural': it is enjoyed by fans, encouraged by the media, and implicit in player-management relations." To punish Washington would not solve the problem: "If Commissioner O'Brien is to bring a little order into the 'sport' of professional basketball, he will need the wisdom of Solomon; for it is, indeed, the entire value system that is out of kilter."[118] For McWilliams, the punch was merely symptomatic of the ruthless system of values taking over the nation in the 1970s—the same neoliberal economic system that had produced urban violence, the attack on organized labor, and increasing wealth inequality.

Regardless of the various efforts to contextualize the fight in terms of its racial and political significance, Rockets fans were outraged at Washington's assault on their star forward. Reporting from Houston on December 14, Nicholas Chriss of the *Los Angeles Times* noted that emotions were "running so high against Washington and the Lakers" that in preparation for the Rockets-Lakers rematch later that evening, the Rockets' management had flooded the local media with messages requesting that fans remain calm.[119] To ensure that no violence broke out in the stands, Houston had forty-one security employees on hand at the game—double the usual number—and six policemen guarding the Lakers' bench. Despite these fears of fan unrest, there was no violence in the stands that night—only booing.[120]

Throughout his suspension, Washington continued to face the re-verberations of his punch. As he told Steve Cady of the *New York Times*, "I never want to go through what I'm going through now again. It's unbearable."[121] Every day he received hate mail and crank calls at his home in Palos Verdes, an affluent Los Angeles suburb. Hundreds of obscene letters arrived filled with racial slurs, death threats, and resolutions demanding that he be banned from the NBA for life. Washington described the content of these letters: "The typical ones said things like, 'All you black niggers are the same. Animals.' Some were signed, 'KKK,' but I know they were really from sick people trying to intimidate me."[122] He left packages unopened, fearing that they contained bombs. Washington's wife, Pat, recalled that because of the incident, a doctor had even refused to deliver their second child.

Washington became a hermit and avoided going out in public: "There weren't a lot of six-eight black men wandering around in the Palos Verdes area. . . . It wasn't like I could go out and not be recognized, especially since my picture was in the paper every day and the tape was on TV every night."[123] The punch had brought him a new-found infamy that he found frightening. People even accosted Pat, asking her what was wrong with her "crazy husband." The fact that Washington had no income was one of his biggest challenges, and he began looking for a job as a substitute high school teacher in Los Angeles. Thanks to his frugality, Washington had saved some money over the past four years, but he supported his blind grandparents and other members of his extended family in addition to his wife and two children. "I had gotten one check this season for $18,000," he explained, "and the league took $10,000 of it. So when I got hurt financially, a lot of people got hurt."[124] Although he was relatively wealthy in comparison to most African Americans, unlike white athletes with generational wealth, he was still heavily reliant on his salary, with much of it going toward caring for relatives.

ON JANUARY 6, 1978, TOMJANOVICH MADE HIS FIRST PUBLIC APpearance since the fight. He looked fit despite his physical trials over the last month. Speaking haltingly to the press through his wired jaw, the Rockets guard said he could forgive Washington but added, "There can be no excuse for what he did." Tomjanovich was the ideal embodiment of a diligent and self-sacrificing white athlete, whose biggest frustration was his inability to work: "For the first time in 16 years, I am out of action. If I'm away from the game for one week, I get edgy." When asked if he would be afraid to return to action after the trauma of the fight, he stated, "I just have to take it one step at a time and not worry how I might feel next year."[125] Although he refused to speak about his recent legal action against the Lakers, Tomjanovich revealed that he would have to undergo another surgery to repair his damaged eyes.

The following month, Commissioner O'Brien allowed Washington to return to the league. In January, Washington had applied for reinstatement and had met with O'Brien at the league headquarters in New York City. In a statement to the press, O'Brien reassured NBA fans of Washington's remorse and rehabilitation: "Mr. Washington acknowledges that his acts were inexcusable, deeply regrets what he did, assured me that he will never again behave in similar fashion and recognizes the need for strong penalties."[126] On the road with his new team, the Boston Celtics (the Lakers had traded him in December 1977), Washington continued to receive death threats and still required extra security.[127] "When I first came back, there was police and FBI at the games," Washington recollected. "They told me I couldn't order food using my own name (in the hotels) because it might be poisoned. I'd get letters sent to me with razor blades in them, and the Boston ballboys would cut their fingers. Finally, I just threw all the mail away."[128] Despite having "done his time," he continued to be the target of racist abuse.

Washington's punch also precipitated two civil lawsuits against the Lakers' parent company, California Sports, Inc. Filed in December 1977, Tomjanovich's suit charged that the Lakers were negligent in failing to control Washington's behavior on the court.[129] In February 1978 his case was transferred to federal court, and he sought $2.6 million in damages. That same month, the Rockets also filed a federal lawsuit, asking for $1.8 million in damages for Tomjanovich's injury.[130] According to both suits, the Lakers were culpable for damages because they had known of Washington's "violent tendencies" and had "failed to take proper measures to control these tendencies."[131] Certainly, the lawyers representing Tomjanovich and the Rockets used this strategy because they knew that California Sports had deeper pockets than Washington and could pay substantial compensation. But in suing Washington's employer, they also fed into popular ideas about Black players' inherent savagery and the ongoing need for white paternalistic control in professional basketball.[132]

Public discussion of Washington's punch continued over the course of the entire season. African American players and sportswriters remained especially critical of Washington's criminalization in the court of public opinion. In March 1978, *Black Sports* focused on the so-called crisis of violence in the NBA and other big-time leagues, presenting a decidedly different analysis from that of the mainstream media. The magazine questioned the continued demonization of

Washington. Clayton Riley challenged the notion that Black male violence was somehow exceptional or pathological, whether in professional basketball or the United States at large. Quoting the militant Black Power activist H. Rap Brown, Riley wrote, "'Violence . . . is as American as cherry pie,' possibly more." Fighting was no longer just confined to the boxing ring; it had become a mainstay of professional hockey and football: "In hockey, the fights are so much a part of what is expected by the audience, that tickets are being sold that might as well be stamped 'At Least One Fight Guaranteed Each Game.'" Riley argued that football was equally violent even though fistfights on the field were rare: "The violence of football can be seen through the injury lists that say things like 'probable starter,' and 'unlikely to play.'" In contrast, violence in the NBA appeared to be more of a problem only because basketball was "a presumably 'non-contact' sport."[133]

According to Riley's diagnosis, "the whole macho thing" was at the root of what was happening on the basketball court. "It's about masculinity, being a man," he insisted.[134] Sports arenas were merely the metaphorical testing ground for American ideals of violent heteropatriarchal manhood: "Being a male athlete in this country carries with it the very real center of the designation 'man' to a great many people." To be aggressive and violent was to be a man in the United States: "The male ethic is to win by force, if necessary, to overwhelm, to hurt, to maim, cripple, all toward the end of achieving victory. Not to fight is to be feminized by implication, and there is nothing that will trigger a fury faster in a male athlete than the suggestion that there is a little 'girl' in him." Tied to this fear of feminization was "a sense of territorial imperative," the desire to take over and dominate space, whether on the basketball court or in other aspects of US private and public life.[135] These deep-seated notions of white American manhood were hardly the fault of a few Black basketball players.

Looking back on the sensationalized coverage of Washington's punch, Riley believed that the media helped to incite violence in professional sport: "The commentators droned on about how sickening the whole thing was, but these commentators from CBS, NBC, ABC, and every independent station around, are the same people who have been promoting the macho scene in sports over the tube."[136] How could one exclusively blame these young men for seeking to embody these masculine norms? Riley argued that the recent *Sports Illustrated* issue on NBA enforcers, which "unfairly portrayed [them] as hatchet men and assassins, was an act of criminal provocation. . . . Players take those media-created images seriously. And then we react so righteously when something happens."[137] Despite their righteous indignation about on-court fights, both the media and the fans were complicit in encouraging violence in sport.

A special report in the same *Black Sports* issue revealed that there was plenty of evidence to suggest that spectators were, in fact, far more rabid and aggressive than the athletes themselves. "No longer content to remain the silent, adoring majority, America's sports fans now want to be part of the action and the action is getting violent," journalist Peter Greenberg declared.[138] In calling them a "silent majority," Greenberg pointed the finger at conservative white fans. Citing numerous examples from the past year, he noted that fan violence in the stands was becoming a regular part of the game in all the big-time professional and NCAA sports. In response, the police presence at games had increased, and stadium architects had started to experiment with designs to help keep unruly crowds away from players.[139]

Greenberg consulted with experts to explore why sports fans seemed to have a growing contempt for today's professional athletes, and he found that white working-class resentments were at the heart of the problem. As behaviorist and UCLA psychiatry professor Arnold Beisser hypothesized, "The socio-economic distance is so great between most fans and highly paid athletes . . . that the athletes don't seem like real people. So the fans are more apt to be callous toward them."[140] This "class warfare" in the sporting realm echoed broader social tensions amid 1970s deindustrialization and stagflation and the white backlash against racial integration.

Moreover, Black sociologist Harry Edwards claimed that the media, particularly television, only aggravated this race and class conflict: "Fueled by previously televised instant replays of football cheap shots, hockey square-offs, and basketball brawls, the fan seeks his new identity."[141] Violence in the stands was therefore constitutive of white sports fans' performance of manhood. For the NBA, a league now dominated by Black athletes, this intersection of racial and class resentments created a potentially explosive situation. Prevailing narratives of rising white victimization at the hands of African Americans and other "special-interest groups" seemed to embolden white fans to lash out at supposedly entitled star Black players.

In the meantime, the NBA instituted several rule changes during the 1978–1979 season, with an eye to reducing player fights. The league went from two to three referees so that they could better police the game, clamping down on hand-checking and dispensing technical fouls for violations of the anti-zone injunction. Although some complained that these modifications were turning pro ball into a "sissy game," Kareem Abdul-Jabbar expressed his approval: "For the first time in years, we're back to playing basketball. . . . It's eliminating a lot of pushing, shoving and holding."[142] Nevertheless, the addition of a third official proved a short-lived experiment. Arguing that it was too costly, the team owners abandoned the practice the following season.[143]

In August 1979, both civil suits against the Lakers finally went to trial in Houston in front of a six-member jury of five men and one woman. By this time, Washington had been traded again and was with the San Diego Clippers. Given the high-profile nature of the case, and the fact that Washington had already been tried and found guilty in the court of public opinion, attorneys questioned forty-one prospective jurors to get to the final six. Making things more difficult for the Lakers, US district court judge John Singleton ruled that an edited film of the incident, put together for Tomjanovich and the Rockets, could be admitted as evidence. Lakers attorneys objected on the grounds that the film had been altered to accentuate Washington's punch. In defending the Lakers against liability, they argued that Tomjanovich had assumed the risk of injury by playing professional basketball and that Washington had acted in self-defense.[144]

Washington felt violated by the process: "The whole trial was about the Lakers' failure to control me, to train me, to keep me from injuring people. It sounded as if they were describing the behavior of some kind of animal."[145] Any hope for absolution in the courts had evaporated.

After two weeks of testimony and five hours of deliberation, the jury awarded Tomjanovich $3.3 million in damages ($1.8 million in actual damages and $1.5 million in punitive damages), far exceeding the player's requested $2.6 million.[146] They even gave $50,000 of those damages to Mrs. Sophie Tomjanovich for the "loss of aid and companionship" during her husband's hospitalization.[147] Although Washington was not personally liable for the damages, his character was still on trial. The jury rejected his claim of self-defense and found that he had committed battery and acted in reckless disregard for the safety of others. They found the Lakers negligent for "failing to train Washington properly" and for employing him even "after they became aware that he had a tendency for violence while playing basketball."[148] The fact that the jury awarded Tomjanovich more money than his suit requested was rare.[149] They had added 50 percent to the $1 million in punitive damages sought by Tomjanovich. As one legal expert explained, "It means that the jury is completely turned off by what has occurred; they believe it was an act with malice and with disregard for a person's safety; it was a brutal act, an act outside the human element."[150] It likely did not help that the edited film of the punch was shown repeatedly throughout the trial. Moreover, shortly after the verdict, Judge Singleton revealed to the lawyers that at least two of the six jurors had asked if Tomjanovich could autograph their copies of the court's legal instructions.[151]

Reflecting on the entire incident, Washington argued that the racial imperatives of the league had contributed to his demonization:

"Who buys the tickets to the game—white people or black people? The answer is white people. So they were going to come down on me, the big black guy who beat up the two white guys. It only made sense."[152] If the roles were reversed, he "might have been fined fifty dollars" or even embraced as a hero. Instead, Washington, like many young Black men of his generation, was presumed criminal.

In some respects, these racialized scripts of violence and punishment in professional basketball helped to shape conventional wisdom about the necessity of establishing "law and order" in African American communities. They also served to legitimize the continued white backlash against efforts at racial integration beyond the court, from busing to affirmative action. And the fact that Black players insisted on being recognized as men only reinforced the class-inflected narratives of white male victimization that fed the rise of conservative politics in the ensuing years. Although the impact of Washington's punch continued to reverberate, violence was just one of the NBA's many worries, for another crisis was right around the corner.

Chapter 7

Undisciplined

The NBA's "Cocaine Crisis"

A lot of people use the word "undisciplined" to describe the NBA. . . . I think that word is pointed at a group more than at a sport. What do they mean by it? On the court? Off the court? What kind of clothes a guy wears? How he talks? How he plays? I think that's a cop-out.

—Al Attles, *Sports Illustrated*, 1979

BERNARD KING WAS AWAKENED BY A LOUD THUMPING NOISE ON DE-cember 18, 1978. The twenty-two-year-old star player for the New Jersey Nets realized that he was sitting in his Corvette. A harsh light blinded him as he looked out the driver's-side window. It was a police officer. "He was rapping on the glass with one hand while shining his flashlight into the car," King later recalled. The NBA sophomore and six-foot-seven forward rolled down his window. The cold December air hit him in the face. The patrolman asked him to exit the vehicle. "I realized my engine was idling," he recounted. "The motor was on. So

241

were my headlights. I'd been slumped over the steering wheel." Still in a daze, King stepped out of his car. He looked around and recognized that he was at the intersection of Stone and Livonia Avenues in Brownsville, Brooklyn. He was double-parked, facing a stop sign. For the life of him, King could not remember how he got there. He had been in Long Island, New York, on Saturday night to attend a sneak preview of *Fast Break*, a movie in which he played the role of "Hustler," a talented teenage ballplayer and pool shark. After the screening, King had gone to a bar. "Everything after that was a blank. How long had I been partying?" he had wondered.[1] The police officer told him it was 5:15 . . . on Monday morning.

King had lost an entire day to his alcohol-fueled bender. He had missed an appearance on Sunday evening at the opening-night festivities for the New Jersey Gems, a women's professional basketball team. The police officer put him in the back of the cruiser and took him to Brooklyn Central Booking at the 84th Precinct—coincidentally, just a ten-minute walk from where he grew up in Fort Greene's Whitman housing project. "I was humiliated, deeply ashamed, and numb with self-disgust," King recalled. "Those feelings would only deepen in the coming hours, when officers at the 84th gave me a partial strip search and found a coke vial containing a small amount of the drug—about ten dollars' worth, according to the police—in my pocket."[2] King was confused. He was a drinker but not a hard-drug user. He wondered if he had sniffed the cocaine while he was inebriated. Later that same morning, the police sent him home with a desk ticket to appear in criminal court for arraignment on January 9. They charged him with a misdemeanor DWI, possession of a controlled substance, and driving without a license.

Despite his humiliating arrest, King was no slouch. In the 1977 NBA draft, he went seventh in the first round to the New Jersey Nets, securing a contract of $800,000 over five years.[3] He quickly distinguished himself as one of the best players on the team. He had strength, speed, and guile. "Bernard is an improvising soloist," Black sportswriter Clayton Riley described. "Even up front he seems to 'read' the court exceptionally well, setting picks, using his body cleverly in the human thunder called NBA rebounding." Meanwhile, off the court, King was controlled. The young forward knew how to say a lot without revealing anything about himself. "He speaks rapidly, big city swift," Riley noted. "All of the questions in the world will draw nothing out of him except what he's already decided to tell you."⁴ King kept his personal thoughts close to his chest, often referring to himself in the third person. Reporters, especially white reporters, were not sure what to make of him.

King had thought that returning to the New York City area to play pro ball would be a dream come true. But he was unhappy. When he was not on the court, he felt empty and alone. He tried to fill his emotional void with partying and casual sex: "After every game, every night, I was drinking." It was the late 1970s, and temptation was just

New Jersey Nets rookie Bernard King drives past Elvin Hayes of the Washington Bullets in Washington, March 26, 1978. (AP Photo)

around the corner in Manhattan. When the Nets were at home, he would drive into the city for the clubs. One night, at Studio 54, King drank so much that he blacked out. Thankfully, former Knicks guard Dean Meminger was there with his wife, and they brought him back to their apartment to sleep it off. They knew he was not capable of driving back to New Jersey.[5]

Most often, however, King drank alone. He kept a bottle in his glove compartment so that he could drink after games. When he was on the road, he traveled with alcohol in his checked luggage. Once, King noticed that his bag was soaked, and he knew the bottle had cracked and leaked. Although the Nets trainer was in charge of handling the players' bags, transporting them from the airport to the hotel, he had said nothing to King. Had he noticed that King's wet bag reeked of booze? For road trips, rookies were assigned roommates, but King always paid the difference to secure his own room. He needed to hide his partying and drinking from the team. He still managed to produce on the court, so no one bothered him. As a rookie, he set a franchise record for the most points scored in a season, and he was a top contender for NBA Rookie of the Year. "I was in denial about my problems, sending them to the back room and shutting the door," King recalled. "That couldn't last. It never does."[6]

It had all come crashing down that morning in December. The day after his arrest in Brooklyn, King was too ashamed to attend the Nets' practice. He could not face his teammates or the media. Although this was not his first brush with the law, he knew that this transgression would garner a lot of press. King shut himself inside his New Jersey condo and tried to ignore the constant ringing of the telephone. He tried to sleep, but mostly he cried: "I couldn't go on the way I was. Unless something changed, I was going to die."[7]

Even though King hid, news of his arrest spread quickly. Most of the stories focused almost exclusively on his illicit drug charge. There was little mention of his alcohol intoxication—the main source of his problems. White sportswriters also highlighted his past run-ins with police while at the University of Tennessee, painting him as a serial offender.[8] Because of that cold December morning, King became a symbol of the NBA's supposed descent into Black decadence and delinquency. He became the face of the league's rising "cocaine crisis."

"NBA: A Real Mess," *Basketball Weekly* decried in June 1978.[9] The league's television ratings had slipped 3 percent from the previous season, and low attendance figures also plagued a number of franchises. "The doomsayers would have us believe these are some of the darkest moments in the uneven history of pro basketball," declared sportswriter Larry Donald.[10] After its reputation took a hit with Kermit Washington's infamous punch, the league was still struggling to find its footing. King's drug scandal could not have come at a worse time.

Years of speculation, overexpansion, and mismanagement on the part of white team owners and league executives had helped to produce much of the NBA's instability in the late 1970s. An ill-fated switch from ABC to CBS in 1973 stuck the NBA with lackadaisical coverage, poor time slots, and tape-delayed games, while erratic scheduling undercut the very team rivalries that had long been the lifeblood of the league.[11] And thanks to the asymmetrical merger agreement, the former ABA teams still struggled under the weight of hefty entry fees.[12] Yet rather than acknowledge the white basketball establishment's role in creating the NBA's Dark Ages, many white sportswriters and fans continued to direct their criticism at the majority-Black players.

For *Basketball Weekly* writer Bob Ryan, the root of the pro game's decline could be traced back to 1967: "The ABA had a completely negative effect on the quality of professional basketball."[13] The talent war had helped to topple the four-year rule, leading to "the influx of untutored players coming out of school too early." It had brought in big-money, no-cut contracts, making the players lazy. The ABA, Ryan charged, had encouraged acrobatic improvisation on offense at the expense of disciplined defense. In a nutshell, the outlaw league had helped to make pro ball a Black game.

Stories like these angered African American players. White racism, they maintained, not Black ballplayers' bad behavior, had caused pro basketball's recent dip in popularity and television ratings. As veteran Black forward for the Seattle SuperSonics and NBPA president Paul Silas told *Sports Illustrated*, "It is a fact that white people in general look disfavorably upon blacks who are making astronomical amounts of money if it appears they are not working hard for that money."[14] Black players were so skilled, he argued, that white sportswriters and fans mistook their seemingly effortless virtuosity for a lack of effort. Achieving that level of skill took a lot of hard work. But it was difficult for Silas and the NBPA to convince white fans of this as they confronted a resurgence in pseudoscientific theories about African Americans' "natural" physical abilities—myths that helped to explain away the rising dominance of Black male athletes in the seventies.[15]

HEIGHTENED PUBLIC CONCERN ABOUT THE NBA's EMERGING "cocaine crisis" exemplified these racial tensions. It also dovetailed with the anti-Black narratives driving the rise of more punitive drug policy, beginning with the Rockefeller drug laws in 1973. States across the nation followed New York's lead, instituting harsh antidrug laws with mandatory minimums, as government officials "got tough" with African American drug users and dealers who supposedly threatened the safety of white American society, especially white children and teens.[16] Even as some liberal politicians considered decriminalizing marijuana well into the late seventies, a moral panic about the violent effects of PCP (phencyclidine), alongside the growth of a powerful white "parents' movement"—a nonpartisan network of suburban antidrug groups—helped keep the rubric of prohibition in place.[17]

Illicit drug use in professional basketball was by no means a new issue, but by mid-decade fears were mounting. In late January 1975 a thirty-nine-page intradepartmental police memo containing allegations of a drug (marijuana) ring involving players in the NFL and ABA was leaked to the press. The story was picked up on the wires and went national. Roxie Ann Rice, a nineteen-year-old African American woman, claimed she had been recruited to be a marijuana courier for professional athletes on seven NFL and two ABA teams.[18] The story seemed plausible enough. Here was a Black woman implicating Black professional athletes in a drug scandal. But after a monthlong investigation, the Drug Enforcement Agency (DEA) dismissed Rice's claims as unsubstantiated.[19]

Even though Rice's allegations of a marijuana ring proved to be untrue, rumors of illicit drug use still sullied professional basketball. Following the scandal, the *Louisville Times* published a damning report claiming that the use of illegal drugs, particularly marijuana, was rampant in the ABA and NBA. The newspaper claimed to have done interviews with sixteen players, coaches, former players, and even a former trainer, all of whom requested anonymity. "How bad is it? Unbelievable, that's how bad," one NBA coach reportedly said. "Everybody's into it."[20] Although cocaine was not yet commonplace, the anonymous sources maintained, marijuana use was widespread, especially among the younger players. The exposé angered ABA and NBA officials. Sure, some players used drugs, they acknowledged, but marijuana use was not exceptional to pro ball. It was an American reality.[21]

To help reassure fans that they had the drug situation under control and that pro ball was still wholesome family entertainment, the NBA insisted that its private network of security offices was staying on top of the players. "My objective is to maintain the integrity of the sport," said league security head Jack Joyce. In addition to inspecting the finances of potential owners and hardship cases, overseeing stadium security, and monitoring point spreads and betting lines, the security officers were supposed to investigate rumors from fans, team personnel, and other players in order to police the athletes' personal lives.[22] Despite these public assurances, league officials did not really clamp down on drug use until cocaine came into the mix. In the late 1970s it was still common for players from both teams to gather in the same hotel room to smoke weed. As long as it stayed out of the newspapers, the NBA turned a blind eye.[23]

Once cocaine arrests, like King's, became more prevalent, NBA surveillance picked up, but it was not applied equally. Some Black players suspected that the league's security agents were racially profiling them, even though white players were also known to use coke. "I've seen plenty of white guys coming to games with their noses running," Darryl Dawkins later recalled. "In fact, there were a couple of white stars who used to sit on the bench with towels over their heads, and the talk among the players was that their noses would start bleeding whenever they sat down."[24] Yet league officials looked the other way.

Although the NBA tried to cloak its security measures in the neutral language of player safety, it was more concerned about repairing its damaged image in the eyes of white fans and protecting the team owners' financial interests. "We aren't trying to catch these guys," Joyce claimed. "We're trying to protect them. The owners have a huge investment in the ballplayers. The blue chips are worth a million dollars or more. If they lose the ballplayers, they lose money." Aryeh Neier, executive director of the American Civil Liberties Union, called these intrusive policing practices "awful" and "dangerous," and Arthur Goldberg, a former US Supreme Court justice who had defended Curt Flood in his reserve-clause case, criticized the league's paternalism and lack of respect for its employees' Fourth Amendment rights: "There's too much invasion of privacy of the players; this security business is just another example of this invasion. Athletes ought to be treated as adults."[25]

Meanwhile, the case of Black NFL defensive linemen Don Reese and Randy Crowder offered a cautionary tale of what could happen if sports leagues failed to adequately supervise and discipline their players. In August 1977 the two Miami Dolphins were convicted of selling a pound of cocaine and sentenced to one year in prison and five years' probation. Around the same time that a judge denied them early release in April 1978, the NBA again reassured fans that it would protect the sanctity of professional basketball from the menace of rising drug crime.[26] "If a player is associating with the wrong type of people or going to a restaurant or bar where we feel he could be subjected to meeting what you call 'undesirables,' we alert him to that fact," security head Joyce maintained. "It's a preventative-type program."[27] It was hard to miss the racial overtones of the NBA's two-pronged mission to save the players from themselves and to save the league from the players. It not only evoked the long history of Black bodies as property but also reinforced contemporary ideas about the dangerous convergence of Black freedom and equality with rising violence and criminality in post–civil rights America.

BERNARD KING'S DECEMBER ARREST SEEMED TO SIGNAL A DISTURB- ing trend among professional athletes. "Sport is filled with problem children who like to tell us that they are misunderstood and really quite sensitive," wrote Mike Lupica of the *Chicago Tribune*. But fans did not owe these "problem children" an ounce of sympathy. Rich, talented, and successful, they had the world in their hands, yet they were always running afoul of the law: "A troubled childhood in a poor neighborhood is not a credit card for life."[28] Lupica appeared to be taking aim at King's history as a hardship case in the 1977 NBA draft; he had no idea that the disgraced Nets player had actually suffered traumatic abuse as a youth. Lupica also seemed clueless about the intense racism and police harassment that King had faced as a college star. Or perhaps, like many other white sportswriters and fans at the time, he did not care.

King already had a bad reputation from his time at the University of Tennessee, where the local press had portrayed the Brooklyn native "as an inner-city hoodlum addicted to drugs and larceny."[29] The Knoxville police had arrested him five times in the span of fifteen months for offenses ranging from drug possession to burglary. One of the arrests was for misdemeanor possession of marijuana (they had found one joint during a search of his vehicle). He pled guilty and was fined $50 and given sixty days' probation.[30] King was also picked up for allegedly stealing university video equipment. But all the players had permission to borrow the equipment to watch game tapes as long as they returned it.[31] The local newspapers had blown everything out of proportion. "He never did anything you wouldn't find most other students doing in modern times," Tennessee coach Ray Mears later told *Black Sports*. "He's no gangster or anything close to it."[32]

Instead, it seemed as if the local authorities had it in for the young Black basketball star. They were intent on sending him a message: "Remember your place, boy." Toward the end of his first season with the Volunteers, King was summoned to Coach Mears's office. The police chief had just come for a visit. "The chief told me he has officers on his staff that 'don't like that uppity nigger,'" Coach Mears warned him.[33] King felt sick. He had already received death threats while playing on the road. Now he had to worry about the very men who were supposed to "serve and protect" him.

The fear and pressure he felt were almost too much to bear. He tried to dull the pain with alcohol and marijuana, and found ways to rationalize his self-medication. "Half the students I knew got high . . . and I told myself I was doing pretty much what everyone else did," King recalled thinking.[34] In retrospect, he realized that drugs and alcohol were only a "temporary remedy," a way to avoid dealing with the root of his pain. Because he was a survivor of child abuse, the police intimidation had triggered something deep within him.

Sure enough, Knoxville law enforcement made good on their threats. They followed his car and even pulled him over and threatened him. Coupled with his unhealed childhood trauma, the constant police intimidation pushed his anxiety into overdrive: "When I wasn't competing, I was in emotional and mental pain, drinking and smoking weed."[35] Still, King had convinced himself that he had everything under control. He just had to persevere and stay focused on making it into the NBA.

He needed to make moves for the sake of his family. Born in 1956, he was the second of six children to Thomas and Thelma King. His parents had come to Brooklyn with their families as part of the Great Migration north from the Carolinas. King spent his formative years in the Walt Whitman housing projects, a city-owned development that stood at the north end of Fort Greene Park, near the Brooklyn Docks. Finances were tight, and he was their ticket out of public housing.

But finances were not their only problem. Childhood abuse was a family secret that King kept hidden for most of his life. Perhaps a vestige of their ancestors' experiences of violence and dehumanization under slavery and the long shadow of southern Jim Crow, intergenerational trauma tormented the Kings. As a young girl, Thelma had been subjected to harsh corporal punishment, and she inflicted that same abuse on her own children. "Sometimes she made me strip out of my clothes and then hit me with the broomstick until my skin was red, swollen, and bruised," King recounted. The beatings seemed arbitrary, unconnected to his behavior. He came to feel a combination of vulnerability, shame, and resentment, but he swallowed his pain and rage. King's unflappability became his signature on the court: "That's where my Game Face came from. . . . It was a mask, a shield. It allowed me to shut out the hurt, protect myself from the outside world."[36]

In basketball, King had found an important emotional outlet. As a teen, he played for Fort Hamilton High School during the year, and youth basketball kept him busy during New York City's hot and steamy summers. However, playing for Tennessee had made him depressed. The racism he faced in Knoxville was overwhelming, so he decided to enter the NBA's hardship draft after his junior year.[37]

Now a pro, King felt the full weight of public disdain on his shoulders. Many white sportswriters did not seem terribly interested in reporting on the complex lives of King and other African American ballplayers. Nor did fans seem to acknowledge their full humanity. Instead, they became simplistic symbols in larger debates about the troubling state of Black America. Lupica's rant about pro sports' "problem children" was indicative of a much broader white backlash against Black financial success and perceived Black "entitlements," from welfare to affirmative action, in the midst of a decade of comparative scarcity and austerity. The fact that King was caught with cocaine, a high-priced drug with upper-class associations, only intensified the popular outcry.

At the time, the average American did not know much about cocaine. Decades had elapsed since the passage of the Harrison Narcotics Tax Act of 1914, which effectively outlawed its sale and use. In the late 1970s it was still seen as a "status drug" of the elite. Part of cocaine's cachet was "its rarity, high price and use by celebrities, musicians and other folk heroes," a 1977 report by the National Institute of Drug Addiction (NIDA) noted. Most cocaine users considered it to be a "social drug" that was relatively safe and had few undesirable side effects. But if cocaine's price fell and it became more widely available, it could become a problem, the report acknowledged.[38] Already there were signs that this might happen. Even though absolute numbers remained small, a NIDA survey of high school seniors from across the nation showed that their rates of cocaine use had "increased sharply" from 1975 to 1979.[39]

Black sportswriter Clayton Riley criticized white reporters for their racist coverage of King's arrest. They had prejudged the young forward, based on his past arrests, without bothering to look into the full story. Riley pointed out that four of the five cases against King in Tennessee had resulted in no convictions. Still, white sportswriters had rushed to paint King as criminal, even crazy, while calling for his swift and strict punishment.[40] For white athletes who faced drug charges, the stock narrative was quite different. When jockey Ronnie Franklin was charged with cocaine possession the following year, his trainer characterized him as a "victim of circumstances," stating that his arrest was likely the result of a "boys-will-be-boys escapade." White sportswriters tended to reproduce this innocent framing of Franklin's arrest. Similar ideas of victimhood also applied to white basketball players caught with drugs, as reporters told redemptive stories of their rehabilitation.[41]

Despite the backlash in the press, to King's surprise his teammates and coaches remained supportive of him. Even the Nets' fans stood behind him at first, giving him a standing ovation at the next home game. Coach Kevin Loughery knew King had an alcohol problem, and so did the entire Nets organization, but they let it slide without directly confronting him. King was their star rookie. They did not want to kill the golden goose.[42] The NBA also lacked a formal prevention program for players suffering from alcohol addiction. They were so focused on illegal "street" drugs that alcohol was not even on their radar. "Alcoholism just isn't a problem in the NBA," league physician Torrey Brown later argued.[43] Prevailing stereotypes that connected urban Black communities with illicit drug use seemed to have blinded the league to the problem of alcohol abuse among its players.

In January 1979, King initially pled innocent to his charges in Brooklyn Criminal Court.[44] However, in February he switched to a guilty plea for the charge of impaired driving. The judge gave King a $50 fine and suspended his driver's license for sixty days. Meanwhile, the other misdemeanor charges—driving without a license and cocaine possession—were held in "adjournment in contemplation of dismissal."[45] If King stayed out of trouble for six months, the judge would drop the two charges. An NBA spokesperson stated that the league would not punish King for the impaired-driving violation; instead, it would await disposition of the other charges before taking any disciplinary action.

After King's January court appearance, the Nets' top brass, including Coach Loughery and GM Charlie Theokas, called him into the office for a meeting. Rather than taking disciplinary action, the team

Bernard King of the New Jersey Nets as he brushes past reporters after his lawyer entered King's plea of innocent to charges of cocaine and driving violations in Brooklyn Criminal Court, January 9, 1979. (AP Photo/Robert Karp)

requested that King see a psychologist. Still deep in denial about his demons, he was reluctant to seek help. Although he finally agreed to give therapy a chance, he was not ready to do the emotional work of recovery: "I wasn't at all prepared to talk about what was hurting me. I could not admit I was an alcoholic. I went to one therapy session; that was it."[46]

THE NETS EVENTUALLY TRADED KING TO THE UTAH JAZZ IN October, right before the start of the 1979–1980 season. Deep down he knew that he had not trained hard enough over the summer and that he was probably drinking too much. Although Coach Loughery said it was a front-office decision to trade him for Utah center Rich Kelley, King knew that there was more to it than that: "I was wounded and angry. The team knew about my partying. They had known for a long time. If they wanted to get rid of me now, it was their choice. But

I knew it wasn't for the reason Loughery gave me."[47] The Nets had looked the other way when he was helping them win, but they were quick to offload him when his use ran out. The Jazz, desperate to fill holes in their lineup, acquired King despite his tarnished reputation. They also picked up Terry Furlow, another talented Black player with a checkered past.

King had a hard time adjusting to life in the lily-white environs of Salt Lake City. He felt like he was under a microscope; he could hardly blend in with his surroundings. Outside of the team, he did not see many other Black faces. When he moved into his rental in a high-rise condominium called Zion Summit, a development owned by the Mormon Church, King discovered that he was the first African American to ever live in the building. Hardly a bastion of racial tolerance in those days, the Church of Jesus Christ of Latter-Day Saints had just lifted its ban on African Americans in the priesthood in 1978, almost a decade after fourteen Black players were released from the University of Wyoming football team for attempting to protest this exclusionary policy.[48]

Things were not much better on the court. The Jazz struggled, racking up a miserable 2–10 record in the first month of the season. Because King had missed the team's training camp, it took him a while to get up to speed on offense. Then, in November, just as he was finally starting to hit his stride, he suffered a serious injury that kept him out for more than a month. Misdiagnosed as an ankle sprain, it turned out to be a foot fracture. With King sidelined, the Jazz kept losing. The young forward started to spiral out of control again: "With the injury keeping me out of the gym, I had a lot of time on my hands and slipped into my old patterns. . . . I was depressed, and isolated, and sought to dull those feelings with alcohol."[49] He sank into a pit of hopelessness and could not seem to pull his way out. In desperation, he telephoned his agent and lawyer, Bill Pollak, on New Year's Eve and begged for help. Pollak urged him to seek treatment, and King agreed to enter rehab.

But before he could make good on his promise, on January 2 he was arrested and booked into the Salt Lake County Jail at 2:00 a.m. for investigation of alleged forcible sexual abuse and cocaine possession.[50] As disturbing details of the night made their way into national newspapers, they seemed to confirm the worst nightmares of white Americans still leery of the effects of racial integration and the rising power of African American men. King and other Black professional athletes, who had access to both white women and illicit drugs, posed a particular threat to the racial status quo.

Rebecca Pratt, a twenty-five-year-old Mormon, had gone to King's apartment on the night of January 1. She told police that when the Jazz star began "making advances," she had tried to leave, but he had forced her to perform oral sex. She then waited for King to fall asleep before fleeing and calling police.[51]

When the arresting officers arrived at King's apartment, they were unable to wake him and had to call in the paramedics. Once he was conscious, they took him to jail, but he was released nine hours later. With the police investigation still underway, there were no charges yet filed against him.[52] In the meantime, the Jazz put King on indefinite suspension without pay, pending the outcome of the investigation. If he was charged with forcible sexual abuse (a felony), he could face up to five years in prison. Police also sent a white powdery substance—found in King's condo during his arrest—to the lab for testing. If it turned out to be cocaine, he could face prosecution under Utah's strict drug laws.[53]

As the investigation continued, there was much speculation and skepticism about what had happened that night in King's apartment. King's attorney, Bob Van Sciver, said Pratt's story was "improbable," and Salt Lake City journalists argued there were "a lot of holes in the report."[54] Regardless of Pratt's whiteness, her gender made her story automatically suspect. However, King had no counter-testimony to offer. Police lie-detector tests showed that he could not even remember most of what had happened during the night of the alleged assault because he had been so intoxicated.[55] His behavior played into well-worn ideas about Black men's hypersexuality and lack of self-control. In the early 1900s, the racist archetype of the dangerous "Negro cocaine fiend," prone to mass murders and the rape of white women, had stoked public support for the drug's prohibition. And the growing uproar surrounding King and other Black ballplayers caught with cocaine echoed these earlier racial scripts.[56]

Regardless of his innocence or guilt, the damage was done. "You're in Utah, not New York, and the stigma of the arrest will be hard to erase," said Mike Carter of the *Salt Lake City Tribune*. In white, conservative, Mormon Utah, King would find little support. There were only around four thousand African Americans living in Salt Lake County. Local sportswriters believed that the "racial angle" of the incident would likely be enough for the Jazz to trade him, whether or not he was convicted. "This is not the thing for a Black guy to get involved in with a white girl. It sounds fishy, but, if they get the drug thing, he's dead. With the Mormons, it could be over," another local reporter said.[57] Patriarchal prerogatives meant that sportswriters were willing to cut King some slack about his alleged assault of Pratt, but drug abuse was apparently grounds for immediate dismissal.

The risk that Jazz GM Frank Layden had taken in acquiring King now seemed to be coming back to haunt him. He announced that King would remain on unpaid suspension until the county attorney decided whether to file charges. Layden believed that he had "to protect the integrity" of both the team and the league.[58]

On Monday, January 7, King was arraigned on sex and drug charges in front of Judge Floyd H. Gowans. In addition to Pratt's formal complaint, the white powdery substance had come back as cocaine. With his preliminary hearing set for February 20, King was up against a wall, facing three counts of forcible sodomy and two counts of forcible sexual abuse (all felonies), and one count of possession of cocaine (a misdemeanor). Still, Gowans allowed King to travel to California to participate in a twenty-one-day alcohol-treatment program at St. Joseph's Hospital in Santa Monica.[59] Gowans's leniency, alongside reporters' skepticism about Pratt's allegations, pointed to the masculine privileges that star Black ballplayers, by virtue of their celebrity and wealth, could increasingly access.

As King awaited his fate, Howie Evans of the *New York Amsterdam News* tried to make sense of the talented forward's "tragic tale." How could a young man with such skill and success—a young man with the world at his feet—fall so far? Rather than blame King alone for his criminal behavior, Evans saw the lack of mentorship and discipline for King, at both the college and pro levels, as symptomatic of the general disregard for Black athletes as full humans. King was there to "function as a piece of meat," and only when his activities off the court affected his performance on the court did teams dispose of him.[60] Indifferent coaches enabled King and other Black players to embrace forms of misogynistic violence without any constructive consequences.

Although critical of King for refusing to "grow up," Evans believed that rehabilitation and redemption were still possible for the troubled forward. He questioned whether harsh punishment and complete banishment were the appropriate solutions to King's problems. "Basketball and the NBA owe Bernard King something," Evans argued. "His is a life that should not be discarded. His is a life that can be saved. But only with love and understanding." Yet Evans did not let King off the hook. The embattled ballplayer had a responsibility to his community: "For all of those kids who idolized him, Bernard must become a man. Nothing else is acceptable."[61]

Trouble and tragedy seemed to follow King. On May 23 his Jazz teammate Terry Furlow died in a gruesome solo car crash. At around 3:10 a.m., Furlow's rented Mercedes had veered out of control along Interstate 71 near West 117th St., close to the Cleveland-Linndale city line. Furlow had arrived in town a few nights earlier to attend a party for his former teammate Clarence "Foots" Walker of the Cavaliers. According to witnesses, the Utah guard had been trying to pass a tractor-trailer when his car slammed into a steel utility pole. He did not appear to have hit the brakes. There were no skid marks on the road.[62] A rescue squad from the Cleveland Fire Department arrived on the scene and spent thirty-five minutes trying to extricate Furlow from the twisted wreckage.[63] They rushed the Utah guard to nearby Deaconess Hospital, but it was too late. Doctors pronounced Furlow dead on arrival at 4:05 a.m.[64]

Police searched and impounded the car, and an autopsy was performed to determine the cause of death. "There's no doubt he died as a result of the accident," announced Cuyahoga County coroner Samuel Gerber. "He had a dislocated and fractured cervical spine and a dislocated and transsection of the brain stem."[65] But what had caused Furlow to swerve out of control in the first place? Speculations started flying. Even though police found open and empty alcoholic beverage containers in the wrecked Mercedes, the press coverage immediately zeroed in on the discovery of a white powdery substance believed to be cocaine and a suspected marijuana cigarette.[66] The suspicious substances were sent for chemical analysis, and the coroner conducted a toxicology test on Furlow's body.[67] They would now have to await the results.

"Terry was a troubled young man," said Jazz head coach Tom Nissalke. "We knew he had a history of problems when he joined us last fall. But he played so well in his first two months with us that we were very encouraged and hoped he may have found the right situation."[68] Furlow had shown such promise at the collegiate level. He was the second-leading scorer at Michigan State University (bested only by Earvin "Magic" Johnson a couple of years later) and third-leading scorer in the nation as a senior (29.4 points per game). But in the NBA he earned more attention for being outspoken and insubordinate than for his production on the court.[69] Selected twelfth overall by the Philadelphia 76ers in the 1976 draft, Furlow had bounced around the league, playing for four teams in four years. His death appeared to be yet another tragic example of a young, unruly Black ballplayer paying the ultimate price for living life in the fast lane—a warning about the dangers of getting too much too soon and becoming caught up in a life of drugs and excess.

In the weeks before Furlow's death, another drug rumor involving Spencer Haywood, now of the Los Angeles Lakers, cast a shadow over the 1980 NBA Finals. Much like King and Furlow, Haywood was a story of lost possibility. Although he had come into the league as a young phenom, having defeated the four-year rule in the courts, he had never quite reached the heights expected of him. Now a thirty-year-old veteran on his fourth team, Haywood had become increasingly unstable.

Although nothing was ever confirmed publicly, by the time of the finals Haywood's cocaine abuse was an open secret in the NBA. Previously, he had never been a heavy drug user. Back in 1978, when he was playing for the Knicks, he had dabbled in cocaine on the party scene in New York City, but he was not a big fan. Like many other ballplayers of his generation, he preferred to smoke marijuana.[70] But after arriving in Los Angeles in September 1979, he descended into a nine-month cycle of addiction. He had discovered freebasing at a friend's party in Beverly Hills. Haywood remembered thinking, "Everyone seems to be having fun; nobody's walking around in a stupor or nodding off like the heroin junkies I've seen. These were upstanding men of the community, having a little fun. What could it hurt to try it, just once?"[71] When he took his first hit, it was an intense high. All of his problems and insecurities seemed to evaporate.

In 1980 doing coke was considered chic. People knew it was illegal, but cocaine wasn't a "street-corner drug" like smack. For Haywood and other Black pro athletes, it opened the door to an elite social world: "In Hollywood in '79 and '80, I was blowin' with the cream of society—the leaders of government, great artists and writers, tycoons of business and industry, the beautiful people from straight off the magazine covers, the actors and producers and directors of the movie and TV business, musicians." However, things really started to go south when he began mixing in other drugs, from quaaludes to Valium, to help take the edge off his highs.[72]

It did not help that his personal life was falling down around him. His then wife, supermodel Iman, had suffered a miscarriage in the middle of the season, and back in Silver City, Mississippi, his mother was dying of cancer. His drug use spiraled further out of control. Haywood dropped nearly twenty pounds and looked terrible. He had gone from the starting lineup to the bench. His concentration was shot; he forgot plays and kept messing up the Lakers' offense.[73] His lack of playing time caused friction with Coach Paul Westhead that frequently spilled out into the press. Haywood later recalled that his cocaine use was pretty much out in the open, yet none of the Lakers—neither his teammates nor the front office—made any kind of real intervention.[74]

Things eventually came to a head when the Lakers took on the Philadelphia 76ers in the NBA Finals. After practice on Thursday, May 1, Haywood went out to smoke at a friend's place. It would not hurt to get a little bit of partying in, he reasoned, because game 1 of the series was not until Sunday. Haywood stayed up all night getting high. The next morning, he had to get himself to practice, so he took a quaalude to help bring him down. As he drove home, he kept falling asleep at the wheel, but he somehow managed to shower, get back in his car, and drive to the Lakers' practice facility in West Los Angeles. During the warm-up, however, he passed out cold in the hurdler's stretch. It took five minutes to rouse him. Furious at Haywood's latest act of disrespect for the team, Coach Westhead sent him home and cut his playing time in the series. When Haywood almost got into a physical fight with one of his teammates after game 2 in Philadelphia, Westhead suspended him for the rest of the season.[75]

The next morning Westhead held a press conference to address the disciplinary action taken against Haywood, but he remained opaque about the situation: "It's kind of an accumulation of things. . . . My feeling for days now is that Spencer's attitude has not been in tune with the rest of the team, and I was hopeful he would snap out of it and get back on track. Unfortunately, it didn't happen."[76] Unless legal proceedings made players' indiscretions public knowledge, the Lakers and the league preferred to keep any discussion of cocaine out of the media. Nevertheless, drug rumors started circulating.

In the meantime, the Lakers beat the 76ers in six games to win the NBA championship—their first in eight years—thanks, in part, to the brilliant play of the effervescent African American rookie Earvin "Magic" Johnson.[77] The championship came with glory, bragging rights, and an extra $345,000 to divvy up among the players. NBPA bylaws stated that anyone who played over sixty games with the winning team was entitled to a full share of the playoff money. Even though Haywood had played eighty-six games with the Lakers—seventy-six regular-season games and eleven playoff games—his teammates were so frustrated with his drug abuse and inconsistent effort that they voted to give him only one-quarter of his designated playoff money.[78] He felt betrayed.

Haywood's cocaine abuse had cost him more than just playoff money. The Lakers barred him from riding in the victory parade, excluded him from the team photo marking their finals win, and denied him a championship ring: "I was probably the only player in the NBA, before or since, to be thrown off a team because of drug problems, with no testing, no warning, no second chance."[79]

Ultimately, Haywood's addiction cost him his career. Technically still under contract with the Lakers, the thirty-year-old veteran hoped that he would be put in the expansion draft, with the potential of being picked up by the new Dallas Mavericks. Instead, the NBA informed him that he would have to play out the remainder of his contract overseas with Carrera Venezia of the Italian professional league. It was a huge blow. Haywood could not help but think back to his embattled entry into the NBA, when he fought the powers that be to overturn the four-year rule. He felt as if the league was now penalizing him for his earlier stand. The NBA had decided to make an example of him as a warning to other players about what could happen if they, too, were caught with cocaine, and his punishment had a chilling effect on those struggling with substance abuse.[80] Yes, Haywood clearly had a drug problem, but it seemed as if NBA officials had enjoyed watching his demise.

ALTHOUGH THE RECENT NBA CHAMPIONSHIP HAD AIRED ON TAPE delay because CBS did not think it would attract enough viewers to warrant a prime-time slot, in the off-season the league could not stay out of the news. Mainstream sportswriters seemed only too eager to provide readers with the unseemly details of a few Black ballplayers' legal troubles. On June 4, Bernard King, dressed in a three-piece gray flannel suit, stood before a Salt Lake County judge to receive his sentence. The prosecutor and King's attorney had come to a plea-bargaining agreement with respect to the sex charges. The three felony charges of forcible sodomy were dropped, and in exchange King pled guilty to misdemeanor charges of forcible sexual abuse. The judge sentenced him to two suspended one-year jail terms and a $2,000 fine so that King could return to basketball and continue his treatment for alcoholism under the supervision of his parole officer. As long as he stayed out of trouble, he would stay out of prison.[81]

With King's misdemeanor cocaine charge still in play, Jazz general manager Frank Layden told reporters, "His status with us is unchanged." He remained on indefinite suspension—now *with pay*.[82] An arbitrator had ordered the Jazz to pay King his full salary for the 1979–1980 season after the NBPA came to his defense, arguing that the original unpaid suspension was instituted without due process.[83] "Bernard's problem is alcoholism, which is an illness," NBPA lawyer Larry Fleisher said. "They can't suspend somebody because of an illness. The rest of the world knows this, but not sports."[84] King suffered from a medical condition, the union argued, and should have been treated for it, not punished. Instead, the Jazz had viewed him as guilty until proven innocent.

In light of King's very public troubles, the NBA began to revisit its drug education and prevention program. Security director Joyce provided Commissioner O'Brien with a list of twelve recommended changes. Some of his suggestions were more substantive in nature: the league should expand its oversight of drugs dispensed by teams and work with the NCAA to develop background information on top college prospects. However, the bulk of his proposals involved stepped-up warnings to the players about the dangers of illicit drugs and various public relations efforts to showcase the league's antidrug stance. Joyce called for drug seminars led by DEA agents at all training camps, the distribution of drug education materials to all clubs, and posted warnings about illegal drugs in all locker rooms. He also recommended that the league encourage players to participate in antidrug spots for TV and radio and to discuss the adverse effects of drugs when conducting basketball clinics with teens.[85]

Just when the NBA could ill afford any more negative publicity, another Black player ran afoul of the law. On Sunday, July 13, at around 7:30 p.m., Atlanta police arrested the Hawks' All-Star guard Eddie Johnson at an intersection in south Fulton County. Although he was known as "Fast Eddie" because of his quickness and agility on the court, the arresting officers claimed that Johnson was "unsteady on his feet, his eyes were glassy, and he was belligerent."[86] A few months earlier, he had been the darling of Atlanta, as Hawks fans voted him team MVP for the 1979–1980 season. Johnson averaged 18.5 points per game, led the Hawks in steals with 120, and was second in assists with 370. Now he found himself embroiled in a messy public scandal. Police charged Johnson with driving under the influence, driving with a suspended license, and possession of cocaine after they found a white powdery substance and drug paraphernalia in the flight bag in the trunk of his rental car.[87] His arrest went out on the wires and appeared in the sports pages of all the major US dailies.

Atlanta's local Black newspaper took a special interest in Johnson's situation. *Daily World* sports columnist Othello "Chico" Renfroe went to visit the embattled guard in the Fulton County Jail. A former shortstop in both the Negro and Mexican leagues in the 1940s and 1950s, Renfroe was no stranger to the pressures of professional sport. He had wondered why the Hawks had just left Johnson in jail. Atlanta's front office later revealed that it had, at first, discouraged any efforts to bail out Johnson. "We wanted to solve Eddie's problem

Eddie Johnson (3) of the Atlanta Hawks drives against Maurice Cheeks of the Philadelphia 76ers on his way to a first-period field-goal try in the first game of the NBA playoff series at Philadelphia, April 6, 1980. (AP Photo/Gene Puskar)

in the long run," Hawks President Michael Gearon subsequently said of their "tough-love" approach. "We had to keep him confined to help him."[88]

Although Renfroe acknowledged that Johnson was "a troubled man," he knew that the county jail was no place for the young ballplayer. Johnson was a sick man who needed support: "I'm convinced that if he seeks help and admits he needs help he can bounce back like Daryl [sic] Porter and Bob Welch."[89] Porter and Welch were two white Major League Baseball players who had struggled with addiction. White athletes with substance-abuse problems received much more sympathetic treatment in the media: their addiction cast as illness and their recovery presented as a portrait of courage and redemption.[90] But Renfroe made it clear that addiction was no respecter of race. African American drug users also deserved a chance at rehabilitation rather than criminalization. He urged Black fans to stand with Johnson in his hour of need, just as they had celebrated his spectacular feats on the court: "Eddie Johnson needs you again, he needs your prayers, your confidence and a pat on the shoulder."[91]

A few days later, Johnson was released on a $26,000 bond. "I'm not guilty," he told reporters as he left the facility. "I was driving a rent-a-car. That stuff (white powder suspected to be cocaine) could have been there when I got the car. The police thought I had a concealed weapon and they treated me that way."[92] He declared that he would dedicate the next season to his former teammate and friend, the late Terry Furlow. Although out on bail, Johnson headed to Ridgeview Institute near Smyrna, Georgia, to undergo a court-ordered psychiatric examination.[93]

It turned out that the white powdery substance in Johnson's rental car was a forty-gram mixture containing 1 percent pure cocaine. Regardless of how it got there, this was hardly a potent elixir: street coke in the Atlanta area typically ranged from 8 to 14 percent pure. "On the facts of this case," Fulton County district attorney Lewis R. Slaton said, "Johnson is not a trafficker, but a user."[94] If convicted,

Johnson would face a lighter sentence; the judge had the authority to impose a sentence from two to fifteen years, with probation or suspension possible for all or part of the term.

Johnson's woes continued, however. Already facing the cocaine possession charge, he was arrested again on July 24, this time for auto theft. As his latest misdeed circulated in national newspapers, it became yet another example of how Black players had plunged the NBA into upheaval. According to the warrant, Atlanta rental agency Luxury Auto Import alleged that Johnson had stolen a $34,000 1980 Porsche 911E from them. Johnson was held on a $2,000 bond and charged with felony motor-vehicle theft because of the high value of the car.[95] He was then ordered to undergo another psychiatric examination at Grady Memorial Hospital in Atlanta.

For their part, the Atlanta Hawks seemed willing to cut their valuable property some slack because of Johnson's integral role as guard. Coach Hubie Brown admitted that he was aware that Johnson dabbled in the drug world during the off-season but argued that "Fast Eddie" had turned over a new leaf. Luckily for Johnson, in early August, Paul Isringhausen, the owner of Luxury Auto Import, decided to drop the charges against him. And around the same time, Johnson was released from Grady Memorial's psychiatric ward after a two-week stay for observation and treatment. For the moment, the Hawks remained optimistic that their All-Star guard would be able to rejoin the team in the fall for the start of the season.[96] He was too important to dispose of—yet.

LESS THAN A WEEK LATER, CHRIS COBBS'S INFAMOUS EXPOSÉ ON rampant cocaine abuse in the NBA went national. Newspapers from across the country reprinted and excerpted the *Los Angeles Times* article, never questioning its veracity. One headline even called it a "study."[97] But Cobbs quoted mostly anonymous sources and relied on a smattering of team executives for his estimates of cocaine use (40 to 75 percent) and freebasing (10 percent) in the NBA. Given that African Americans composed about 75 percent of the league's players, the racial connotations were impossible to miss: this was a Black drug crisis. Cobbs's allegations quickly made their way onto television, but *CBS News* could not even get the story right. Anchor Charles Kuralt later had to apologize for two errors in their report: they accidentally used a photo of David Thompson for Eddie Johnson and featured footage of college teams. Apparently, they had trouble distinguishing one Black ballplayer from the next.[98]

Even though cocaine was most popular among wealthy white professionals, socialites, and celebrities in 1980, the majority-Black league became the target of moral panic. With their lucrative contracts, young Black players were able to afford the expensive drug, which sold for $90 to $125 per gram (around $315 to $438 in today's dollars).[99] Cocaine had gotten into the hands of the wrong kind of people—young and entitled Black men who by fluke of athletic talent were living well above their proper socioeconomic station in life.

The exposé inflamed concerns about a rising freebase problem in the league. "Free base is as dangerous as heroin, and it's a serious problem," Gearon reportedly told Cobbs.[100] It did not help that Cobbs's article came out just two months after African American comedian Richard Pryor had set himself on fire while freebasing cocaine and drinking rum, a story that made the national news and became another disturbing omen of growing Black degeneracy.[101] Foreshadowing the racialized panic surrounding crack cocaine in the mid-1980s, freebase was the latest demon drug, treated with growing hysteria in the press. The media helped peddle the erroneous idea that freebase was far more addictive than powder cocaine because it created such an intense euphoria that users inevitably succumbed to multiday binges costing thousands of dollars. With Republican presidential candidate Ronald Reagan campaigning that summer on an anti-Black platform of rolling back civil rights and social welfare while ramping up law and order, Cobbs's article was an unexpected gift.[102] It inflamed racialized fears about cocaine-addled African American players that set the stage for the punitive turn in Reagan's War on Drugs.

Cobbs's shocking revelations put NBA officials on the defensive. Commissioner O'Brien responded by issuing a prepared statement: "It is obvious that professional athletes are not immune from the same temptations that have, unfortunately, caused drug usage to increase in society generally." He noted that the league had a well-established drug education program in place and that, over the summer, he had formed a special antidrug committee composed of owners, general managers, coaches, trainers, and physicians to review the situation.[103] "Any player proved having engaged in the use or sale of illegal drugs will forfeit his right to play in the NBA," O'Brien told reporters. "But we don't and won't act on hearsay and whim. Nothing will be done unless charges are proved."[104]

Behind the scenes, those interviewed and named in the exposé, including Stan Kasten (Atlanta Hawks GM), Frank Layden (Utah Jazz GM), Paul Westphal (Seattle SuperSonics guard), and Michael Gearon (Atlanta Hawks president), insisted that Cobbs had misquoted them and taken their words out of context. They denied giving the reporter percentage estimates of cocaine use in the league.[105] Meanwhile, O'Brien and security head Joyce scheduled a September meeting of the antidrug committee. In addition to all of Joyce's proposed changes from the summer, the agenda included legal questions pertaining to player rights in the context of drug investigations and NBA policy regarding rehabilitation and disciplinary action for those caught using drugs.[106]

Team and league officials positioned themselves as the protectors of the purity and integrity of the game amid this latest wave of Black contamination. Nets GM Charley Theokas, a member of O'Brien's antidrug committee, chastised the majority-Black players with the rhetoric of personal responsibility, stressing their ultimate obligation to the league's largely white fan base: "Professional basketball players should realize theirs is no 9-to-5 job. . . . They are public figures. They belong to the public 24 hours a day and they should lead by example."[107] As NBA officials called for greater control over the players' labor and leisure, they summoned long-standing racial scripts of white ownership over Black bodies.

The NBPA recognized that it was caught between a rock and a hard place. "I have no idea what the percentage is," said union lawyer Larry Fleisher, "but I know that 75 percent is ludicrous." Still, Fleisher acknowledged that public perception, regardless of its accuracy, could harm the NBA's financial stability: "We have to think about television ratings, ticket prices and all sorts of ramifications." As the league's top brass aligned themselves with the fans in opposition to the players, the NBPA felt that it had to adopt a more hardline position, too. "We've become very militant in our view now," Fleisher declared. "We'll be less prone to help a player convicted of a drug offense."[108] Although the NBPA refused to join Commissioner O'Brien's newly appointed antidrug committee, it agreed to cooperate with the group. And during the preseason, Fleisher visited all of the teams to gather policy recommendations from the players.[109]

In September the league went ahead with its planned drug seminars.[110] Joyce and two federal drug-enforcement officers met with the New York Knicks for a little more than an hour. Although the discussion touched lightly on the medical risks of taking cocaine, most of it centered on the legal ramifications of being caught with street drugs. The players would face closer scrutiny by police, the officers warned, because catching public figures helped local departments "get more federal funds for investigative purposes."[111] There were also more than a thousand informants working with federal, state, and local law enforcement in the New York area who would jump at the chance to rat out professional athletes to bolster their credibility. NBA players could easily become collateral damage in the expanding War on Drugs.

As league and team officials looked ahead to the future, many of them saw drugs through the lens of punishment rather than rehabilitation. So ingrained was the idea that ballplayers had criminal tendencies that one NBA administrator even suggested having teams hold practice sessions at nearby maximum-security prisons. "While this should be positioned solely as a 'community relations' appearance," he advised, "the basic reason for the practice and visit is to expose the players to the hardship of prison life."[112] Perhaps the league could scare them straight.

The rest of the major leagues followed the NBA's lead, going on the defensive in the wake of Cobbs's damning exposé. Their campaigns to "clean up" pro sports were by no means racially neutral. Arrested in Toronto on charges of possession of cocaine, marijuana, and hashish, just days after Cobbs's story broke, the Texas Rangers' Black Canadian pitcher Ferguson Jenkins became the face of Major League Baseball's drug problem, with his photo splashed all over the nightly television news.[113] One league official even asserted that teams with a higher proportion of Black and Latino players were more likely to have serious drug issues. "For an executive to say that blacks are more likely to use drugs and not back up that statement with documentation is irresponsible," said Cleveland Indians African American first baseman Andre Thornton. Likewise, NFLPA executive director Ed Garvey noted the continuing double standard in professional football: "Owners and commissioners are too quick to condemn the players for anything. . . . The security forces are always examining what the players are up to but not the owners."[114]

NHL executives, in contrast, argued that their league's drug problem was negligible compared to that of the other leagues because a third of their teams were located in Canada, where access to drugs was more restricted. The implication of their claim was that the drug crisis was a US problem, and, given the overwhelming whiteness of the NHL, a Black problem. There were relatively few NHL players charged with, and even fewer convicted of, drug-related offenses. However, its majority-white players were not the targets of law enforcement. After being arrested in the Toronto airport, Don Murdoch of the New York Rangers was one of the few NHL players convicted of cocaine possession.[115]

Still, not everyone in the NBA accepted Cobbs's sensationalist findings at face value. Chicago Bulls GM Rod Thorn was one of a few dissenting voices among NBA managers: "This cocaine thing has been blown way out of proportion. . . . I'm not going to say that some players don't take cocaine, but that 75 per cent figure is totally fallacious." He added, "I think what the story should say is that a lot of players may have TRIED cocaine or marijuana but didn't go any farther."[116] The idea that anyone, especially Black athletes, could use but not abuse drugs seemed completely outside of the public imagination.

African American players were the most vocal in their opposition to Cobbs's smearing of the league. "How can any sport operate with 75 percent of its players on drugs?" asked Maurice Lucas of the New Jersey Nets.[117] Julius Erving also balked at the high figure and felt that the league's singular focus on player drug use was misguided: "There's a greater alcohol-abuse problem in sports in general than a drug problem. . . . And some coaches have been known to be the worst offenders."[118] Indeed, alcoholism in professional sports received little traction in the news cycle. Against the backdrop of urban decay, drugs became fused with popular narratives of Black criminality, so it was hardly surprising that the NBA treated cocaine as its sole scourge. Illicit drugs were a much bigger PR nightmare for a majority-Black league endeavoring to expand its appeal among white suburban families. Meanwhile, rookie New York Knicks center Marvin Webster challenged the media's particular demonization of professional athletes: "[Drug use] is a national social problem—not just [in] the NBA, football or baseball. It's a problem for the armed services, the entertainment business."[119] But somehow the drug problem had become its problem alone.

Amid all of the public consternation over the NBA's supposed "cocaine crisis," David Israel was one of the few journalists to offer a systemic analysis of the place of drugs in professional sports: "Sports drug culture begins in the locker room, not on the street. . . . You need Dexedrine to play, you need Seconal to come down, you need marijuana to kill the pain, you need cocaine to level off and reach some kind of socially acceptable state of coherent euphoria." Echoing the long-standing critiques of New Left athletic activists such as Jack Scott, Israel pointed the finger at the commercial sporting establishment and its quest for profit at the expense of the players' well-being. "The problem is not Eddie Johnson or Ferguson Jenkins. They are not the truly sick ones. They are the victims," Israel declared. "The truly sick people are the owners and executives who demand consistently high levels of performance, levels they know are impossible to reach without drugs; the villains are the guys who want faster, faster, faster and better, better, better at any cost and by any means. It is, after all the only way to keep the customer satisfied."[120]

All of the hype and hand-wringing were hypocritical. "You are conditioned to abuse your body and betray your sensibilities," Israel noted, "but only on company time." As he saw it, the pro leagues' latest antidrug campaign was more about face-saving appearances than fundamental change: "Jocks don't indulge in drugs any more than other members of an affluent privileged class, and they have better reasons. But they are only charming until they get caught and become criminals. Then we fret about what an awful influence they must be on our children."[121]

In November, Commissioner O'Brien and NBPA attorney Fleisher took the unusual step of sending a joint memo about drugs to the players. They believed that the seriousness of the situation warranted it. "Remember, millions of Americans, and especially young people, look upon you as heroes," they entreated. "If you are abusing drugs, STOP! If you are thinking about abusing drugs, DON'T!" Two years before Nancy Reagan first used her famous antidrug phrase, they called on NBA players to "just say no."[122] As the Blackest professional sports league and as one still struggling to find its financial footing, the NBA felt an intense pressure to protect its reputation in the eyes of its majority-white fans. How could NBA officials pitch the sport as wholesome family entertainment if their players kept getting caught with illegal drugs? How could they expand their market share, especially among white middle-class suburbanites, without the right kind of role models?

UPON CLOSER EXAMINATION, THE VERY CASES THAT HAD HELPED TO spark Cobbs's cocaine exposé were hardly straightforward morality tales about the dangers of Black decadence and drug addiction. As mainstream sportswriters sought to make sense of Terry Furlow's untimely death, they cast him as a selfish, moody, and petulant troublemaker who had turned to cocaine because he could not handle the rigors of pro basketball. But Furlow's story was more complicated than this simplistic caricature suggested. His brash and charismatic personality had long made it difficult for him to silently stomach the racism he confronted in big-time basketball. As a college athlete at Michigan State, he was known to keep a photo of Muhammad Ali in his locker. During his junior season with the Spartans, Furlow was one of ten African American players who walked out of a team meeting to protest racism in the basketball program—particularly Coach Gus Ganakas's decision to start a white player named Jeff Tropf ahead of several more-skilled Black teammates. Refusing to cow down to white authority, the outspoken Furlow often exchanged heated words with Ganakas.[123]

Furlow continued to be vocal and defiant in the NBA, two characteristics that made the young Black player a liability, and he found himself shunted from club to club. Although he had been a college standout, Furlow spent most of his rookie season riding the pine with the Philadelphia 76ers. He had the unfortunate luck of being a talented newcomer on a team chock-full of NBA All-Stars, including Dr. J, George McGinnis, and Steve Mix. However, Furlow was not shy about expressing his discontent.[124] Branded a nuisance, the chip on his shoulder only grew.

After just one season, Philadelphia traded him to the Cleveland Cavaliers. Unfortunately for Furlow, bad luck struck again. Following a spectacular showing in preseason exhibition games, a nasty viral infection sidelined him for two months. When he returned, he found himself coming off the bench behind yet another superstar, the newly acquired veteran Walt Frazier. Although Furlow became a fan favorite thanks to his shooting ability, he constantly clashed with Cavs coach and general manager Bill Fitch. Known for his one-on-one play, Furlow chafed against the constraints of Fitch's team-oriented system. A season and a half into his time there, and after a heated on-court shouting match with Fitch, Cleveland shipped Furlow to the Atlanta Hawks. "I wasn't getting paid for taking verbal abuse," Furlow commented on the trade. "I hope the situation is right in Atlanta."[125]

His move to the Hawks proved even more disastrous. Now on his third team in three years, Furlow found himself once again fighting for a starting position, this time against Eddie Johnson at Atlanta's training camp. Johnson emerged victorious, snatching a place in the starting lineup, something that Furlow had trouble handling despite his friendship with Johnson. And if Furlow thought Fitch was abusive, Hawks coach Hubie Brown's style was even more severe. Furlow often fought with Brown, who was known for goading and berating his players. "I wouldn't conform totally to what Hubie Brown wanted," Furlow once said. "Some players cannot take that on-your-back, taunting, cursing, swearing, hounding, you're-getting-your-ass-whupped kind of stuff. I'll tell you something else: When you play for the Atlanta Hawks, Hubie Brown is in control of your life."[126] Only twenty-one games into the 1979–1980 season, Hawks officials announced their decision to trade Furlow to the Utah Jazz "because he refused to accept a subservient role."[127] Feeling isolated in Utah, Furlow became depressed. In the months before his deadly automobile accident, there were rumors that he was behaving bizarrely and possibly freebasing. Although the mainstream sports media had been quick to blame his fatal crash on drugs, the coroner had found only trace amounts of cocaine and Valium in the late player's blood.[128]

Ironically, even though Johnson had beaten Furlow out of a starting guard position, his own fall from grace came not long after. With Johnson's drug and auto-theft arrests in the summer of 1980, sportswriters had begun to characterize the Hawks' star as a young man who abused cocaine because he was ill-equipped to handle his newfound fame and fortune. However, those close to Johnson wondered if there was also something deeper at work. The abrupt change in Johnson's personality had shocked his cousin and teammate Wayne "Tree" Rollins. "I couldn't believe the way Eddie was acting," Rollins told the *New York Times*. "Eddie was always a quiet guy, never hung out in discos or stuff like that. All of a sudden, Eddie was like a different guy."[129]

When Johnson was released to Grady Hospital after his second arrest in mid-July, his psychiatrist, Lloyd T. Baccus, put him on sedation and waited for him to calm down. "It took a couple of days for him to stop being so belligerent, so hyper, much longer than it would if his problem had been drugs," Baccus later told reporters at a press conference in September. "We are treating Mr. Johnson for a manic-depressive disorder."[130] (Untreated sufferers of this serious mental illness, now known as bipolar disorder, often self-medicate by using alcohol and drugs.) Baccus prescribed Johnson lithium, and the young guard seemed to stabilize. "His prognosis is excellent," Baccus said. "He will be productive and able to carry on his duties."[131] Hawks president Gearon admitted that Atlanta's front office had jumped to conclusions about the star guard's issues: "At the time, we thought Eddie had a drug problem. . . . We didn't realize he had a manic-depressive problem."[132]

Looking contrite and subdued, and dressed in a three-piece suit, Johnson had also appeared at the September press conference. He apologized to both the Hawks and the city of Atlanta for his arrests and said he would be present for the start of the team's training camp.[133] It was, in some respects, a stunning scene. To repair his own image and that of the franchise, Johnson had thrown himself on the mercy of the press, revealing all of his private medical information. It was better to be sick than a simple criminal. Both he and the Hawks had too much riding on his return to play.

Perhaps some of the stunning scene had to do with Johnson's upcoming trial for cocaine possession. Even though the young guard's arrest had occurred before Commissioner O'Brien's threat to ban any player convicted of illegal drug use, a cloud of uncertainty hung over his career. "The commissioner cannot take more power than the Congress of the United States," said Johnson's attorney, Robert Fierer. "Mr. O'Brien cannot create a retroactive law that affects Eddie Johnson."[134] If Johnson was convicted for possession but the judge decided to give him a suspended sentence in light of his mental illness, would O'Brien choose to be harsher than the judge in order to make a point? Just in case, Johnson's lawyers were ready to take legal action if the NBA suspended him.

An Atlanta judge later ended up throwing out the cocaine evidence that police had gathered from Johnson's rental car, and prosecutors dropped the case.[135] Still, Johnson's mental illness and cocaine use continued to plague him during and after his career in the NBA. In October 1981 the Hawks had him committed to Grady Hospital's psychiatric ward for treatment. Johnson had apparently gone off his medication and was behaving erratically. Although he stabilized after his week-long stay at Grady, Johnson remained suspicious about the motives behind Atlanta's decision to have him confined against his will. "I'm concerned about myself as a person," he told reporters, "and they're concerned about me only because of how I reflect on the team."[136] It seemed as if they were most concerned about the optics— and his ability to produce on the court.[137]

To counter all of this negative publicity, the NBA marketed itself as a benevolent institution of racial uplift, helping to transform wayward Black players into respectable, law-abiding men, with just the right dose of pizzazz on the court.[138] The league announced new drug-rehabilitation initiatives, including the hiring of a confidential, twenty-four-hour counseling service for its players. Any player or member of his family could call a toll-free number to reach the counselors from the Life Extension Institute. Additionally, they had access to "four clinics staffed with 30 full-time and 30 part-time psychologists, social workers, lawyers and financial and physical rehabilitation specialists."[139] The NBA pledged to help its ailing athletes rid themselves of their personal demons.

Mainstream sportswriters tended to uncritically reproduce this narrative of reform. If players got clean, they had the league to thank. When Bernard King made a comeback with the Golden State Warriors in fall 1980, Scott Ostler of the *New York Times* dubbed him a "reclamation project from Brooklyn."[140] Even though two years earlier, journalists had been quick to label King a criminal, Ostler now described him as "amiable, accommodating and, above all, well spoken." Ostler marveled, "Although he's a ghetto graduate, he speaks in the quiet, precise, clipped and cultivated manner of Sidney Poitier playing a college professor. Not a curse word or a 'you-know' to be heard." King attended Alcoholics Anonymous meetings and hoped to serve as an inspiration for others struggling with addiction. "I hope my coming forward will make it easier for others to come forward, to know that if they suffer from alcoholism, they can do it," the young forward said. Apparently, discipline and the right amount of "finishing" had changed King from delinquent to role model.

This tidy story of racial uplift and rehabilitation obscured a much longer and more complex reality. As late as spring 1993, several weeks after King's retirement from basketball, he fell into a deep depression. This time around, he sought help: "My therapy was slow. It was painful. I cried during most sessions. Over time, I learned that the core of my pain emanated from my mother's lack of connection. The beatings in the kitchen, the lack of a single hug, had left me with a gaping hole in my heart. Throughout my life, I'd try to blunt my pain with alcohol and sex, but the emotional wounds were still fresh and the void hadn't been filled."[141]

Of course, King and other African American ballplayers of the 1970s were complicated humans with their own personal challenges. Yet the media often framed them as undisciplined—as a band of immoral and hedonistic criminals responsible for bringing all of the pathologies of urban Black America into the professional ranks. In some respects, their highly publicized cocaine scandals helped to sanction the increasingly punitive turn in US drug policy. They became prime examples of young Black men who needed harsher law and order, the very embodiment of the imagined connection between Black freedom and prosperity and Black degeneracy in the post–civil rights era. This imagined connection not only made them suspect but also set the stage for the unprecedented regime of racially determined policing and mass incarceration that would affect generations to come.

Though more famous and financially successful, Black ballplayers, just like other Black youths of the seventies, struggled with the impact of intergenerational poverty, trauma, and the stress of trying to "make it" in the face of so many obstacles. They occupied an often-confusing, liminal space in the shifting racial terrain of the United States. They were feted and showered with money but simultaneously portrayed as subhuman, treated as criminals, and made to feel like mere commodities for the edification of mostly white fans. Washington Bullets guard Dave Bing perhaps best described this frustrating and disorienting experience: "Very seldom do people give players credit for being able to think. They should play basketball and that's it. . . . And I think that management, the media, and some fans think that we don't have feelings, . . . we don't hurt, we don't pain."[142] All of that bothered him, and Bing and other Black athletes were no longer willing to just shut up and play.

Epilogue

In fall 1979, Larry Bird (Boston Celtics) and Earvin "Magic" Johnson (Los Angeles Lakers) made their professional debuts. It was a welcome development for the NBA's top brass, who had high hopes for a turnaround after another season of shrinking gates and declining television audiences. Ratings for CBS's *Game of the Week* had fallen 27 percent from the previous year. League executives hired a high-priced public relations firm and scrambled to figure out why fans seemed to be abandoning the NBA. Was it because of the fall of the New York Knicks and other major-market teams, or because 79 percent of the players were Black when more than 75 percent of the fans were white? They also wondered what steps they could take to increase fan interest. Did they need to add a three-point shot or remove the recent ban on hand-checking?[1]

Even as rookies, Bird and Johnson were no strangers to basketball fans. They had played against each other in the 1979 NCAA championship game, and the NBA seized on their budding, cross-racial rivalry to help restore its battered reputation. As they battled it out for college supremacy, the two could not have been more different. A point guard known for his expert passing and athleticism, Johnson was gregarious and ebullient, whereas Bird, a forward and a talented shooter, was introverted and serious. Although both were six-foot-nine, sophomore

Johnson was ripped and conventionally attractive, while senior Bird was awkward looking and lacked muscular definition.

When Magic and his Michigan State Spartans prevailed over Bird and his Indiana State Sycamores (75–64), the final made both players household names. It was the highest-rated championship in history, with a Nielsen rating of 24.1 and 40 million viewers.[2] As the NBA promoted these "clean-cut" rookies from opposite sides of the color line, it began to fashion itself as a space of both colorblindness and multiculturalism—one that could embrace both an exuberant, ever-smiling Black star and a hardworking, self-described "hick" from small-town Indiana. Yet race was at the center of not only the NBA's marketing and management strategies but also its sports media coverage in the early 1980s.

Bird appeared to be the Great White Hope that the Celtics and the NBA needed. Even before he stepped on the court, Celtics fans bought an unprecedented six thousand season tickets.[3] Bird did not disappoint: he won Rookie of the Year in 1980 and helped to reverse the Celtics' declining fortunes alongside a roster of aging stars, including JoJo White, Dave Cowens, and Don Chaney. Thanks to Bird's arrival, Boston went from having the second-worst record in the league in the 1978–1979 season to winning the NBA championship in 1981. And he accomplished all of this without the "natural" athletic abilities that his Black counterparts possessed in droves. As the popular narrative went, though not a particularly fast runner or high jumper, Bird worked hard and played smart to overcome his physical limitations. He had also overcome a childhood marked by financial hardship and trauma to become the NBA's biggest star.[4]

As Bird revived the Celtics' long-standing ideal of "humility, teamwork, and excellence," he inspired white fans' nostalgia for the good old days, before integration and commercialization had ruined the game. "Bird, in fact, carries his humility to an extreme," noted John Papanek of *Sports Illustrated*. "He spurns publicity (and untold thousands of dollars) and doesn't enjoy sharing with strangers his innermost—or, for that matter, outermost—feelings."[5] The same reticent behavior that had turned the white media against Kareem Abdul-Jabbar a decade earlier was now an asset when performed by the NBA's only white superstar. Old friends from the Hoosier state said that fame and money had not changed Bird one bit. He still dressed in jeans and baseball hats, and liked to hunt, fish, and drink beer in his spare time. He was the epitome of white, blue-collar American manhood.[6]

Unlike Bird, Magic Johnson reveled in the spotlight. But his big smile and unadulterated enthusiasm for the game seemed to soften any threatening edge to his self-confidence. Johnson had helped to revive Michigan State basketball. Thanks to his dynamic play and force of personality, he filled the Jenison Field House with fans, landed the Spartans on national TV, led them to an NCAA title, and—perhaps most importantly—brought the MSU program a windfall of revenue.[7] The NBA hoped he would work his magic for them.

When Johnson entered the college draft as a sophomore in 1979, the Los Angeles Lakers chose him number one in the first round. Magic was hardly the archetypal African American "hardship draft" player. Unlike Bird, the Lansing, Michigan, native grew up with a strong sense of family and relative financial security. His father had a full-time job at General Motors, and his mother worked as a school custodian.[8] Johnson's rise to basketball stardom became a reassuring story of *American* success—one that seemed to counter continued Black grievances about persistent racism and inequality. "In a way I suppose the case of Earvin Johnson is the best evidence available that the free enterprise system still works in America," argued Larry Donald of *Basketball Weekly*. "That a young man with talent, diligent effort and a few breaks can make it in this country."[9]

Whereas the ailing Celtics saw Bird as their savior, the Lakers viewed Johnson as a dynamic playmaker who could contribute to an already talented, mostly Black roster, including the likes of Jabbar, Norm Nixon, Jamaal Wilkes, and Michael Cooper. Johnson was faster and more fluid on the court than Bird, yet sportswriters tended to highlight his effervescence while critiquing his flashy and "selfish" style. They often cast his labor on the court as play. Whereas Bird worked hard to win, Johnson played cheerfully for the fun of it. Still, Johnson more than lived up to the Lakers' expectations. In his rookie season, Los Angeles had the second-best record in the NBA and won the league championship with Johnson named the series' Most Valuable Player.[10]

Representing East Coast versus West Coast, traditional versus modern, and white versus Black, the young stars and their teams embodied the culture wars of the 1980s. Although the Celtics and Lakers were the two most successful franchises of the decade, Boston, the whitest team in the league, stood in sharp contrast to the predominantly Black Los Angeles squad. CBS played up this rivalry, broadcasting doubleheaders with Boston in one game and Los Angeles in the next, and their direct matchups always garnered much higher ratings than other NBA games. Even their sneaker deals with Converse played on popular notions of racial difference: Bird, ironically, wore black, and Johnson wore white. Through the Magic-Bird rivalry the NBA began to figure out how to monetize US racial tensions and repackage aspects of African American urban culture and aesthetics into a safe spectacle for fans.[11]

When Boston met Los Angeles in the 1984 NBA Finals, their racial contest played out on pro basketball's biggest stage. The series seemed to be a referendum on Black ball versus white ball. Speed, agility, and creativity characterized the Lakers' game, whereas the Celtics were slower and more methodical in their approach. The teams traded victories in the first two games, but when Los Angeles won game 3 by a large margin (137–104), many thought they would go on to grab the title. However, Boston bumped their way back with physical play that slowed the lightning-quick Lakers, taking both game 4 and game 5. Los Angeles managed to hold them off in game 6 with a 119–108 win, but the Celtics triumphed in game 7, seizing the NBA title. For his part, Bird had a second championship under his belt and a pair of Most Valuable Player awards for the season and the series. As mainstream sportswriters praised Bird and the blue-collar Celtics for outworking and outsmarting Johnson and the more athletic Lakers, they fed into timeworn narratives of anti-Blackness. Ultimately, though, the NBA proved to be the real winner in this racial clash, riding the Magic-Bird rivalry all the way to the bank, with increased attendance, television ratings, and profits by the end of the decade.[12]

INITIALLY, THE NBA REMAINED ON SHAKY GROUND. EVEN WITH the help of Johnson and Bird, the permanent addition of the three-point shot, and the introduction of a new team (Dallas Mavericks), the league still struggled to expand its fan base in the early eighties.[13] Since the late seventies, overall game attendance had fluctuated up and down in the range of nine million fans, breaking the ten-million mark only in the 1983–1984 season. The widest swings happened at the franchise level, especially among some of the more established teams. For example, the New York Knicks went from a high of 791,031 fans in 1972–1973 to a low of 438,823 fans in 1982–1983.[14]

If anyone had the know-how to repair the league's respectability in the eyes of white fans and white advertisers, it was attorney David Stern. He had worked with the league since 1966, helping it to navigate the upsurge of Black players during the NBA-ABA talent war, the wave of Black-led antitrust lawsuits that exposed the practice of blacklisting and brought down the four-year rule and the option clause, and the rough waters of on-court violence and drug scandals during the so-called Dark Ages. Although Lawrence O'Brien was still league commissioner in the early 1980s, Stern spearheaded various initiatives from behind the scenes to help contain the NBA's negative associations with urban Blackness. Building on their strategies from the seventies, Stern and company introduced stricter policies of player discipline while also seeking the support of fans in opposition to the players' rights and contract demands.

New game rules and several changes to the Collective Bargaining Agreement (CBA) brought tighter restrictions on player conduct and tougher penalties for infractions. In fall 1980 the league instituted an official ban on all jewelry on the court. Though ostensibly introduced for safety reasons, many viewed the "Darryl Dawkins amendment" as a rule directed at the Philadelphia 76ers' brash Black star, who liked to wear earrings and layer gold chains with pendants.[15] In turn, any player who committed a flagrant foul, defined as "unnecessary contact committed by a player against an opponent," would now face automatic ejection from the game.[16]

The 1980 CBA also expanded and institutionalized the harsh punishment deployed against Kermit Washington for fighting back in 1977. According to the league's constitution, the commissioner now had the broad and unilateral power to suspend and/or fine a player as much as $10,000 if he felt the player's conduct was "prejudicial to or against the best interests of the Association or the game of basketball." And if a player sought to appeal his punishment for this vaguely worded offense, the commissioner was also in charge of the entire appeals process.[17] The idea of league officials as the ultimate protectors of the game became codified in NBA bylaws and contracts as disciplinary measures became more sweeping and autocratic.

Meanwhile, the team owners continued to publicly blame the players for their economic troubles. Much as they had during the previous decade, they claimed that rising labor costs, alongside the league's ongoing image crisis, were responsible for the NBA's purported multimillion-dollar losses. But their own pattern of greed and mismanagement shared much of the guilt. The revolving door of team owners—twenty-two sales from 1972–1982—led to instability, short-term thinking, and wild spending. If a franchise failed, some owners reasoned, they could just sell it to the highest bidder to recoup any losses. However, by 1982, there were few interested buyers. The pro basketball bubble generated by club owners' rampant speculation had burst.[18] Now they looked to Johnson and Bird to restore their profitability while they attempted to claw back some of the players' hard-won labor rights.

Two months after the CBA expired in June 1982, the NBA sent a formal offer to the NBPA for negotiation. The list of proposals was provocative, to say the least. It included a "salary moderation" plan (essentially a salary cap) and called for an end to "guaranteed contracts, no-trade clauses, renegotiation of existing contracts, and even incentive and performance bonuses." Adding insult to injury, the league called on players earning over $100,000 to fund their own benefits, and it proposed coach-class air travel for all players.[19] Bob Lanier, the Black head of the NBPA, was incensed; with the help of union attorney Larry Fleisher and outside counsel Jim Quinn, he wrote a scathing reply: "It is inconceivable that any management group, even in the worst of times, would have proposed something as barbaric as the six pages you sent us."[20]

In all of the professional sports leagues, players were struggling to defend the labor gains they had made in the seventies. In 1981 MLB players had gone on strike over the owners' attempts to restrict their free agency with a compensation plan, and in fall 1982 NFL players, embittered by their own limited free agency, went on strike for a greater share of league revenues.[21] Beyond the sporting world, a wider campaign to delegitimize and defang the power of labor unions was also underway in the midst of a dire recession and the decline of the American steel and car industries. In 1981 US automakers had forced the once-powerful United Auto Workers to provide givebacks, and President Ronald Reagan had fired over eleven thousand striking air-traffic controllers, leading to the decertification of the Professional Air Traffic Controllers Association. In this climate of austerity, NBA officials carefully framed the contentious CBA negotiations, appealing to the racial and economic grievances of the league's still majority-white fans. After all, if regular (white) workers had to share in the pain of hard times, highly paid Black professional basketball players should as well.[22]

Continued reports of African American players' drug abuse in the press further compromised the NBPA's bargaining power. In January 1982, Washington Bullets point guard John Lucas publicly admitted to having a cocaine problem. After entering an outpatient rehabilitation program and assuring Commissioner O'Brien that he was clean, Lucas was permitted to resume playing.[23]

Yet, some two years after its publication, Chris Cobbs's infamous cocaine exposé still loomed over the league. "People in the NBA who have drug problems get the publicity," Jabbar complained to the *Washington Post*. "We are all highly visible, but we are no more or less susceptible to the problem than the rest of the society."[24] When former defensive lineman and convicted drug criminal Don Reese published a *Sports Illustrated* feature on widespread cocaine use in the NFL in June 1982, its impact reverberated throughout professional sports.[25] The NBA went on the defensive. League officials insisted that drug testing would be part of their CBA negotiations with the union, but the players pushed back. "I ain't no damned guinea pig," union president Lanier declared. "Drug testing would be an invasion of a guy's personal and private life."[26]

In the meantime, these "cocaine crises" in the NBA and NFL helped smooth the way for President Reagan's declaration of a renewed and more repressive War on Drugs in October 1982. Although at the time less than 2 percent of the US public saw drugs as the most significant social problem confronting the country, the image of the Black pro athlete as cocaine criminal had become increasingly ubiquitous.[27] Discussions about the need to discipline the delinquent, drug-ridden Black players who endangered the sanctity of America's sports leagues mirrored broader calls for a crackdown on Black dealers and drug users in order to protect the nation. By December 1982, President Reagan had invited commissioners, player representatives, security directors, lawyers, and general managers from the various professional sports leagues to the White House, hoping to enlist them in his mounting antidrug crusade.[28] For the time being, however, the NBPA was able to resist league officials' efforts to insert mandatory drug testing into the CBA.

The team owners had underestimated the strength of the players' resolve, and after months of back and forth, the CBA negotiations were stalled. Determined to defend their rights, the NBPA came out of the All-Star Weekend in February 1983 with a plan to strike if there was still no satisfactory agreement in place by April 2.[29] The NBA responded with warnings of its own, including the stoppage of insurance coverage and all payments (regular salaries, deferred compensation, and incentives) in the event of a strike. They even threatened to strip veteran free agents of their right to negotiate or sign new contracts. The league also sought to discredit the players' stance in the media. NBA officials once again cried poor, claiming that a strike would imperil the league's survival, and they impugned NBPA attorney Fleisher (and the players' intelligence), arguing that he was deliberately misleading the union membership.[30] As the league waged its public relations campaign, the fans turned on the players. In Philadelphia, the 76ers' Black NBPA representative Clint Richardson received hate mail from factory workers and faced a barrage of verbal abuse from hometown spectators.[31]

The players held strong, and on March 31 the two sides reached an agreement in principle, thereby averting a strike. By maintaining a unified front, the NBPA had managed to rebuff most of the draconian rollbacks in the NBA's initial proposal. Although the new four-year contract contained a salary cap, it also provided players with a guaranteed cut of the league's revenues, including television revenues, and protected their right to free agency. It was a historic profit-sharing pact that paved the way for the success of the league in years to come.[32] With an eye to the future and a nod to the past, NBPA head Lanier said, "I may not reap the benefits of this agreement, but we have worked on behalf of the younger brothers and those who are still to come. Guys like Oscar Robertson and Paul Silas sacrificed for me. We won because the guys stuck together."[33]

But the players' image problems were far from over. John Lucas's public struggles with cocaine continued, and the Bullets eventually cut him in January 1983. In the months that followed, revelations of drug abuse involving Utah Jazz forward John Drew, New Jersey Nets guard Micheal Ray Richardson, and Seattle SuperSonics guard David Thompson also hit the press.[34] By September, Commissioner O'Brien and the NBPA had collaborated to establish a new, more punitive drug policy.

Sportswriters heralded the NBA's "war on drugs" as comprehensive and groundbreaking—a model for other leagues to follow.[35] Under the new plan, any player who was convicted of, or pled guilty to, a crime involving the use or distribution of cocaine or heroin would be permanently banned from the league. The NBA could also test players without notice, and if they were caught using cocaine or heroin, they would face expulsion.[36] Yet marijuana control was noticeably absent from the program, and there was still a degree of mercy for those who voluntarily came forward about their cocaine or heroin use. The first time a player sought help, there would be no penalty or loss of salary, and the team would pay for his treatment. The second time, he would be suspended without pay during the treatment period but would face no other penalty. The third time, he would be out. Although the penalty of permanent dismissal for drug use was mandatory, after two years a banned player could apply for reinstatement in the league.[37] In the face of an increasingly conservative political climate, marked by antiunionism and anti-Blackness, the NBPA made a strategic choice to get tough on drugs. The players were tired of being portrayed as junkies and hoped that the harsh policy would improve their image and usher in a new era of prosperity.

Although the plan helped rehabilitate the league's overall reputation, Black players faced disproportionate surveillance and punishment. In the first two years of the program, all seven of those disciplined for drugs were African American.[38] The NBA's plan also foreshadowed broader policy shifts, including the expansion of employee drug testing in the public and private sectors (late 1980s) and the passage of state-level "three-strikes" laws for repeat offenders (mid-1990s). The sporting war on drugs spilled out into the rest of society.

DAVID STERN HAD REMAINED LARGELY IN THE BACKGROUND, BUT his imprint was all over the league's latest CBA and drug policy. When he finally took over as commissioner in February 1984, almost twenty years into his work with the NBA, the diminutive forty-one-year-old lawyer hit the ground running in his efforts to make the majority-Black league palatable for white consumption. "This is the first sport where it became fashionable and allowable to talk about race," Stern told the *New York Times* later that December. "Our problem was that sponsors were flocking out of the N.B.A. because it was perceived as a bunch of high-salaried, drug-sniffing black guys." Rather than shy away from the NBA's racial dilemma, Stern leaned in, approaching it as a "marketing problem."[39]

In the first years of the decade, Stern had laid the groundwork for handling the NBA's "race problem" by priming the league's publicity machine. Step one involved raising the NBA's visibility through broadcast marketing, the syndication of games, and better scheduling. In winter 1981 he orchestrated a new four-year television deal with CBS, USA, and ESPN worth $88 million, a minimal increase from the NBA's previous contract and a relatively small amount in contrast to the soaring revenues scored by the NFL and MLB. Despite these drawbacks, the decision to shift more of the league's presence to cable proved especially fortuitous by the latter part of the decade. Starting the season later in November was also advantageous for the NBA's ratings. Home openers no longer overlapped with the World Series in October, and the NBA Finals, now played in June, no longer had to compete with sweeps programming.[40]

Secondly, Stern believed that the NBA's long-term success would hinge on the development of meaningful corporate and media relationships. Although he had difficulty selling the league to Madison Avenue at first, Stern and his growing PR team worked to implement a uniform game format with extended timeouts across all of its broadcasts so that viewers knew what to expect when they tuned in, and teams could make more money from commercials.[41] He also began to build the NBA as a full-fledged entertainment corporation with multiple streams of revenue and an expanding international reach that was more akin to Disney and Time Warner than to the NFL and MLB.[42]

Perhaps most importantly, timing was on Stern's side. A few months after he became commissioner in 1984, the Chicago Bulls drafted Michael "Air" Jordan. One of the greatest players of all time, the Hall of Famer won numerous accolades throughout his career: Rookie of the Year, five-time league MVP, six-time NBA champion, six-time NBA Finals MVP, ten-time All-NBA First Team, nine-time NBA All-Defensive First Team, Defensive Player of the Year, fourteen-time NBA All-Star, three-time NBA All-Star MVP, 50th Anniversary All-Time Team, and ten scoring titles.[43] Jordan was not just an athletic phenomenon but also a cultural icon who helped spur the globalization of the NBA. He came into the league alongside the growth of cable, which increased the number of televised games, bringing in more fans and bigger revenues.

Through Jordan, and with the help of greater television exposure and the marketing expertise of shoe companies such as Nike, the NBA expanded its popularity by promoting a highly curated brand of American Blackness—one emptied of contemporary political content and any reference to past struggles.[44] Arguably, all of the characteristics that became the cornerstone of the NBA's global profitability in the age of Jordan, from gravity-defying Black athleticism to Black masculine cool, were already in place long before his arrival. However, the various efforts of African American players to fundamentally

reshape the game both on and off the court in the seventies were quietly submerged.

This overall strategy paid off handsomely. The NBA went from an
average of 10,021 fans per game (58 percent capacity) in 1980–1981 to
15,245 fans per game (89 percent capacity) in 1990–1991. In the first
seven years of Stern's tenure, the league's gross annual revenue (non-
retail money from game tickets and TV deals) rose from $160 million
to $700 million. Player salaries also increased by 177 percent, and the
average value of NBA franchises tripled. Even though all the other
US professional sports leagues saw their television numbers fall over
the course of the 1980s, the NBA's ratings went up by 21 percent.[45]

Buoyed by these rising numbers, the NBA went one step further.
In the early 1990s the league began to link itself more actively to
the Black urban aesthetics of hip-hop, hoping to expand its fan base
among some of the exploding music genre's biggest supporters: white
suburban youths with disposable incomes. Players wore extra-baggy
shorts as part of their official uniforms, and hip-hop stars produced
promotional songs for the league—but all within "respectable" limits.
The NBA provided a safe space for fans to engage in "racial voy-
eurism" detached from any real engagement with everyday African
American people and their social realities. Through the careful promotion of its Black stars, the league peddled a packaged form of masculine rebellion that appealed to young people in the United States
and across the globe.[46]

However, the NBA's tenuous racial and labor peace had begun to
unravel by the late nineties. Pushing through the opening created
by the league's own marketing plan, Black players of the hip-hop
generation asserted themselves on their own terms. Allen Iverson,
Gary Payton, Latrell Sprewell, Ron Artest (Metta World Peace), and
others pushed back against the still-narrow confines of NBA deco-
rum by defiantly displaying their youthful, urban Black style on and
off the court. They dunked at every opportunity. They taunted and
trash talked. They flashed obscene gestures at coaches and fans. They

sported baggy jeans, puffer jackets, gold chains, cornrows, and tattoos. They recorded rap songs. As more of their "street" ways permeated the NBA, fans and sportswriters alike characterized them as "pimps and thugs" who were corrupting the game.[47] The league, once again, found itself in an image crisis.

To reckon with what Phil Taylor of *Sports Illustrated* dubbed the NBA's "Dunk Ages," Commissioner Stern responded with strategies that he had learned from the league's Dark Ages.[48] In November 2004 a notorious brawl later dubbed the "Malice in the Palace" took place between Indiana Pacers players and Detroit fans at the Pistons' arena in Auburn Hills, Michigan. After Pacers forward Ron Artest fouled Pistons center Ben Wallace with less than sixty seconds left in the game, Wallace pushed Artest, and a fight broke out between several players. Even though the players' fight had ended, an angry Pistons fan threw a drink at Artest. Artest charged him, igniting a clash between the largely Black players and the mostly white spectators. Stern responded by suspending nine players for a combined total of 146 games, representing roughly $11 million in lost salary. He attempted to clamp down on the league's negative associations with Black urban youth culture by instituting a dress code (no baggy jeans or chains), setting nineteen as the minimum age for new players, and compiling a list of prohibited establishments where players were barred from socializing. He even reached out to Republican strategist Matthew Dowd for ideas on how to improve the league's "red state appeal."[49]

Stern and the team owners also pulled straight from the 1970s playbook during the lockouts of the 1998–1999 and 2011–2012 seasons. With team owners crying financial hardship, the league locked the players out, hoping to force them into giving back some of their share of the profits. Much as it had in the past, the NBA sought the support of fans in opposition to the supposedly overpaid, ungrateful, and financially illiterate Black players who by 2011 made up 78 percent of the league.[50]

Although they have achieved another racial and labor détente with league officials, today's players understand that they must remain vigilant. The NBA's relative "wokeness" in the professional sports world is by no means a given. As recently as 2014, the leaked audio of onetime Los Angeles Clippers owner Donald Sterling making racist comments sent NBA executives into damage control. His racism had been an open secret within the organization for decades, but the league purged Sterling only after his sins became public knowledge and calls for an NBA boycott grew louder.[51]

The resurgence of Black athletic activism during the last decade has created new challenges and opportunities for the NBA and its players. On social media and in other public forums, many players have expressed vocal support for the broader #BlackLivesMatter movement. Rather than go against the very powerful players association, the NBA has decided to embrace its athletes' political statements. Commissioner Adam Silver was quick to declare that the league supports the players' freedom of speech.[52] But if the NBA has become more open to the concerns of its African American players, it is only because earlier generations pushed league executives and team owners to recognize their racial and economic rights. Indeed, the current commissioner's own father, Ed Silver, a negotiator for the team owners' side in the early seventies, once argued that any changes to the pro basketball system that empowered the players would lead to chaos.[53]

Most recently, at the height of the COVID-19 pandemic in summer 2020, NBA players used the unprecedented opportunity of playing in the league's "bubble" at Walt Disney World to organize in support of racial justice. Just two months after the police murder of George Floyd in Minneapolis on May 25, which propelled millions of people across the United States and around the world to demonstrate in the streets, NBA players took to the court wearing uniforms donning political messages, from "Black Lives Matter" to "Say Their Names" to "I Can't Breathe," rather than their own names.[54] When the state violence continued, they intensified their efforts. On August 26 the

Milwaukee Bucks refused to take the court for their scheduled playoff game against the Orlando Magic in protest of the police shooting of a Black man named Jacob Blake in Kenosha, Wisconsin.

The Bucks' decision to strike for social justice, though not unique to the NBA, owed a largely unacknowledged debt to the labor protections produced by decades of NBA players' individual and collective resistance.[55] If the NBA now has a reputation for being not only the coolest but the most progressive of all the US professional leagues, it's because the players made it so by fighting against the paternalistic and profit-driven practices of the white basketball establishment. Both on and off the court, generations of Black players worked to make the modern NBA into what fans from across the globe cheer for today.

THE 1998–1999 NBA LOCKOUT HAPPENED DURING MY SECOND SEA-son as a Toronto Raptors dancer. I was then a naive twenty-three-year-old, and I recall being confused about the significance of the

Members of the Milwaukee Bucks and the Boston Celtics kneel around a Black Lives Matter logo before the start of an NBA basketball game on July 31, 2020, in Lake Buena Vista, Florida. (Photo by Ashley Landis-Pool/Getty Images)

fight between the players and the team owners. The sports media tended to portray the players as greedy and arrogant ingrates who thought they were bigger than the game, but I knew there had to be more to the story. In the meantime, the dancers and other nonsalaried staff who worked at the games became collateral damage in this labor battle. For me, the lockout could not have come at a worse time. I had just graduated from university and had not yet lined up full-time employment. During those months, I earned no income from the team, except for payment for the odd practice and corporate appearance. Thankfully, I had relatives who graciously agreed to take me in.

Although the players have reshaped the industry for members of their bargaining unit, there is still so much work to be done. Now more than ever, the sports industry as a whole is ripe for a more expansive vision of racial and labor politics: one that reaches back to aid former NBA and ABA players who lacked today's labor protections and now struggle to make ends meet; one that embraces the multitude of workers who make all aspects of the games possible, from concessions to uniforms to halftime entertainment; one that stands in support of "amateurs" in the NCAA who are striving for better working conditions and fair compensation; and one that rejects the heteropatriarchal structure of sporting culture and raises its voice in support of women, trans, and nonbinary athletes' calls for equal pay and treatment. This is the sports labor movement of the future, and because of their relative power and fame and their enduring commitment to justice, NBA players can help make it happen.

Acknowledgments

THIS BOOK COMES IN THE WAKE OF SOME PROFOUND LOSSES AND transitions in my life. Working on it helped to restore my equilibrium and my faith in myself as a scholar, writer, and person. There are simply too many people to thank here. It takes way more than a village to write a book.

First, I would like to thank my Raptors "OG" Dance Pak friends, who continue to inspire me, especially Madonna Gimotea, Tamara Mose, Karen Burthwright, Melanie Allison, Vanessa Cobham, and Kim Deline. You took an awkward "bunhead" from Kitchener and transformed me into a confident dancer and woman. I have so many great memories of our fun times together. Thanks also to Kevin Willis for giving me a small glimpse of the life of a pro ballplayer so many years ago.

I want to acknowledge Katy O'Donnell, who first saw promise in me and this project, and encouraged me to write a trade book. I also owe a special thank-you to Deirdre Mullane, who has been the most enthusiastic agent and writing guru. You "got" this project immediately and understood what I was trying to accomplish. A huge thanks goes out to the entire team at Bold Type Books, especially Hillary Brenhouse and Claire Zuo. The folks at Hachette, including Clive Priddle, Lindsay Fradkoff, Jocelynn Pedro, Miguel Cervantes, Pete Garceau, and Melissa Veronesi, have also been so supportive of this project.

Thank you to the faculty and staff in the departments of History and Critical Race, Gender, and Culture Studies at American University, especially those who cut me slack and offered support as I wrote this book during a global pandemic with an energetic preschooler at home: professors Eric Lohr, Kate Haulman, Eileen Findlay, Mary Ellen Curtin, and Lily Wong and administrators Gabriella Folsom, Sara Gerard-Sharp, and Allison Johntry. To my former PhD advisee and fellow hoops fan Dr. Curtis Harris (@ProHoopsHistory): your research has enriched this book immensely.

Over the years, numerous scholarly interlocutors have offered helpful commentary on different iterations of this project. Chapter 6 is adapted by permission from my article "Punishing the Punch: Constructions of Black Criminality During the NBA's 'Dark Ages,'" published in the *Journal of African American History* 104, no. 3 (Summer 2019): 445–473. Editor Pero Dagbovie and the anonymous reviewers offered many valuable suggestions. A particular note of thanks goes out to the Sports Studies Caucus of the American Studies Association, including its founding coordinator, Noah Cohan, and members Lucia Trimbur, Tyran Steward, Dan Gilbert, Amira Rose Davis, Frank Guridy, and David J. Leonard. My professional mentors, including Matthew Frye Jacobson, Kevin Kelly Gaines, and Adrian Burgos Jr., offered their unwavering support, writing recommendation letters for the fellowships that made this book possible.

I could not have completed a project of this magnitude as a mid-career woman-of-color scholar and mother without the financial support of a number of institutions. As a visiting faculty fellow in the Inclusion Imperative program at the Dresher Center for the Humanities (University of Maryland, Baltimore County), I spent a year conceptualizing and researching *Black Ball* alongside a dynamic group of thinkers, including Jessica Berman, Courtney Hobson, Rachel Brubaker, Nicole King, Michelle Scott, Dawn Biehler, and so many others. The Public Scholars program of the National Endowment for the Humanities gave me additional time to get into the thick of writing.

I had a very ambitious research plan when I first started out, but then COVID-19 intervened. Although the pandemic limited my ability to consult traditional archives and do interviews, it forced me to amass my own extensive collection of published memoirs and digitized materials. Before COVID hit, George Rugg made my research in the University of Notre Dame's Joyce Sports Research Collection a breeze, and afterward, Jeffrey Monseau of Springfield College sent me scans of key materials from the Lawrence F. O'Brien National Basketball Association papers. Thanks also to Nathan Jones of the Vanderbilt Television News Archives and to Jared Browsh, who sourced important articles in the *Denver Post* for Chapter 2.

I have benefited from the gentle prodding of various accountability groups who have seen me through the ups and downs of this journey, including my Faculty Success Program buddies (Michelle King, Janice Pata, and Cabeiri Robinson), the "5:30 a.m. writing crew" (Danielle McGuire, Melissa Stuckey, Crystal Sanders, and Amira Rose Davis), the "Second Book Club" (Julie Weise and Julian Lim), and the "Peloton Babes" (Karie Cotrone and Mary Sheridan), who kept my fitness on point.

My friends have also sustained me during what have been some of the hardest yet most rewarding times of my life. A huge thanks goes out to my Baltimore ladies, the "Snack Chat Mamas" (Rachel Scott, Nicole Fisher Sullivan, and Kyle Kingsley), and the "Buffalo Gals" (Theresa McCarthy, Carole Emberton, Lakisha Simmons, and Cindy Wu), who have listened to me complain, cheered me on, and made me laugh out loud. I could not have crossed the finish line without the help of "#DDT" (Aureliano DeSoto and Lisa Guerrero) and the "Snark Club" (Jeanne-Marie Jackson and Tyran Steward), whose irreverent memes and general hilarity kept me going. Thanks also to Maryjane Viejo, the Chigwidas, Liz Thornberry, and Vesla Weaver for your support.

My son was two years old when this project started to pick up. I could not have focused on it without the community of child-care workers and educators who have worked with him over the years. Sarah Malphrus, Zari Press, and Zenia Gates have helped our family immeasurably. My heartfelt thanks goes out to everyone on "Team Gus," including Dr. Susan Grant, Julie Hemmeter, Adeline Stang, Katie Kuhn, Andrea Bennett, and all of the special-education crew at Hampden Elementary, especially Mrs. Limiac, teacher extraordinaire. This project would not have been possible without you, and my son is happier and healthier because of you.

Last but not least, my family has been there through it all. I owe a debt of gratitude to my late father, John Runstedtler, for inspiring my curiosity for history and politics and my enduring belief in the importance of unions. I wish that you could have seen this book. To my mom, Elisea Runstedtler: you are the strongest, most generous person I know. To my brother, Allan Runstedtler: thanks for encouraging me in the final stretch. A special thanks to my mother-in-law, Veronique Clark, for being such a wonderful Grandma. To my husband, Joe: thank you for seeing me through this crazy journey and for still loving me in the end. Like a good former Marine, you were always there to remind me to "normalize" struggle and to "walk with one foot at a time." And to Gus, my special little boy: you have made me a better person. Finally, I am eternally grateful to my furry ride-or-die Billie, who sat next to me for countless hours during the writing of this book. Rest in peace, dear girl. Till we meet again at the Rainbow Bridge.

Notes

Introduction

1. Chris Cobbs, "NBA and Cocaine: Nothing to Snort At," *Los Angeles Times*, 19 August 1980.

2. "Californians Captured Three of the Four Awards Announced Monday," United Press International, 19 January 1981, accessed 20 December 2021, https://upi.com/4196752.

3. See Matthew Schneider-Mayerson, "'Too Black': Race in the 'Dark Ages' of the National Basketball Association," *International Journal of Sport and Society* 1, no. 1 (2010): 223–233; FreeDarko, *The Undisputed Guide to Pro Basketball History* (New York: Bloomsbury, 2010), 99–103.

4. Santiago Colás, *Ball Don't Lie: Myth, Genealogy, and Invention in the Cultures of Basketball* (Philadelphia: Temple University Press, 2016), 21–24; Curtis Matthew Harris, "From the Triangle to the Cage: Basketball's Contested Origins, 1891–1910" (MA thesis, American University, 2014), 76–77; Curtis Matthew Harris, "Hardwood Revolution: The NBA's Growth and Player Revolt, 1950–1976" (PhD diss., American University, 2021), 1.

5. Colás, *Ball Don't Lie*, 39; Harris, "Hardwood Revolution," 1–2.

6. Ron Thomas, *They Cleared the Lane: The NBA's Black Pioneers* (Lincoln: University of Nebraska Press, 2002), 26–27.

7. Harris, "Hardwood Revolution," 63–64.

8. Thomas, *They Cleared the Lane*, 57.

9. Thomas, 67.

10. Harris, "Hardwood Revolution," 109.

11. Harris, 96–98, 117.

12. Harris, 109–115.

13. Harris, 81–85. For more on Maurice Stokes's life and career, see Pat Farabaugh, *An Unbreakable Bond: The Brotherhood of Maurice Stokes and Jack Twyman* (Haworth, NJ: St. Johann, 2014).

14. Harris, "Hardwood Revolution," 88–90.

15. Oscar P. Robertson, *The Big O: My Life, My Times, My Game* (Lincoln: University of Nebraska Press, 2013), 179.

16. Harris, "Hardwood Revolution," 116.

17. Robertson, *Big O*, 181–183; Harris, "Hardwood Revolution," 122.

18. Robertson, *Big O*, 183–185.

19. Robertson, 185; Harris, "Hardwood Revolution," 123.

20. Harris, 102.

21. Colás, *Ball Don't Lie*, 19–20.

22. Theresa Runstedtler, *Jack Johnson, Rebel Sojourner: Boxing in the Shadow of the Global Color Line* (Berkeley: University of California Press, 2012); Howard Bryant, *The Heritage: Black Athletes, a Divided America, and the Politics of Patriotism* (Boston: Beacon, 2018), vii.

23. For the original use of this term, see W. E. B. Du Bois, "The Strivings of the Negro People," *Atlantic*, August 1897, 194–195.

Chapter 1: Exile: Connie Hawkins's Long Journey to the NBA

1. Bob Voelker, "Pipers Explode in Third to Grab Playoff Contest," *Morning Herald* (Uniontown, PA), 5 April 1968.

2. "Pipers Top Muskies, Win Eastern Title," *New York Times*, 15 April 1968.

3. "Reveal Offers to Shift ABA Team," *Chicago Daily Defender*, 9 May 1968; Emily Ruby, "The Year That Rocked Pittsburgh," *Western Pennsylvania History* 96, no. 1 (2013): 27.

4. David Wolf, *Foul: The Connie Hawkins Story* (New York: Holt, Rinehart and Winston, 1972), 144.

5. Terry Pluto, *Loose Balls: The Short, Wild Life of the American Basketball Association* (New York: Simon and Schuster, 2007), 79. See also Howie Evans, "Sort of Sporty," *New York Amsterdam News*, 6 May 1967; and Wolf, *Foul*, 102–147.

6. Wolf, *Foul*, 147, 232.

7. David Wolf, "The Unjust Exile of a Superstar," *Life*, 16 May 1969, 52.

8. Wolf, *Foul*, 231, 234, 148.

9. *Cornelius Hawkins v. National Basketball Association*, 288 F. Supp. 614 (W.D.Pa. 1968), 615 (hereafter *Hawkins v. NBA*).

10. Wolf, *Foul*, 147–148, 210.

11. Wolf, "Unjust Exile," 55.

12. Wolf, 55.

13. Pluto, *Loose Balls*, 80.

14. Wolf, *Foul*, 41; Wolf, "Unjust Exile," 55.

15. Wolf, 55.

16. Wolf, 57; Wolf, *Foul*, 63.

17. Wolf, "Unjust Exile," 55.

18. Wolf, 55; "Rap with Connie Hawkins and David Wolf on All Levels of Basketball," *Black Sports*, September 1972, 22–23.

19. Carl Suddler, *Presumed Criminal: Black Youth and the Justice System in Postwar New York* (New York: New York University Press, 2019), 125.

20. Wolf, "Unjust Exile," 56; Wolf, *Foul*, 85.

21. "Implicate 12 More Players in Basketball Bribery Scandal," *Chicago Daily Tribune*, 25 May 1961; Wolf, "Unjust Exile," 52.

22. "No Justice for Players Who Failed to Report Bribe Offers," *Philadelphia Tribune*, 13 June 1961.

23. "Iowa Five Loses Frosh Phenom," *Philadelphia Inquirer Public Ledger*, 17 May 1961.

24. *Jacob L. Molinas v. National Basketball Association*, 190 F. Supp. 241 (S.D.N.Y. 1961), 242–243. See also Wolf, *Foul*, 50. The other antitrust suit against the NBA, filed in 1960, involved white center Bill Spivey. The NBA had banned Spivey because of his alleged involvement in a point-shaving scandal at the University of Kentucky in the early 1950s. The two sides settled out of court for $10,000. See "Bill Spivey Opens Suit Against NBA: Asks $820,000 Damages," *Chicago Daily Defender*, 5 January 1960; "Charges Blacklisting: Spivey Sues Podoloff, NBA for $820,000," *Washington Post*, 4 January 1960; Jim Murray, "A Case for Zola," *Los Angeles Times*, 1 November 1961.

25. Dan Klores, "Blackballing in the NBA Kept Cleo Hill from Becoming a Star," *Andscape*, 25 October 2018, accessed 14 October 2019, https://andscape .com/features/blackballing-in-the-nba-kept-cleo-hill-from-becoming-a-star. See also Thomas, *They Cleared the Lane*, 138–151; and "Rap: Cleo Hill, Ronnie Blye and Phil Harris Candidly Discuss the Alleged Practice of Blacklisting in Pro Sports," *Black Sports*, October 1971.

26. "Connie Hawkins Charges Blackball, Sues N.B.A. For $6 Million," *Baltimore Sun*, 4 November 1966; "$6 Million Suit Filed," *Washington Post*, 4 November 1966.

27. Thomas, *They Cleared the Lane*, 134.

28. Wolf, *Foul*, 154.

29. Pluto, *Loose Balls*, 42.

30. Joe Jares, "Labor Pains of a New League," *Sports Illustrated*, 13 February 1967. See also Wolf, *Foul*, 153; and "'Lively League' to Duel with NBA," *Basketball News*, 1 February 1967.

31. Pluto, *Loose Balls*, 39–40.

32. Pluto, 41–42.

33. Mikan claimed that the performance bond was $100,000. "'We're Ready to Go,' Says Mikan of Cage League," *Los Angeles Times*, 25 June 1967.

34. Jares, "Labor Pains."

35. Pluto, *Loose Balls*, 43.

36. Bob Fowler, "The Opening Toss," *Cage Stars* 1, no. 1 (1967): 1, 5.

37. Pluto, *Loose Balls*, 60, 59.

38. "10-Team A.B.A. Official Entry in Pro Sports," *Chicago Tribune*, 3 February 1967.

39. Jares, "Labor Pains."

40. Fowler, "Opening Toss," 3.

41. Pluto, *Loose Balls*, 44.

42. Pluto, 80 (italics in original).

43. Seymour S. Smith, "Hawkins Finds Cage Future Rests Now with New A.B.A.," *Baltimore Sun*, 7 June 1967; "Summer Basketball Tourney," *New York Amsterdam News*, 10 June 1967.

44. "Will Thurmond Go to ABA's Oakland?," *Los Angeles Sentinel*, 20 April 1967.

45. Wolf, *Foul*, 236. See also *Hawkins v. NBA*, 615.

46. Wolf, *Foul*, 155.

47. Pluto, *Loose Balls*, 79–80.

48. Wolf, *Foul*, 155.

49. "Ellis Decides to Continue in NBA," *Chicago Daily Defender*, 27 April 1967; Leslie Matthews, "The Sports Whirl," *New York Amsterdam News*, 6 May 1967.

50. Wolf, *Foul*, 211 (italics in original).

51. Wolf, 155.

52. "Rap with Connie Hawkins," 70.

53. Pluto, *Loose Balls*, 79.

54. Wolf, "Unjust Exile," 59.

55. Pluto, *Loose Balls*, 48–49.

56. "Wilt Ponders Bids from A.B.A.," *Baltimore Sun*, 29 June 1967. See also "Barry Jumps to ABA for $500,000," *Washington Post*, 21 June 1967. The *Post* reported that six additional NBA players—Wayne Hightower, Bob Love, Jim Barnes, Clyde Lee, Joe Strawder, and Chico Vaughn—were jumping to the ABA. However, only two, Hightower and Vaughn, actually made the move, to Denver and Pittsburgh, respectively.

57. "'Lively League' to Duel."

58. "Barry Jumps to ABA."

59. Pluto, *Loose Balls*, 49–50.

60. Al Stump, "Rick Barry Today," *Sport*, January 1968, 11.

61. "Rick Barry Vaulting Heats Up NBA-ABA War," *Chicago Daily Defender*, 22 June 1967.

62. "Barry Jumps to ABA."

63. "Barry Jumps to ABA."

64. Dave Brady, "Barry Case Challenges NBA's Reserve Clause," *Washington Post*, 21 June 1967.

65. "NBA Wins in Court . . . But," *Basketball News*, 16 September 1967. See also "Warriors Upheld on Option Clause: Court Rules Barry Is Bound to Club One More Year," *New York Times*, 9 August 1967.

66. Pluto, *Loose Balls*, 51.

67. Stump, "Rick Barry Today," 12; "Hoosiers in Love with Their Pacers," *Basketball News*, 15 November 1967, 8.

68. Stump, "Rick Barry Today," 13.

69. Stump, 11–12.

70. Smith, "Hawkins Finds Cage Future."

71. Wolf, *Foul*, 159.

72. Wolf, 158–159.

73. "New Chance for Connie Hawkins," *Vidette-Messenger* (Valparaiso, IN), 24 October 1967.

74. "Hawkins Leads Pipers' Foray," *New Pittsburgh Courier*, 21 October 1967.

75. Wolf, *Foul*, 161.

76. "Connie Finest in ABA," *New Pittsburgh Courier*, 2 December 1967.

77. Wolf, *Foul*, 161.

78. He scored 34, 19, 29, 28, and 20 points in the first five games. See "Connie Hawkins 1967–68 Game Log," *Basketball Reference*, accessed 3 December 2019, www.basketball-reference.com/players/h/hawkico01/gamelog/1968/aba.

79. Wolf, *Foul*, 162.

80. "Connie Finest in ABA."

81. Lawrence Casey, "Sports Ledger," *Chicago Daily Defender*, 2 April 1968.

82. "Pipers Defeat New Orleans in Playoff Opener, 120–112," *New York Times*, 19 April 1968.

83. "Pipers Even Series, 106–105," *Los Angeles Times*, 26 April 1968.

84. "Hawkins Lost to Pipers," *Chicago Daily Defender*, 30 April 1968.

85. "Pipers Win, Even Series," *Los Angeles Times*, 2 May 1968; "Hawkins Sparks Pipers' Win," *Chicago Daily Defender*, 4 May 1968.

86. Wolf, *Foul*, 175–180; "Pipers Vanquish Bucs, Win Title," *New York Times*, 5 May 1968.

87. Wolf, *Foul*, 159.

88. "Connie Hawkins 'One of the Greatest,'" *Basketball News*, October 1968; Huel Washington, "Oaks Meet Pipers in Championship Preview," *Sun Reporter* (San Francisco), 14 December 1968; "Hawkins, Daniels Head ABA 'Stars,'" *Chicago Daily Defender*, 4 May 1968. See also "Connie Hawkins," *Basketball Reference*, accessed 19 May 2022, www.basketball-reference.com/players/h/hawkico01.html.

89. *Hawkins v. NBA*, 615, 622.

90. Wolf, *Foul*, 237.

91. Wolf, 184–185.

92. Wolf, 185–186.

93. Wolf, 189.

94. Tanisha C. Ford, *Liberated Threads: Black Women, Style, and the Global Politics of Soul* (Chapel Hill: University of North Carolina Press, 2015), 4–5.

95. Wolf, *Foul*, 191–192.

96. Harry Edwards, *The Revolt of the Black Athlete* (New York: Free Press, 1970), 104. See also Amy Bass, *Not the Triumph but the Struggle: The 1968 Olympics and the Making of the Black Athlete* (Minneapolis: University of Minnesota Press, 2002); and Douglas Hartmann, *Race, Culture, and the Revolt of the Black Athlete: The 1968 Olympic Protests and Their Aftermath* (Chicago: University of Chicago Press, 2003).

97. "Barry a Success in Debut, Gate; New Franchises a Dud in ABA," *Basketball News*, 1 November 1968.

98. Wolf, *Foul*, 206.

99. Wolf, 213–215, 216–217, 218.

100. Wolf, 219.

101. Wolf, 234–235.

102. Wolf, "Unjust Exile," 56, 52b.

103. Wolf, 59.

104. Wolf, 60.

105. Wolf, 52b.

106. David Wolf, "$1 Million End to an Unjust Exile," *Life*, 27 June 1969, 67; Wolf, *Foul*, 259.

107. Wolf, 260.

108. Wolf, 260, 261.

109. Wolf, 260.

110. Wolf, 268–269.

111. Alan Goldstein, "Hawkins's Ban Lifted 3 Weeks Ago," *Baltimore Sun*, 21 June 1969.

112. Sam Lacy, "Milk and Honey from the Mouth of the NBA," *Baltimore Afro-American*, 28 June 1969.

Chapter 2: Hardship: Spencer Haywood vs. the White Basketball Establishment

1. "ABA All-Stars on TV," *Basketball Weekly*, 5 January 1970.

2. The allusion is to the infamous *Heidi* Game, a 1968 AFL contest between the Oakland Raiders and the visiting New York Jets. The game ran long, and NBC cut away from it at 7:00 p.m. EST and began to broadcast *Heidi*, a made-for-TV movie scheduled for the 7:00 slot. The Raiders scored two late touchdowns and won the game, but viewers did not get to see this exciting conclusion.

3. Don Cronin, "ABA Flirts with Oblivion," *Anderson (IN) Daily Bulletin*, 26 January 1970; Dave Pierce, "ABA All-Star Game Is First Class Show," *Basketball Weekly*, 2 February 1970.

4. Cronin, "ABA Flirts"; "West Rocket Power Downs East, 128–98," *Anderson (IN) Daily Bulletin*, 26 January 1970; Pierce, "ABA All-Star Game."

5. "Larry Jones Sets Record in Star Tilt," *Gettysburg (PA) Times*, 26 January 1970.

6. "ABA Stages All-Star Game in Lull in War with NBA," *Circleville (OH) Herald*, 24 January 1970; "Larry Jones Sets Record"; Spencer Haywood with Scott Ostler, *Spencer Haywood: The Rise, the Fall, the Recovery* (New York: Amistad, 1992), 137.

7. Odie Lindsey, "Spencer Haywood," *Mississippi Encyclopedia*, 14 April 2018, accessed 12 April 2019, https://mississippiencyclopedia.org/entries/spencer-haywood; "Spencer Haywood: College Stats," *Basketball Reference*, accessed 23 May 2022, www .basketball-reference.com/players/h/haywosp01.html#all_all_college_stats.

8. Curry Kirkpatrick, "The Team That Went over the Hill," *Sports Illustrated*, 15 April 1968, 91; Lew Alcindor with Jack Olsen, "My Story: A Year of Turmoil and Decision," *Sports Illustrated*, 10 November 1969, 35–36; John Matthew Smith, "'It's Not Really My Country': Lew Alcindor and the Revolt of the Black Athlete," *Journal of Sport History* 36, no. 2 (2009): 224.

9. Edwards, *Revolt of the Black Athlete*, 90–100.

10. Haywood with Ostler, *Spencer Haywood*, 104–107, 118. Statistics from Lindsey, "Spencer Haywood."

11. Haywood with Ostler, *Spencer Haywood*, 114. See also Marc J. Spears and Gary Washburn, *The Spencer Haywood Rule: Battles, Basketball, and the Making of an American Iconoclast* (Chicago: Triumph, 2020), 53–54.

12. Haywood with Ostler, *Spencer Haywood*, 127.

13. Adam Criblez, *Tall Tales and Short Shorts: Dr. J, Pistol Pete, and the Birth of the Modern NBA* (Lanham, MD: Rowman & Littlefield, 2017), 1. The NCAA's ban on dunking remained in effect until 1976.

14. Spears and Washburn, *Spencer Haywood Rule*, 62–64.

15. Haywood with Ostler, *Spencer Haywood*, 128, 131, 130.

16. Haywood with Ostler, 133.

17. Bill Libby, "Spencer Haywood: The Fun Is Just Beginning," *Sport*, August 1970, 69.

18. Mike Hall, "Post Man," *Oakland Post*, 10 July 1969.

19. Haywood with Ostler, *Spencer Haywood*, 133–134.

20. Pluto, *Loose Balls*, 182.

21. Pluto, 182.

22. Bill Libby and Spencer Haywood, *Stand Up for Something: The Spencer Haywood Story* (New York: Grosset & Dunlap, 1972), 45.

23. Libby and Haywood, 13–14; Haywood with Ostler, *Spencer Haywood*, 30, 33.

24. Haywood with Ostler, 52–53. See also Spears and Washburn, *Spencer Haywood Rule*, 21–26.

25. Haywood with Ostler, *Spencer Haywood*, 61. See also Spears and Washburn, *Spencer Haywood Rule*, 27–30.

26. Haywood with Ostler, *Spencer Haywood*, 66.

27. Pete Daniel, *Lost Revolutions: The South in the 1950s* (Chapel Hill: University of North Carolina Press, 2000), 294.

28. Haywood with Ostler, *Spencer Haywood*, 72–80; Stevie Wonder, "Living for the City," Genius, accessed 20 May 2022, https://genius.com/Stevie-wonder-living -for-the-city-lyrics.

29. Libby and Haywood, *Stand Up for Something*, 60.

30. Libby and Haywood, 176–177. Bill Ringsby's sons, Don and Gary, were equal one-third owners of the Rockets.

31. Haywood with Ostler, *Spencer Haywood*, 134; Libby and Haywood, *Stand Up for Something*, 62. Although the press initially reported that his contract was worth $250,000, subsequent discussions of it set the value much higher, at $325,000 and even $450,000.

32. "Detroit to Protest Haywood Signing," *Washington Post*, 26 August 1969. See also "Haywood Signs Contract with ABA Rockets," *Washington Post*, 24 August 1969.

33. "Spencer Haywood Makes Rockets Happy," *Los Angeles Sentinel*, 11 September 1969.

34. Haywood with Ostler, *Spencer Haywood*, 134. See Daniel Geary, "The Moynihan Report: An Annotated Edition, *Atlantic*, 14 September 2015, accessed 2 August 2021, www.theatlantic.com/politics/archive/2015/09/the-moynihan-report-an -annotated-edition/404632; Daniel Geary, *Beyond Civil Rights: The Moynihan Report and Its Legacy* (Philadelphia: University of Pennsylvania Press, 2015).

35. "Move a Preventive Measure," *New Journal and Guide* (Norfolk, VA), 13 September 1969.

36. "Detroit to Protest Haywood Signing"; "Dee to Urge Banning of A.B.A. Scouts," *Chicago Tribune*, 6 September 1969. See also "Coaches Tell ABA to Keep Its Hands Off," *Chicago Tribune*, 11 September 1969.

37. Pluto, *Loose Balls*, 183.

38. Greene, quoted in "Black Athletic Power," *Chicago Daily Defender*, 26 August 1969.

39. Sheep Jackson, "Saturday Review," *Call and Post* (Cleveland), 6 September 1969.

40. Libby and Haywood, *Stand Up for Something*, 46.

41. "NBA Quits Merger Talks After ABA 'Breach of Faith,'" *Washington Post*, 26 August 1969.

42. Sam Lacy, "Did Connie Start It?," *Baltimore Afro-American*, 20 September 1969; "Murphy, Lanier Turn Down Pros," *Chicago Daily Defender*, 8 September 1969.

43. Haywood with Ostler, *Spencer Haywood*, 135, 136, 137.

44. Dan Hafner, "Haywood Gets Education in Pro Basketball," *Los Angeles Times*, 28 October 1969.

45. Haywood with Ostler, *Spencer Haywood*, 138.

46. Hafner, "Haywood Gets Education."

47. Libby and Haywood, *Stand Up for Something*, 181, 62.

48. Libby and Haywood, 62–63.

49. Pluto, *Loose Balls*, 178. On the Dolgoff Plan, see Pluto, 177–179.

50. Libby and Haywood, *Stand Up for Something*, 1; Libby, "Spencer Haywood," 42.

51. Libby, "Spencer Haywood," 40. See also "Denver Rockets Whip Indiana," *Colorado Springs Gazette-Telegraph*, 28 February 1970.

52. Libby, "Spencer Haywood," 40, 42.

53. Haywood with Ostler, *Spencer Haywood*, 140; Libby and Haywood, *Stand Up for Something*, 5–6.

54. Libby and Haywood, 182.

55. Libby, "Spencer Haywood," 42.

56. Pluto, *Loose Balls*, 185.

57. Libby and Haywood, *Stand Up for Something*, 5.

58. Tracey Salisbury, "*Black Sports* Magazine," in *African Americans in Sports*, ed. David Kenneth Wiggins (New York: Routledge, 2015), 35.

59. "Peacock Alley," *Black Sports*, August 1973, 44.

60. "Haywood Gets into Six-Figure Act in New Pact," *Baltimore Afro-American*, 4 April 1970. See also Claude Harrison Jr., "NBA-ABA Feud Producing Instant Millionaires and Paupers," *Philadelphia Tribune*, 31 March 1970.

61. "Haywood Gets into Six-Figure Act."

62. Haywood with Ostler, *Spencer Haywood*, 142.

63. "Haywood Proving Worth in $Million-Plus Play," *Baltimore Afro-American*, 18 April 1970; Haywood with Ostler, *Spencer Haywood*, 138, 143.

64. Libby, "Spencer Haywood," 43.

65. Roger Stanton, "Maravich Worth a Million," *Basketball Weekly*, 2 February 1970; "Millionaire at 22, Bob Lanier Stuck with Short Stilts," *Baltimore Afro-American*, 4 April 1970.

66. Harrison, "NBA-ABA Feud."

67. Haywood with Ostler, *Spencer Haywood*, 142, 143.

68. Haywood with Ostler, 143.

69. Libby and Haywood, *Stand Up for Something*, 75, 76.

70. Pluto, *Loose Balls*, 185.

71. Haywood with Ostler, *Spencer Haywood*, 143–144. See also "Haywood Sidelined by Break," *Washington Post*, 9 October 1970; and "Haywood Wants Pact 'Clarified,'" *Washington Post*, 27 October 1970.

72. Libby and Haywood, *Stand Up for Something*, 76, 70. See also Ralph Moore, "Haywood Lays Groundwork for Rocket Suit," *Denver Post*, 27 October 1970.

73. Spencer Haywood, "Why I Jumped to Seattle," *Sport*, March 1971, 7, 94. This is confirmed in *Denver Rockets, etc. v. All-Pro Management Inc.*, 325 F. Supp. 1049 (CD Ca. 1971), 1053 (hereafter *Denver v. All-Pro*).

74. Haywood with Ostler, *Spencer Haywood*, 144.

75. Ralph Moore, "Rockets Stand Fast on Site for Haywood Contract Talks," *Denver Post*, 27 October 1970; "Rockets Say Contract Talks Only at Home," *Chicago Daily Defender*, 3 November 1970.

76. "Haywood Case Taken to Court," *Denver Post*, 16 November 1970; "Set Battle Lines in Haywood Tiff," *Chicago Daily Defender*, 21 November 1970.

77. "Rockets File $1 Million Action Against Center," *Baltimore Afro-American*, 28 November 1970.

78. Jim Graham, "Open Letter to Haywood," *Denver Post*, 25 November 1970.

79. Ralph Moore, "Rockets Granted Court Injunction in Haywood Case," *Denver Post*, 17 November 1970. See also "Set Battle Lines in Haywood Tiff"; and Dave Overpeck, "Stars Surprise College Backers," *Basketball Weekly*, 10 December 1970.

80. "Haywood Says He's Thru with Rockets," *Chicago Tribune*, 24 November 1970.

81. "Haywood Case Goes to Court," *Washington Post*, 25 November 1970.

82. Ralph Moore, "Haywood Blasts Ringsbys on Rocket Pact," *Denver Post*, 17 November 1970.

83. "Haywood Judge Asks for Advice," *Washington Post*, 27 November 1970.

84. Dave Overpeck, "Scheer Says New Merger Vote 'Almost Certainly Would Fail,'" *Basketball Weekly*, 30 November 1970. See also "Freeman Is Happy to Be Traded," *Basketball Weekly*, 25 January 1971.

85. Roger Stanton, "Basketball Weekly Backs Harding," *Basketball Weekly*, 10 December 1970.

86. Vesla Weaver, "Frontlash: Race and the Development of Punitive Crime Policy," *Studies in American Political Development* 21, no. 2 (2007): 230; Keeanga-Yamahtta Taylor, *From #Blacklivesmatter to Black Liberation* (Chicago: Haymarket, 2016), 65–69; Elizabeth Kai Hinton, *From the War on Poverty to the War on Crime: The Making of Mass Incarceration in America* (Cambridge, MA: Harvard University Press, 2016), 180–184.

87. "Haywood-Rockets Dispute Sends Attendance Down," *Baltimore Sun*, 8 December 1970. See also Ralph Moore, "Rockets to Stand Firm on Haywood Contract," *Denver Post*, 7 December 1970; and Dave Overpeck, "Rockets Troubled," *Basketball Weekly*, 15 February 1971.

88. Haywood with Ostler, *Spencer Haywood*, 144, 145.

89. Libby and Haywood, *Stand Up for Something*, 77.

90. "Spencer Haywood Signs Multi-Year Pact with Seattle," *Los Angeles Times*, 31 December 1970.

91. Haywood with Ostler, *Spencer Haywood*, 145.

92. "Another Jumping: Cage War Looms in Hardwood Case," *Baltimore Afro-American*, 9 January 1971.

93. A. S. "Doc" Young, "Good Morning Sports!," *Chicago Daily Defender*, 14 January 1971; Bob Greene, "Haywood Plays for Seattle; Milwaukee Joins Protesters," *Greeley (CO) Daily Tribune*, 5 January 1971; Peter Carry, "Anybody Else Care to Bid for Spencer Haywood?," *Sports Illustrated*, 25 January 1971.

94. Haywood with Ostler, *Spencer Haywood*, 149. See also "Court Trips Slow Haywood," *Chicago Daily Defender*, 9 January 1971.

95. Spears and Washburn, *Spencer Haywood Rule*, 101.

96. Roger Stanton, "Pro Basketball Must Mature," *Basketball Weekly*, 18 January 1971.

97. Libby and Haywood, *Stand Up for Something*, 78, 79.

98. Libby and Haywood, 79.

99. "Haywood Gets 10-Day Grace," *Chicago Daily Defender*, 11 January 1971. See also "Ok Haywood to Seattle," *Chicago Daily Defender*, 23 January 1971.

100. Carry, "Anybody Else Care to Bid," 53.

101. *Spencer Haywood v. National Basketball Association*, 401 U.S. 1204 (1971), 1205 (hereafter *Haywood v. NBA*). See also *Denver v. All-Pro*, 1054.

102. Sarah K. Fields, "Odd Bedfellows: Spencer Haywood and Justice William O. Douglas," *Journal of Sport History* 34, no. 2 (2007): 196.

103. Leonard Koppett, "Gentleman's Agreement," *New York Times*, 10 January 1971. For similar critiques, see John Crittenden, "ABA Forces NCAA into Corner," *Basketball Weekly*, 8 February 1971; and Dave Overpeck, "Reporter's Eyes Pop on Contract," *Basketball Weekly*, 8 February 1971.

104. Koppett, "Gentleman's Agreement."

105. Koppett.

106. *Denver v. All-Pro*, 1058.

107. District court ruling, quoted in *Haywood v. NBA*, 1205. See also Fields, "Odd Bedfellows," 196–197.

108. "NBA Panel Benches Haywood," *Chicago Daily Defender*, 18 February 1971.

109. *Haywood v. NBA*, 1206.

110. "Strife Irks Haywood," *Chicago Daily Defender*, 20 February 1971.

111. "Strife Irks Haywood."

112. Libby and Haywood, *Stand Up for Something*, 61.

113. Fields, "Odd Bedfellows," 198, 197–200.

114. *Haywood v. NBA*, 1205–1206.

115. "Supreme Court Favors Haywood," *Chicago Daily Defender*, 2 March 1971; "NBA Appeals Haywood Order," *Chicago Daily Defender*, 4 March 1971.

116. Haywood, "Why I Jumped to Seattle," 7.

117. Haywood, 7, 94. This is confirmed in *Denver v. All-Pro*, 1053.

118. Haywood, "Why I Jumped to Seattle," 94, 95.

119. Haywood, 95.

120. Roger Stanton, "No Sympathy for Spencer," *Basketball Weekly*, 8 March 1971.

121. *Denver v. All-Pro.*, 1054–1055, 1067.

122. *Denver v. All-Pro*, 1051.

123. *Denver v. All-Pro*, 1053.

124. *Denver v. All-Pro*, 1057.

125. *Denver v. All-Pro*, 1061, 1056.

126. Gar Yarbro, "From the Barbershop: Pros Must Be Stopped," *Basketball Weekly*, 29 March 1971.

127. "Cavs' Pick Carr, Bulls Rival ABA in Draft Battle," *Chicago Daily Defender*, 30 March 1971.

128. "Haywood Free," *Chicago Daily Defender*, 1 April 1971; "Rockets Start Over, at Home," *Chicago Daily Defender*, 8 April 1971.

129. Sam Lacy, "More Power to Haywood and Others," *Baltimore Afro-American*, 3 April 1971.

Chapter 3: Bondage: Overthrowing the Option Clause

1. Robertson, *Big O*, 278.

2. US Senate, Subcommittee on Antitrust and Monopoly of the Committee on the Judiciary, *S.2373 A Bill to Allow the Merger of Two or More Professional Basketball Leagues, Part 1*, September 21–23, 1971, 303 (hereafter Hearing on S.2373, part 1). See also "Oscar Robertson, President of the NBA Players Association and a Player for the Milwaukee Bucks, Reads a Prepared Statement to the Senate Subcommittee," NBC News Archives, 22 September 1971, accessed 25 April 2022, www.gettyimages.com

/detail/video/oscar-robertson-president-of-the-nba-players-association-news-footage
/1272065985.

3. Hearing on S.2373, part 1, 303. For more on the Senate hearings, see Harris, "Hardwood Revolution," 170–204.

4. Hearing on S.2373, part 1.

5. Robertson, *Big O*, 180–185, 212–213.

6. Robert Michael Goldman, *One Man Out: Curt Flood Versus Baseball* (Lawrence: University Press of Kansas, 2008); Michael Oriard, *Brand NFL: Making and Selling America's Favorite Sport* (Chapel Hill: University of North Carolina Press, 2007), 59–60.

7. Taylor, *From #Blacklivesmatter to Black Liberation*, 57–59; Lane Windham, *Knocking on Labor's Door: Union Organizing in the 1970s and the Roots of a New Economic Divide* (Chapel Hill: University of North Carolina Press, 2017), 2–3, 7–8.

8. Robertson, *Big O*, 135, 193.

9. Robertson, 136, 193–195.

10. Alan Goldstein, "Cagers Seek End to Reserve Plan," *Baltimore Sun*, 9 June 1966.

11. Joshua Mendelsohn, *The Cap: How Larry Fleisher and David Stern Built the Modern NBA* (Lincoln: University of Nebraska Press, 2020), 6–9.

12. Robertson, *Big O*, 195.

13. George Vecsey, "Behind Oscar Robertson's Discontent," *Sport*, December 1967, 36.

14. Vecsey, "Behind Oscar Robertson's Discontent," 37.

15. Vecsey, 38.

16. Vecsey, 39.

17. "Pros Can't Meet Big O's Salary Demands," *Los Angeles Times*, 18 April 1970; "Cincinnati's 'Big O' Ponders Jump to ABA," *New Journal and Guide* (Norfolk, VA), 18 April 1970.

18. "Big O Traded to Milwaukee," *Chicago Daily Defender*, 22 April 1970; "Royals Trade Robertson to Bucks for Robinson and Paulk," *New York Times*, 22 April 1970. See also Robertson, *Big O*, 232–234, 242, 245. The Bucks gave him a three-year contract for a reported $175,000 per year.

19. Robertson, *Big O*, 249.

20. "Antitrust Suit Filed by Cagers," *Baltimore Sun*, 17 April 1970; "NBA Players File Suit to Block Merger," *Los Angeles Times*, 17 April 1970; Leonard Koppett, "N.B.A. Players Sue to Block Merger," *New York Times*, 17 April 1970. See also Hearing on S.2373, part 1, 297.

21. *Oscar Robertson et al. v. National Basketball Association*, 389 F. Supp. 867 (SD NY 1975), 872–873 (hereafter *Robertson v. NBA*).

22. *Robertson v. NBA*, 873.

23. "Players' Suit Halts All Merger Plans for Now," *Basketball Weekly*, 10 May 1970; Koppett, "N.B.A. Players Sue."

24. *Robertson v. NBA*, 873. See also Hearing on S.2373, part 1, 24–26.

25. Howie Evans, "An Open Message to Black Athletes," *New York Amsterdam News*, 4 April 1970.

26. Roger Stanton, "Common Sense About Some Colors," *Basketball Weekly*, 10 May 1970.

27. Citing *United Mineworkers v. Pennington* (1965), Judge Carter argues that "an agreement reached in collective bargaining does not automatically exempt the parties

from scrutiny for antitrust violations." Daniel J. Murphy, "Oscar Robertson: The Player and the Case," in *Sports and the Law: Major Legal Cases*, ed. Charles E. Quirk (New York: Garland, 1996), 196. See also *Robertson v. NBA*, 876, 881–882.

28. "NBA, ABA Agree on Merger Terms," *Basketball News*, July 1970; Sam Goldaper, "N.B.A. and A.B.A. Agree to Merge, Subject to Approval of Congress," *New York Times*, 19 June 1970.

29. Goldaper, "N.B.A. and A.B.A. Agree to Merge."

30. Bill Mokray, "Pro Notes," *Basketball News*, October 1970, 4.

31. "Four General Managers Sound Off," *Sport*, September 1970.

32. Bill Mokray, "NBA Notes," *Basketball News*, August 1970.

33. Bob Maisel, "The Morning After," *Baltimore Sun*, 20 June 1970.

34. "Time Out with the Editors: Let's Stop the Price Escalation for Sporting Events," *Sport*, September 1970.

35. Robertson, *Big O*, 265–267; Leonard Koppett, "Bucks Sweep Bullets, Take Crown: Robertson Star as Milwaukee Wins, 118–106," *New York Times*, 1 May 1971.

36. Sam Lacy, "Merger Has 'O' in Mackey Spot," *Baltimore Afro-American*, 15 May 1971.

37. Lacy, "Merger Has 'O' in Mackey Spot." See also Roger Stanton, "NBA-ABA Merger Very Close," *Basketball Weekly*, 15 May 1971.

38. Fred Girard, "Black . . . Not So Beautiful on Paper," *St. Petersburg Times*, 22 January 1973. See also Philip H. Dougherty, "Black Sports Magazine Is Set," *New York Times*, 12 January 1971; and "New Black Magazines Planned," *New York Times*, 8 December 1971. Newspaper reports of the time estimated the magazine's circulation at more than 200,000 copies per month.

39. "Rap: Oscar Robertson, Ned Doyle, Joe Caldwell, Marshall Emery and Sam Jones Rap on Drafting, Salaries, Contracts and Merger in Pro Basketball," *Black Sports*, August 1971.

40. "Rap," 30–31.

41. "Rap," 31, 46.

42. "Rap," 46.

43. "Rap," 48.

44. "Rap," 61.

45. "NBA Cagers Warned of Fines," *Baltimore Sun*, 20 August 1971.

46. "NBA Cagers Warned."

47. Edmund S. Nish, Chairman of NBA Negotiating Committee, to Lawrence Fleisher, Attorney for NBPA, 2 September 1971, in Hearing on S.2373, part 1, 95–96.

48. Sam Goldaper, "N.B.A. Players Spurn Offer by Owners as Senate Hearings on Merger Near," *New York Times*, 19 September 1971.

49. Hearing on S.2373, part 1, 1.

50. "Southern Manifesto on Integration (March 12, 1956)," accessed 17 September 2019, www.thirteen.org/wnet/supremecourt/rights/sources_document2.html. See also "Sam Ervin: A Featured Biography," accessed 17 September 2019, www.senate.gov /artandhistory/history/common/generic/Featured_Bio_ErvinSam.htm.

51. Hearing on S.2373, part 1, 250. Section 14(b) opened the door to state-level "right-to-work" laws, which prohibit compulsory union membership dues and "fees" as a condition of employment.

52. Robertson, *Big O*, 277.

53. Hearing on S.2373, part 1, 12.

54. Hearing on S.2373, part 1, 14.

55. Hearing on S.2373, part 1, 15.

56. Hearing on S.2373, part 1, 17.

57. Hearing on S.2373, part 1, 17, 18, 19.

58. Hearing on S.2373, part 1, 21.

59. Hearing on S.2373, part 1, 155–156, 159.

60. Hearing on S.2373, part 1, 160, 174.

61. Hearing on S.2373, part 1, 170.

62. Hearing on S.2373, part 1, 228–229.

63. Hearing on S.2373, part 1, 304.

64. Hearing on S.2373, part 1, 306.

65. Hearing on S.2373, part 1, 306. See also Robertson, *Big O*, 280.

66. Hearing on S.2373, part 1, 307, 308.

67. Hearing on S.2373, part 1, 312, 313.

68. Findings from Hearing on S.2373, part 1, 340–342. Also see Mark Asher, "Loopholes Pull Basketball Owners out of Hole," *Washington Post*, 24 September 1971.

69. Hearing on S.2373, part 1, 347, 348.

70. Hearing on S.2373, part 1, 364. Beyond these examples, their research showed that several other NBA teams (Seattle, Phoenix, Chicago, and Boston) were within the realm of being profitable. The remaining NBA franchises had operating losses of no more than $200,000 to $400,000 a year.

71. Hearing on S.2373, part 1, 365–366.

72. Hearing on S.2373, part 1, 368, 397.

73. Charles Maher, "War on Sports," *Los Angeles Times*, 21 October 1971.

74. Taylor, *From #Blacklivesmatter to Black Liberation*, 89.

75. Leonard Koppett, "New Sports Arena," *New York Times*, 3 October 1971.

76. "Hearings on Merger Rescheduled," *Washington Post*, 6 November 1971.

77. US Senate, Subcommittee on Antitrust and Monopoly of the Committee on the Judiciary, *S.2373 A Bill to Allow the Merger of Two or More Professional Basketball Leagues, Part 2*, November 15, 1971, and January 25, March 6, and May 3 and 9, 1972, 539 (hereafter Hearing on S.2373, part 2); Alan Goldstein, "Senators Told ABA Needs Merger to Survive," *Baltimore Sun*, 16 November 1971.

78. Sam Lacy, "Backs Against Wall," *Baltimore Afro-American*, 25 December 1971.

79. Joelle Jackson, "Bryant Gumbel (1948–)," Black Past, 23 June 2011, accessed 12 September 2019, www.blackpast.org/african-american-history/gumbel-bryant -1948.

80. Bryant C. Gumbel, "S.2373 Formula for Life or Death?," *Black Sports*, January 1972, 27.

81. Gumbel, "S.2373 Formula for Life or Death?"

82. "Hearing Resumes on Basketball Merger Monday," *Washington Post*, 5 March 1972.

83. "Players Oppose Leagues Merging," *Chicago Daily Defender*, 7 March 1972.

84. Hearing on S.2373, part 2, 757.

85. Leonard Shapiro, "Pro Basketball Merger Bill Held Up," *Washington Post*, 25 May 1972.

86. "NBA Merger Denied by Senate," *Chicago Daily Defender*, 15 June 1972.

87. "Stars of 2 Cage Loops Join Hands for Charity," *Baltimore Afro-American*, 20 May 1972.

88. Leonard Koppett, "N.B.A. All-Stars Sink A.B.A., 106–104," *New York Times*, 26 May 1972; Gary Kale, "NBA Nips ABA, Lanier Is MVP," *Daily Messenger* (Canandaigua, NY), 26 May 1972.

89. "Stars of 2 Cage Loops"; "Players Threaten Strike for $3,300 All-Star Fines," *New Pittsburgh Courier*, 24 June 1972; "Robertson Says Players May Strike If NBA Fines Stick," *Jet*, 6 July 1972.

90. US Senate, Committee on Commerce, *S.3445 A Bill to Protect the Public Interest in the Field of Professional Team Spectator Sports*, June 16, 19, 23, and 28, 1972; US House of Representatives, Antitrust Subcommittee of the Committee on the Judiciary, *Hearings on the Antitrust Laws and Organized Professional Team Sports Including Consideration of the Proposed Merger of the American and National Basketball Associations*, July 27, August 2, 9, and September 7, 1972. See also "NBA Merger Denied by Senate."

91. "Cage Merger Bill 'Kills' Reserve Clause," *Baltimore Sun*, 8 September 1972.

92. "Pro-Basketball Merger Receives Authorization of Senate Trust Panel," *Wall Street Journal*, 8 September 1972.

93. "N.B.A.-A.B.A. Bill Receives Backing," *New York Times*, 8 September 1972. Although the Supreme Court had just ruled against Curt Flood in his case against the reserve clause on June 19, it had argued that Congress had the power to remove baseball's antitrust exemption and that the reserve clause was a matter for collective bargaining.

94. "Pro-Basketball Merger Receives Authorization."

95. Leonard Koppett, "Ifs, Ands and Buts of Basketball Merger Here Again," *New York Times*, 16 November 1972.

Chapter 4: Troubled: Black Players Flood the Leagues

1. Roger Kahn, "Lew Alcindor's Life as a Pro," *Sport*, February 1970, 59.

2. Kahn, "Lew Alcindor's Life," 59.

3. Kahn, 59.

4. Smith, "'It's Not Really My Country,'" 225.

5. Kahn, "Lew Alcindor's Life," 59.

6. Kahn, 63. See also "Bucks Win in Overtime Without Alcindor," *Philadelphia Inquirer Public Ledger*, 1 November 1969; and Claude Harrison Jr., "Alcindor's Inexperience Shows Against 76ers, Says He'll Get Better," *Philadelphia Tribune*, 4 November 1969.

7. Kahn, "Lew Alcindor's Life," 63.

8. Written with the help of veteran reporter Jack Olsen, Alcindor's memoirs appeared in three installments. See Alcindor with Olsen, "My Story," *Sports Illustrated*, 27 October 1969; "My Story: UCLA Was a Mistake," *Sports Illustrated*, 3 November 1969; "My Story: A Year of Turmoil and Decision," *Sports Illustrated*, 10 November 1969.

9. Kahn, "Lew Alcindor's Life," 64.

10. Kahn, 63. See also "Bucks Edge 'Sonic Five," *Daily Chronicle* (Centralia, WA), 22 November 1969.

11. Kahn, "Lew Alcindor's Life," 63.

12. Alcindor with Olsen, "My Story," 84.

13. Kahn, "Lew Alcindor's Life," 65.

14. Jeff Prugh, "Alcindor to Get Advice—for Free," *Los Angeles Times*, 28 March 1969.

15. "'Millionaire' Lew Signs, Buys into Buck Team," *Los Angeles Times*, 3 April 1969. See also Kareem Abdul-Jabbar and Peter Knobler, *Giant Steps: The Autobiography of Kareem Abdul-Jabbar* (New York: Bantam, 1983), 191–192.

16. Jabbar and Knobler, *Giant Steps*, 193.

17. Kahn, "Lew Alcindor's Life," 64, 65.

18. "Alcindor Unveils Bride, New Name," *Baltimore Afro-American*, 12 June 1971.

19. See Damion L. Thomas, *Globetrotting: African American Athletes and Cold War Politics* (Urbana: University of Illinois Press, 2012).

20. "Alcindor Unveils Bride." See also Aram Goudsouzian, "From Lew Alcindor to Kareem Abdul-Jabbar: Race, Religion, and Representation in Basketball, 1968–1975," *Journal of American Studies* 51, no. 2 (2017): 445–446.

21. Terence Smith, "Biggest Name in N.B.A.: Jabbar," *New York Times*, 4 June 1971. He first mentioned his new name in the press in Alcindor with Olsen, "My Story: A Year of Turmoil and Decision," 37.

22. Jabbar and Knobler, *Giant Steps*, 235.

23. "Alcindor Unveils Bride."

24. Smith, "Biggest Name in N.B.A."

25. Kenneth Denlinger, "Alcindor Becomes 'Jabbar': African Trip Begins," *Washington Post*, 4 June 1971.

26. Terry Bledsoe, "White Man's Games a Path to the Black Man's Salvation," *Los Angeles Times*, 10 June 1973.

27. "The Role of Sport in the Black Man's Struggle for Survival," *Black Sports*, May/June 1972, 49; Martin Kane, "An Assessment of 'Black Is Best,'" *Sports Illustrated*, 18 January 1971, 73.

28. Jefferson Cowie, *Stayin' Alive: The 1970s and the Last Days of the Working Class* (New York: New Press, 2010), 7, 12.

29. Michelle Alexander, *The New Jim Crow: Mass Incarceration in the Age of Color-blindness* (New York: New Press, 2010), 50–51; Taylor, *From #Blacklivesmatter to Black Liberation*, 53–54; Philip Jenkins, *Decade of Nightmares: The End of the Sixties and the Making of Eighties America* (New York: Oxford University Press, 2006), 66. For a more in-depth discussion of structural unemployment and urban fiscal crisis, see William Julius Wilson, *When Work Disappears: The World of the New Urban Poor* (New York: Vintage, 1997), and *The Truly Disadvantaged: The Inner City, the Underclass, and Public Policy* (Chicago: University of Chicago Press, 1990).

30. James A. Michener, *Sports in America* (New York: Random House, 1976), 171.

31. "Jabbar on Black Journal," *Tri-State Defender* (Memphis), 29 April 1972; "Jocks Cash in on Sports' Bidding Wars," *Chicago Tribune*, 18 October 1972. The Bucks did not reveal the actual dollar amount, but reports estimated the deal to be worth anywhere from $1.4 million to $1.6 million.

32. Lacy J. Banks, "The Black Majority," *Philadelphia Inquirer*, 7 February 1973.

33. Leonard Koppett, "In Pro Salaries, N.B.A. Is No. 1," *New York Times*, 11 March 1973. However, these averages were somewhat deceptive because the superstars' salaries skewed things higher. In 1973, $17,500 was the minimum salary in both pro basketball leagues. See also "Money Income in 1973 of Families and Persons in the United

States," *Current Population Reports: Consumer Income*, series P–60, no. 7, January 1975, 5, accessed 3 May 2022, www2.census.gov/library/publications/1975/demographics /p60-97.pdf.

34. "The Earl Monroe Statement," *Basketball News*, 29 November 1971; "Rap with Earl Monroe on the Many Facets of a Super Star," *Black Sports*, February 1972, 22, 56; Earl Monroe with Quincy Troupe, *Earl the Pearl: My Story* (New York: Rodale, 2013), 162–163, 292.

35. "Rap with Earl Monroe," 20.

36. "Rap with Earl Monroe," 20.

37. Monroe with Troupe, *Earl the Pearl*, xv.

38. "Rap with Earl Monroe," 19. See also Monroe with Troupe, *Earl the Pearl*, 95–96, 150, 161–163, 181, 196.

39. Monroe with Troupe, 184, v, 188.

40. Monroe with Troupe, 196, 197.

41. Monroe with Troupe, 210.

42. Clayton Riley, "Earl: The First and Last Word in Guard," *Black Sports*, April 1977, 36.

43. Monroe with Troupe, *Earl the Pearl*, 211.

44. Monroe with Troupe, 213. See also 169–173.

45. "Rap with Earl Monroe," 57.

46. Riley, "Earl," 36.

47. Eric Lincoln, "Dr. J., Dr. J! Jitter-Jiving and Fleeazoating," *Black Sports*, March 1973, 12.

48. Julius Erving with Karl Taro Greenfeld, *Dr. J: The Autobiography* (New York: Harper, 2013), 5.

49. Lincoln, "Dr. J., Dr. J!," 16–17.

50. Erving with Greenfeld, *Dr. J*, 90–91, 103.

51. Erving with Greenfeld, 104–106.

52. Erving with Greenfeld, 105, 36, 134, 163.

53. Erving with Greenfeld, 205, 208.

54. Erving with Greenfeld, 247, 248. For more on Dr. J's time at the Rucker, see Vincent M. Mallozzi, *Asphalt Gods: An Oral History of the Rucker Tournament* (New York: Doubleday, 2003), 111–146.

55. Erving with Greenfeld, 263.

56. Lincoln, "Dr. J., Dr. J!," 17.

57. Erving with Greenfeld, *Dr. J*, 530–531.

58. Wayne Embry with Mary Schmitt Boyer, *The Inside Game: Race, Power, and Politics in the NBA* (Akron, OH: University of Akron Press, 2004), 215.

59. Embry with Boyer, *Inside Game*, 215–216.

60. Embry with Boyer, 192.

61. "Wayne Embry Appointed to Administrative Post," *Sun Reporter* (San Francisco), 18 March 1972. See also "Taking Care of Business with Wayne Embry," *Black Sports*, February 1973.

62. "Jabbar Exonerated After Drug Arrest," *Washington Post*, 7 October 1972; "Jabbar Jailed on Pot," *Tri-State Defender* (Memphis), 14 October 1972.

63. "Bucks' Jabbar Freed After Drugs Arrest," *Chicago Tribune*, 7 October 1972.

64. "Jabbar Jailed, Cleared on Marijuana Charge," *Los Angeles Times*, 7 October 1972.

65. Embry with Boyer, *Inside Game*, 216.

66. "Bucks' Jabbar Freed"; "Jabbar Exonerated"; "Jabbar Jailed."

67. Embry with Boyer, *Inside Game*, 217–218.

68. "Jabbar Exonerated."

69. *CBS Evening News*, 6 October 1972; *NBC Nightly News*, 6 October 1972.

70. Alexander, *New Jim Crow*, 46; Weaver, "Frontlash," 237.

71. Elizabeth Hinton, "'A War Within Our Own Boundaries': Lyndon Johnson's Great Society and the Rise of the Carceral State," *Journal of American History* 102, no. 1 (2015): 102. See also Hinton, *From the War on Poverty to the War on Crime*; and Julilly Kohler-Hausmann, *Getting Tough: Welfare and Imprisonment in 1970s America* (Princeton, NJ: Princeton University Press, 2017).

72. Matthew D. Lassiter, "Impossible Criminals: The Suburban Imperatives of America's War on Drugs," *Journal of American History* 102, no. 1 (2015): 134–135.

73. Koppett, "In Pro Salaries, N.B.A. Is No. 1."

74. Stan Love and Ron Rapoport, *Love in the NBA: A Player's Uninhibited Diary* (New York: Saturday Review Press, 1975), 37.

75. Jabbar and Knobler, *Giant Steps*, 247–248, 250. Sportswriter Charley Rosen corroborates Jabbar's observations about white drug use and admits to supplying Steve Patterson of the Cleveland Cavaliers with marijuana during his trips to New York City in the early 1970s. Charley Rosen, *Sugar: Michael Ray Richardson, Eighties Excess, and the NBA* (Lincoln: University of Nebraska Press, 2018), 28.

76. Wolf, *Foul*, 317. Hawkins also made similar observations about the racial segregation on team buses (285–288).

77. Alexander, *New Jim Crow*, 67.

78. "Wally Blasts Philly Cops, Fight Youth Gang Killings," *Chicago Daily Defender*, 1 January 1972.

79. Wayne Lynch, *Season of the 76ers: The Story of Wilt Chamberlain and the 1967 NBA Champion Philadelphia 76ers* (New York: St. Martin's, 2002), 236.

80. Thomas Boswell, "Now, Wali Wonder," *Washington Post*, 28 November 1972; George Solomon, "Wali Jones' Drug Clinic Visits D.C.," *Washington Post*, 28 June 1973.

81. "Wally Blasts Philly Cops."

82. Lynch, *Season of the 76ers*, 236; Wally Jones and Jim Washington, *Black Champions Challenge American Sports* (New York: David McKay, 1972).

83. Herb Taft, "Concerned Athletes Give Out T-Shirts and Anti-Drug Advice," *Bay State Banner* (Dorchester, MA), 14 December 1972.

84. "Wali Jones Denies Use of Cocaine," *Baltimore Sun*, 26 May 1973.

85. "Wali Jones Settles with Milw. Bucks," *Philadelphia Tribune*, 26 May 1973.

86. "NBA Players Group Not Asked to Aid Jones," *Baltimore Sun*, 24 December 1972; Al Harvin, "People in Sports: Wali Jones," *New York Times*, 23 December 1972.

87. Love and Rapoport, *Love in the NBA*, 90.

88. "Wally Jones Sues N.B.A. for $5-Million in Damages," *New York Times*, 2 November 1971; "Wally Blasts Philly Cops." See also "Bucks Cut Jones," *Chicago Daily Defender*, 10 January 1973.

89. Bill Mokray, "Pro Notes," *Basketball News*, 10 January 1972.

90. Boswell, "Now, Wali Wonder."

91. Boswell.

92. "Jones Files Grievance with NBA," *Washington Post*, 2 January 1973.

93. "Attorney Seeks Pay for Wali Jones," *Baltimore Sun*, 2 January 1973.

94. "Wali Jones Suspension Clarified by Bucks," *Baltimore Sun*, 6 January 1973.

95. "Disciplinary Reason Is Given in Bucks-vs.-Wali Jones Case," *New York Times*, 6 January 1973.

96. "Bucks Place Wali Jones on Waivers," *Washington Post*, 10 January 1973.

97. "Bucks Cut Jones"; "Jones Put on Waivers by Milwaukee Bucks," *Baltimore Sun*, 10 January 1973.

98. "Jones Put on Waivers."

99. "Jones Blasts Bucks," *Chicago Tribune*, 14 January 1973; "Wali Jones Says Bucks Defamed Him," *Baltimore Sun*, 14 January 1973.

100. Sandy Padwe, "In Pro Basketball, Drug Usage Leads to Warnings and Worries," *Newsday*, 30 April 1973, quoted in US Senate, Subcommittee to Investigate Juvenile Delinquency of the Committee on the Judiciary, *Proper and Improper Use of Drugs by Athletes*, June 18, July 12 and 18, 1973, 362, 365 (hereafter *Proper and Improper Use*). The article was the second installment of a four-part series in which Padwe explored drug abuse in professional and amateur sports.

101. Curtis Mayfield, "Pusherman," Genius, 1972, accessed 20 May 2022, https://genius.com/Curtis-mayfield-pusherman-lyrics.

102. Robert E. Weems Jr., *Desegregating the Dollar: African American Consumerism in the Twentieth Century* (New York: New York University Press, 1998), 83–84.

103. Padwe, "In Pro Basketball," quoted in *Proper and Improper Use*, 362.

104. Padwe, 363.

105. "Ridge's Suit Claims Football Allowed Harmful Drugs' Use," *Washington Post*, 18 April 1970.

106. Padwe, "In Pro Basketball," quoted in *Proper and Improper Use*, 363.

107. Seymour S. Smith, "NBA Takes Steps in Drug Problem," *Baltimore Sun*, 25 June 1973.

108. Padwe, "In Pro Basketball," quoted in *Proper and Improper Use*, 364.

109. "The Wali Jones Case Is Closed, but Not Tightly," *New York Times*, 25 May 1973.

110. "Bucks and Jones Settle a Dispute," *New York Times*, 23 May 1973.

111. Dave Begel, "'Made Sacrificial Lamb by Bucks,' Says Wali Jones After Settlement," *Washington Afro-American*, 29 May 1973; "Wali Jones Case Is Closed"; "Facts in Jones Case Raise Many Questions," *Milwaukee Journal*, 25 May 1973.

112. "Facts in Jones Case."

113. Begel, "Made Sacrificial Lamb."

114. Begel. See also "Wali Jones Denies Use of Cocaine."

115. "Wali Jones Working to Fight Drugs," *Washington Post*, 5 June 1973.

116. Solomon, "Wali Jones' Drug Clinic Visits D.C." See also *Proper and Improper Use*, 123–124; and Taft, "Concerned Athletes."

117. *Proper and Improper Use*, 109, 111, 120.

118. *Proper and Improper Use*, 105.

119. *Proper and Improper Use*, 106, 107.

120. *Proper and Improper Use*, 107. For a contemporary discussion about the overwhelming pressure for athletes to play while injured or in pain, see Dwight Chapin, "Playing in Pain," *Los Angeles Times*, 12 February 1974.

121. *Proper and Improper Use*, 108.

122. Sam Lacy, "Jim Crow in Reverse," *Baltimore Afro-American*, 1 April 1972; Rosen, *Sugar*, 9.

Chapter 5: Professional: Simon Gourdine and the NBA's White Ceiling

1. "The Best of All Worlds for a Black Pro," *Ebony*, January 1975, 97.

2. "1975 All-Star Game," *Basketball Weekly*, 23 January 1975.

3. Byron Rosen, "Buddy Young, NFL Great, Killed in Highway Wreck," *Washington Post*, 6 September 1983; "Buddy Young NFL Appointee," *New Journal and Guide* (Norfolk, VA), 19 June 1965; "Buddy Young to NFL Staff," *Chicago Daily Defender*, 15 June 1965; Dick Edwards, "Ex-Giant Monte Irvin Gets Top Baseball Spot," *New York Amsterdam News*, 24 August 1968; "Baseball Job to Irvin," *Baltimore Afro-American*, 24 August 1968.

4. Dave Anderson, "Simon Gourdine Approaches 'Some Day,'" *New York Times*, 8 November 1974.

5. "The Man: Simon Gourdine," *Black Sports*, March 1972, 36.

6. Morton Mintz, "GM Responds to Charges of Job Discrimination," *Washington Post*, 2 May 1970.

7. Jessica Levy, "Black Power in the Boardroom: Corporate America, the Sullivan Principles, and the Anti-Apartheid Struggle," *Enterprise & Society* 21, no. 1 (2020): 171–172.

8. Embry with Boyer, *Inside Game*, 192.

9. Marcia Chatelain, *Franchise: The Golden Arches in Black America* (New York: Liveright, 2020), 66, 13. For more on the concept of "Black capitalism" and the connection between Black business and Black progress in this period, see Laura Warren Hill and Julia Rabig, eds., *The Business of Black Power: Community Development, Capitalism, and Corporate Responsibility in Postwar America* (Rochester, NY: University of Rochester Press, 2012); Dean Kotlowski, "Black Power—Nixon Style: The Nixon Administration and Minority Business Enterprise," *Business History Review* 72, no. 3 (1998): 409–445.

10. Embry with Boyer, *Inside Game*, 193, 194.

11. Embry with Boyer, *Inside Game*, 194.

12. "The Man: Simon Gourdine," 37, 36.

13. "Progress Report 1964–1974: A Decade of Struggle," *Ebony*, January 1975, 28.

14. Michael Farber, "A Man of Moderate Mien," *Sports Illustrated*, 7 May 1995.

15. "The Man: Simon Gourdine," 36–37.

16. "The Man: Simon Gourdine," 62.

17. Anderson, "Simon Gourdine Approaches"; Richard Goldstein, "Simon P. Gourdine, Pioneer in Sports Management, Dies at 72," *New York Times*, 19 August 2012; "Rap with Simon Gourdine," *Black Sports*, March 1975, 18.

18. "The Man: Simon Gourdine," 37.

19. "The Man: Simon Gourdine," 37.

20. "Progress Report 1964–1974," 27, 34. See also Terry H. Anderson, *The Pursuit of Fairness: A History of Affirmative Action* (New York: Oxford University Press, 2004).

21. "The Man: Simon Gourdine," 37, 48, 62.

22. "The Man: Simon Gourdine," 62.

23. "The Man: Simon Gourdine," 62 (italics in original).

24. "Basketball Integration Leader," *New York Amsterdam News*, 15 June 1974.

25. Bob Stewart, "Bill Russell's Biggest Challenge," *Pro Basketball Illustrated, 1966–1967*, Winter 1966, 18, 36.

26. "NBA Plans to Select New Leader," *Baltimore Sun*, 18 June 1974; "N.B.A. Fails to Choose New Chief," *New York Times*, 20 June 1974; William Barry Furlong, "This Morning: NBA Governors Raise Bickering to a Fine Art," *Washington Post*, 21 June 1974.

27. Furlong, "This Morning."

28. Furlong.

29. Sheep Jackson, "From the Sidelines," *Call and Post* (Cleveland), 7 December 1974.

30. "Gourdine Selected by NBA," *Baltimore Sun*, 8 November 1974. See also "Gourdine Deputy NBA Commissioner," *Chicago Tribune*, 8 November 1974; "Black Named NBA Deputy Commissioner," *Washington Post*, 8 November 1974; and "NBA Elects Black as Deputy Chief," *Los Angeles Times*, 8 November 1974.

31. Anderson, "Simon Gourdine Approaches."

32. "White House Congrats Telephoned to Gourdine," *Baltimore Afro-American*, 23 November 1974.

33. "Simon P. Gourdine Named NBA Deputy Commissioner," *Philadelphia Tribune*, 12 November 1974.

34. Sam Lacy, "Black Lawyer Nears Top Post in Pro Sports," *Baltimore Afro-American*, 16 November 1974.

35. "Choice of Gourdine Is Hailed in NBA," *Baltimore Afro-American*, 23 November 1974.

36. "The Business of Sports," *Black Enterprise*, December 1974, 43. See also Ulish Carter, "Black Players Dominate NBA but Ignored for Jobs," *Tri-State Defender* (Memphis), 16 February 1974.

37. Bob Logan, "Discontent Unfolds Around NBA Camps," *Chicago Tribune*, 2 October 1974.

38. "Love Hurting Bulls' Cause," *Chicago Tribune*, 8 October 1974.

39. "Fan Tired of Paying Freight for the Pros," *Chicago Tribune*, 22 October 1974.

40. "Lagging Economy Takes Its Toll," *Basketball Weekly*, 23 January 1975.

41. Bob Logan, "NBA Set Example with Love, Van Lier," *Chicago Tribune*, 23 October 1974.

42. "Love, Van Lier Case, an Example for Others," *Basketball Weekly*, 5 December 1974.

43. "Overdue Payments Threat to New Orleans Future," *Basketball Weekly*, 2 January 1975.

44. "Rap with Simon Gourdine," 8.

45. "Rap with Simon Gourdine," 8, 17.

46. "Rap with Simon Gourdine," 17–18.

47. "Rap with Simon Gourdine," 18, 57.

48. The efforts of the McDonald's Corporation to place Black franchise owners in Black neighborhoods is a clear example of this trend. See Chatelain, *Franchise*, Chapter 2, "Burgers in the Age of Black Capitalism."

49. "Rap with Simon Gourdine," 57.

50. On Blaxploitation and Hollywood's efforts to capture the urban Black movie-going public, see Weems, *Desegregating the Dollar*, 80–90.

51. "Business of Sports," 45.

52. "Rap with Simon Gourdine," 60.

53. "Rap with Simon Gourdine," 18.

54. Simon Gourdine, interview by Roscoe C. Brown Jr., *Soul of Reason*, WNBC/WNYU, 14 April 1975, Folder 151, Box 53, Subseries A, Subseries IV, Records of the Institute of Afro-American Affairs, New York University Archives, Elmer Holmes Bobst Library, New York, accessed 16 January 2020, http://hdl.handle.net/2333.1/3r2286n9.

55. Simon Gourdine, interview by Roscoe C. Brown Jr.

56. "O'Brien Picked to Run NBA," *Washington Post*, 29 April 1975.

57. Stephen Isaacs, "O'Brien Rejected 1st Offer by NBA," *Washington Post*, 30 April 1975.

58. "Report Larry O'Brien New NBA Commissioner," *Chicago Tribune*, 29 April 1975; "NBA Said to Name O'Brien Its Head," *Baltimore Sun*, 29 April 1975; Sam Goldaper, "N.B.A. Picks O'Brien as New Commissioner," *New York Times*, 29 April 1975; Sarah Pileggi, "Scorecard: Commish with a Mission," *Sports Illustrated*, 12 April 1975.

59. Alan Goldstein, "Another Day," *Baltimore Sun*, 18 May 1975.

60. David DuPree, "No Room at NBA's Top for Gourdine," *Washington Post*, 1 May 1975.

61. Brad Pye Jr., "Prying Pye: Bypassed Gourdine," *Los Angeles Sentinel*, 1 May 1975.

62. DuPree, "No Room at NBA's Top."

63. Evans, "Sort of Sporty," *New York Amsterdam News*, 14 May 1975. See also "Basketball Not Ready for Black," *New York Amsterdam News*, 7 May 1975.

64. Sam Goldaper, "N.B.A. Owners Look for Political Ladder," *New York Times*, 1 May 1975.

65. DuPree, "No Room at NBA's Top."

66. "Sen. McCall Calls 'Foul' on the NBA," *New York Amsterdam News*, 7 May 1975.

67. Goldaper, "N.B.A. Owners Look for Political Ladder."

68. "Rap with Rev. Jesse Jackson," *Black Sports*, May 1975, 24. See also Ulish Carter, "NBA By Pass [*sic*] Black Deputy Commissioner for Political Reasons," *New Pittsburgh Courier*, 10 May 1975.

69. "Bypass of Black as Commissioner Triggers Call for NBA Boycott," *Baltimore Afro-American*, 10 May 1975.

70. "Bypass of Black as Commissioner." See also Goldstein, "Another Day."

71. Thomas, *They Cleared the Lane*, 224.

72. Bill Nunn Jr., "Fans Miffed over 'Coach-of-Year' Balloting," *Chicago Defender*, 15 May 1975.

73. "Phil Johnson, NBA Coach of Year Moves," *Atlanta Daily World*, 4 May 1975.

74. "Best of All Worlds for a Black Pro," 98.

75. "Washington Bullets Duel Warriors for NBA Crown," *Atlanta Daily World*, 25 May 1975; "Warriors Head Home, Bullets Task Harder," *Chicago Defender*, 20 May 1975; Thomas, *They Cleared the Lane*, 225; "10 Blacks and Barry," *Black Sports*, March 1975, 42, 52.

76. Sam Lacy, "Title Series Coaches Enhance Image of NBA," *Baltimore Afro-American*, 24 May 1975.

77. Thomas, *They Cleared the Lane*, 227–229; Rudy Langlais, "K.C. Didn't Panic," *Black Sports*, July 1974, 22, 24.

78. Thomas, *They Cleared the Lane*, 229–231; Langlais, "K.C. Didn't Panic," 24.

79. Paul Lecesne, "Same Guy, Same Spirit, New Role: Al Attles," *Black Sports*, February 1972, 51.

80. Roy S. Johnson, "Attles Coaches in a Personal Way," *New York Times*, 28 January 1982.

81. Johnson, "Attles Coaches in a Personal Way."

82. Wells Twombly, "Alvin Attles Works Miracles," *Sport*, April 1974, 56; Thomas, *They Cleared the Lane*, 137.

83. "Al Attles," *Basketball Reference*, accessed 24 May 2022, www.basketball -reference.com/players/a/attleal01.html; Thomas, *They Cleared the Lane*, 221. See also "Alvin Attles," NBA.com, accessed 23 March 2020, www.nba.com/warriors/staff /alvin-attles.

84. Thomas, *They Cleared the Lane*, 223.

85. See, for example, Bob Logan, *Basketball Weekly*, 2 January 1974; Ted Green, "Hubie's Hawks Hustle," *Basketball Weekly*, 27 December 1978.

86. Komozi Woodard, *A Nation Within a Nation: Amiri Baraka (Leroi Jones) and Black Power Politics* (Chapel Hill: University of North Carolina Press, 1999), 159–160, 184–185.

87. Langlais, "K.C. Didn't Panic," 26.

88. Langlais, 26.

89. Bob Logan, "Some Notes and Thoughts at Various NBA Stops," *Basketball Weekly*, 26 December 1974.

90. Langlais, "K.C. Didn't Panic," 31.

91. Larry Donald, "Cool Hand K.C. Jones Keeps Bullets Rolling," *Basketball Weekly*, 9 January 1975.

92. See, for example, Frank Saunders, "No More 'Ray Who?,'" *Black Sports*, July 1974; "An Interview with Lenny Wilkens," *Black Sports*, April 1978.

93. Eric Lincoln, "The Hot Seat: Al Attles," *Black Sports*, June 1973, 51.

94. Lecesne, "Same Guy, Same Spirit," 52, 53.

95. Twombly, "Alvin Attles Works Miracles," 54.

96. Lincoln, "Hot Seat," 56.

97. Mark Engel, "Clifford Ray: The Quiet Workman Who Believes," *Basketball Weekly*, 13 February 1975.

98. "Bullets, Warriors to Start Today in Final Test of Coaching Strategy," *Baltimore Sun*, 18 May 1975.

99. John Branch, "When the Warriors Lost Home-Court Advantage to the Ice Follies," *New York Times*, 7 June 2015; Paul Henniger, "Viewing Sports: Winter Games Winding Down," *Los Angeles Times*, 24 May 1975; Ulish Carter, "Black Coaches Battle for NBA Title," *New Pittsburgh Courier*, 24 May 1975; "Warriors Head Home, Bullets Task Harder"; Alan Goldstein, "Bullets Upset in Opener: Golden State Rallies for 101–95 Win," *Baltimore Sun*, 19 May 1975.

100. Branch, "When the Warriors Lost Home-Court Advantage"; "Attles Wants to Make It Easy," *Los Angeles Times*, 23 May 1975.

101. David DuPree, "Barry Unstoppable in 109–101 Romp," *Washington Post*, 24 May 1975.

102. DuPree, "Barry Unstoppable."

103. David DuPree, "Bullets Lose Their Last Chance, 96–95," *Washington Post*, 26 May 1975; Kenneth Denlinger, "This Morning: Analyst Barry Says the Bullets 'Gave Up,'" *Washington Post*, 26 May 1975; Leonard Koppett, "Warriors Capture Title on 4–0 Sweep," *New York Times*, 26 May 1975.

104. Koppett, "Warriors Capture Title."

105. Rick Booker, "Rick Booker Comments. . . . The Babes Shall Lead Them," *Sun Reporter* (San Francisco), 31 May 1975.

106. Brad Pye Jr., "Prying Pye: Black Coaches' Day," *Los Angeles Sentinel*, 29 May 1975.

107. Booker, "Rick Booker Comments."

108. Richard Rothschild, "Fun Facts About the 1975 NBA Finals, the Warriors' Last Trip to Title Series," *Sports Illustrated*, 3 June 2015, accessed 31 March 2020, www .si.com/nba/2015/06/03/nba-finals-1975-warriors-bullets-rick-barry-jamaal-wilkes -cavaliers.

109. Carter, "Black Coaches Battle."

110. Henniger, "Viewing Sports."

111. "Locker Room Chatter," *Black Sports*, August 1976, 6.

112. Ulish Carter, "NBA Excludes Black Coaches When Rehiring," *New Pittsburgh Courier*, 6 November 1976.

113. Thomas, *They Cleared the Lane*, 231, 214. See also Allan P. Barron, "Publisher's Statement," *Black Sports*, May 1976.

Chapter 6: Criminal: Kermit Washington's Infamous Punch

1. John Feinstein, *The Punch: One Night, Two Lives, and the Fight That Changed Basketball Forever* (New York: Back Bay, 2002), 21.

2. Ted Green, "O'Brien Hits Washington with $53,560 Haymaker," *Los Angeles Times*, 13 December 1977. It stood as the longest non-drug-related suspension in the NBA until Stern banned Latrell Sprewell for a year for attacking Golden State coach P. J. Carlisimo in 1997. See also Paul Buker, "Washington Says Punch Will Haunt Him for Life," *Oregonian*, 26 January 1998.

3. Feinstein, *Punch*, 56.

4. Hal Bock, "A Punch That Was Felt Around the NBA," *Philadelphia Inquirer*, 25 April 1993.

5. Buker, "Washington Says Punch Will Haunt Him."

6. Feinstein, *Punch*, 3–6, 10–13. For a television clip of the punch, see YouTube, accessed 17 July 2022, www.youtube.com/watch?v=vM2CLRnR2cQ. Although there are competing accounts of the altercation, this chapter is less concerned with the "truth" of what happened than with the discussions and actions that the incident inspired.

7. Memo from George G. Gallantz to Commissioner Walter Kennedy, 7 March 1975, 3, in Box 17, Folder 7, Lawrence F. O'Brien National Basketball Association Papers, Springfield College, Springfield, MA (hereafter LOB).

8. Criblez, *Tall Tales and Short Shorts*, 141, 173–174.

9. Criblez, 141–142.

10. Pluto, *Loose Balls*, 26.

11. "Documentary on 1976 Slam Dunk Contest," accessed 18 August 2020, YouTube, www.youtube.com/watch?v=mpZtiLTOZrQ.

12. "A Shattering Legal Week for Pro Sports," *Skanner* (Portland, OR), 19 February 1976; Ulish Carter, "Player-Owner Negotiations Changing Sports Structure," *New Pittsburgh Courier*, 28 February 1976; "Players, NBA Settle Suit out of Court," *Los Angeles Times*, 4 February 1976; Mendelsohn, *Cap*, 90.

13. "A Shattering Legal Week."

14. "A Shattering Legal Week."

15. Carter, "Player-Owner Negotiations." For all the settlement details, see Memo from Lawrence F. O'Brien to NBA Owners & General Managers, "Synopsis of the Stipulation and Settlement Agreement," 21 May 1976, 1–16, in Box 17, Folder 12, LOB.

16. "Players, NBA Settle Suit out of Court."

17. Carter, "Player-Owner Negotiations."

18. Robertson, *The Big O*, 309, 307.

19. "Locker Room Chatter," *Black Sports*, May 1976.

20. "NBA Held Offering Merger Proposal," *Baltimore Sun*, 4 June 1976; "Pro Basketball Merger Is Reported Near," *Washington Post*, 4 June 1976.

21. "ABA Quints See Merger," *Baltimore Afro-American*, 12 June 1976.

22. "NBA and ABA Set to Merge," *Philadelphia Tribune*, 19 June 1976; "NBA-ABA Merger," *New Pittsburgh Courier*, 26 June 1976.

23. Lester Carson, "News from the Editor: Sad Day for Basketball," *Black Sports*, July 1976, 8.

24. Harris, "Hardwood Revolution," 3–4, 205; Rosen, *Sugar*, 76.

25. "Rap with Chet Walker," *Black Sports*, June 1976, 46. See also "In the Matter of Chester Walker and Chicago Bulls and the National Basketball Association, Report of the Special Master," 70 Civ. 1526 (S.D.N.Y. 1978), 1–2, in Box 17, Folder 14, LOB.

26. "Rap with Chet Walker," 46.

27. "Rap with Chet Walker," 58, 61.

28. Ted Green, "The NBA: Where It's Legal to Mug a Fellow Worker," *Los Angeles Times*, 3 March 1976.

29. Jenkins, *Decade of Nightmares*, 66–67, 137–138.

30. Green, "NBA."

31. Sam Goldaper, "N.B.A. Issues Memo Seeking a Curb on Violence," *New York Times*, 1 March 1977.

32. Allan P. Barron, "Publisher's Statement," *Black Sports*, March 1977.

33. Goldaper, "N.B.A. Issues Memo."

34. Goldaper.

35. Goldaper.

36. Mark Asher, "NBA Assigns Standbys After Refs' Strike Vote," *Washington Post*, 8 April 1977.

37. Sam Goldaper, "N.B.A. Acts to Cut Down on Fighting," *New York Times*, 8 March 1977.

38. Sam Goldaper, "Lakers' Kermit Washington Fined $10,000," *New York Times*, 13 December 1977; Nancy Scannell, "O'Brien Fears Fan Fights," *Washington Post*, 16 December 1977.

39. Goldaper, "N.B.A. Acts."

40. Paul L. Montgomery, "Abdul-Jabbar Fined $5,000 for One Punch," *New York Times*, 21 October 1977.

41. Stephen J. Gulotta Jr., "Torts in Sports—Deterring Violence in Professional Athletics," *Fordham Law Review* 49, no. 5 (1980): 768n28. In the MLB the league presidents could suspend a player indefinitely, but any fines above $500 were subject to arbitration. See also Scannell, "O'Brien Fears Fan Fights." Several NHL players involved in fights in the 1970s were charged with assault; however, the NHL did not institute harsher sanctions for fighting until implementing the "third-man-in" rule in 1977. It stipulated that any player coming off the bench to join a fight would be ejected from the game. Mike Chambers, "History of Fighting in Hockey," *Denver Post*, 1 December 2013, accessed 1 October 2018, www.denverpost.com/2013/12/01/history-of-fighting-in-hockey.

42. *Time*, 10 March 1975, 62, quoted in Gulotta, "Torts in Sports," 769n34. The president of the NHL said that his league accepted "violence as part of its games."

43. Scott Young, "Recycling the Old Line," *Globe and Mail* (Toronto), 14 December 1977. See also "'Part of Hockey,'" *Washington Post*, 14 December 1977.

44. Mark Engel, "In Defense of Kermit," *Basketball Weekly*, 16 February 1978.

45. Feinstein, *Punch*, 21.

46. Sam Goldaper, "76ers Win Again, 107–89; Fight Erupts," *New York Times*, 27 May 1977; Bill Simmons, *The Book of Basketball: The NBA According to the Sports Guy* (New York: Ballantine, 2010), 130.

47. Bob Logan, "76ers Beat Up Trail Blazers," *Chicago Tribune*, 27 May 1977.

48. Goldaper, "76ers Win Again."

49. Curry Kirkpatrick, "There's No Place Like Home Court," *Sports Illustrated*, 6 June 1977, 23.

50. David DuPree, "76ers Romp in Brawl-Marred Game to Take 2–0 Lead," *Washington Post*, 27 May 1977.

51. DuPree, "76ers Romp."

52. Ted Green, "Fists Fly and So Do 76ers Again, 107–89," *Los Angeles Times*, 27 May 1977.

53. DuPree, "76ers Romp." See also Green, "Fists Fly" and Darryl Dawkins and Charley Rosen, *Chocolate Thunder: The Uncensored Life and Times of the NBA's Original Showman* (Toronto: Sport Media, 2003), 79.

54. Sam Goldaper, "O'Brien Fines Dawkins, Lucas $2,500 Apiece," *New York Times*, 28 May 1977. See also "O'Brien Fines Lucas, Dawkins," *Baltimore Sun*, 28 May 1977; "Dawkins, Lucas Are Fined $2,500 Each for Fighting," *Los Angeles Times*, 28 May 1977; "Fight in Playoffs Costs Dawkins, Lucas $2,500," *Washington Post*, 28 May 1977; and Bob Logan, "Dawkins, Lucas Fined $2,500," *Chicago Tribune*, 28 May 1977.

55. "19-Year-Old Moses Malone Signs $3 Million Pro Basketball Contract," *Black Panther*, 7 September 1974, 54; Don Kowet, "Moses Malone: Undergraduate in the ABA," *Sport*, January 1975, 76; Harry Xanthakos, "Moses Malone: No Miracles . . . Just Victories," *Black Sports*, January 1975, 38.

56. Larry Donald, "Malone Case Bares Evil Which Plagues Basketball," *Basketball Weekly*, 21 November 1974; Dwight Chapin, "Moses the Manchild Is Making It," *Los Angeles Times*, 18 December 1974.

57. Rod Sieb, "Did Moses' Crossing Open the Floodgates?," *Basketball Weekly*, 13 February 1975.

58. Sam Goldaper, "2 Schoolboys on N.B.A. List," *New York Times*, 9 May 1975.

59. "High School Cager a Jumper for Pro Pact," *Chicago Defender*, 3 June 1975.

60. John Rhodes, "Daryl Dawkins, the 76ers First Draft Choice Plans to Work as a Professional Ball Player," *Philadelphia Tribune*, 1 July 1975.

61. Dawkins and Rosen, *Chocolate Thunder*, 20.

62. "76ers Draft 6-10 Florida Schoolboy in First Round," *Philadelphia Tribune*, 31 May 1975; James Tuite, "Issue and Debate," *New York Times*, 10 May 1975.

63. See Goldaper, "2 Schoolboys on N.B.A. List," and "Dawkins 76ers' Prime Pupil," *New York Times*, 12 August 1975. Median income figure from US Bureau of the Census, Current Population Reports, P-60, No. 105, "Money Income in 1975 of Families and Persons in the United States," 1977, 1, accessed 3 May 2022, www2.census.gov /library/publications/1978/demographics/p60-117.pdf.

64. "NBA's 76ers Announce Signing of Dawkins," *Baltimore Sun*, 1 June 1975; "Teen-Agers Taken," *Los Angeles Times*, 30 May 1975.

65. Goldaper, "Dawkins 76ers' Prime Pupil"; Green, "Fists Fly."

66. Kirkpatrick, "There's No Place Like Home Court."

67. Ted Green, "He Dunks Like King Kong," *Los Angeles Times*, 26 May 1977.

68. Kirkpatrick, "There's No Place Like Home Court."

69. David DuPree, "Walton and Family Blazers Seek Antidote to Doctor," *Washington Post*, 22 May 1977.

70. Kirkpatrick, "There's No Place Like Home Court."

71. "Playoff Notes," *Los Angeles Times*, 26 May 1977.

72. Green, "He Dunks Like King Kong," and "Walton Gives 'Em a Title and the Shirt off His Back," *Los Angeles Times*, 6 June 1977.

73. Feinstein, *Punch*, 194.

74. "Blazers Hope to Break Hex of Magic Number Again," *Baltimore Sun*, 31 May 1977.

75. "Blazers Maul Philadelphia, 130–98," *Baltimore Sun*, 1 June 1977.

76. Green, "Walton Gives 'Em a Title."

77. Goudsouzian, "From Lew Alcindor to Kareem Abdul-Jabbar," 450. See also Ron Miller, *ABC Evening News*, 19 October 1977.

78. Montgomery, "Abdul-Jabbar Fined $5,000."

79. Montgomery.

80. Feinstein, *Punch*, 22.

81. Memo to the files from Lawrence F. O'Brien, "Meeting with Kareem Abdul-Jabbar," 10 November 1977, 1, in Box 17, Folder 26, LOB.

82. Bill Jauss, "Jack Scott: NBA Fights Owners' Fault," *Chicago Tribune*, 18 April 1977.

83. Simmons, *Book of Basketball*, 132.

84. John Papanek, "The Enforcers," *Sports Illustrated*, 31 October 1977, 43.

85. For Benson's photo spread, see Papanek, "Enforcers," 38–42.

86. Paul Attner, "Washington's Friends Say Fight out of Character for Gentle Giant," *Washington Post*, 14 December 1977. Calvin Murphy had a similar story about his own appearance in the issue.

87. Feinstein, *Punch*, 40–41.

88. Papanek, "Enforcers," 44

89. See Feinstein, *Punch*, chapters 8, 10.

90. Scannell, "O'Brien Fears Fan Fights." See also Sam Goldaper, "O'Brien Places Stress on the Uncovering of 'Root Causes,'" *New York Times*, 15 December 1977.

91. On the Kerner Commission, see Elizabeth Hinton, *America on Fire: The Untold History of Police Violence and Black Rebellion Since the 1960s* (New York: Liveright, 2021), 171–172.

92. John W. Joyce, "Violence Committee Meeting, January 19, 1978," 4, in Box 5, Folder 51, LOB.

93. Scannell, "O'Brien Fears Fan Fights."

94. Seymour S. Smith, "Growing On-Court Violence Becomes Big NBA Problem," *Baltimore Sun*, 21 December 1977.

95. Buker, "Washington Says Punch Will Haunt Him."

96. Mark Engel, "Rudy Tomjanovich and His Long Stroll with Anonymity," *Basketball Weekly*, 2 January 1975.

97. Feinstein, *Punch*, 124–126.

98. Matthew Frye Jacobson, *Roots Too: White Ethnic Revival in Post–Civil Rights America* (Cambridge, MA: Harvard University Press, 2006), 98.

99. Ted Green, "Tomjanovich Is in Intensive Care After Laker Punchout," *Los Angeles Times*, 11 December 1977; Sam Goldaper, "Lakers Get Dantley in Aftermath of Violent Brawl," *New York Times*, 14 December 1977; Goldaper, "O'Brien Places Stress on the Uncovering of 'Root Causes'"; "Basketball as Combat Sport," *New York Times*, 16 December 1977.

100. Nicholas C. Chriss, "Rockets' Fans Warned," *Los Angeles Times*, 14 December 1977; "NBA Slaps Cager with Suspension," *Baltimore Sun*, 13 December 1977.

101. Goldpaper, "Lakers' Kermit Washington Fined $10,000."

102. Clayton Riley, "Close Encounters of the NBA Kind," *Black Sports*, March 1978, 20.

103. Earl Gustkey, "A Fine Can Be Worse Than a Pulled Hamstring," *Los Angeles Times*, 5 January 1978.

104. Green, "O'Brien Hits Washington."

105. Goldaper, "Lakers' Kermit Washington Fined $10,000." See also "NBA Slaps Cager with Suspension."

106. "Letters: The Aftermath," *Los Angeles Times*, 17 December 1977.

107. Green, "Tomjanovich Is in Intensive Care"; "Tomjanovich's Jaw Fractured," *Washington Post*, 12 December 1977; "Jaw to Be Wired Shut," *Los Angeles Times*, 15 December 1977; "Tomjanovich Still Improving," *New York Times*, 15 December 1977.

108. "Surgery Successful on Tomjanovich," *Washington Post*, 18 December 1977; "Tomjanovich Ponders Future, Discusses Plans," *Baltimore Sun*, 7 January 1978.

109. "The Newswire: Tomjanovich to Fly Home Today, Faces More Surgery," *Los Angeles Times*, 24 December 1977; "Tomjanovich Returning Home for Christmas," *New York Times*, 24 December 1977.

110. Goldaper, "Lakers' Kermit Washington Fined $10,000."

111. Green, "O'Brien Hits Washington."

112. Attner, "Washington's Friends."

113. "N.B.A. Enforcers in Spotlight," *Black Panther*, 24 December 1977, 60.

114. Thomas Giles, "Commentary: Washington Won't Be Scapegoat for NBA," *Bay State Banner* (Dorchester, MA), 19 January 1978.

115. Carl Nesfield, "Is Violence in Sports Being Overplayed?," *New York Amsterdam News*, 24 December 1977.

116. Evans, "Sort of Sporty," *New York Amsterdam News*, 31 December 1977.

117. Paul L. Montgomery, "Players' Leader Is Disturbed by Fights," *New York Times*, 14 December 1977. See also Nesfield, "Is Violence in Sports Being Overplayed?"; "A Coach's Opinion: Al Attles," *Black Sports*, March 1978; "A Player's Opinion: Rick Barry," *Black Sports*, March 1978; and David DuPree, "Pushing, Then Punching," *Washington Post*, 9 February 1978.

118. Carey McWilliams, "Out of Kilter," *Nation*, 31 December 1977, 709.

119. Chriss, "Rockets' Fans Warned."

120. "Lakers Win Quietly in Houston Under a Heavy Guard," *New York Times*, 15 December 1977.

121. Steve Cady, "Washington Is Reeling from Punch He Threw," *New York Times*, 30 December 1977.

122. Ted Green, "Kermit Washington Tries to Leave All of the Ugliness Behind Him," *Los Angeles Times*, 15 February 1978.

123. Feinstein, *Punch*, 91.

124. Green, "Kermit Washington Tries."

125. "Tomjanovich Ponders Future."

126. "Washington Can Resume Career, O'Brien Rules," *Los Angeles Times*, 2 February 1978.

127. Ted Green, "Lakers Trade Pair for Charlie Scott," *Los Angeles Times*, 28 December 1977; Feinstein, *Punch*, 221.

128. Buker, "Washington Says Punch Will Haunt Him."

129. "Rockets' Tomjanovich Files Damage Suit Against Lakers," *Los Angeles Times*, 30 December 1977.

130. "Tomjanovich Suit Transferred to Federal Court," *Baltimore Sun*, 14 February 1978; Donald Huff, "Jury Selected to Hear Kermit Washington Case," *Washington Post*, 7 August 1979.

131. "The $3 Million Punch," *Washington Post*, 21 August 1979.

132. Both suits used the doctrine of *respondeat superior* in suing the Lakers rather than Washington. Typically, there are three rationales behind this strategy: (1) the employer has deeper pockets than the employee, (2) any damages incurred because of the tortious activity of employees should be considered part of the cost of doing business, and (3) the employer has a duty to maintain control over its employees. Gulotta, "Torts in Sports," 777–778.

133. Riley, "Close Encounters of the NBA Kind," 16, 18.

134. "News from the Editor," *Black Sports*, March 1978, 4.

135. Riley, "Close Encounters of the NBA Kind," 18.

136. Riley.

137. "News from the Editor," 4.

138. Peter S. Greenberg, "Wild in the Stands," *Black Sports*, March 1978, 9. Article reprinted from *New Times* magazine. See also Clark Whelton, "Take Me out of the Ball Game," *Black Sports*, April 1978, 6–12.

139. Greenberg, "Wild in the Stands," 14, 60.

140. Greenberg, 13.

141. Harry Edwards, quoted in Greenberg, 14.

142. Bob Logan, *Basketball Weekly*, 20 December 1978, 11.

143. Not until the 1988–1989 season did the NBA make the third referee a permanent change. Sam Goldaper, "N.B.A. May Add a Third Referee," *New York Times*, 22 March 1988.

144. Huff, "Jury Selected."

145. Feinstein, *Punch*, 265.

146. "It's a $3.3 Million Haymaker," *Los Angeles Times*, 18 August 1979.

147. "NBA's MVP Sees Warning in $3-Million Fight Award," *Jet*, 13 September 1979.

148. "It's a $3.3 Million Haymaker."

149. "The $3 Million Punch."

150. "It's a $3.3 Million Haymaker."

151. Feinstein, *Punch*, 267. The Lakers appealed the verdict, and the two sides eventually agreed to a $2 million settlement before the case was heard on appeal. Most of the money was placed in an annuity set up for Tomjanovich's children.

152. Feinstein, 78.

Chapter 7: Undisciplined: The NBA's "Cocaine Crisis"

1. Bernard King and Jerome Preisler, *Game Face: A Lifetime of Hard-Earned Lessons on and off the Basketball Court* (New York: De Capo, 2017), 170, 171.

2. King and Preisler, *Game Face*, 171. For contemporaneous reports of King's arrest, see "Nets' King Is Charged in Drug Case," *Baltimore Sun*, 19 December 1978; "Drug Arrest," *Chicago Tribune*, 19 December 1978; "The Newswire," *Los Angeles Times*, 19 December 1978; Mike Lupica, "Many Pros Think Adulthood Is Just Another Game," *Chicago Tribune*, 20 December 1978.

3. Clayton Riley, "Sports Opinion: Bernard King a Victim of Writers' Racism," *Chicago Tribune*, 11 February 1979.

4. Clayton Riley, "The Creation of a King," *Black Sports*, June 1978, 11–12.

5. King and Preisler, *Game Face*, 152, 153.

6. King and Preisler, 154–155.

7. King and Preisler, 172.

8. "Drug Arrest"; "Nets' King Is Charged."

9. Bob Ryan, "NBA: A Real Mess," *Basketball Weekly*, 15 June 1978.

10. Larry Donald, "What Will the NBA Do?," *Basketball Weekly*, 15 March 1979.

11. Criblez, *Tall Tales and Short Shorts*, 182–183; Simmons, *Book of Basketball*, 137; Donald, "What Will the NBA Do?" After switching from ABC to CBS in the 1973–1974 season, the league's television ratings plummeted by 20 percent and continued to decline over the course of the decade. CBS proved to be a bad fit for the NBA: the network did little to effectively package and broadcast the games.

12. "NBA All Ok," *Basketball Weekly*, 16 February 1978, 8; Criblez, *Tall Tales and Short Shorts*, 175, 211.

13. Bob Ryan, *Basketball Weekly*, 18 January 1979.

14. John Papanek, "There's an Ill Wind Blowing for the NBA," *Sports Illustrated*, 26 February 1979, 22.

15. See, for example, Kane, "An Assessment of 'Black Is Best.'"

16. On the rise of punitive drug policies, often targeted at African Americans, that drove the expansion of the US carceral state in the 1970s, see Kohler-Hausmann, *Getting Tough*, 79–120.

17. Lassiter, "Impossible Criminals," 136; Jenkins, *Decade of Nightmares*, 125–129.

18. "Police Investigate Possible Drug Ring Activity in Sports," *Los Angeles Times*, 23 January 1975; "FDA to Look into Substance of NFL Drug Ring," *Mexia (TX) Daily News*, 24 January 1975; "Inquiries Pressed in Drug Case," *New York Times*, 23 January 1975; "Drug Ring Uncovered in NFL, ABA?," *Xenia (OH) Daily Gazette*, 23 January 1975; "Woman's Tale of NFL Drug Trafficking Is Called False," *Baltimore Sun*, 8 February 1975.

19. Paul Delaney, "Drug Inquiry Clears Players," *New York Times*, 8 February 1975.

20. "Pro Players Accused of Drug Use," *Corbin (KY) Times-Tribune*, 12 February 1975.

21. "Pro Basketball Has Gone to Pot, It Is Reported," *Los Angeles Times*, 13 February 1975. See also "Drug Abuse Reported in ABA, NBA," *Washington Post*, 13 February 1975.

22. "Security, FBI-Style: Pro Athletes Under Tight Surveillance," *Los Angeles Times*, 6 January 1976.

23. Rosen, *Sugar*, 28–29.

24. Rosen, 65.

25. "Security, FBI-Style."

26. For more on Reese and Crowder, see Art Dunn, "Don Reese: I'm a Man Now," *Chicago Tribune*, 12 August 1977; Prentis Rogers, "Rogers' Two Cents," *Atlanta Daily World*, 5 March 1978; Ed Kiersh, "Snowstorm over Miami," *Black Sports*, February 1978.

27. "NBA 'Cop' Uncovers Little Wrong," *Baltimore Sun*, 5 April 1978.

28. Lupica, "Many Pros Think."

29. Riley, "Creation of a King," 13.

30. "Nets' King Is Charged"; King and Preisler, *Game Face*, 109; Lupica, "Many Pros Think."

31. Riley, "Sports Opinion."

32. Riley, "Creation of a King," 13.

33. King and Preisler, *Game Face*, 103.

34. King and Preisler, 105.

35. King and Preisler, 107–108.

36. King and Preisler, 6, 11.

37. King and Preisler, 124.

38. Robert C. Petersen and Richard C. Stillman, eds., *Cocaine: 1977*, NIDA Research Monograph 13 (Rockville, Maryland: Department of Health, Education, and Welfare, Public Health Service, Alcohol, Drug Abuse, and Mental Health Administration, 1977), 32, vi, 9.

39. Patrick M. O'Malley, Lloyd D. Johnson, and Jerald G. Bachman, "Drug Use Among American Youth, 1975–79," *Economic Outlook*, Spring 1980, 41. Federal lawmakers were also concerned about cocaine. See *Cocaine: A Major Drug Issue of the Seventies*, Hearings Before the Select Committee on Narcotics Abuse and Control, House of Representatives, Ninety-Sixth Congress, First Session, July 24, 26; October 10, 1979.

40. Riley, "Sports Opinion."

41. "Franklin Will Ride for Delp," *Washington Post*, 22 June 1979; Tom Duffy, "Delp to Let Franklin Ride," *Chicago Tribune*, 22 June 1979; Bill Vergin, "How Drugs Could Have Ended Swen Nater's Career," *Basketball Digest*, June 1980.

42. King and Preisler, *Game Face*, 172–173.

43. Sheila Moran, "Alcohol: An Occupational Hazard for Athletes," *Los Angeles Times*, 23 May 1980.

44. "Transitions: Basketball," *Washington Post*, 10 January 1979.

45. "Nets' King Draws $50 Fine," *Baltimore Sun*, 17 February 1979.

46. King and Preisler, *Game Face*, 173, 174.

47. King and Preisler, 181.

48. Carey Holwell Hamilton, "The Wyoming Black Fourteen (1969)," BlackPast, 1 September 2016, accessed 15 May 2022, www.blackpast.org/african-american-history /wyoming-black-fourteen-1969.

49. King and Preisler, *Game Face*, 183.

50. "Jazz Suspends Bernard King," *Washington Post*, 3 January 1980.

51. Tom Duffy, "Sports Briefing: Bernard King Arrested Again," *Chicago Tribune*, 3 January 1980; Jane Gross, "Police to Ask King Prosecution," *New York Times*, 4 January 1980.

52. "Jazz Suspends Bernard King"; "King, Forward for Jazz, Arrested on Sex Charge," *New York Times*, 3 January 1980.

53. "NBA Player Accused of Sexually Abusing Ex-missionary," *Philadelphia Tribune*, 4 January 1980.

54. "NBA Player Accused."

55. Byron Rosen, "NBA Hopes to Discover Dawkins-Proof Boards," *Washington Post*, 5 June 1980.

56. Doris Marie Provine, *Unequal Under Law: Race in the War on Drugs* (Chicago: University of Chicago Press, 2007), 74–78.

57. "NBA Player Accused"; population data from US Census Bureau, Census 1980, General Population Characteristics, part 46, Utah, PC80-1-B46, table 15, accessed 3 May 2022, www2.census.gov/prod2/decennial/documents/1980a_utABCD -02.pdf.

58. Gross, "Police to Ask King Prosecution."

59. "Jazz's Bernard King Arraigned on Six Charges," *Chicago Tribune*, 8 January 1980; Sheila Moran, "Baseball Just Seems to Be a Natural Mix for Booze," *Los Angeles Times*, 22 May 1980.

60. Howie Evans, "Bernard King: A Tragic Tale," *New York Amsterdam News*, 12 January 1980.

61. Evans, "Bernard King."

62. "Furlow, Guard for Jazz, Killed in Ohio Car Crash," *Los Angeles Times*, 24 May 1980; "Terry Furlow Dies in Auto Accident," *Chicago Tribune*, 24 May 1980.

63. Carrie Seidman, "Furlow of Utah Jazz Dies in Crash in Ohio," *New York Times*, 24 May 1980.

64. "Stellar NBA Guard Furlow Crash Victim," *Baltimore Afro-American*, 31 May 1980.

65. "Terry Furlow Dies."

66. "Stellar NBA Guard Furlow."

67. "Terry Furlow Dies."

68. "Furlow, Guard for Jazz, Killed."

69. Seidman, "Furlow of Utah Jazz Dies."

70. Haywood with Ostler, *Spencer Haywood*, 182; Spears and Washburn, *Spencer Haywood Rule*, 144.

71. Haywood with Ostler, *Spencer Haywood*, 189.

72. Haywood with Ostler, 193, 196–197.

73. Haywood with Ostler, 198, 200–202.

74. Spears and Washburn, *Spencer Haywood Rule*, 146.

75. Haywood with Ostler, *Spencer Haywood*, 205–207; Spears and Washburn, *Spencer Haywood Rule*, 150–152.

76. Scott Ostler, "Haywood Gets More Time—for Sleeping, Not Playing," *Los Angeles Times*, 9 May 1980.

77. "Stellar NBA Guard Furlow."

78. Haywood with Ostler, *Spencer Haywood*, 208. See also "Haywood Gets a Laker Slight," *New York Times*, 20 May 1980.

79. Haywood with Ostler, *Spencer Haywood*, 211. See also Spears and Washburn, *Spencer Haywood Rule*, 152.

80. Spears and Washburn, *Spencer Haywood Rule*, 153; David Thompson with Sean Stormes and Marshall Terrill, *Skywalker* (Champaign, IL: Sports Publishing, 2003), 219–220.

81. "King Pleads Guilty, Escapes Prison Term," *New York Times*, 5 June 1980.

82. "King Pleads Guilty."

83. "Jazz Ordered to Pay King," *New York Times*, 3 June 1980.

84. George Vecsey, "Relief Is on Way for Players Who Drink," *New York Times*, 21 April 1980.

85. Memo from John W. Joyce to Lawrence F. O'Brien, "Recommended Additions to NBA Drug Education and Prevention Program," 9 July 1980, in Box 8, Folder 1, LOB.

86. "Hawks Eddie Johnson Bound Over for Drug, Traffic Mishaps," *Atlanta Daily World*, 17 July 1980.

87. "Hawks Eddie Johnson Bound Over"; "Hawks' Johnson Arrested Again," *Washington Post*, 26 July 1980.

88. George Vecsey, "A Life Ends; Another Is Cause for Concern," *New York Times*, 15 September 1980.

89. Chico Renfroe, "Eddie Johnson Needs Your Help," *Atlanta Daily World*, 17 July 1980.

90. Moran, "Baseball Just Seems to Be a Natural Mix for Booze."

91. Renfroe, "Eddie Johnson Needs Your Help."

92. Byron Rosen, "Johnson: Furlough or Furlow?," *Washington Post*, 17 July 1980.

93. "Hawks' Johnson to Be Tried as Drug User, Not as Seller," *Los Angeles Times*, 19 July 1980.

94. "Hawks' Johnson to Be Tried as Drug User." See also "NBA Star Faces Rap," *Baltimore Afro-American*, 26 July 1980.

95. "Atlanta's Eddie Johnson Charged with Auto Theft," *Los Angeles Times*, 25 July 1980; "Eddie Johnson of Hawks Charged with Stealing Car," *New York Times*, 26 July 1980.

96. "Auto Theft Charges Against Eddie Johnson Dropped," *Atlanta Daily World*, 10 August 1980.

97. Cobbs, "NBA and Cocaine." See also "3 of 4 NBA Players Are Said to Use Cocaine," *Baltimore Sun*, 20 August 1980; Chris Cobbs, "Widespread Cocaine Use by Players Alarms NBA," *Washington Post*, 20 August 1980; and Jim Walker, "Sports Briefing: NBA Drug Use Up, Says Study," *Chicago Tribune*, 20 August 1980.

98. Original report on *CBS Evening News*, 19 August 1980, and corrections offered on 20 and 21 August 1980.

99. Cobbs, "NBA and Cocaine."

100. Cobbs.

101. See *ABC World News Tonight*, 11 June 1980 and *CBS Evening News*, 11 June 1980.

102. Michael Schaller, *Ronald Reagan* (New York: Oxford University Press, 2011), 29–30.

103. "Statement by NBA Commissioner Lawrence F. O'Brien," in Box 4, Folder 39, LOB.

104. Bart Barnes and David DuPree, "Sports and Drugs: Uneasy Partners," *Washington Post*, 4 September 1980. See also "The Drug Department," *Chicago Tribune*, 27 August 1980 and "O'Brien Says NBA Will Take a Hard Line on Cocaine Use," *Los Angeles Times*, 21 August 1980.

105. Memo from John W. Joyce to Lawrence F. O'Brien, "Quotations and Statements Attributed to NBA Personnel Appearing in the *Los Angeles Times*, August 19, 1980, by Chris Cobbs," 25 August 1980, in Box 4, Folder 49, LOB.

106. Memo from John W. Joyce to Lawrence F. O'Brien, "Proposed Agenda for the Drug Prevention and Education Committee, September 8, 1980," 25 August 1980, in Box 4, Folder 49, LOB.

107. "NBA Tries to Curtail Drugs," *Washington Post*, 22 August 1980.

108. Barnes and DuPree, "Sports and Drugs."

109. Confidential memo from Michael Burke, Head of the Antidrug Committee, to Lawrence F. O'Brien, 10 September 1980, in Box 8, Folder 1, LOB.

110. "NBA to Sponsor Drug Seminars," *Baltimore Sun*, 10 September 1980.

111. Memo from Edward J. Donovan to Michael Burke, "Knicks/NBA Drug Seminar," 17 September 1980, in Box 4, Folder 49, LOB.

112. Memo from Ed Falk to Lawrence F. O'Brien, "Drug Program," 23 September 1980, in Box 4, Folder 49, LOB.

113. "Drug Department." See also *CBS Nightly News*, 25 August 1980.

114. Barnes and DuPree, "Sports and Drugs."

115. "Transitions," *Washington Post*, 13 September 1977; Tom Duffy, "Sports Briefing: Potpourri," *Chicago Tribune*, 26 July 1978.

116. Richard Dozer, "Drug Charge Overblown—Bulls' Thorn," *Chicago Tribune*, 21 August 1980. Los Angeles Lakers GM Jerry Buss also disputed the figure of 75 percent. See "O'Brien Says NBA Will Take a Hard Line."

117. Seymour S. Smith, "Reports of NBA Drug Use Draw Varied Player Reaction," *Baltimore Sun*, 6 September 1980.

118. "The Doctor Is In," *Chicago Tribune*, 15 November 1980. See also "Erving Cites Alcohol," *Baltimore Sun*, 16 November 1980. For similar sentiments, see Vecsey, "Relief Is on Way for Players Who Drink." The Los Angeles Dodgers of Major League Baseball was the first pro sports franchise to form a company program for alcohol abuse.

119. Smith, "Reports of NBA Drug Use."

120. David Israel, "Athletes Use Drugs to Meet Demand for Excellence," *Chicago Tribune*, 28 August 1980.

121. Israel, "Athletes Use Drugs to Meet Demand."

122. Memo to players from Lawrence F. O'Brien and Lawrence Fleisher, 11 November 1980, in Box 8, Folder 1, LOB. See also Pierre-Marie Loizeau, *Nancy Reagan: The Woman Behind the Man* (New York: Nova History, 2004), 105.

123. Vecsey, "A Life Ends"; Dave Kindred, "Furlow Set for Boos, Headlines," *Washington Post*, 29 April 1979; Mike Sielski, "The Troubling, Tragic, and Mysterious Story of Former Sixers Draft Pick Terry Furlow," *Philadelphia Inquirer*, 21 May 2020.

124. "Terry Furlow Unhappy Picking up 'Splinters' on the 76ers' Bench," *Philadelphia Tribune*, 4 June 1977.

125. "Furlow, Lee Call Trade Good Deal," *New York Times*, 2 February 1979. See also Sam Goldaper, "Cavaliers Beat Nets, 123 to 114," *New York Times*, 25 January 1979; Seidman, "Furlow of Utah Jazz Dies"; Peter P. Spudich Jr., "Terry Furlow Loses Life in Car Mishap," *Atlanta Daily World*, 25 May 1980; and Vecsey, "A Life Ends."

126. Sielski, "Troubling, Tragic, and Mysterious Story."

127. Vecsey, "A Life Ends."

128. "The Newswire," *Los Angeles Times*, 26 June 1980. See also "Furlow Blood Shows Drugs," *Chicago Tribune*, 26 June 1980.

129. Vecsey, "A Life Ends."

130. Baccus quoted in Vecsey.

131. "Eddie Johnson Apologizes to Atlanta and Teammates," *Los Angeles Times*, 12 September 1980. See also "Hawks Johnson Says He Is in Good Condition, Ready to Play," *Atlanta Daily World*, 14 September 1980.

132. Vecsey, "A Life Ends."

133. "Eddie Johnson Apologizes"; "Hawks Johnson Says."

134. George Vecsey, "Sports of the Times: Judges and Drugs," *New York Times*, 27 September 1980.

135. Barry Cooper, "Drugs, Personal Problems Slowing Fast Eddie's Career Down," *Orlando Sentinel*, 6 December 1987.

136. David DuPree, "Eddie Johnson Works at Coping with Manic-Depressive Disorder," *Washington Post*, 19 November 1981.

137. For his part, Johnson could not seem to shake his demons. He played ten years in the league and made the All-Star team twice, but the NBA, after suspending him for cocaine use several times, banned him for life in 1987. Over the next twenty years, Johnson was in and out of prison. But then in 2008 he received a mandatory life sentence for sexually assaulting an eight-year-old girl, and he died in Santa Rosa Correctional Institution in Milton, Florida, in November 2020. See "Two-Time NBA All-Star 'Fast Eddie' Johnson Dies at 65," *Pittsburgh Post Gazette*, 3 November 2020.

138. Glyn Hughes, "Managing Black Guys: Representation, Corporate Culture, and the NBA," *Sociology of Sport Journal* 21, no. 2 (2004): 174.

139. "Athletes Not Immune to Ravages of Alcohol, Drugs," *Baltimore Sun*, 8 April 1981.

140. Scott Ostler, "The Land of the Free and Home of the King," *Los Angeles Times*, 10 December 1980.

141. King and Preisler, *Game Face*, 291.

142. "An Interview with Dave Bing," *Black Sports*, April 1977, 31.

Epilogue

1. All percentages from John Matthew Smith, "'Gifts That God Didn't Give': White Hopes, Basketball, and the Legend of Larry Bird," *Massachusetts Historical Review* 13, no. 1 (2011): 6–7. See also Sam Goldaper, "Issue and Debate," *New York Times*, 3 April 1979.

2. Patrick Ferrucci and Earnest Perry, "Double Dribble: The Stereotypical Narrative of Magic and Bird," *Journalism History* 41, no. 2 (2015): 93; Pamela Grundy, Murry Nelson, and Mark Dyreson, "The Emergence of Basketball as an American National Pastime: From a Popular Participant Sport to a Spectacle of Nationhood," *International Journal of the History of Sport* 31, nos. 1–2 (2014): 147.

3. Mark Engel, "John Havlicek Man of the Year," *Basketball Weekly*, 4 January 1979; Smith, "'Gifts That God,'" 9.

4. John Papanek, "Gifts That God Didn't Give," *Sports Illustrated*, 9 November 1981, 85–86; Smith, "'Gifts That God,'" 2–3, 7–8; Ferrucci and Perry, "Double Dribble," 96.

5. Papanek, "Gifts," 85. See also Larry Donald, "The Selling of Larry Bird," *Basketball Weekly*, 8 March 1979.

6. Papanek, "Gifts," 86–88.

7. Larry Donald, "Goodbye Earvin, Hello Magic," *Basketball Weekly*, 15 June 1979.

8. Ferrucci and Perry, "Double Dribble," 96.

9. Donald, "Goodbye Earvin."

10. Ferrucci and Perry, "Double Dribble," 96, 97; Ed Davis, "Magic Outfunks Chocolate Thunder," *Los Angeles Sentinel*, 22 May 1980.

11. Ferrucci and Perry, "Double Dribble," 93, 96; Smith, "'Gifts That God,'" 3, 12.

12. Scores from "1984 NBA Finals: Lakers vs. Celtics," *Basketball Reference*, accessed 25 March 2022, www.basketball-reference.com/playoffs/1984-nba-finals-lakers-vs -celtics.html. See also Ferrucci and Perry, "Double Dribble," 98; and Smith, "'Gifts That God,'" 17–18, 23.

13. Scott Ostler, "NBA: More Rebounding and More Chickens?," *Los Angeles Times*, 8 October 1980.

14. James Quirk and Rodney D. Fort, *Pay Dirt: The Business of Professional Team Sports* (Princeton, NJ: Princeton University Press, 2018), 498, 500.

15. Richard Dozer, "Trends: Some Jewels Among Changes in NBA Rules," *Chicago Tribune*, 26 September 1980. See also Bob Ryan, "NBA Wraps Up Good Time Meetings," *Boston Globe*, 5 June 1980 and "NBA Rule Changes," *Skanner* (Portland, OR), 3 September 1980.

16. Ryan, "NBA Wraps Up"; "NBA Rule Changes."

17. NBA Collective Bargaining Agreement, 10 October 1980, 46, 18–19, in Box 18, Folder 29, LOB.

18. Mendelsohn, *Cap*, 23, 25.

19. Mendelsohn, 47.

20. Bob Lanier, letter to O'Brien, 6 August 1982, LOB, quoted in Mendelsohn, 51.

21. Mendelsohn, 30.

22. Jenkins, *Decade of Nightmares*, 181–182; Mendelsohn, *Cap*, 168.

23. David DuPree, "Bullets' Lucas Admits That Problems Are Drug-Related," *Washington Post*, 19 January 1982; "After Drug Disclosure Lucas Gets Ok to Play," *Baltimore Sun*, 21 January 1982.

24. David DuPree, "NBA Drug Use: High-Risk Recreation," *Washington Post*, 21 March 1982.

25. Don Reese, "I'm Not Worth a Damn," *Sports Illustrated*, 14 June 1982.

26. Bart Barnes, "NBA Will Urge Drug Tests," *Washington Post*, 2 July 1982; Lanier, quoted in Mendelsohn, *Cap*, 295. See also "Roundup," *Washington Post*, 2 August 1982.

27. Alexander, *New Jim Crow*, 49.

28. Dave Kindred, "Life's Realities Hit Hardest on Easy Street," *Washington Post*, 19 December 1982.

29. Mendelsohn, *Cap*, 231–234.

30. Sam Goldaper, "Brief N.B.A. Labor Talks Held," *New York Times*, 2 March 1983; Phil Jasner, "NBA Owners Voice Striking Words," *Philadelphia Daily News*, 7 March 1983; David DuPree, "NBA: Strike Would Cancel Free Agency," *Washington Post*, 6 March 1983. See also Mendelsohn, *Cap*, 242–245.

31. Bill Livingston, "Richardson: NBA Strike Would Draw Fans' Wrath," *Philadelphia Inquirer*, 28 February 1983.

32. Phil Jasner, "No April Foolin': NBA Settles," *Philadelphia Daily News*, 1 April 1983; David DuPree, "Strike Is Averted as NBA, Players Agree in Principle," *Washington Post*, 1 April 1983; "NBA, Players Put Faith, Hope in Parity," *Washington Post*, 2 April 1983. For more details on this complex agreement, see Mendelsohn, *Cap*, 278–281.

33. Sam Goldaper, "Revenue Sharing Instituted," *New York Times*, 1 April 1983.

34. Roy S. Johnson, "An Athlete, a Cocaine Addict: John Drew Fights for His Life," *New York Times*, 27 February 1983; "Richardson Supported by Nets," *New York Times*, 2 April 1983; "Thompson to Be Treated at Alcohol, Drug Center," *Washington Post*, 7 May 1983; Susan Reimer, "Teams, Leagues Get Involved," *Baltimore Sun*, 10 May 1983; "Lucas's Drug Pattern Began to Repeat Itself," *Baltimore Sun*, 12 May 1983; Roy S. Johnson, "Richardson Says Addiction Is Cured," *New York Times*, 14 June 1983. See also Thompson with Sean Stormes and Marshall Terrill, *Skywalker*, 210–223 and Rosen, *Sugar*, 54–56.

35. "NBA Starts 'War on Drugs,'" *Chicago Defender*, 29 September 1983; Phil Jasner, "NBA and Players Declare War Against Drug Abuse," *Philadelphia Daily News*, 29 September 1983; Larry Whiteside, "NBA, Players Assn. Unite to Drive out Drug Abusers," *Boston Globe*, 29 September 1983.

36. Sam Goldaper, "N.B.A. Will Ban Drug Users: Stern Plan Adopted," *New York Times*, 29 September 1983.

37. NBA Press Release, "NBA and Its Players Association Announce New Drug Program," in Box 16, Folder 26, LOB.

38. Rosen, *Sugar*, 66. The players included John Lucas, John Drew, Quintin Daley, David Thompson, Marques Johnson, Michael Ray Richardson, and Walter Davis.

39. Jane Gross, "N.B.A.'s Rebuilding Program Is Showing Results," *New York Times*, 23 December 1984. For more on the racial dimensions of the NBA's marketing efforts, see Hughes, "Managing Black Guys."

40. Mendelsohn, *Cap*, 21–22.

41. Mendelsohn, 162–164.

42. David L. Andrews, "Whither the NBA, Whither America?," *Peace Review* 11, no. 4 (1999): 506. See also Walter LaFeber, *Michael Jordan and the New Global Capitalism*

(New York: W.W. Norton, 2002) and Pete Croatto, *From Hang Time to Prime Time: Business, Entertainment, and the Birth of the Modern-Day NBA* (New York: Atria, 2020).

43. "Legends Profile: Michael Jordan," NBA.com, 14 September 2021, accessed 15 April 2022, www.nba.com/news/history-nba-legend-michael-jordan.

44. See David L. Andrews, "Deconstructing Michael Jordan: Reconstructing Postindustrial America," *Sociology of Sport Journal* 13, no. 4 (1996): 315–318; Andrews, "The Fact(s) of Michael Jordan's Blackness: Excavating a Floating Racial Signifier," in *Michael Jordan, Inc.: Corporate Sport, Media Culture, and Late Modern America*, ed. David L. Andrews (Albany: SUNY Press, 2001), 107–152.

45. E. M. Swift, "From Corned Beef to Caviar," *Sports Illustrated*, 3 June 1991, 78, 84.

46. Lisa Guerrero, "One Nation Under a Hoop: Race, Meritocracy, and Messiahs in the NBA," in *Commodified and Criminalized: New Racism and African Americans in Contemporary Sports*, ed. David J. Leonard and C. Richard King (Lanham, MD: Rowman & Littlefield, 2011), 133–134.

47. Guerrero, "One Nation Under a Hoop," 134.

48. David Shields, *Black Planet: Facing Race During an NBA Season* (New York: Crown, 1999); Phil Taylor, "Swish . . . Clank!," *Sports Illustrated*, 7 November 1994.

49. Dave Zirin, "Economics, Race, and the N.B.A. Lockout," *New Yorker*, 24 October 2011, accessed 15 April 2022, www.newyorker.com/sports/sporting-scene/economics -race-and-the-n-b-a-lockout. For an in-depth racial analysis of the "Malice in the Palace," see David J. Leonard, *After Artest: The NBA and the Assault on Blackness* (Albany: State University of New York Press, 2012).

50. Zirin, "Economics, Race, and the N.B.A. Lockout"; demographic information from Richard Lapchick et al., "The 2011 Racial and Gender Report Card: National Basketball Association, Executive Summary," 16 June 2011, 3, accessed 24 May 2022, www.tidesport.org/_files/ugd/7d86e5_b3ce57a63e1a48dd8154a2e768e5d0d5.pdf.

51. Rosen, *Sugar*, 80–81.

52. Ahiza Garcia, "The NBA Is Not Afraid to Lead on Social Justice," CNN.com, 19 February 2018, accessed 10 August 2019, www.money.cnn.com/2018/02/16/news /companies/nba-adam-silver-player-activism/index.html.

53. Mendelsohn, *Cap*, 87.

54. The Undefeated, "Social Justice Messages Each NBA Player Is Wearing on His Jersey," Andscape.com, 31 July 2020, accessed 20 May 2022, www.andscape.com /features/social-justice-messages-each-nba-player-is-wearing-on-his-jersey.

55. Sean Gregory, "Why Jacob Blake's Shooting Sparked an Unprecedented Sports Boycott," Time.com, 27 August 2020, www.time.com/5883892/boycott-nba-mlb -wnba-jacob-blake; Theresa Runstedtler, "The Milwaukee Bucks Led the Way as Athletes Took a Stand over Jacob Blake," Time.com, 28 August 2020, accessed 25 April 2022, www.time.com/5884624/milwaukee-bucks-nba-history.

Index

Theresa Runstedtler is a scholar of African American history whose research focuses on the intersection of race, masculinity, labor, and sport. She is the author of *Jack Johnson, Rebel Sojourner: Boxing in the Shadow of the Global Color Line*, which won the 2013 Phillis Wheatley Book Prize from the Northeast Black Studies Association. She is a professor at American University and lives in Baltimore with her husband and son.